Amazon Web Services in Action

Amazon Web Services
in Action

MICHAEL WITTIG
ANDREAS WITTIG

MANNING
Shelter Island

Manning Publications Co.	Development editor: Dan Maharry
20 Baldwin Road	Technical development editor Jonathan Toms
PO Box 761	Copyeditor: Tiffany Taylor
Shelter Island, NY 11964	Proofreader: Melody Dolab
	Technical proofreader: Doug Warren
	Typesetter: Gordan Salinovic
	Cover designer: Marija Tudor

ISBN 9781617292880
Printed in the United States of America
5 6 7 8 9 10 – EBM – 20 19 18 17 16

brief contents

contents

foreword

Throughout the late 90s and early 2000s, I worked in the rank and file of system administrators who endeavored to keep network services online, secure, and available to users. At that time, working with systems was a tedious, monotonous affair involving cable slinging, server racking, operating system installation from optical media, and manual software configuration. Any businesses wishing to engage in the emerging online marketplace bore the burden of managing physical servers, accepting the associated capital and operating costs, and hoping for enough success to justify those expenses.

When Amazon Web Services emerged in 2006, it signaled a shift in the industry. Many of the previously repetitive, time-consuming tasks became unnecessary, and the cost of launching new services plummeted. Suddenly anyone with a good idea and the ability to execute could build a global business on world-class infrastructure at a starting cost of just a few cents per hour. In terms of cumulative disruption of an established market, a few technologies stand above all others, and AWS is among them.

Today the march of progress continues unabated. In November 2014, at its annual re:Invent conference in Las Vegas, AWS announced to more than 13,000 live attendees that the number of major new features and services had nearly doubled each year since 2008. Usage of existing services grew on a similar scale, with a roughly 100% year-over-year increase for S3 and EC2. This growth offers new opportunities for the engineers and businesses that strive to solve some of the most challenging problems in building an online marketplace.

Needless to say, this unprecedented power and flexibility comes at the expense of considerable complexity. In response to and often in anticipation of customer demand, AWS has assembled dozens of services with thousands of features that enable yet confound new users. The benefits are accompanied by a brand-new lexicon and distinct architectural and technical best practices. This motley collection of sometimes overlapping services usually intimidates the beginner.

Amazon Web Services in Action slices through the challenges of learning AWS by using examples to cement knowledge in the minds of readers. Andreas and Michael focus on the most prominent services and features that users are likely to encounter. Security considerations are placed front and center, helping to establish that hosting systems in the cloud can be safe for even the most sensitive applications. And because many readers will be footing the bill from AWS personally, any examples that incur charges are called out explicitly throughout the text.

As a consultant, author, and, at heart, an engineer, I celebrate all efforts to introduce the wonderful world of cloud computing to new users. *Amazon Web Services in Action* is at the head of the pack as a confident, practical guide through the maze of the industry's leading cloud platform.

With this book as your sidekick, what will you build on the AWS cloud?

BEN WHALEY
AWS COMMUNITY HERO AND AUTHOR OF
THE UNIX AND LINUX SYSTEM ADMINISTRATION HANDBOOK

preface

When we started to develop software, we didn't care about operations. We wrote code, and someone else was responsible for deployment and operations. There was a huge gap between software development and IT operations. On top of that, releasing new features was a huge risk because it was impossible to test all the changes to software and infrastructure manually. Every six months, when new features needed to be deployed, we experienced a nightmare.

Time passed, and we became responsible for a product. Our goal was to iterate quickly and to be able to release new features to the product every week. Our software was responsible for managing money, so the quality of the software and infrastructure was as important as the ability to innovate. But the inflexible on-premises infrastructure and the outdated process of deploying software made that goal impossible to reach. We started to look for a better way.

Our search lead us to Amazon Web Services, which offered us a flexible and reliable way to build and operate our applications. The possibility of automating every part of our infrastructure was fascinating. Step by step, we dove into the different AWS services, from virtual servers to distributed message queues. Being able to outsource tasks like operating a SQL database or terminating HTTPS connections on a load balancer saved us a lot of time. We invested this time in automating testing and operations for our entire infrastructure.

Technical aspects weren't the only things that changed during this transformation to the cloud. After a while the software architecture changed from a monolithic application to microservices, and the separation between software development and operations disappeared. Instead we built our organization around the core principle of DevOps: you build it, you run it.

Our company became the first bank running on AWS in Germany. We learned a lot about Amazon Web Services, microservices, and DevOps during this journey.

Today we work as consultants, helping our clients to get the most out of AWS. The interesting thing is that most of them aren't concerned about saving money. Instead, they're transforming their organizations to benefit from the innovative space that AWS offers to outperform their competitors.

We were completely surprised when we were asked to write a book about AWS in January 2015. But, after experiencing the level of professionalism at Manning Publications during our first phone calls, we became more and more confident. We love reading books as well as teaching and sharing our knowledge, so writing a book seemed to be a perfect fit.

Due to the tremendous support from Manning Publications and our MEAP readers, we were able to finish this book in only nine months. We enjoyed the feedback loop among ourselves, our editors, and MEAP readers. And it was a lot of fun to create and improve all the examples that are part of *Amazon Web Services in Action*.

acknowledgments

Writing a book is time consuming. We invested our time, and other people did as well. We think that time is the most valuable resource on Earth, and we want to honor every minute spent by the people who helped us with this book.

To all the readers who bought the MEAP edition of the book, who motivated us by their confidence in us to finish the book, and who shared their interest in AWS: thank you for reading the book. We hope you learned a lot.

Thank you to all the people who posted comments in the book's Author Online forum and who provided excellent feedback that improved the book.

Thank you to all the reviewers who provided detailed comments from the first to the last page: Arun Allamsetty, Carm Vecchio, Chris Bridwell, Dieter Vekeman, Ezra Simeloff, Henning Kristensen, Jani Karhunen, Javier Muñoz Mellid, Jim Amrhein, Nestor Narvaez, Rambabu Posa, Scott Davidson, Scott M. King, Steffen Burzlaff, Tidjani Belmansour, and William E. Wheeler. Your input helped shape this book—we hope you like it as much as we do.

We also want to thank Manning Publications for placing their trust in us. This is our first book, so we know this was a high-risk venture for them. We want to thank the following staff at Manning for their excellent work:

- Dan Maharry, who helped us to teach AWS without missing important steps. Thanks for your patience when we made the same mistake multiple times. We also want to thank Jennifer Stout and Susanna Kline for helping out when Dan was on vacation.

- Jonathan Thoms, who helped us think about how our code teaches the ideas behind it.
- Doug Warren, who checked that our code examples worked as expected.
- Tiffany Taylor, who perfected our English. We know you had a hard time with us, but our mother tongue is German, and we thank you for your efforts.
- Candace Gillhoolley and Ana Romac, who helped us to promote this book.
- Benjamin Berg, who answered our many questions regarding the technical aspects of writing a book.
- Mary Piergies, Kevin Sullivan, Melody Dolab, and all the others who worked behind the scenes and who took our rough draft and turned it into a real book.

Many thanks to Ben Whaley for contributing the foreword to our book.

Thanks also to Christoph Metzger, Harry Fix, and the Tullius Walden Bank team for providing us with an incredible workplace where we acquired many of our AWS skills by migrating the IT of the first bank in Germany to do so to AWS.

Last but not least, we want to thank the significant people in our lives who supported us as we worked on the book. Andreas wants to thank his wife Simone, and Michael wants to thank his partner Kathrin, for their patience and encouragement during the past nine months.

about this book

This book introduces the most important AWS services and how you can combine them to get the most out of Amazon Web Services. Most of our examples use typical web applications to demonstrate important points. We pay a lot of attention to security topics, so we followed the principle of "least privilege" in this book. And we used official AWS tools whenever possible.

Automation sneaks in throughout the book, so by the end you'll be comfortable with using the automation tool CloudFormation to set up everything you've learned in an automated way; this will be one of the most important things you will learn from our book.

You'll find three types of code listings in this book: Bash, JSON, and Node.js/JavaScript. We use Bash to create tiny scripts to interact with AWS in an automated way. JSON is used to describe infrastructure in a way that CloudFormation can understand. And we use the Node.js platform to create small applications in JavaScript when programming is required to use services.

We focus on Linux as the operating system for virtual servers in the book. Examples are based on open source software whenever possible.

Roadmap

Chapter 1 introduces cloud computing and AWS. You'll learn about key concepts and basics, and you'll create and set up your AWS account.

Chapter 2 brings Amazon Web Services into action. You'll spin up and dive into a complex cloud infrastructure with ease.

Chapter 3 is about working with a virtual server. You'll learn about the key concepts of EC2 services with the help of a handful of practical examples.

Chapter 4 presents different approaches to automating your infrastructure. You'll learn how to use infrastructure as code by using three different approaches: your terminal, a programming language, and a tool called CloudFormation.

Chapter 5 introduces three different ways to deploy software to AWS. You'll use each of the tools to deploy an application to AWS in an automated fashion.

Chapter 6 is about security. You'll learn how to secure your system with private networks and firewalls. You'll also learn how to protect your AWS account.

Chapter 7 introduces S3, a service offering object storage, and Glacier, a service offering long-term storage. You'll learn how to integrate object storage into your applications to implement a stateless server by creating an image gallery.

Chapter 8 is about block-level storage for virtual servers offered by AWS. This is interesting if you plan to operate legacy software on block-level storage. You also take some performance measurements to get a good idea of the options available on AWS.

Chapter 9 introduces RDS, a service offering you managed relational database systems like PostgreSQL, MySQL, Oracle, and Microsoft SQL Server. If your applications use such a relational database system, this is an easy way to implement a stateless server architecture.

Chapter 10 introduces DynamoDB, a service offering a NoSQL database. You can integrate this NoSQL database into your applications to implement a stateless server. You'll implement a to-do application in this chapter.

Chapter 11 lays the foundation for becoming independent of losing a single server or a complete data center. You'll learn how to recover a single EC2 instance in the same or in another data center.

Chapter 12 introduces the concept of decoupling your system to increase reliability. You'll learn how to use synchronous decoupling with the help of load balancers on AWS. Asynchronous decoupling is also part of this chapter; we explain how to use SQS, a distributed queuing service, to build a fault-tolerant system.

Chapter 13 shows you how to use many services you've learned about to build a fault-tolerant application. In this chapter, you'll learn everything you need to design a fault-tolerant web application based on EC2 instances, which aren't fault-tolerant by default.

Chapter 14 is all about flexibility. You'll learn how to scale the capacity of your infrastructure based on a schedule or based on the current load of your system.

Code conventions and downloads

All source code in listings or in text is in a `fixed-width font like this` to separate it from ordinary text. Code annotations accompany many of the listings, highlighting important concepts. In some cases, numbered bullets link to explanations that follow the listing, and sometimes we needed to break a line into two or more to fit on the page. In our Bash code we used the continuation backslash. In our JSON and Node.js/ JavaScript code, an artificial line break is indicated by this symbol: ➥.

The code for the examples in this book is available for download from the publisher's website at www.manning.com/books/amazon-web-services-in-action and from GitHub at https://github.com/AWSinAction/code.

Author Online

Purchase of *Amazon Web Services in Action* includes free access to a private web forum run by Manning Publications where you can make comments about the book, ask technical questions, and receive help from the authors and from other users. To access the forum and subscribe to it, point your web browser to www.manning.com/ books/amazon-web-services-in-action. This page provides information on how to get on the forum once you're registered, what kind of help is available, and the rules of conduct on the forum.

Manning's commitment to our readers is to provide a venue where a meaningful dialog between individual readers and between readers and the authors can take place. It isn't a commitment to any specific amount of participation on the part of the authors, whose contribution to the AO forum remains voluntary (and unpaid). We suggest you try asking the authors some challenging questions, lest their interest stray!

The AO forum and the archives of previous discussions will be accessible from the publisher's website as long as the book is in print.

about the authors

Andreas Wittig and **Michael Wittig** work as software engineers and consultants focusing on AWS and web and mobile application development. They work with clients around the globe. Together, they migrated the complete IT infrastructure of a German bank to AWS—the first bank in Germany to do so. They have expertise in distributed system development and architecture, algorithmic trading, and real-time analytics. Andreas and Michael are proponents of the DevOps model. They are both AWS Certified Solutions Architects, Professional Level.

about the cover illustration

The figure on the cover of *Amazon Web Services in Action* is captioned "Paysan du Canton de Lucerne," or a peasant from the canton of Lucerne in central Switzerland. The illustration is taken from a collection of dress costumes from various countries by Jacques Grasset de Saint-Sauveur (1757-1810), titled *Costumes de Différent Pays,* published in France in 1797. Each illustration is finely drawn and colored by hand.

The rich variety of Grasset de Saint–Sauveur's collection reminds us vividly of how culturally apart the world's towns and regions were just 200 years ago. Isolated from each other, people spoke different dialects and languages. In the streets or in the countryside, it was easy to identify where they lived and what their trade or station in life was just by their dress.

The way we dress has changed since then and the diversity by region, so rich at the time, has faded away. It is now hard to tell apart the inhabitants of different continents, let alone different towns, regions, or countries. Perhaps we have traded cultural diversity for a more varied personal life—certainly for a more varied and fast-paced technological life.

At a time when it is hard to tell one computer book from another, Manning celebrates the inventiveness and initiative of the computer business with book covers based on the rich diversity of regional life of two centuries ago, brought back to life by Grasset de Saint-Sauveur's pictures.

Part 1

Getting started

Have you watched a blockbuster on Netflix, bought a gadget on Amazon.com, or synced files with Dropbox today? If so, you've used Amazon Web Services (AWS) in the background. As of December 2014, AWS operated 1.4 million servers and therefore is a big player in the cloud computing market. The data centers of AWS are distributed throughout the United States, Europe, Asia, and South America. But the cloud doesn't consist of hardware and computing power alone. Software is part of every cloud platform and makes the difference for you as a customer. The information technology research firm Gartner has classified AWS as a leader in the Magic Quadrant for Cloud Infrastructure as a Service in 2015 for the fourth time. The speed and quality of innovation on the AWS platform is extremely high.

The first part of this book will guide you through your first steps with AWS and give you an idea of how you can use AWS to improve your IT infrastructure. Chapter 1 introduces cloud computing and AWS; you'll learn about key concepts and basics. Chapter 2 brings Amazon Web Service into action; you'll dive into a complex cloud infrastructure with ease.

What is
Amazon Web Services?

This chapter covers

- Overview of Amazon Web Services
- Benefits of using Amazon Web Services
- Examples of what you can do with Amazon Web Services
- Creating and setting up an Amazon Web Services account

Amazon Web Services (AWS) is a platform of web services offering solutions for computing, storing, and networking, at different layers of abstraction. You can use these services to host web sites, run enterprise applications, and mine tremendous amounts of data. The term *web service* means services can be controlled via a web interface. The web interface can be used by machines or by humans via a graphical user interface. The most prominent services are EC2, which offers virtual servers, and S3, which offers storage capacity. Services on AWS work well together; you can use them to replicate your existing on-premises setup or design a new setup from scratch. Services are charged for on a pay-per-use pricing model.

3

As an AWS customer, you can choose among different data centers. AWS data centers are distributed in the United States, Europe, Asia, and South America. For example, you can start a virtual server in Japan in the same way you can start a virtual server in Ireland. This enables you to serve customers worldwide with a global infrastructure.

The map in figure 1.1 shows the data centers available to all customers.

> **Which hardware powers AWS?**
>
> AWS keeps secret the hardware used in its data centers. The scale at which AWS operates computing, networking, and storage hardware is tremendous. It probably uses commodity components to save money compared to hardware that charges extra for a brand name. Handling of hardware failure is built into real-world processes and software.[1]
>
> AWS also uses hardware especially developed for its use cases. A good example is the Xeon E5-2666 v3 CPU from Intel. This CPU is optimized to power virtual servers from the c4 family.

In more general terms, AWS is known as a *cloud computing platform.*

1.1   *What is cloud computing?*

Almost every IT solution is labeled with the term *cloud computing* or just *cloud* nowadays. A buzzword may help to sell, but it's hard to work with in a book.

Cloud computing, or the cloud, is a metaphor for supply and consumption of IT resources. The IT resources in the cloud aren't directly visible to the user; there are layers of abstraction in between. The level of abstraction offered by the cloud may vary from virtual hardware to complex distributed systems. Resources are available on demand in enormous quantities and paid for per use.

Figure 1.1   AWS data center locations

---

[1]   Bernard Golden, "Amazon Web Services (AWS) Hardware," *For Dummies,* http://mng.bz/k6lT.

Here's a more official definition from the National Institute of Standards and Technology:

Cloud computing is a model for enabling ubiquitous, convenient, on-demand network access to a shared pool of configurable computing resources (e.g., networks, servers, storage, applications, and services) that can be rapidly provisioned and released with minimal management effort or service provider interaction.

—The NIST Definition of Cloud Computing,
National Institute of Standards and Technology

Clouds are often divided into the following types:

- *Public*—A cloud managed by an organization and open to use by the general public
- *Private*—A cloud that virtualizes and shares the IT infrastructure within a single organization
- *Hybrid*—A mixture of a public and a private cloud

AWS is a public cloud. Cloud computing services also have several classifications:

- *Infrastructure as a service (IaaS)*—Offers fundamental resources like computing, storage, and networking capabilities, using virtual servers such as Amazon EC2, Google Compute Engine, and Microsoft Azure virtual machines
- *Platform as a service (PaaS)*—Provides platforms to deploy custom applications to the cloud, such as AWS Elastic Beanstalk, Google App Engine, and Heroku
- *Software as a service (SaaS)*—Combines infrastructure and software running in the cloud, including office applications like Amazon WorkSpaces, Google Apps for Work, and Microsoft Office 365

The AWS product portfolio contains IaaS, PaaS, and SaaS. Let's take a more concrete look at what you can do with AWS.

1.2 What can you do with AWS?

You can run any application on AWS by using one or a combination of services. The examples in this section will give you an idea of what you can do with AWS.

1.2.1 Hosting a web shop

John is CIO of a medium-sized e-commerce business. His goal is to provide his customers with a fast and reliable web shop. He decided to host the web shop on-premises, and three years ago he rented servers in a data center. A web server handles requests from customers, and a database stores product information and orders. John is evaluating how his company can take advantage of AWS by running the same setup on AWS, as shown in figure 1.2.

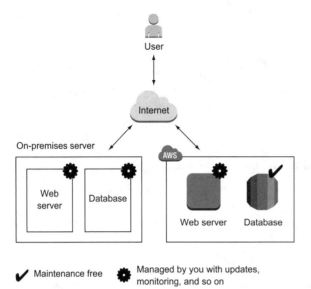

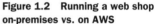

✔ Maintenance free   ⚙ Managed by you with updates, monitoring, and so on

Figure 1.2   Running a web shop on-premises vs. on AWS

John realized that other options are available to improve his setup on AWS with additional services:

- The web shop consists of dynamic content (such as products and their prices) and static content (such as the company logo). By splitting dynamic and static content, John reduced the load for his web servers and improved performance by delivering the static content over a content delivery network (CDN).
- John uses maintenance-free services including a database, an object store, and a DNS system on AWS. This frees him from managing these parts of the system, decreases operational costs, and improves quality.
- The application running the web shop can be installed on virtual servers. John split the capacity of the old on-premises server into multiple smaller virtual servers at no extra cost. If one of these virtual servers fails, the load balancer will send customer requests to the other virtual servers. This setup improves the web shop's reliability.

Figure 1.3 shows how John enhanced the web shop setup with AWS.

John started a proof-of-concept project and found that his web application can be transferred to AWS and that services are available to help improve his setup.

1.2.2   *Running a Java EE application in your private network*

Maureen is a senior system architect in a global corporation. She wants to move parts of the business applications to AWS when the company's data-center contract expires in a few months, to reduce costs and gain flexibility. She found that it's possible to run enterprise applications on AWS.

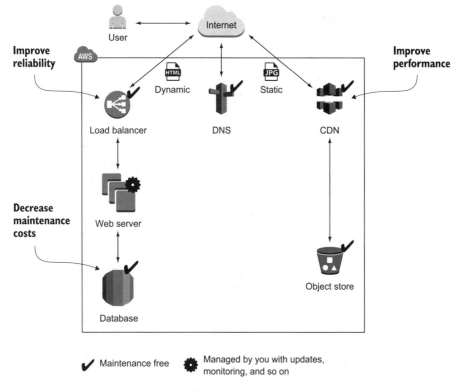

Figure 1.3 Running a web shop on AWS with CDN for better performance, a load balancer for high availability, and a managed database to decrease maintenance costs

To do so, she defines a virtual network in the cloud and connects it to the corporate network through a virtual private network (VPN) connection. The company can control access and protect mission-critical data by using subnets and control traffic between them with access-control lists. Maureen controls traffic to the internet using Network Address Translation (NAT) and firewalls. She installs application servers on virtual machines (VMs) to run the Java EE application. Maureen is also thinking about storing data in a SQL database service (such as Oracle Database Enterprise Edition or Microsoft SQL Server EE). Figure 1.4 illustrates Maureen's architecture.

Maureen has managed to connect the on-premises data center with a private network on AWS. Her team has already started to move the first enterprise application to the cloud.

1.2.3 Meeting legal and business data archival requirements

Greg is responsible for the IT infrastructure of a small law office. His primary goal is to store and archive all data in a reliable and durable way. He operates a file server to

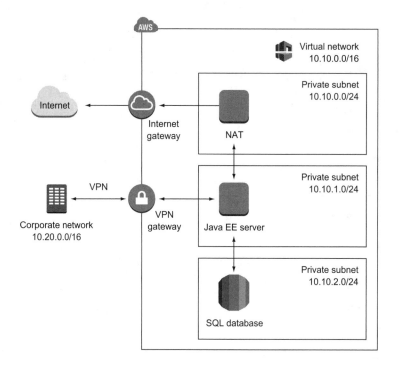

Figure 1.4   Running a Java EE application with enterprise networking on AWS

offer the possibility of sharing documents within the office. Storing all the data is a challenge for him:

- He needs to back up all files to prevent the loss of critical data. To do so, Greg copies the data from the file server to another network-attached storage, so he had to buy the hardware for the file server twice. The file server and the backup server are located close together, so he is failing to meet disaster-recovery requirements to recover from a fire or a break-in.
- To meet legal and business data archival requirements, Greg needs to store data for a long time. Storing data for 10 years or longer is tricky. Greg uses an expensive archive solution to do so.

To save money and increase data security, Greg decided to use AWS. He transferred data to a highly available object store. A storage gateway makes it unnecessary to buy and operate network-attached storage and a backup on-premises. A virtual tape deck takes over the task of archiving data for the required length of time. Figure 1.5 shows how Greg implemented this use case on AWS and compares it to the on-premises solution.

Greg is fine with the new solution to store and archive data on AWS because he was able to improve quality and he gained the possibility of scaling storage size.

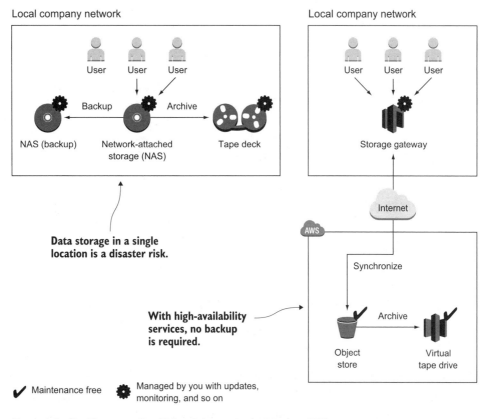

Local company network

Local company network

User User User

User User User

NAS (backup)   Network-attached   Tape deck
                storage (NAS)

Backup   Archive

Storage gateway

Data storage in a single location is a disaster risk.

Internet

AWS

Synchronize

With high-availability services, no backup is required.

Object store   Archive   Virtual tape drive

✔ Maintenance free   ⚙ Managed by you with updates, monitoring, and so on

Figure 1.5   Backing up and archiving data on-premises and on AWS

1.2.4   *Implementing a fault-tolerant system architecture*

Alexa is a software engineer working for a fast-growing startup. She knows that Murphy's Law applies to IT infrastructure: anything that can go wrong, will go wrong. Alexa is working hard to build a fault-tolerant system to prevent outages from ruining the business. She knows that there are two type of services on AWS: fault-tolerant services and services that can be used in a fault-tolerant way. Alexa builds a system like the one shown in figure 1.6 with a fault-tolerant architecture. The database service is offered with replication and failover handling. Alexa uses virtual servers acting as web servers. These virtual servers aren't fault tolerant by default. But Alexa uses a load balancer and can launch multiple servers in different data centers to achieve fault tolerance.

So far, Alexa has protected the startup from major outages. Nevertheless, she and her team are always planning for failure.

You now have a broad idea of what you can do with AWS. Generally speaking, you can host any application on AWS. The next section explains the nine most important benefits AWS has to offer.

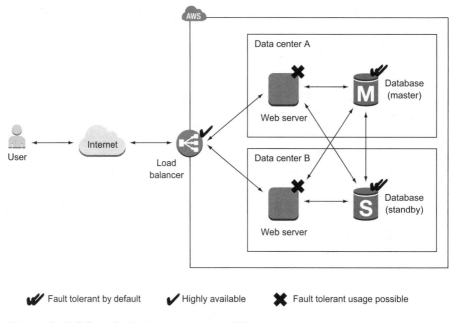

Figure 1.6   Building a fault-tolerant system on AWS

1.3   How you can benefit from using AWS

What's the most important advantage of using AWS? Cost savings, you might say. But saving money isn't the only advantage. Let's look at other ways you can benefit from using AWS.

1.3.1   Innovative and fast-growing platform

In 2014, AWS announced more than 500 new services and features during its yearly conference, re:Invent at Las Vegas. On top of that, new features and improvements are released every week. You can transform these new services and features into innovative solutions for your customers and thus achieve a competitive advantage.

The number of attendees to the re:Invent conference grew from 9,000 in 2013 to 13,500 in 2014.[2] AWS counts more than 1 million businesses and government agencies among its customers, and in its Q1 2014 results discussion, the company said it will continue to hire more talent to grow even further.[3] You can expect even more new features and services in the coming years.

---

[2] Greg Bensinger, "Amazon Conference Showcases Another Side of the Retailer's Business," *Digits*, Nov. 12, 2014, http://mng.bz/hTBo.

[3] "Amazon.com's Management Discusses Q1 2014 Results - Earnings Call Transcript," *Seeking Alpha*, April 24, 2014, http://mng.bz/60qX.

1.3.2 Services solve common problems

As you've learned, AWS is a platform of services. Common problems such as load balancing, queuing, sending email, and storing files are solved for you by services. You don't need to reinvent the wheel. It's your job to pick the right services to build complex systems. Then you can let AWS manage those services while you focus on your customers.

1.3.3 Enabling automation

Because AWS has an API, you can automate everything: you can write code to create networks, start virtual server clusters, or deploy a relational database. Automation increases reliability and improves efficiency.

The more dependencies your system has, the more complex it gets. A human can quickly lose perspective, whereas a computer can cope with graphs of any size. You should concentrate on tasks a human is good at—describing a system—while the computer figures out how to resolve all those dependencies to create the system. Setting up an environment in the cloud based on your blueprints can be automated with the help of infrastructure as code, covered in chapter 4.

1.3.4 Flexible capacity (scalability)

Flexible capacity frees you from planning. You can scale from one server to thousands of servers. Your storage can grow from gigabytes to petabytes. You no longer need to predict your future capacity needs for the coming months and years.

If you run a web shop, you have seasonal traffic patterns, as shown in figure 1.7. Think about day versus night, and weekday versus weekend or holiday. Wouldn't it be nice if you could add capacity when traffic grows and remove capacity when traffic shrinks? That's exactly what flexible capacity is about. You can start new servers within minutes and throw them away a few hours after that.

The cloud has almost no capacity constraints. You no longer need to think about rack space, switches, and power supplies—you can add as many servers as you like. If your data volume grows, you can always add new storage capacity.

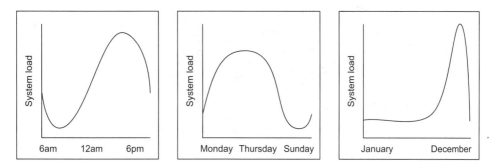

Figure 1.7 Seasonal traffic patterns for a web shop

Flexible capacity also means you can shut down unused systems. In one of our last projects, the test environment only ran from 7:00 a.m. to 8:00 p.m. on weekdays, allowing us to save 60%.

1.3.5   *Built for failure (reliability)*

Most AWS services are fault-tolerant or highly available. If you use those services, you get reliability for free. AWS supports you as you build systems in a reliable way. It provides everything you need to create your own fault-tolerant systems.

1.3.6   *Reducing time to market*

In AWS, you request a new virtual server, and a few minutes later that virtual server is booted and ready to use. The same is true with any other AWS service available. You can use them all on demand. This allows you to adapt your infrastructure to new requirements very quickly.

Your development process will be faster because of the shorter feedback loops. You can eliminate constraints such as the number of test environments available; if you need one more test environment, you can create it for a few hours.

1.3.7   *Benefiting from economies of scale*

At the time of writing, the charges for using AWS have been reduced 42 times since 2008:

- In December 2014, charges for outbound data transfer were lowered by up to 43%.
- In November 2014, charges for using the search service were lowered by 50%.
- In March 2014, charges for using a virtual server were lowered by up to 40%.

As of December 2014, AWS operated 1.4 million servers. All processes related to operations must be optimized to operate at that scale. The bigger AWS gets, the lower the prices will be.

1.3.8   *Worldwide*

You can deploy your applications as close to your customers as possible. AWS has data centers in the following locations:

- United States (northern Virginia, northern California, Oregon)
- Europe (Germany, Ireland)
- Asia (Japan, Singapore)
- Australia
- South America (Brazil)

With AWS, you can run your business all over the world.

1.3.9   *Professional partner*

AWS is compliant with the following:

- *ISO 27001*—A worldwide information security standard certified by an independent and accredited certification body

- *FedRAMP & DoD CSM*—Ensures secure cloud computing for the U.S. Federal Government and the U.S. Department of Defense
- *PCI DSS Level 1*—A data security standard (DSS) for the payment card industry (*PCI*) to protect cardholders data
- *ISO 9001*—A standardized quality management approach used worldwide and certified by an independent and accredited certification body

If you're still not convinced that AWS is a professional partner, you should know that Airbnb, Amazon, Intuit, NASA, Nasdaq, Netflix, SoundCloud, and many more are running serious workloads on AWS.

The cost benefit is elaborated in more detail in the next section.

1.4 How much does it cost?

A bill from AWS is similar to an electric bill. Services are billed based on usage. You pay for the hours a virtual server was running, the used storage from the object store (in gigabytes), or the number of running load balancers. Services are invoiced on a monthly basis. The pricing for each service is publicly available; if you want to calculate the monthly cost of a planned setup, you can use the AWS Simple Monthly Calculator (http://aws.amazon.com/calculator).

1.4.1 Free Tier

You can use some AWS services for free during the first 12 months after you sign up. The idea behind the Free Tier is to enable you to experiment with AWS and get some experience. Here is what's included in the Free Tier:

- 750 hours (roughly a month) of a small virtual server running Linux or Windows. This means you can run one virtual server the whole month or you can run 750 virtual servers for one hour.
- 750 hours (or roughly a month) of a load balancer.
- Object store with 5 GB of storage.
- Small database with 20 GB of storage, including backup.

If you exceed the limits of the Free Tier, you start paying for the resources you consume without further notice. You'll receive a bill at the end of the month. We'll show you how to monitor your costs before you begin using AWS. If your Free Tier ends after one year, you pay for all resources you use.

You get some additional benefits, as detailed at http://aws.amazon.com/free. This book will use the Free Tier as much as possible and will clearly state when additional resources are required that aren't covered by the Free Tier.

1.4.2 Billing example

As mentioned earlier, you can be billed in several ways:

- *Based on hours of usage*—If you use a server for 61 minutes, that's usually counted as 2 hours.

- *Based on traffic*—Traffic can be measured in gigabytes or in number of requests.
- *Based on storage usage*—Usage can be either provisioned capacity (for example, 50 GB volume no matter how much you use) or real usage (such as 2.3 GB used).

Remember the web shop example from section 1.2? Figure 1.8 shows the web shop and adds information about how each part is billed.

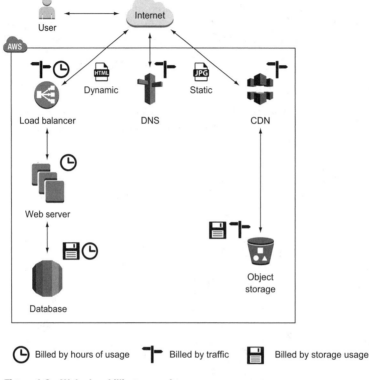

Figure 1.8   Web shop billing example

Let's assume your web shop started successfully in January, and you decided to run a marketing campaign to increase sales for the next month. Lucky you: you were able to increase the number of visitors of your web shop fivefold in February. As you already know, you have to pay for AWS based on usage. Table 1.1 shows your bills for January and February. The number of visitors increased from 100,000 to 500,000, and your monthly bill increased from 142.37 USD to 538.09 USD, which is a 3.7-fold increase. Because your web shop had to handle more traffic, you had to pay more for services, such as the CDN, the web servers, and the database. Other services, like the storage of static files, didn't experience more usage, so the price stayed the same.

With AWS, you can achieve a linear relationship between traffic and costs. And other opportunities await you with this pricing model.

Table 1.1 How an AWS bill changes if the number of web shop visitors increases

Service	January usage	February usage	February charge	Increase
Visits to website	100,000	500,000		
CDN	26 M requests + 25 GB traffic	131 M requests + 125 GB traffic	113.31 USD	90.64 USD
Static files	50 GB used storage	50 GB used storage	1.50 USD	0.00 USD
Load balancer	748 hours + 50 GB traffic	748 hours + 250 GB traffic	20.30 USD	1.60 USD
Web servers	1 server = 748 hours	4 servers = 2,992 hours	204.96 USD	153.72 USD
Database (748 hours)	Small server + 20 GB storage	Large server + 20 GB storage	170.66 USD	128.10 USD
Traffic (outgoing traffic to internet)	51 GB	255 GB	22.86 USD	18.46 USD
DNS	2 M requests	10 M requests	4.50 USD	3.20 USD
Total cost			538.09 USD	395.72 USD

1.4.3 Pay-per-use opportunities

The AWS pay-per-use pricing model creates new opportunities. You no longer need to make upfront investments in infrastructure. You can start servers on demand and only pay per hour of usage; and you can stop using those servers whenever you like and no longer have to pay for them. You don't need to make an upfront commitment regarding how much storage you'll use.

A big server costs exactly as much as two smaller ones with the same capacity. Thus you can divide your systems into smaller parts, because the cost is the same. This makes fault tolerance affordable not only for big companies but also for smaller budgets.

1.5 Comparing alternatives

AWS isn't the only cloud computing provider. Microsoft and Google have cloud offerings as well.

OpenStack is different because it's open source and developed by more than 200 companies including IBM, HP, and Rackspace. Each of these companies uses OpenStack to operate its own cloud offerings, sometimes with closed source add-ons. You could run your own cloud based on OpenStack, but you would lose most of the benefits outlined in section 1.3.

Comparing cloud providers isn't easy, because open standards are mostly missing. Functionality like virtual networks and message queuing are realized differently. If you know what features you need, you can compare the details and make your decision.

Otherwise, AWS is your best bet because the chances are highest that you'll find a solution for your problem.

Following are some common features of cloud providers:

- Virtual servers (Linux and Windows)
- Object store
- Load balancer
- Message queuing
- Graphical user interface
- Command-line interface

The more interesting question is, how do cloud providers differ? Table 1.2 compares AWS, Azure, Google Cloud Platform, and OpenStack.

Table 1.2 Differences between AWS, Microsoft Azure, Google Cloud Platform, and OpenStack

	AWS	Azure	Google Cloud Platform	OpenStack
Number of services	Most	Many	Enough	Few
Number of locations (multiple data centers per location)	9	13	3	Yes (depends on the OpenStack provider)
Compliance	Common standards (ISO 27001, HIPAA, FedRAMP, SOC), IT Grundschutz (Germany), G-Cloud (UK)	Common standards (ISO 27001, HIPAA, FedRAMP, SOC), ISO 27018 (cloud privacy), G-Cloud (UK)	Common standards (ISO 27001, HIPAA, FedRAMP, SOC)	Yes (depends on the OpenStack provider)
SDK languages	Android, Browsers (JavaScript), iOS, Java, .NET, Node.js (JavaScript), PHP, Python, Ruby, Go	Android, iOS, Java, .NET, Node.js (JavaScript), PHP, Python, Ruby	Java, Browsers (JavaScript), .NET, PHP, Python	-
Integration into development process	Medium, not linked to specific ecosystems	High, linked to the Microsoft ecosystem (for example, .NET development)	High, linked to the Google ecosystem (for example, Android)	-
Block-level storage (attached via network)	Yes	Yes (can be used by multiple virtual servers simultaneously)	No	Yes (can be used by multiple virtual servers simultaneously)
Relational database	Yes (MySQL, PostgreSQL, Oracle Database, Microsoft SQL Server)	Yes (Azure SQL Database, Microsoft SQL Server)	Yes (MySQL)	Yes (depends on the OpenStack provider)
NoSQL database	Yes (proprietary)	Yes (proprietary)	Yes (proprietary)	No
DNS	Yes	No	Yes	No

Table 1.2 Differences between AWS, Microsoft Azure, Google Cloud Platform, and OpenStack *(continued)*

	AWS	Azure	Google Cloud Platform	OpenStack
Virtual network	Yes	Yes	No	Yes
Pub/sub messaging	Yes (proprietary, JMS library available)	Yes (proprietary)	Yes (proprietary)	No
Machine-learning tools	Yes	Yes	Yes	No
Deployment tools	Yes	Yes	Yes	No
On-premises data-center integration	Yes	Yes	Yes	No

In our opinion, AWS is the most mature cloud platform available at the moment.

1.6 Exploring AWS services

Hardware for computing, storing, and networking is the foundation of the AWS cloud. AWS runs software services on top of the hardware to provide the cloud, as shown in figure 1.9. A web interface, the API, acts as an interface between AWS services and your applications.

You can manage services by sending requests to the API manually via a GUI or programmatically via a SDK. To do so, you can use a tool like the Management Console, a web-based user interface, or a command-line tool. Virtual servers have a peculiarity: you can connect to virtual servers through SSH, for example, and gain administrator

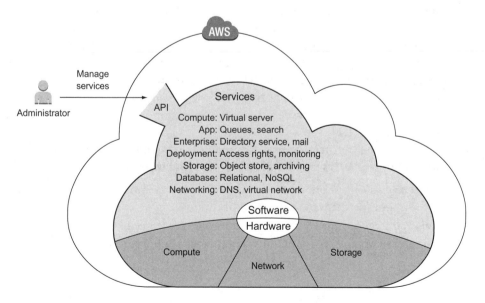

Figure 1.9 The AWS cloud is composed of hardware and software services accessible via an API.

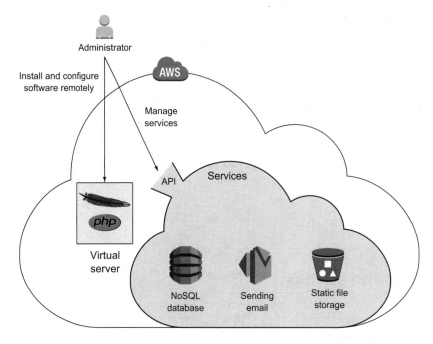

Figure 1.10   Managing a custom application running on a virtual server and dependent services

access. This means you can install any software you like on a virtual server. Other services, like the NoSQL database service, offer their features through an API and hide everything that's going on behind the scenes. Figure 1.10 shows an administrator installing a custom PHP web application on a virtual server and managing dependent services such as a NoSQL database used by the PHP web application.

Users send HTTP requests to a virtual server. A web server is installed on this virtual server along with a custom PHP web application. The web application needs to talk to AWS services in order to answer HTTP requests from users. For example, the web application needs to query data from a NoSQL database, store static files, and send email. Communication between the web application and AWS services is handled by the API, as figure 1.11 shows.

The number of different services available can be scary at the outset. The following categorization of AWS services will help you to find your way through the jungle:

- *Compute services* offer computing power and memory. You can start virtual servers and use them to run your applications.
- *App services* offer solutions for common use cases like message queues, topics, and searching large amounts of data to integrate into your applications.

- *Enterprise services* offer independent solutions such as mail servers and directory services.
- *Deployment and administration services* work on top of the services mentioned so far. They help you grant and revoke access to cloud resources, monitor your virtual servers, and deploy applications.
- *Storage* is needed to collect, persist, and archive data. AWS offers different storage options: an object store or a network-attached storage solution for use with virtual servers.
- *Database storage* has some advantages over simple storage solutions when you need to manage structured data. AWS offers solutions for relational and NoSQL databases.
- *Networking services* are an elementary part of AWS. You can define private networks and use a well-integrated DNS.

Be aware that we cover only the most important categories and services here. Other services are available, and you can also run your own applications on AWS.

Now that we've looked at AWS services in detail, it's time for you to learn how to interact with those services.

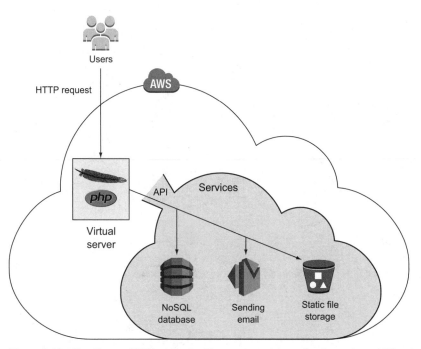

Figure 1.11 Handling an HTTP request with a custom web application using additional AWS services

1.7   *Interacting with AWS*

When you interact with AWS to configure or use services, you make calls to the API. The API is the entry point to AWS, as figure 1.12 demonstrates.

Next, we'll give you an overview of the tools available to make calls to the AWS API. You can compare the ability of these tools to automate your daily tasks.

1.7.1   *Management Console*

You can use the web-based Management Console to interact with AWS. You can manually control AWS with this convenient GUI, which runs in every modern web browser (Chrome, Firefox, Safari $\geq$ 5, IE $\geq$ 9); see figure 1.13.

If you're experimenting with AWS, the Management Console is the best place to start. It helps you to gain an overview of the different services and achieve success quickly. The Management Console is also a good way to set up a cloud infrastructure for development and testing.

1.7.2   *Command-line interface*

You can start a virtual server, create storage, and send email from the command line. With the command-line interface (CLI), you can control everything on AWS; see figure 1.14.

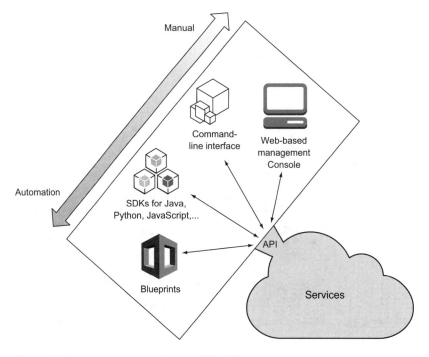

Figure 1.12   Tools to interact with the AWS API

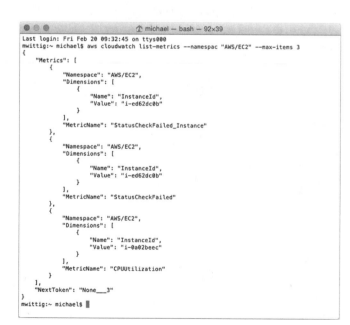

Figure 1.13 Management Console

```
● ● ●                          ⌂ michael — bash — 92×39
Last login: Fri Feb 20 09:32:45 on ttys000
mwittig:~ michael$ aws cloudwatch list-metrics --namespac "AWS/EC2" --max-items 3
{
    "Metrics": [
        {
            "Namespace": "AWS/EC2",
            "Dimensions": [
                {
                    "Name": "InstanceId",
                    "Value": "i-ed62dc0b"
                }
            ],
            "MetricName": "StatusCheckFailed_Instance"
        },
        {
            "Namespace": "AWS/EC2",
            "Dimensions": [
                {
                    "Name": "InstanceId",
                    "Value": "i-ed62dc0b"
                }
            ],
            "MetricName": "StatusCheckFailed"
        },
        {
            "Namespace": "AWS/EC2",
            "Dimensions": [
                {
                    "Name": "InstanceId",
                    "Value": "i-0a02beec"
                }
            ],
            "MetricName": "CPUUtilization"
        }
    ],
    "NextToken": "None___3"
}
mwittig:~ michael$ ▊
```

Figure 1.14 Command-line interface

The CLI is typically used to automate tasks on AWS. If you want to automate parts of your infrastructure with the help of a continuous integration server like Jenkins, the CLI is the right tool for the job. The CLI offers a convenient way to access the API and combine multiple calls into a script.

You can even begin to automate your infrastructure with scripts by chaining multiple CLI calls together. The CLI is available for Windows, Mac, and Linux, and there's also a PowerShell version available.

1.7.3 SDKs

Sometimes you need to call AWS from within your application. With SDKs, you can use your favorite programming language to integrate AWS into your application logic. AWS provides SDKs for the following:

- Android
- Browsers (JavaScript)
- iOS
- Java
- .NET

- Node.js (JavaScript)
- PHP
- Python
- Ruby
- Go

SDKs are typically used to integrate AWS services into applications. If you're doing software development and want to integrate an AWS service like a NoSQL database or a push-notification service, an SDK is the right choice for the job. Some services, such as queues and topics, must be used with an SDK in your application.

1.7.4 Blueprints

A *blueprint* is a description of your system containing all services and dependencies. The blueprint doesn't say anything about the necessary steps or the order to achieve the described system. Figure 1.15 shows how a blueprint is transferred into a running system.

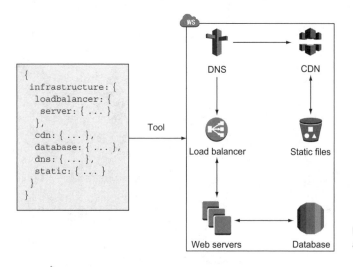

Figure 1.15   Infrastructure automation with blueprints

Consider using blueprints if you have to control many or complex environments. Blueprints will help you to automate the configuration of your infrastructure in the cloud. You can use blueprints to set up virtual networks and launch different servers into that network, for example.

A blueprint removes much of the burden from you because you no longer need to worry about dependencies during system creation—the blueprint automates the entire process. You'll learn more about automating your infrastructure in chapter 4.

It's time to get started creating your AWS account and exploring AWS practice after all that theory.

1.8 Creating an AWS account

Before you can start using AWS, you need to create an account. An AWS account is a basket for all the resources you own. You can attach multiple users to an account if multiple humans need access to the account; by default, your account will have one root user. To create an account, you need the following:

- A telephone number to validate your identity
- A credit card to pay your bills

> **Using an old account?**
>
> You can use your existing AWS account while working on the examples in this book. In this case, your usage may not be covered by the Free Tier, and you may have to pay for your usage.
>
> Also, if you created your existing AWS account before December 4, 2013, you should create a new one: there are legacy issues that may cause trouble when you try our examples.

1.8.1 Signing up

The sign-up process consists of five steps:

1 Provide your login credentials.
2 Provide your contact information.
3 Provide your payment details.
4 Verify your identity.
5 Choose your support plan.

Point your favorite modern web browser to https://aws.amazon.com, and click the Create a Free Account / Create an AWS Account button.

1. PROVIDING YOUR LOGIN CREDENTIALS

The Sign Up page, shown in figure 1.16, gives you two choices. You can either create an account using your Amazon.com account or create an account from scratch. If you create the account from scratch, follow along. Otherwise, skip to step 5.

Fill in your email address, and select I Am a New User. Go on to the next step to create your login credentials. We advise you to choose a strong password to prevent misuse

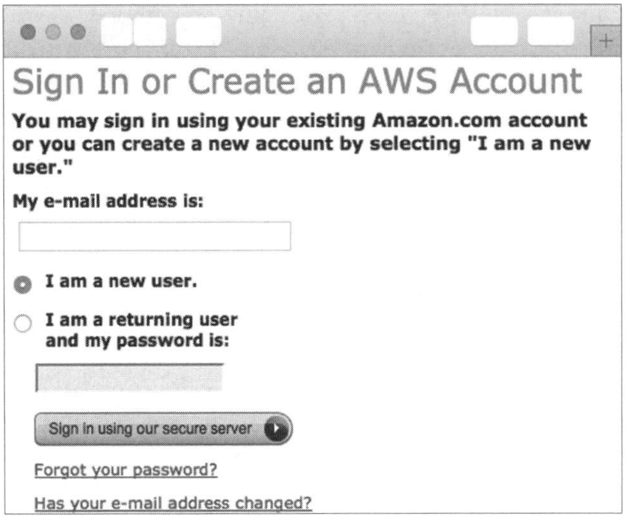

Figure 1.16   Creating an
AWS account: Sign Up page

of your account. We suggest a password with 16 characters, numbers, and symbols. If someone gets access to your account, they can destroy your systems or steal your data.

2. PROVIDING YOUR CONTACT INFORMATION

The next step, as shown in figure 1.17, is to provide your contact information. Fill in all the required fields, and continue.

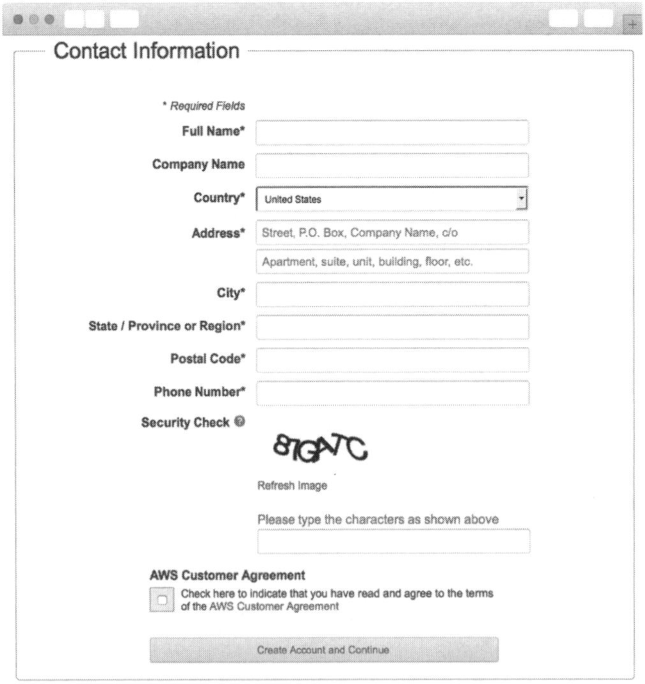

Figure 1.17   Creating an
AWS account: providing
your contact information

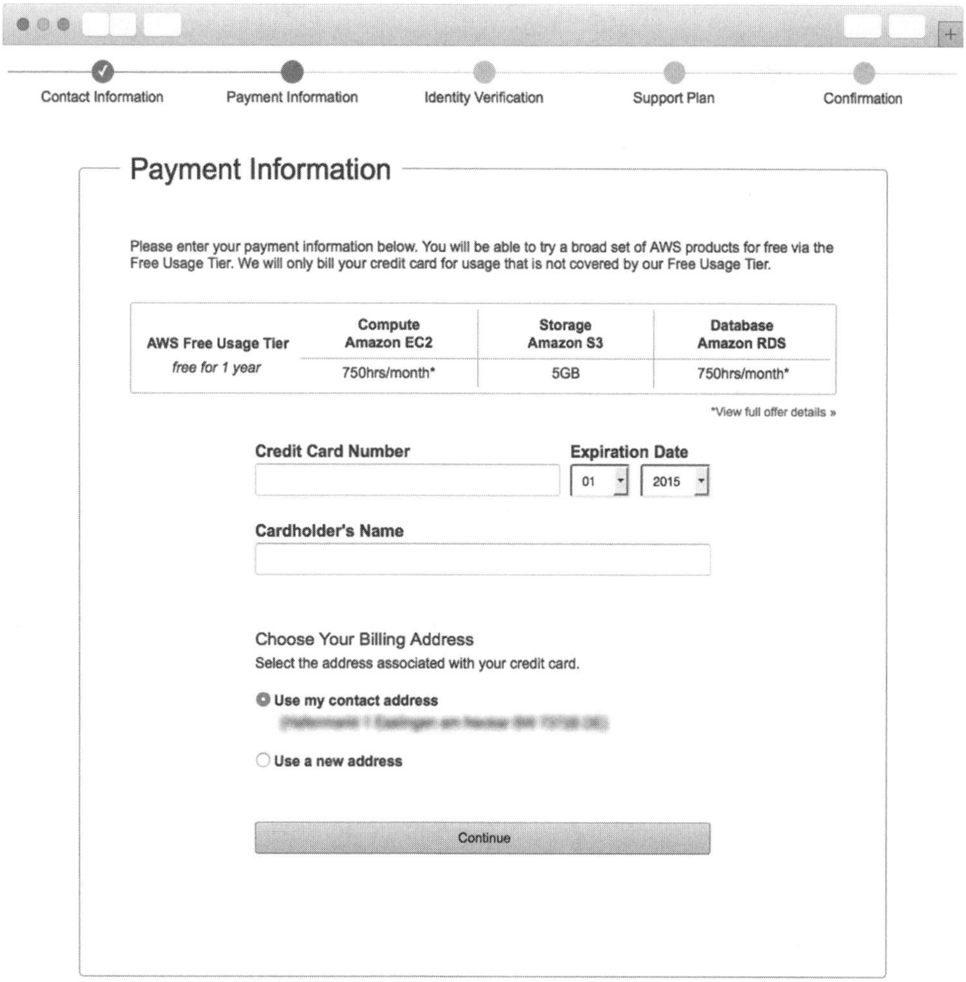

Figure 1.18 Creating an AWS account: providing your payment details

3. PROVIDE YOUR PAYMENT DETAILS

Now the screen shown in figure 1.18 asks for your payment information. AWS supports MasterCard and Visa. You can set your preferred payment currency later, if you don't want to pay your bills in USD; supported currencies are EUR, GBP, CHF, AUD, and some others.

4. VERIFYING YOUR IDENTITY

The next step is to verify your identity. Figure 1.19 shows the first step of the process.

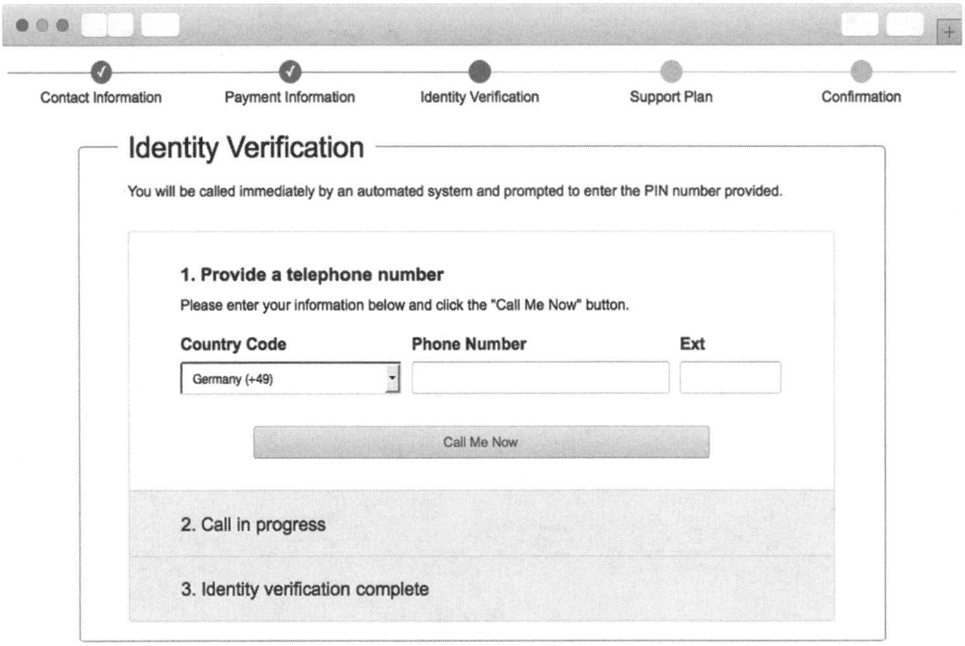

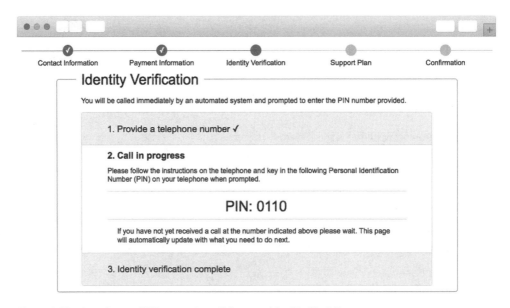

Figure 1.19   Creating an AWS account: verifying your identity (1 of 2)

After you complete the first part, you'll receive a call from AWS. A robot voice will ask you for your PIN, which will be like the one shown in figure 1.20. Your identity will be verified, and you can continue with the last step.

Figure 1.20   Creating an AWS account: verifying your identity (2 of 2)

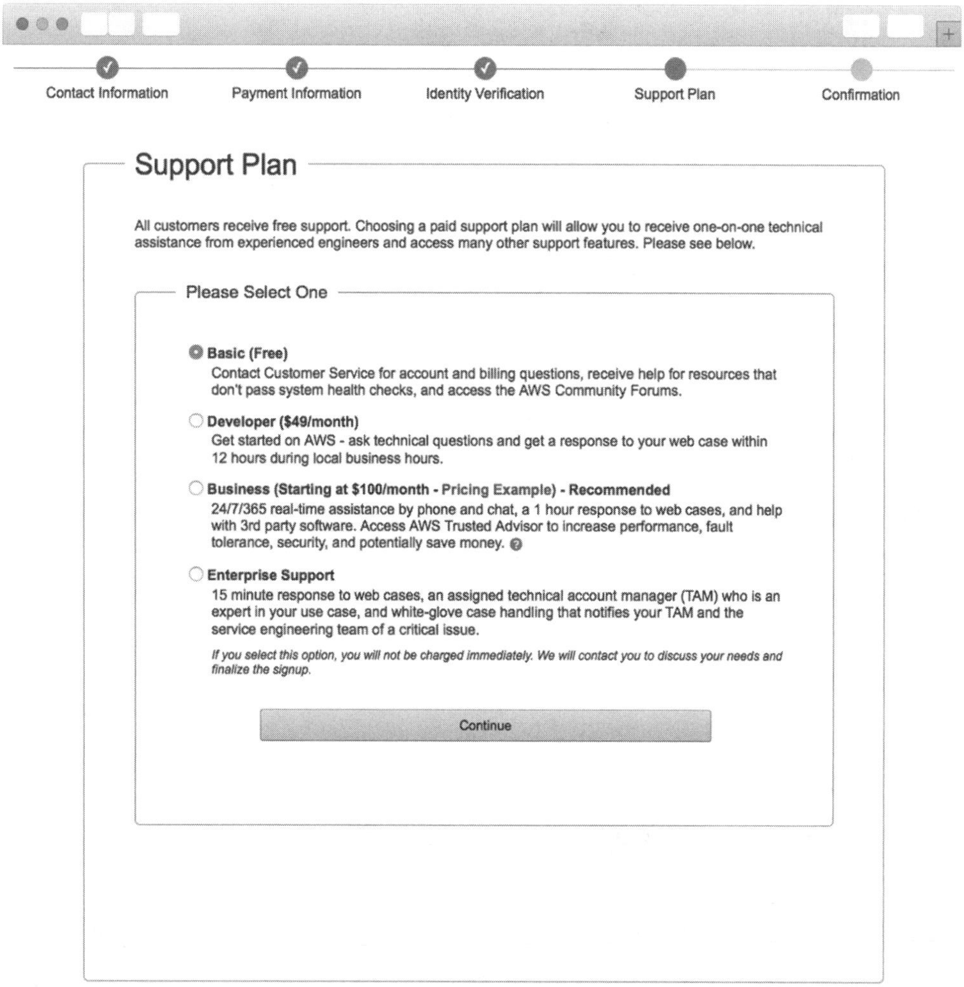

Figure 1.21   Creating an AWS account: choosing your support plan

5. CHOOSING YOUR SUPPORT PLAN

The last step is to choose a support plan; see figure 1.21. In this case, select the Basic plan, which is free. If you later create an AWS account for your business, we recommend the Business support plan. You can even switch support plans later.

High five! You're done. Now you can log in to your account with the AWS Management Console.

1.8.2   Signing In

You have an AWS account and are ready to sign in to the AWS Management Console at https://console.aws.amazon.com. As mentioned earlier, the Management Console is a web-based tool you can use to control AWS resources. The Management Console

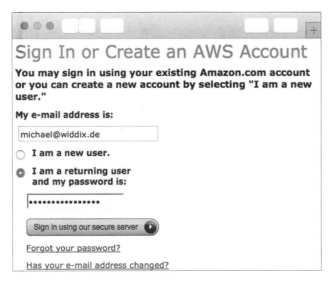

Figure 1.22   Sign in to the Management Console.

uses the AWS API to make most of the functionality available to you. Figure 1.22 shows the Sign In page.

Enter your login credentials and click Sign In Using Our Secure Server to see the Management Console, shown in figure 1.23.

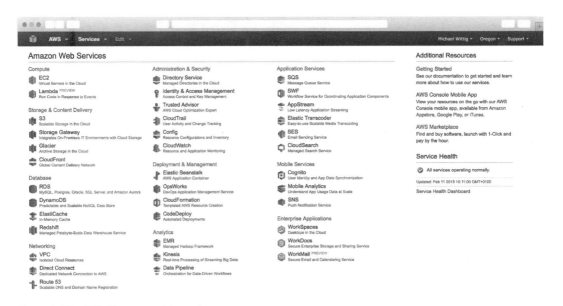

Figure 1.23   AWS Management Console

The most important part is the navigation bar at the top; see figure 1.24. It consists of six sections:

- *AWS*—Gives you a fast overview of all resources in your account.
- *Services*—Provides access to all AWS services.
- *Custom section (Edit)*—Click Edit and drag-and-drop important services here to personalize the navigation bar.
- *Your name*—Lets you access billing information and your account, and also lets you sign out.
- *Your region*—Lets you choose your region. You'll learn about regions in section 3.5. You don't need to change anything here now.
- *Support*—Gives you access to forums, documentation, and a ticket system.

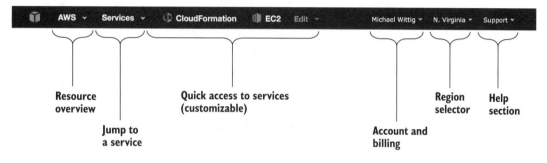

Figure 1.24   AWS Management Console navigation bar

Next, you'll create a key pair so you can connect to your virtual servers.

1.8.3   Creating a key pair

To access a virtual server in AWS, you need a *key pair* consisting of a private key and a public key. The public key will be uploaded to AWS and inserted into the virtual server. The private key is yours; it's like your password, but much more secure. Protect your private key as if it's a password. It's your secret, so don't lose it—you can't retrieve it.

To access a Linux server, you use the SSH protocol; you'll authenticate with the help of your key pair instead of a password during login. You access a Windows server via Remote Desktop Protocol (RDP); you'll need your key pair to decrypt the administrator password before you can log in.

The following steps will guide you to the dashboard of the EC2 service, which offers virtual servers, and where you can obtain a key pair:

1 Open the AWS Management Console at https://console.aws.amazon.com.
2 Click Services in the navigation bar, find the EC2 service, and click it.
3 Your browser shows the EC2 Management Console.

The EC2 Management Console, shown in figure 1.25, is split into three columns. The first column is the EC2 navigation bar; because EC2 is one of the oldest services, it has many

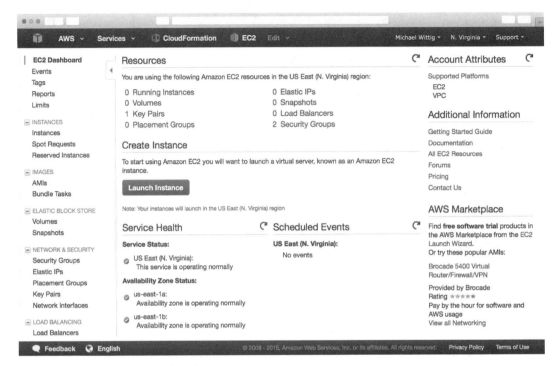

Figure 1.25   EC2 Management Console

features that you can access via the navigation bar. The second column gives you a brief overview of all your EC2 resources. The third column provides additional information.

Follow these steps to create a new key pair:

1 Click Key Pairs in the navigation bar under Network & Security.
2 Click the Create Key Pair button on the page shown in figure 1.26.
3 Name the Key Pair mykey. If you choose another name, you must replace the name in all the following examples!

During key-pair creation, you downloaded a file called mykey.pem. You must now prepare that key for future use. Depending on your operating system, you may need to do things differently, so please read the section that fits your OS.

Using your own key pair

It's also possible to upload the public key part from an existing key pair to AWS. Doing so has two advantages:

- You can reuse an existing key pair.
- You can be sure that only you know the private key part of the key pair. If you use the Create Key Pair button, AWS knows (at least briefly) your private key.

We decided against that approach in this case because it's less convenient to implement in a book.

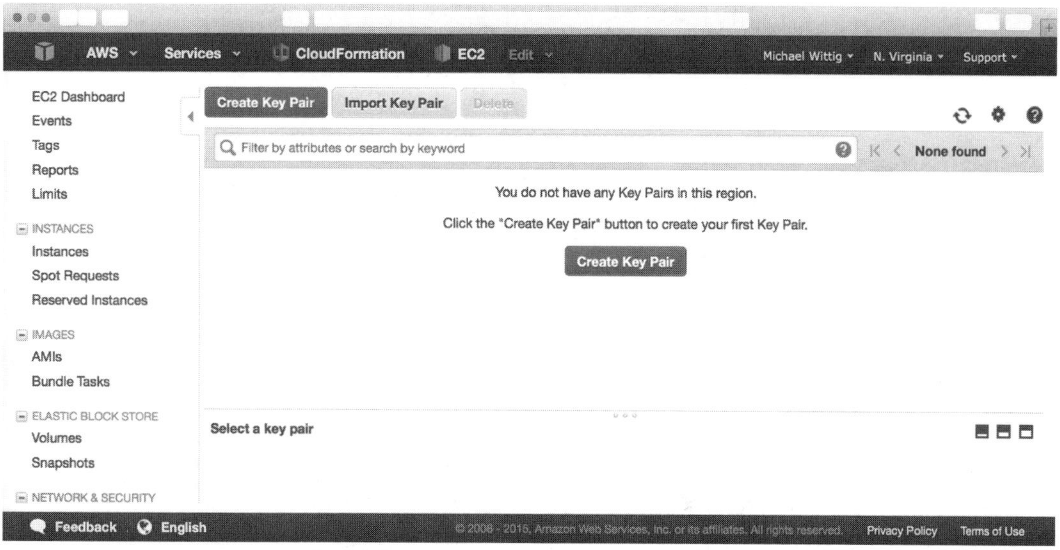

Figure 1.26   EC2 Management Console key pairs

LINUX AND MAC OS X

The only thing you need to do is change the access rights of mykey.pem so that only you can read the file. To do so, run `chmod 400 mykey.pem` in the terminal. You'll learn about how to use your key when you need to log in to a virtual server for the first time in this book.

WINDOWS

Windows doesn't ship a SSH client, so you need to download the PuTTY installer for Windows from http://mng.bz/A1bY and install PuTTY. PuTTY comes with a tool called PuTTYgen that can convert the mykey.pem file into a mykey.ppk file, which you'll need:

1   Run the application PuTTYgen. The screen shown in figure 1.27 opens.
2   Select SSH-2 RSA under Type of Key to Generate.
3   Click Load.
4   Because PuTTYgen displays only *.pkk files, you need to switch the file extension of the File Name field to All Files.
5   Select the mykey.pem file, and click Open.
6   Confirm the dialog box.
7   Change Key Comment to `mykey`.
8   Click Save Private Key. Ignore the warning about saving the key without a passphrase.

Your .pem file is now converted to the .pkk format needed by PuTTY. You'll learn how to use your key when you need to log in to a virtual server for the first time in this book.

Figure 1.27 PuTTYgen allows you to convert the downloaded .pem file into the .pkk file format needed by PuTTY.

1.8.4 Creating a billing alarm

Before you use your AWS account in the next chapter, we advise you to create a billing alarm. If you exceed the Free Tier, an email is sent to you. The book warns you whenever an example isn't covered by the Free Tier. Please make sure that you carefully follow the cleanup steps after each example. To make sure you haven't missed something during cleanup, please create a billing alarm as advised by AWS: http://mng.bz/M7Sj.

1.9 Summary

- Amazon Web Services (AWS) is a platform of web services offering solutions for computing, storing, and networking that work well together.
- Cost savings aren't the only benefit of using AWS. You'll also profit from an innovative and fast-growing platform with flexible capacity, fault-tolerant services, and a worldwide infrastructure.
- Any use case can be implemented on AWS, whether it's a widely used web application or a specialized enterprise application with an advanced networking setup.

- You can interact with AWS in many different ways. You can control the different services by using the web-based GUI; use code to manage AWS programmatically from the command line or SDKs; or use blueprints to set up, modify, or delete your infrastructure on AWS.
- Pay-per-use is the pricing model for AWS services. Computing power, storage, and networking services are billed similarly to electricity.
- Creating an AWS account is easy. Now you know how to set up a key pair so you can log in to virtual servers for later use.

A simple example: WordPress in five minutes

This chapter covers:

- Creating a blogging infrastructure
- Analyzing costs of a blogging infrastructure
- Exploring a blogging infrastructure
- Shutting down a blogging infrastructure

In chapter 1, we looked at why AWS is such a great choice to run web applications in the cloud. In this chapter, you'll evaluate migrating the blogging infrastructure of your imaginary company to AWS.

Example is 100% covered by the Free Tier

The example in this chapter is covered by the Free Tier. As long as you don't run this example longer than a few days, you won't pay anything for it. Keep in mind that this applies only if you created a fresh AWS account for this book and there are no other things going on in your AWS account. Try to complete the chapter within a few days, because you'll clean up your account at the end of the chapter.

34

Your imaginary company currently uses WordPress to host over 1,000 blogs on your own servers. The blogging infrastructure must be highly available, because customers don't tolerate outages. To evaluate whether a migration is possible, you need to do the following:

- Set up a highly available blogging infrastructure
- Estimate monthly costs of the infrastructure

WordPress is written in PHP and uses a MySQL database to store data. Apache is used as the web server to serve the pages. With this information in mind, it's time to map your requirements to AWS services.

2.1 Creating your infrastructure

You'll use four different AWS services to copy the old infrastructure to AWS:

- *Elastic Load Balancing (ELB)*—AWS offers a load balancer as a service. The Elastic Load Balancer (ELB) distributes traffic to a bunch of servers behind it. It's highly available by default.
- *Elastic Compute Cloud (EC2)*—A virtual server is provided by the Elastic Compute Cloud (EC2) service. You'll use a Linux server with an optimized distribution called Amazon Linux to install Apache, PHP, and WordPress. You aren't limited to Amazon Linux; you could also choose Ubuntu, Debian, Red Hat, or Windows. Virtual servers can fail, so you need at least two of them. The load balancer will distribute the traffic between them. In case of a server failure, the load balancer will stop sending traffic to the failed server, and the remaining server will need to handle all the requests until the failed server is replaced.
- *Relational Database Service (RDS) for MySQL*—WordPress relies on the popular MySQL database. AWS provides MySQL as a Relational Database Service (RDS). You choose the database size (storage, CPU, RAM), and RDS takes care of the rest (backups, updates). RDS can also provide a highly available MySQL database by replication.
- *Security groups*—Security groups are a fundamental service of AWS to control network traffic like a firewall. Security groups can be attached to a lot of services like ELB, EC2, and RDS. With security groups, you can configure your load balancer so that it only accepts requests on port 80 from the internet, web servers only accept connections on port 80 from the load balancer, and MySQL only accepts connections on port 3306 from the web servers. If you want to log in to your web servers via SSH, you must also open port 22.

Figure 2.1 shows all the parts of the infrastructure in action. Sounds like a lot of stuff to set up, so let's get started!

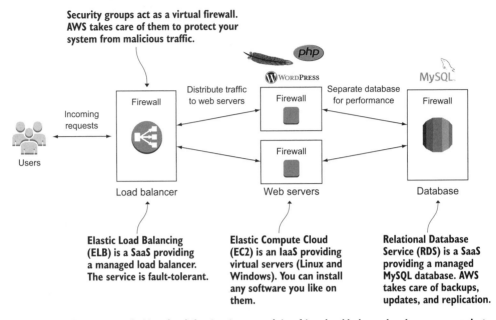

Figure 2.1   **The company's blogging infrastructure consists of two load-balanced web servers running WordPress and a MySQL database server.**

If you expect pages of instructions, you'll be happy to know that you can create all that with a few clicks. The following tasks are performed automatically in the background:

1 Creating an ELB
2 Creating a RDS MySQL database
3 Creating and attaching security groups
4 Creating two web servers:
   - Creating two EC2 virtual servers
   - Installing Apache and PHP via `yum install php`, `php-mysql`, `mysql`, `httpd`
   - Downloading and extracting the latest version of WordPress from http://wordpress.org/latest.tar.gz
   - Configuring WordPress to use the created RDS MySQL database
   - Starting Apache

To create the blogging infrastructure, open the AWS Management Console at https://console.aws.amazon.com. Click Services in the navigation bar, and click the Cloud-Formation service. You'll see a page like the one shown in figure 2.2.

NOTE All examples in this book use *N. Virginia* (also called *us-east-1*) as the default region. Exceptions are indicated. Please make sure you switch to the region *N. Virginia* before working on an example. When using the AWS Management Console, you can check and switch the region on the right side of the main navigation bar.

**Click to create a
new infrastructure
from a blueprint.**

**Reload
the page.**

**You haven't created
an infrastructure from a
blueprint at the moment.**

Figure 2.2   CloudFormation screen

Click Create Stack to start the four-step wizard, as shown in figure 2.3.

Step 1 of 4

**Name your
infrastructure.**

**Here you select the blueprint
for the infrastructure. You
can select a sample,
upload, or provide an
URL. Insert URL of
CloudFormation
template.**

Figure 2.3   Creating a blogging infrastructure: step 1 of 4

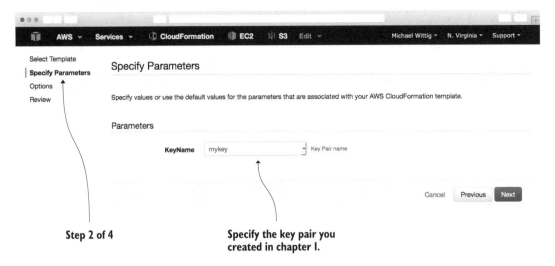

Figure 2.4   Creating a blogging infrastructure: step 2 of 4

Enter wordpress as the Name. For Source, select Specify an Amazon S3 Template URL, and copy this URL: https://s3.amazonaws.com/awsinaction/chapter2/template .json. Click Next to set the KeyName to mykey, as shown in figure 2.4.

Click Next to create a tag for your infrastructure. A tag consists of a key-value pair and can be used add information to all parts of your infrastructure. You can use tags to differentiate between testing and production resources, add the cost center to easily track costs in your organization, or mark resources that belong to a certain application if you host multiple applications in the same AWS account.

> **Pitfall: media uploads and plugins**
>
> WordPress uses a MySQL database to store articles and users. But by default, Word-Press stores media uploads (images) and plugins in a folder called wp-content on the local file system: the server isn't stateless. Using multiple servers isn't possible by default because each request will be served by another server, but media uploads and plugins are stored on only one of the servers.
>
> The example in this chapter is incomplete because it doesn't handle this problem. If you're interested in a solution, see chapter 14, where plugins are installed automatically during bootstrapping virtual servers and media uploads are outsourced to an object-storage service.

In this example, you'll use a tag to mark all resources that belong to the wordpress system. This will help you later to easily find your infrastructure. Use system as the key and wordpress as the value. Figure 2.5 shows how to configure the tag.

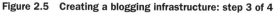

Figure 2.5   Creating a blogging infrastructure: step 3 of 4

Click Next. Finally, you'll see a confirmation page, as shown in figure 2.6. In the Estimate Cost row, click Cost. This will open a new browser tab in the background; you'll deal with it in the next section. Switch back to the original browser tab and click Create.

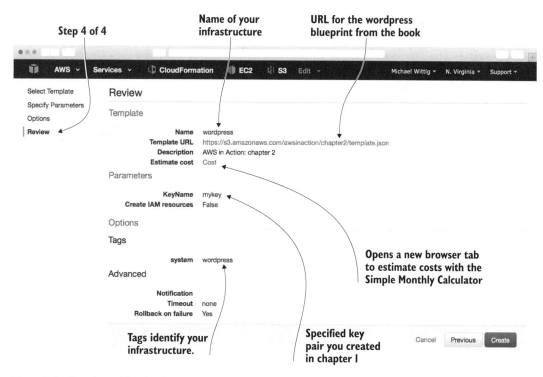

Figure 2.6   Creating a blogging infrastructure: step 4 of 4

**Reload
the page.**

**Infrastructure
is being created.**

**You have created one
infrastructure from a
blueprint at the moment.**

Figure 2.7   Review screen

Your infrastructure will now be created. Figure 2.7 shows that wordpress is in state
CREATE_IN_PROGRESS. It's a good time to take a break; come back in 5-15 minutes,
and you'll be surprised.

Take a look at the result by refreshing the page. Select the Wordpress row, where
Status should be CREATE_COMPLETE. If the status is still CREATE_IN_PROGRESS, be
patient until the status becomes CREATE_COMPLETE. Switch to the Outputs tab, as
shown in figure 2.8. There you'll find the URL to your wordpress system; click it to
visit the system.

**Infrastructure
has been created**

**URL to your newly
created WordPress**

Figure 2.8   Blogging infrastructure result

You may ask yourself, how does this work? The answer is *automation*.

Automation references

One of the key concepts of AWS is automation. You can automate everything. In the background, your blogging infrastructure was created based on a blueprint. You'll learn more about blueprints and the concept of programming your infrastructure in chapter 4. You'll learn to automate the installation of software in chapter 5.

You'll explore the blogging infrastructure in the next section to get a better understanding of the services you're using.

2.2 *Exploring your infrastructure*

Now that you've created your blogging infrastructure, let's take a closer look at it. Your infrastructure consists of the following:

- Web servers
- Load balancer
- MySQL database

You'll use the resource groups feature of the Management Console to get an overview.

2.2.1 *Resource groups*

A *resource group* is a collection of AWS resources. *Resource* is an abstract term for something in AWS like an EC2 server, a security group, or a RDS database. Resources can be tagged with key-value pairs. Resource groups specify what tags are needed for a resource to belong to the group. Furthermore, a resource group specifies the region(s) the resource must reside in. You can use resource groups to group resources if you run multiple systems in the same AWS account.

Remember that you tagged the blogging infrastructure with the key system and the value wordpress. From now on, we'll use this notation for key-value pairs: (system:wordpress). You'll use that tag to create a resource group for your WordPress infrastructure. In the AWS part of the navigation bar in figure 2.9, click Create a Resource Group.

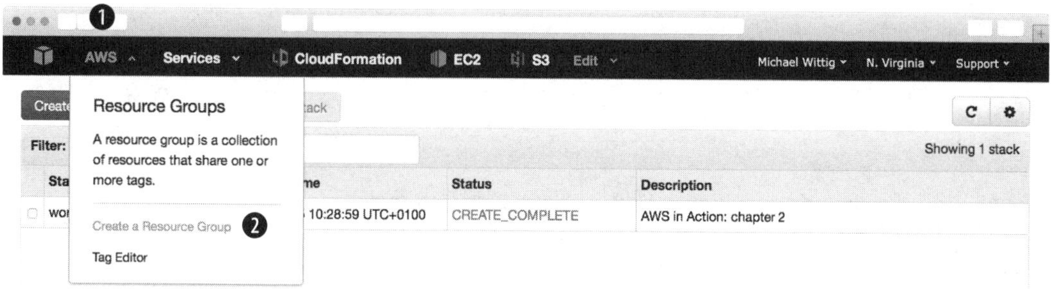

Figure 2.9 Creating a new resource group

> **Figures with cueballs**
> In some figures, as in figure 2.9, you'll see numbered cueballs. They mark the order of clicks you should follow to execute the process being discussed in the surrounding text.

You'll now create a new resource group:

1   Set Group Name to wordpress or whatever you like.
2   Add the tag system with the value wordpress.
3   Select the region N. Virginia.

The form should look like figure 2.10. Save the resource group.

2.2.2   *Web servers*

Now you'll see the screen shown in figure 2.11. Select Instances under EC2 on the left to see your web servers. By clicking the arrow icon in the Go column, you can easily jump to the details of a single web server.

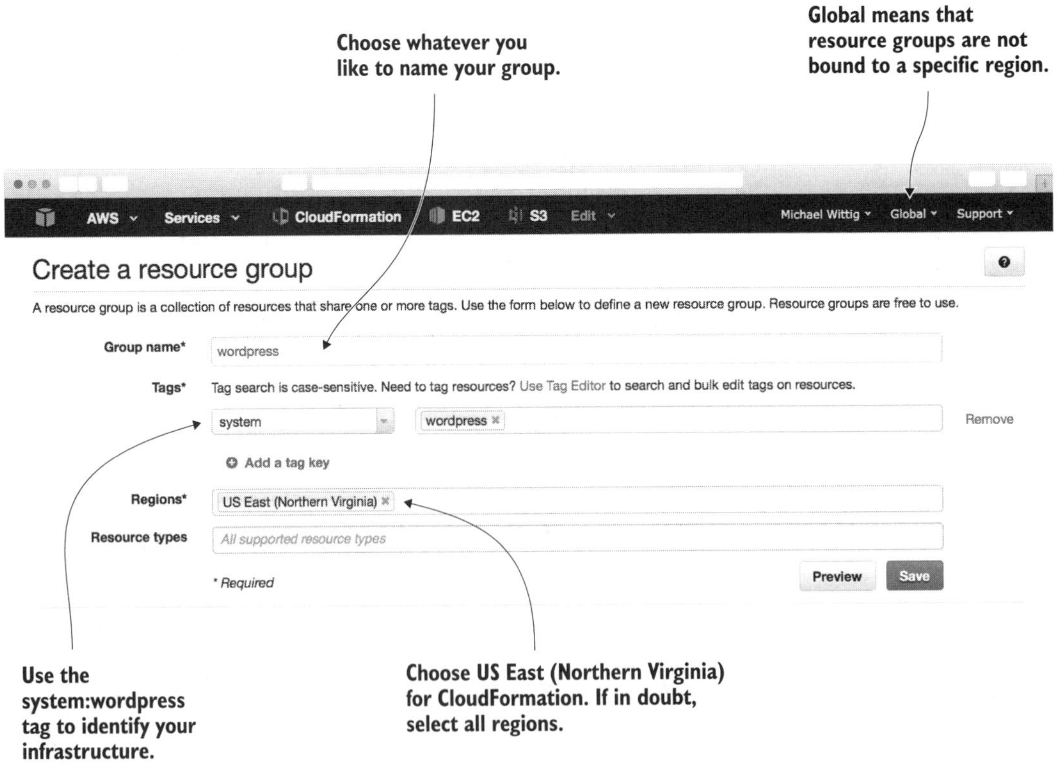

Choose whatever you like to name your group.

Global means that resource groups are not bound to a specific region.

AWS ⌄   Services ⌄   CloudFormation   EC2   S3   Edit ⌄   Michael Wittig ⌄   Global ⌄   Support ⌄

Create a resource group

A resource group is a collection of resources that share one or more tags. Use the form below to define a new resource group. Resource groups are free to use.

Group name*   wordpress

Tags*   Tag search is case-sensitive. Need to tag resources? Use Tag Editor to search and bulk edit tags on resources.

system   wordpress ✕   Remove

⊕ Add a tag key

Regions*   US East (Northern Virginia) ✕

Resource types   All supported resource types

* Required   Preview   Save

Use the system:wordpress tag to identify your infrastructure.

Choose US East (Northern Virginia) for CloudFormation. If in doubt, select all regions.

Figure 2.10   Creating a resource group for your blogging infrastructure

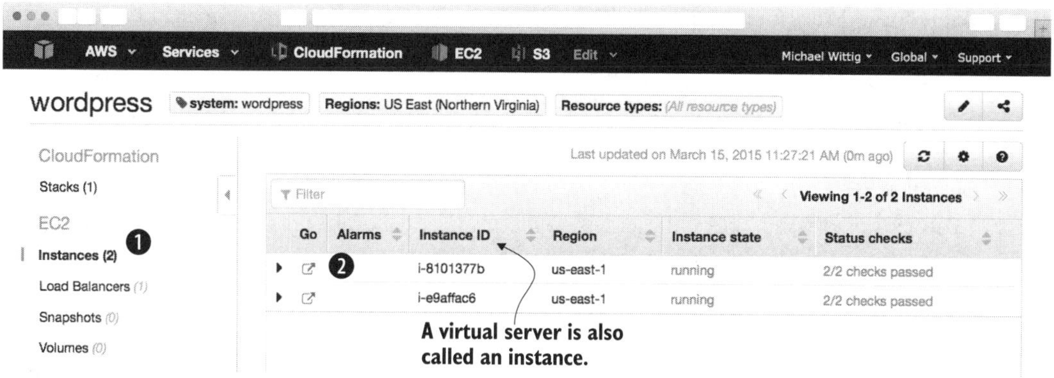

Figure 2.11 Blogging infrastructure web servers via resource groups

You're now looking at the details of your web server, also called an EC2 instance. Figure 2.12 shows an extract of what you see. The interesting details are as follows:

- *Instance type*—Tells you about how powerful your instance is. You'll learn more about instance types in chapter 3.
- *Public IP address*—The IP address that's reachable over the internet. You can use that IP address to connect to the server via SSH.
- *Security groups*—If you click View Rules, you'll see the active firewall rules like the one that enabled port 22 from all sources (0.0.0.0/0).
- *AMI ID*—Remember that you used the Amazon Linux operating system (OS). If you click the AMI ID, you'll see the version number of the OS, among others.

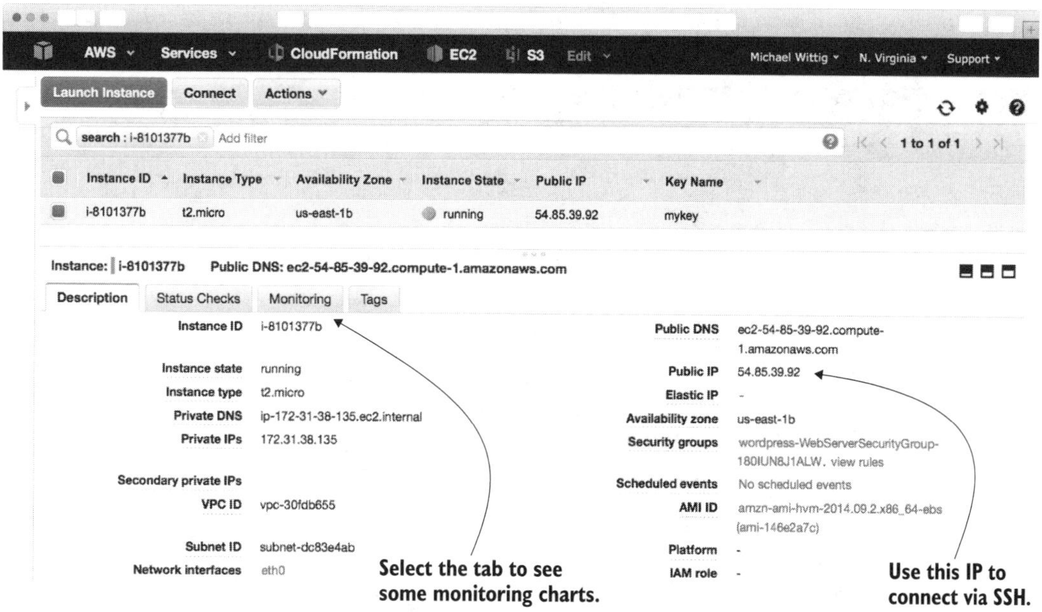

Figure 2.12 Details of web servers running the blogging infrastructure

Select the Monitoring tab to see how your web server is utilized. This will become part of your job: really knowing how your infrastructure is doing. AWS collects some metrics and shows them in the Monitoring section. If the CPU is utilized more than 80%, you should add a third server to prevent page load times from increasing.

2.2.3   *Load balancer*

You can find your load balancer by selecting Load Balancers under EC2 on the left to open the page shown in figure 2.13. By clicking the arrow icon in the Go column, you can easily jump to the details of the load balancer.

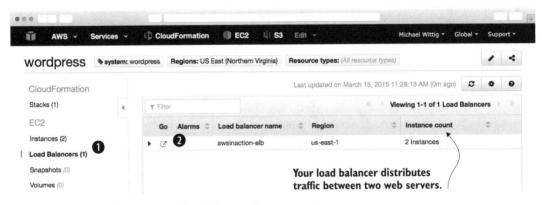

Figure 2.13   Blogging infrastructure load balancer via resource groups

You're now looking at the details of your load balancer. Figure 2.14 shows an extract of what you'll see. The most interesting part is how the load balancer forwards traffic

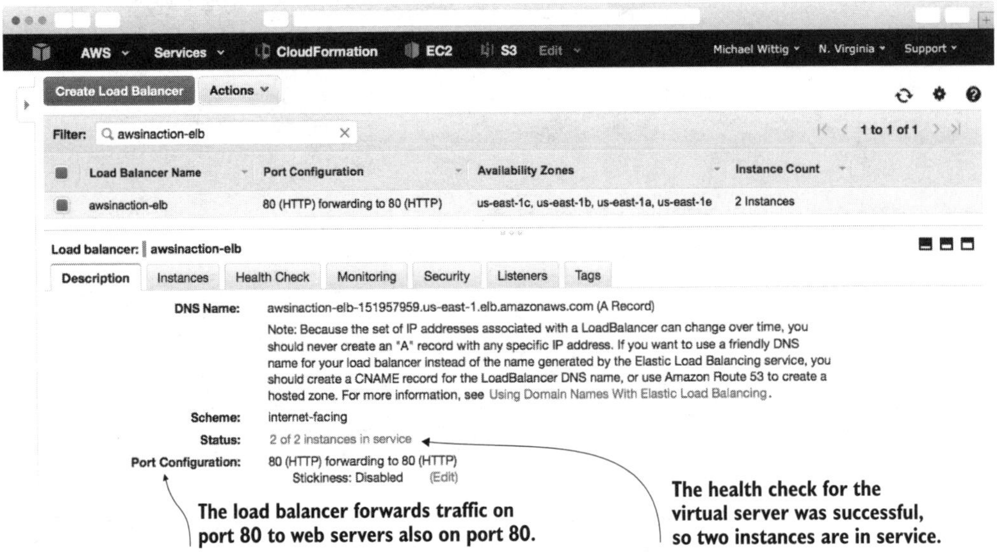

Figure 2.14   Details of load balancers serving the blogging infrastructure

to the web servers. The blogging infrastructure runs on port 80, which is the default HTTP port. The load balancer accepts only HTTP connections to forward to one of the web servers that also listen on port 80. The load balancer performs a health check on the virtual servers attached. Both virtual servers are working as expected, so the load balancer routes traffic to them.

As before, there's a Monitoring tab where you can find interesting metrics that you should watch in production. If the traffic pattern changes suddenly, this indicates a potential problem with your system. You'll also find metrics indicating the number of HTTP errors, which will help you to monitor and debug your system.

2.2.4 MySQL database

Last but not least, let's look at the MySQL database. You can find your database in a resource group named `wordpress`. Select DB Instances under RDS at left. By clicking the arrow icon in the Go column (shown in figure 2.15), you can easily jump to the details of the database.

The details of your MySQL database are shown in figure 2.16. The benefit of using RDS is that you no longer need to worry about backups because AWS performs them automatically. Updates are performed by AWS in a custom maintenance window. Keep in mind that you can choose the right database size in terms of storage, CPU, and RAM, depending on your needs. AWS offers many different instance classes,

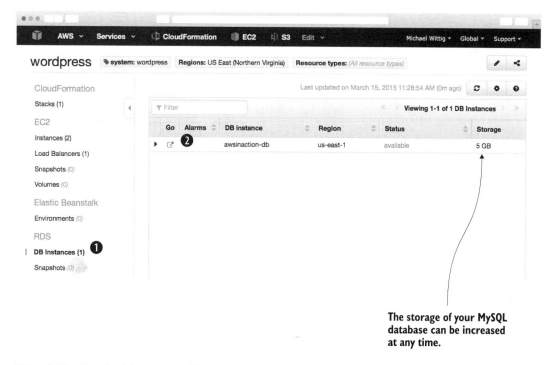

The storage of your MySQL database can be increased at any time.

Figure 2.15   Blogging infrastructure MySQL via resource groups

Your MySQL database uses normal disks at the moment. You could also use SSD disks to improve performance.

AWS ⌄   Services ⌄   ⫿ CloudFormation   ▮ EC2   ⫿ S3   Edit ⌄   Michael Wittig ⌄   N. Virginia ⌄   Support ⌄

DB Instances > awsinaction-db

Details   Recent Events & Logs

Endpoint: awsinaction-db.cnrzexj3is99.us-east-1.rds.amazonaws.com:3306 (authorized) ⓘ

Configuration Details

Engine	MySQL 5.6.22
License Model	General Public License
Created Time	March 15, 2015 at 10:36:59 AM UTC+1
DB Name	wordpress
Username	wordpress
Option Group	default:mysql-5-6 (in-sync)
Parameter Group	default.mysql5.6 (in-sync)

Security and Network

Availability Zone	us-east-1a
VPC	vpc-30fdb655
Subnet Group	default (Complete)
Subnets	subnet-dc83e4ab
	subnet-b0b8f38a
	subnet-d4319cff
	subnet-61b33738
Security Groups	Security Group sg-349a0950 (active)
Publicly Accessible	Yes
Port	3306
Certificate Authority	rds-ca-2015 (Mar 5, 2020)

Instance and IOPS

Instance Class	db.t2.micro ⓘ
Storage Type	Magnetic ◄
IOPS	disabled
Storage	5 GB

Encryption Details **Availability and Durability**

DB Instance Status	available
Multi AZ	No
Automated Backups	Enabled (1 Day) ◄
Latest Restore Time	Mar 15, 2015 11:45:00 AM UTC+1

Maintenance Details

Auto Minor Version Upgrade	Yes
Maintenance Window	wed:07:58-wed:08:28
Backup Window	08:49-09:19
Maintenance Details	None

AWS takes care of backing up your data.

You can specify a window when AWS can apply updates to your database.

Figure 2.16   Details of the MySQL database storing data for the blogging infrastructure

from 1 core with 1 GB RAM up to 32 cores with 244 GB RAM. You'll learn more about this in chapter 9.

Now it's time to evaluate costs. You'll analyze the costs of your blogging infrastructure in the next section.

2.3   How much does it cost?

Part of the evaluation is a cost estimation. To analyze the cost of your blogging infrastructure, you'll use the AWS Simple Monthly Calculator. Remember that you clicked the Cost link in the previous section to open a new browser tab. Switch to that browser tab, and you'll see a screen like figure 2.17. If you closed the tab, go to https://s3.amazonaws.com/awsinaction/chapter2/cost.html instead. Click

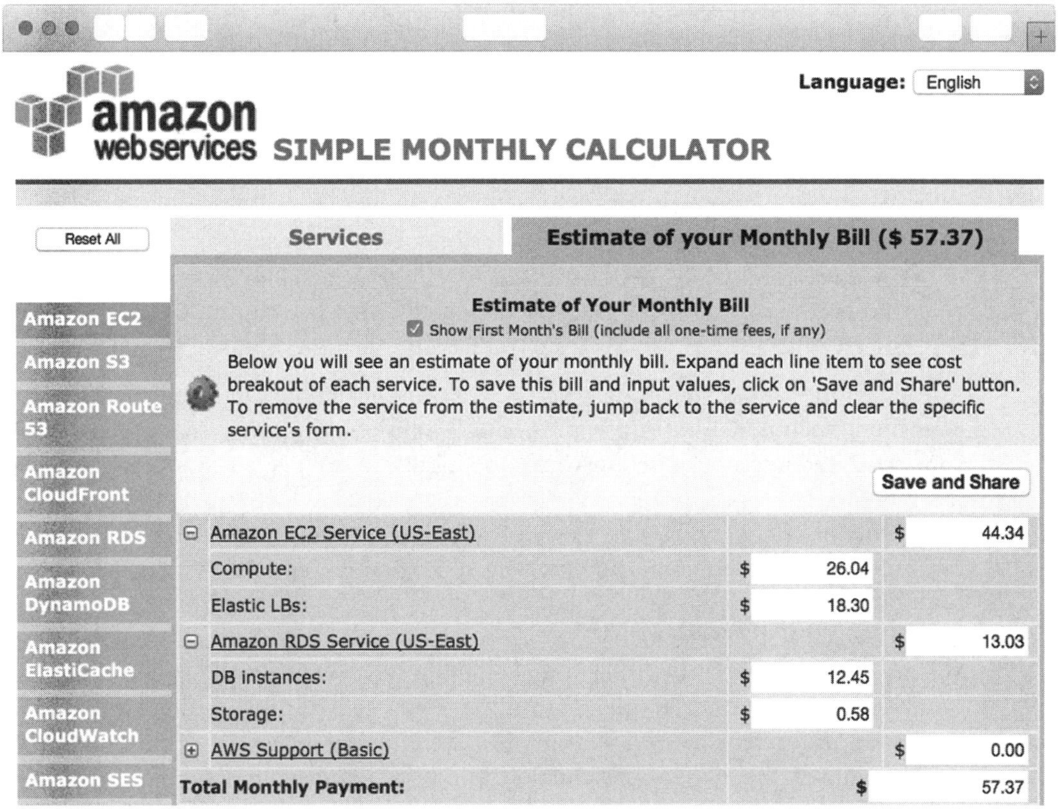

Figure 2.17 Blogging infrastructure cost calculation

Estimate of Your Monthly Bill, and expand the Amazon EC2 Service and Amazon RDS Service rows.

In this example, your infrastructure will cost around $60 per month. Table 2.1 shows the detailed costs of this infrastructure.

Table 2.1 Blogging infrastructure cost calculation with AWS Simple Monthly Calculator

AWS service	Infrastructure	Monthly cost
Amazon EC2 compute	Web servers	$ 26.04
Amazon EC2 elastic LBs	Load balancer	$ 18.30
Amazon RDS DB instances	MySQL database	$ 12.45
Amazon RDS storage	MySQL database	$ 0.58
		$ 57.37

Keep in mind that this is only an estimate. You're billed based on actual use at the end of the month. Everything is on-demand and usually billed by hours of usage or by gigabytes of usage. But what influences usage for this infrastructure?

- *Traffic processed by the load balancer*—Expect costs to go down in December and the summer when people are on vacation and not looking at blogs.
- *Storage needed for the database*—If your company increases the number of blogs, the database will grow, so the cost of storage will increase.
- *Number of web servers needed*—A single web server is billed by hours of usage. If two web servers aren't enough to handle all the traffic during the day, you may need a third server. In that case, you'll consume more hours of virtual servers.

Estimating the cost of your infrastructure is a complicated task, but that's true even if your infrastructure doesn't run in AWS. The benefit of using AWS is that it's flexible. If your estimated number of web servers is too high, you can get rid of a server and stop paying for it.

Now that you've had an overview of the blogging infrastructure, it's time to shut down the infrastructure and complete your migration evaluation.

2.4   *Deleting your infrastructure*

You successfully determined that your company can migrate its blogging infrastructure to AWS for around $60 per month. Now you can decide whether a migration should be performed.

To complete the migration evaluation, you need to delete the blogging infrastructure and get rid of all the resources. You don't need to worry about losing data because you only created useless data during the evaluation.

Go to the CloudFormation service in the Management Console and do the following:

1 Select the Wordpress row.
2 Click Delete Stack, as shown in figure 2.18.

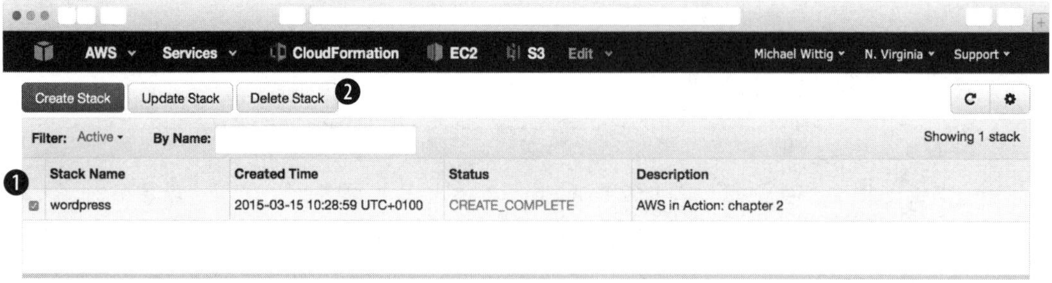

Figure 2.18   Delete your blogging infrastructure.

Figure 2.19 Confirm deletion of your blogging infrastructure.

After you confirm the deletion of the infrastructure, as shown in figure 2.19, it takes a few minutes for AWS to delete all of the infrastructure's dependencies.

This is an efficient way to manage your infrastructure. Just as the infrastructure's creation was automated, its deletion is also completely automated. You can create and delete infrastructure on-demand whenever you like, and you only pay for infrastructure when you create and run it.

2.5   *Summary*

- Creating a blogging infrastructure can be fully automated.
- Infrastructure can be created at any time on-demand without any up-front commitment for how long you'll use it.
- You pay for your infrastructure depending on how many hours you use it.
- Infrastructure consists of several parts, such as virtual servers, load balancers, and databases.
- Infrastructure can be deleted with one click. The process is powered by automation.

Part 2

Building virtual infrastructure with servers and networking

Computing power and network connectivity have become basic needs for private households, medium-sized enterprises, and big corporations alike. Operating hardware in-house or in outsourced data centers covered these needs in the past. Today, the cloud is revolutionizing the way we access computing power. Virtual servers can be started and stopped on demand to fulfill computing needs within minutes. Being able to install software on virtual servers enables you to execute computing tasks without having to buy or rent hardware.

If you want to understand AWS, you have to dive into the possibilities offered by the API working behind the scenes. You can control every service on AWS by sending requests to a REST API. Based on this API, a variety of solutions can help you to automate your overall infrastructure. Infrastructure automation is a major advantage of the cloud, compared to on-premises solutions.

This part of the book will introduce you to infrastructure orchestration and automated deployment of applications. Creating virtual networks allows you to build closed, secure network environments on AWS and to connect them with your home or corporate network. Chapter 3 explores working with a virtual server; you'll learn key concepts of the EC2 service. Chapter 4 discusses approaches to automating your infrastructure and using infrastructure as code. Chapter 5 shows you three different ways to deploy software to AWS. Finally, chapter 6 is about networking; you'll learn how to secure your system with a virtual private network and firewalls.

Using virtual servers: EC2

This chapter covers

- Launching a virtual server with Linux
- Controlling a virtual server remotely via SSH
- Monitoring and debugging a virtual server
- Reducing costs for virtual servers

It's impressive what you can achieve with the computing power of the smartphone in your pocket or the laptop in your bag. But if your task requires massive computing power or high network traffic or needs to run reliably 24/7, a virtual server is a better fit. With a virtual server, you'll get a part of a server located in a data center. On AWS, virtual servers are offered by the service called Elastic Compute Cloud (EC2).

3.1 Exploring a virtual server

A virtual server is part of a physical server that's isolated by software from other virtual servers on the same physical server; it consists of CPUs, memory, networking interfaces, and storage. The physical server is also called the *host server*, and the virtual servers running on it are called *guests*. A hypervisor is responsible for

Not all examples are covered by the Free Tier

The examples in this chapter are *not* all covered by the Free Tier. A special warning message appears when an example incurs costs. As long as you don't run all other examples longer than a few days, you won't pay anything for them. Keep in mind that this applies only if you created a fresh AWS account for this book and nothing else is going on in your AWS account. Try to complete the examples of the chapter within a few days; you'll clean up your account at the end of each example.

isolating the guests from each other and for scheduling requests to the hardware. Figure 3.1 shows these layers of server virtualization.

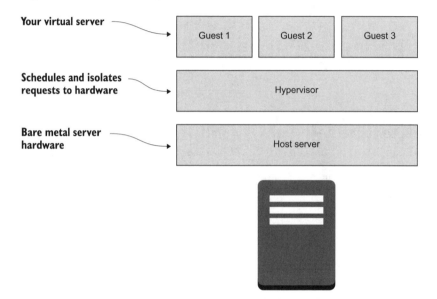

Figure 3.1 Layers of server virtualization

Typical use cases for a virtual server are as follows:

- Hosting a web application
- Executing enterprise applications
- Transforming or analyzing data

3.1.1 *Launching a virtual server*

It takes only a few clicks to launch a virtual server:

1   Open the AWS Management Console at https://console.aws.amazon.com.
2   Make sure you're in the N. Virginia (US East) region (see figure 3.2), because we optimized our examples for this region.

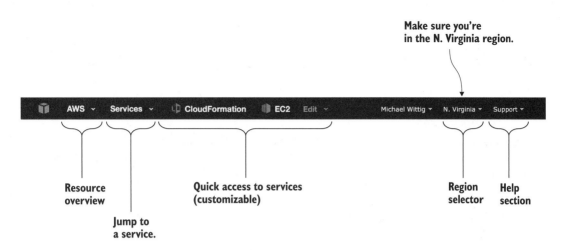

Figure 3.2   Making sure you're in the correct region

3   Find the EC2 service in the navigation bar under Services and click it. You'll see a page like the one shown in figure 3.3.

4   To start the wizard for launching a virtual server, click Launch Instance.

AWS ⌄   Services ⌄   Edit ⌄

EC2 Dashboard

Events

Tags

Reports

Limits

⊟ INSTANCES

Instances

Spot Requests

Reserved Instances

⊟ IMAGES

AMIs

Bundle Tasks

Resources

You are using the following Amazon EC2 resources in the US East (N. Virginia) region:

0   Running Instances   0   Elastic IPs
0   Volumes   0   Snapshots
1   Key Pairs   0   Load Balancers
0   Placement Groups   2   Security Groups

Create Instance

To start using Amazon EC2 you will want to launch a virtual server, known as an Amazon instance.

Launch Instance

Note: Your instances will launch in the US East (N. Virginia) region

**Starting a new
virtual server**

Figure 3.3   Overview of the EC2 service for virtual servers, with the Launch Instance button

The wizard will guide you through the following steps:

1 Selecting an OS
2 Choosing the size of your virtual server
3 Configuring details
4 Reviewing your input and selecting a key pair for SSH

SELECTING AN OS

The first step is to choose a bundle of an OS and preinstalled software for your virtual server, called an Amazon Machine Image (AMI). Select Ubuntu Server 14.04 LTS (HVM) for your virtual server, as shown in figure 3.4.

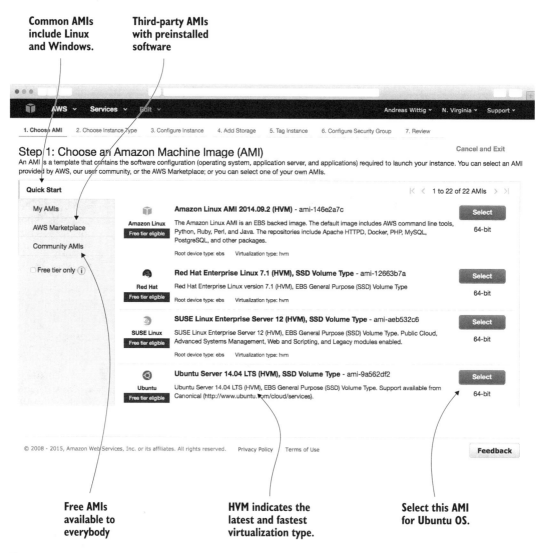

Figure 3.4   Choosing an OS for the virtual server

An AMI is the basis your virtual server starts from. AMIs are offered by AWS, by third-party providers, and by the community. AWS offers the Amazon Linux AMI, which includes a Red Hat Enterprise Linux derivative optimized for use with EC2. You'll also find popular Linux distributions and AMIs with Microsoft Windows Server. In addition, the AWS Marketplace offers AMIs with preinstalled third-party software.

Virtual appliances on AWS

A *virtual appliance* is an image containing an OS and preconfigured software that can be run on a hypervisor. It's the hypervisor's job to run one or more virtual appliances. Because a virtual appliance contains a fixed state, every time you start the virtual appliance, you'll get exactly the same result. You can reproduce virtual appliances as often as needed, so you can use them to eliminate the cost of installing and configuring complex stacks of software. Virtual appliances are used by virtualization tools from VMware, Microsoft, and Oracle and for infrastructure as a service offerings in the cloud.

The AMI is the virtual appliance image in AWS. It's a special virtual appliance for use with the EC2 service for virtual servers. An AMI technically consists of a read-only filesystem including the OS, additional software, and configuration; it doesn't include the kernel of the OS. The kernel is loaded from an Amazon Kernel Image (AKI). You can also use AMIs for deploying software on AWS.

AWS uses Xen, an open source hypervisor, as the underlying technology for the EC2 service. The current generations of virtual servers on AWS use hardware-assisted virtualization. The technology is called Hardware Virtual Machine (HVM) and uses the Intel VT-x platform. A virtual server run by an AMI based on HVM uses a fully virtualized set of hardware and can take advantage of hardware extensions that provide fast access to the underlying hardware.

Using a 3.8+ kernel for your virtual Linux servers will provide the best performance. To do so, you should use at least Amazon Linux 13.09, Ubuntu 14.04, or RHEL7. If you're starting new virtual servers, make sure you're using HVM images.

CHOOSING THE SIZE OF YOUR VIRTUAL SERVER

It's now time to choose the computing power needed for your virtual server. Figure 3.5 shows the next step of the wizard. On AWS, computing power is classified into instance types. An instance type primarily describes the number of CPUs and the amount of memory.

Instance types and families

The names for different instance types are all structured in the same way. The *instance family* groups instance types for the same focus. AWS releases new instance types and families from time to time; the different versions are called and marked as *generations*. The *instance size* defines the capacity of CPU, memory, storage, and networking.

(continued)
For example, the instance type *t2.micro* tells you the following:

1 The instance family is *t*. It groups small, cheap virtual servers with low base-line CPU performance but with the ability to burst significantly over baseline CPU performance for a short time.
2 You're using generation *2* of this instance type.
3 The size is *micro*, indicating that the instance is very small.

Table 3.1 shows examples of instance types for different use cases. All prices in USD are valid for US East (N. Virginia) and a virtual server based on Linux on April 14, 2015.

Table 3.1 Overview of instance families and instance types

Instance type	Virtual CPUs	Memory	Description	Typical use case	Hourly cost (USD)
t2.micro	1	1 GB	Smallest and cheapest instance type, with moderate baseline performance and the ability to burst CPU performance above the baseline	Testing and development environments, and applications with low traffic	0.013
m3.large	2	7.5 GB	Has a balanced ratio of CPU, memory, and networking performance	All kinds of applications, such as medium databases, HTTP servers, and enterprise applications	0.140
r3.large	2	15 GB	Optimized for memory-intensive applications with extra memory	In-memory caches and enterprise application servers	0.175

There are also instance types and families optimized for compute-intensive workloads, workloads with high networking I/O, and storage-intensive workloads. Other instance types provide access to GPUs for server-side graphics workloads. Our experience indicates that you'll over-estimate the resource requirements for your applications. We recommend that you try to start your application with a smaller instance type than you first think you need.

Computers are getting faster and more specialized. AWS is constantly introducing new instance types and families. Some of them are improvements of existing instance families, and others are focused on specific workloads. For example, instance family d2 was introduced in March 2015. It provides instances for workloads requiring high sequential read and write access, such as some databases and log processing.

The smallest and cheapest virtual server will be enough for your first experiments. In the wizard screen shown in figure 3.5, choose the instance type t2.micro. Then click Next: Configure Instance Details to proceed.

Filter by special operation purpose.

Filter outdated instance types.

HDs connected to the server

Select t2.micro for your server.

Only network-attached storage is available.

Click here to proceed.

Figure 3.5 Choose the size of the virtual server.

INSTANCE DETAILS, STORAGE, FIREWALL, AND TAGS

The next four steps of the wizard are easy because you don't need to change the defaults. You'll learn about these settings in detail later in the book.

Figure 3.6 shows the next step of the wizard. You can change the details for your virtual server, such as the network configuration or the number of servers to launch. For now, keep the defaults, and click Next: Add Storage to proceed.

Start one or
multiple virtual
servers at once.

Network settings for
the virtual server

Access control for
server accessing
other AWS services

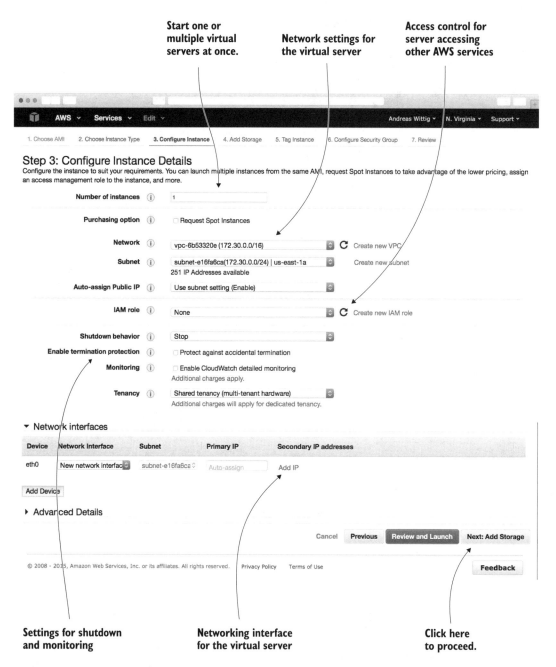

Settings for shutdown
and monitoring

Networking interface
for the virtual server

Click here
to proceed.

Figure 3.6   Details for the virtual server

There are different options for storing data on AWS, which we'll cover in detail in the
following chapters. Figure 3.7 shows the possibility of adding network-attached storage to your virtual server. Keep the defaults, and click Next: Tag Instance.

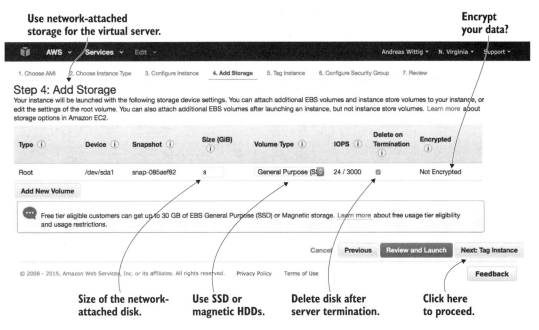

Figure 3.7 Add network-attached storage to your virtual server.

A tidy house indicates a tidy mind. Tags help you to organize resources on AWS. A tag is nothing more than a key-value pair. Add at least a Name tag to your resources to help you find your stuff later. Use Name as the key and myserver as the value, as figure 3.8 shows. Then click Next: Configure Security Group.

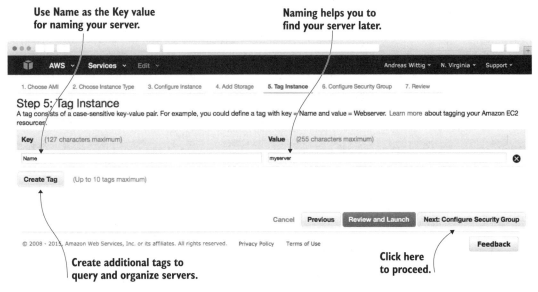

Figure 3.8 Name your virtual server with a Name tag.

A firewall helps to secure your virtual server. Figure 3.9 shows the settings for a default firewall allowing access via SSH from anywhere. This is exactly what you need, so keep the defaults and click Review and Launch.

REVIEWING YOUR INPUT AND SELECTING A KEY PAIR FOR SSH

You're almost finished. The wizard should show a review of your new virtual server (see figure 3.10). Make sure you chose Ubuntu Server 14.04 LTS (HVM) as the OS and t2.micro as the instance type. If everything is fine, click the Launch button.

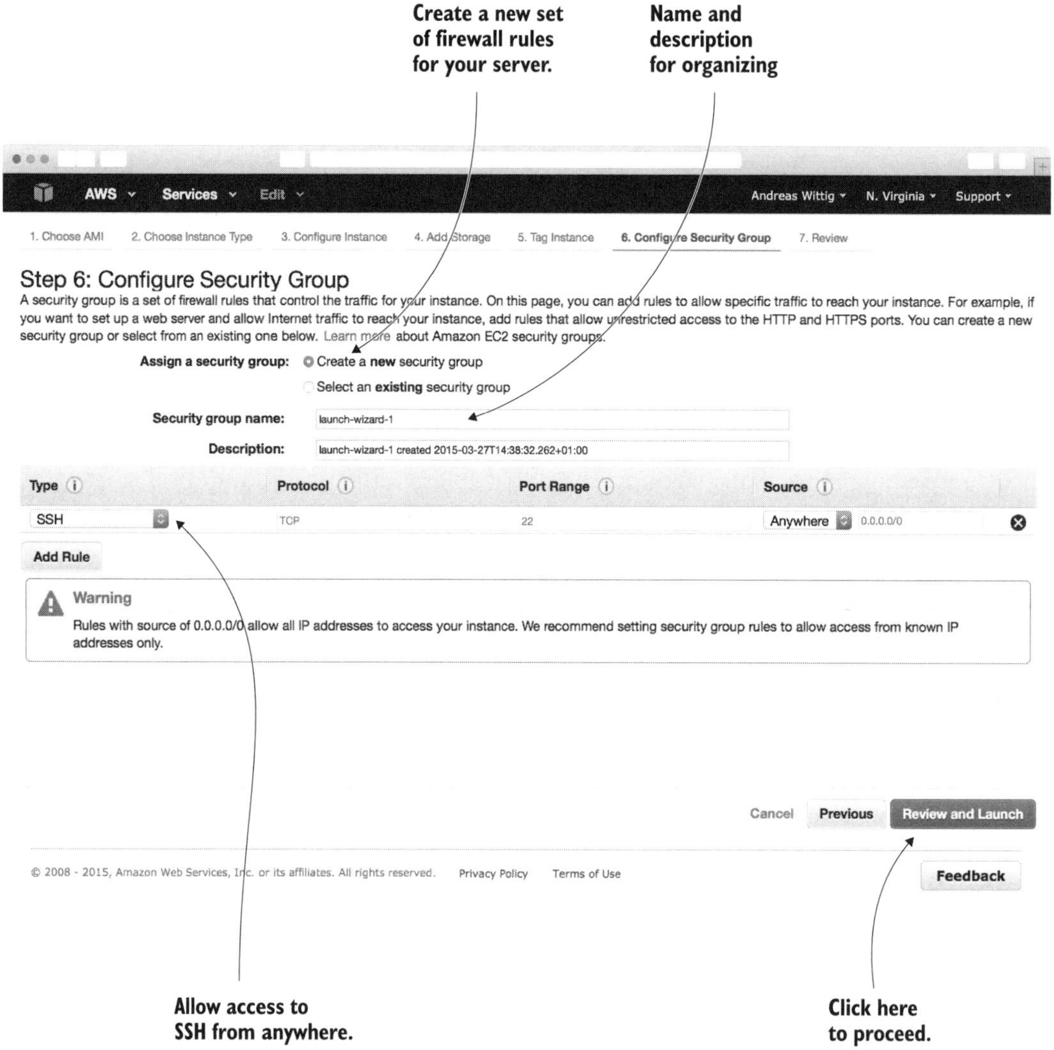

Figure 3.9   Configuring the firewall for your virtual server

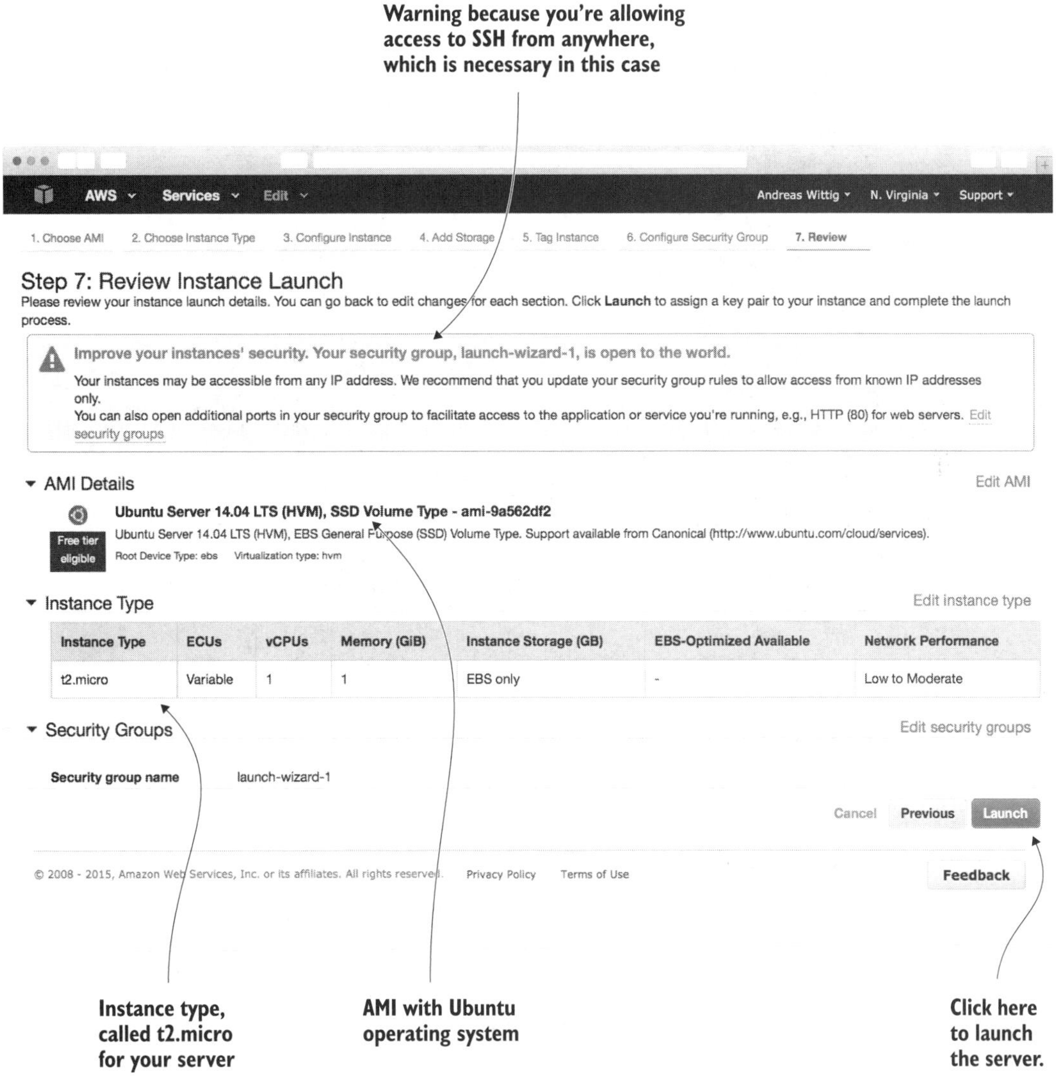

Warning because you're allowing
access to SSH from anywhere,
which is necessary in this case

Figure 3.10   Review the instance launch for the virtual server.

Last but not least, the wizard asks for your new virtual server's key.

Missing your key?

Logging in to your virtual server requires a key. You use a key instead of a password to authenticate yourself. A key is much more secure than a password, and using keys for SSH is enforced for virtual servers running Linux on AWS. If you skipped the creation of a key in section 1.8.3, follow these steps to create a personal key:

(continued)

1 Open the AWS Management Console at https://console.aws.amazon.com. Find the EC2 service in the navigation bar under Services and click it.
2 Switch to Key Pair via the submenu.
3 Click Create Key Pair.
4 Enter `mykey` for Key Pair Name, and click Create. Your browser downloads the key automatically.
5 Open a terminal and switch to your download folder.
6 OS X and Linux only: change the access rights of the file mykey.pem by running `chmod 400 mykey.pem` in the console.

Windows only: Windows doesn't ship a SSH client, so you need to install PuTTY. PuTTY comes with a tool called PuTTYgen that can convert the mykey.pem file into a mykey.ppk file, which you'll need. Open PuTTYgen and select SSH-2 RSA under Type of Key to Generate. Click Load. Because PuTTY-gen displays only *.pkk files, you need to switch the file extension of the File Name Input to All Files. Now you can select the mykey.pem file and click Open. Confirm the dialog box. Change Key Comment to mykey and Click Save Private Key. Ignore the warning about saving the key without a passphrase. Your .pem file is now converted to the .pkk format needed by PuTTY.

You'll find a more detailed explanation about how to create a key in chapter 1.

Choose the option Choose an Existing Key Pair, select the key pair mykey, and click Launch Instances (see figure 3.11).

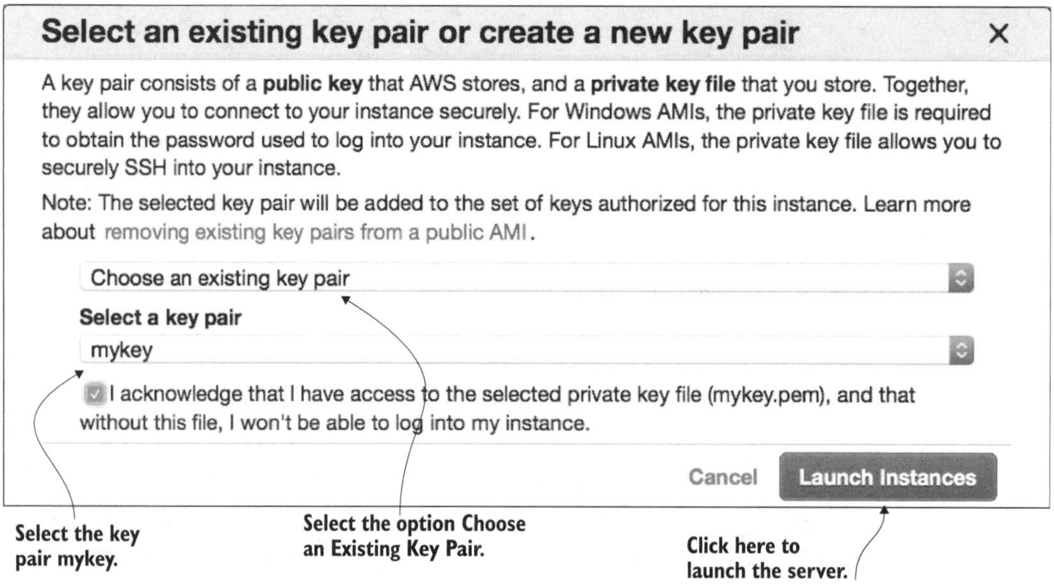

Select an existing key pair or create a new key pair   ✕

A key pair consists of a **public key** that AWS stores, and a **private key file** that you store. Together, they allow you to connect to your instance securely. For Windows AMIs, the private key file is required to obtain the password used to log into your instance. For Linux AMIs, the private key file allows you to securely SSH into your instance.

Note: The selected key pair will be added to the set of keys authorized for this instance. Learn more about removing existing key pairs from a public AMI.

Choose an existing key pair

Select a key pair

mykey

☑ I acknowledge that I have access to the selected private key file (mykey.pem), and that without this file, I won't be able to log into my instance.

Cancel   **Launch Instances**

Select the key pair mykey.   Select the option Choose an Existing Key Pair.   Click here to launch the server.

Figure 3.11   Choosing a key pair for the virtual server

Your virtual server launches. Open an overview by clicking View Instances, and wait until the server reaches the Running state. To take full control over your virtual server, you need to log in remotely.

3.1.2 Connecting to a virtual server

Installing additional software and running commands on your virtual server can be done remotely. To log in to the virtual server, you have to figure out its public IP address:

1 Click the EC2 service in the navigation bar under Services and click Instances in the submenu at left to jump to an overview of your virtual server.
2 Select the virtual server from the table by clicking it. Figure 3.12 shows the server overview and the available actions.
3 Click Connect to open the instructions for connecting to the virtual server.
4 Figure 3.13 shows the dialog with instructions to connect to the virtual server. Find the public IP address of your virtual server, such as 52.4.216.201 in our example.

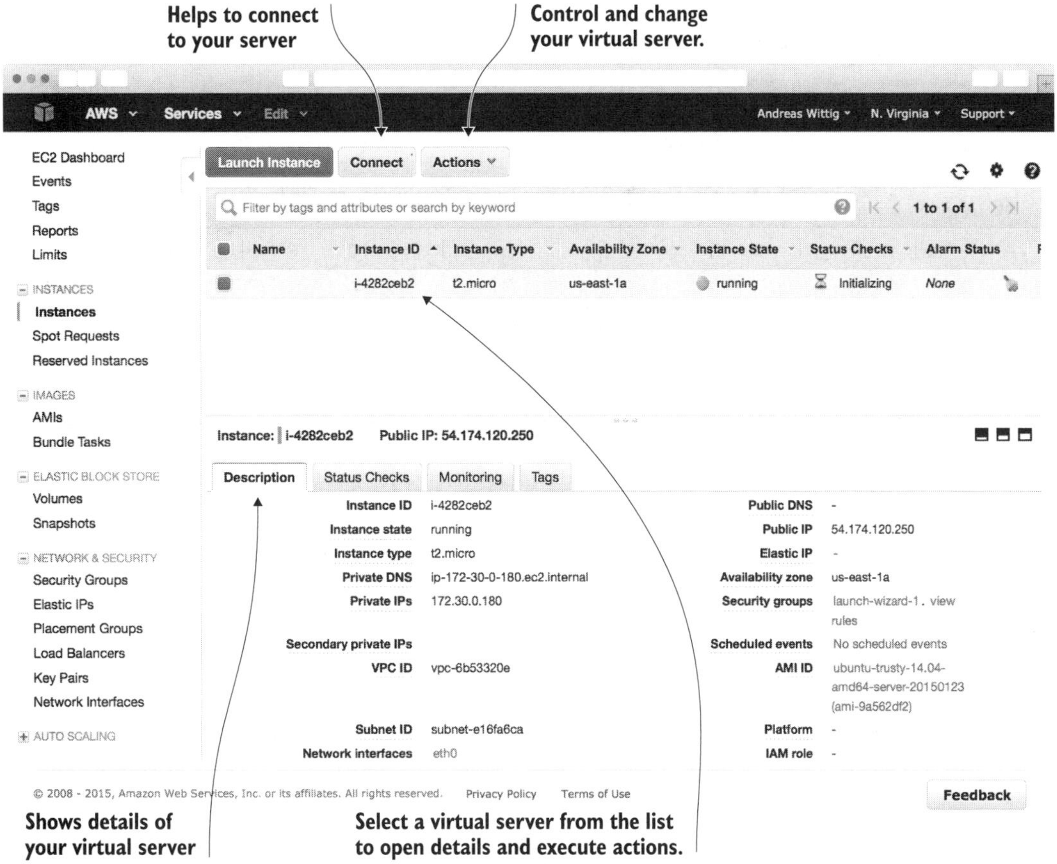

Figure 3.12   Overview of your virtual server with actions to control it

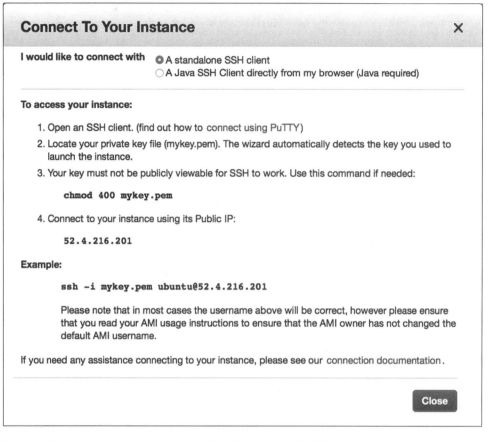

Figure 3.13   Instructions for connecting to the virtual server with SSH

With the public IP address and your key, you can connect to your virtual server. Continue with the next sections, depending on your OS on your local machine.

LINUX AND MAC OS X

Open your terminal and type `ssh -i $PathToKey/mykey.pem ubuntu@$PublicIp`, replacing `$PathToKey` with the path to the key file you downloaded in section 1.8.3 and `$PublicIp` with the public IP address shown in the connect dialog in the AWS Management Console. Answer Yes to the security alert regarding the authenticity of the new host.

WINDOWS

Follow these steps:

1 Find the mykey.ppk file you created in section 1.8.3 and open it by double-clicking.

2 PuTTY Pageant should appear in the task bar as an icon. If not, you may need to install or reinstall PuTTY as described in section 1.8.3.

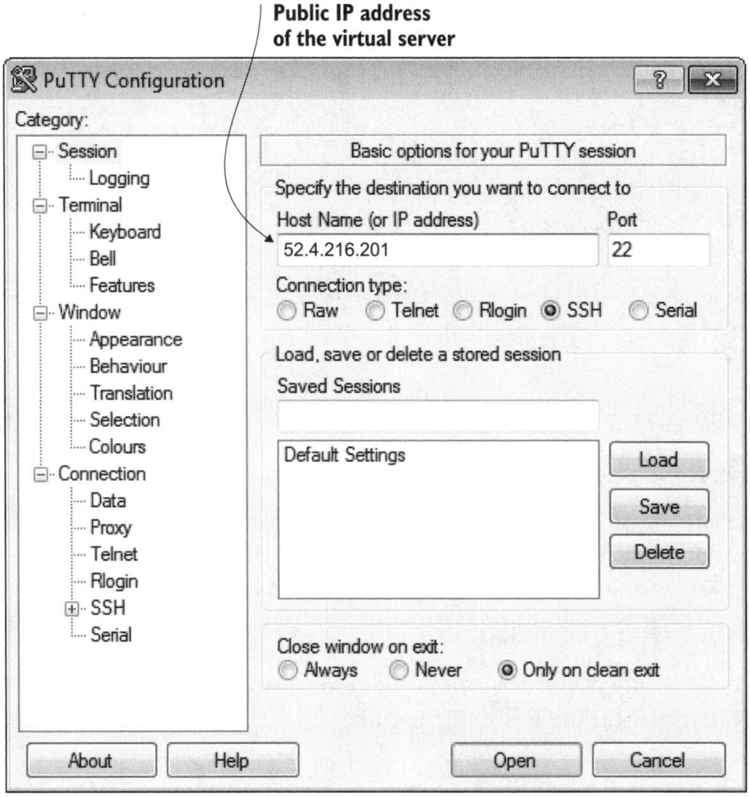

**Public IP address
of the virtual server**

Figure 3.14   **Connecting to the virtual server with PuTTY on Windows**

3   Start PuTTY. Fill in the public IP address shown in the Connect dialog in the
AWS Management Console, and click Open (see figure 3.14).

4   Answer Yes to the security alert regarding the authenticity of the new host, and
type ubuntu as the login name. Press Enter.

LOGIN MESSAGE

Whether you're using Linux, Mac OS X, or Windows, after a successful login you
should see a message like the following:

```
ssh -i ~/Downloads/mykey.pem ubuntu@52.4.216.201
Warning: Permanently added '52.4.216.201' (RSA) to the list of known hosts.
Welcome to Ubuntu 14.04.1 LTS (GNU/Linux 3.13.0-44-generic x86_64)

 * Documentation:  https://help.ubuntu.com/

  System information as of Wed Mar  4 07:05:42 UTC 2015

  System load: 0.24               Memory usage: 5%   Processes:       83
  Usage of /:  9.8% of 7.74GB     Swap usage:   0%   Users logged in: 0

  Graph this data and manage this system at:
    https://landscape.canonical.com/
```

```
    Get cloud support with Ubuntu Advantage Cloud Guest:
       http://www.ubuntu.com/business/services/cloud

0 packages can be updated.
0 updates are security updates.


The programs included with the Ubuntu system are free software;
the exact distribution terms for each program are described in the
individual files in /usr/share/doc/*/copyright.

Ubuntu comes with ABSOLUTELY NO WARRANTY, to the extent permitted by
applicable law.

~$
```

You're now connected to your virtual server and ready to run a few commands.

3.1.3 *Installing and running software manually*

You've started a virtual server with an Ubuntu OS. It's easy to install additional software with the help of the package manager apt. To begin, you'll install a tiny tool called linkchecker that allows you to find broken links on a website:

```
$ sudo apt-get install linkchecker -y
```

Now you're ready to check for links pointing to websites that no longer exist. To do so, choose a website and run the following command:

```
$ linkchecker https://...
```

The output of checking the links looks something like this:

```
[...]
URL        `http://www.linux-mag.com/blogs/fableson'
Name       `Frank Ableson's Blog'
Parent URL http://manning.com/about/blogs.html, line 92, col 27
Real URL   http://www.linux-mag.com/blogs/fableson
Check time 1.327 seconds
Modified   2015-07-22 09:49:39.000000Z
Result     Error: 404 Not Found

URL        `/catalog/dotnet'
Name       `Microsoft & .NET'
Parent URL http://manning.com/wittig/, line 29, col 2
Real URL   http://manning.com/catalog/dotnet/
Check time 0.163 seconds
D/L time   0.146 seconds
Size       37.55KB
Info       Redirected to `http://manning.com/catalog/dotnet/'.
           235 URLs parsed.
Modified   2015-07-22 01:16:35.000000Z
Warning    [http-moved-permanent] HTTP 301 (moved permanent)
           encountered: you should update this link.
Result     Valid: 200 OK
[...]
```

Depending on the number of web pages, the crawler may need some time to check all of them for broken links. At the end, it lists the broken links and gives you the chance to find and fix them.

3.2   *Monitoring and debugging a virtual server*

If you need to find the reason for an error or misbehavior of an application, it's important to have access to tools that can help with monitoring and debugging. AWS provides tools that let you monitor and debug your virtual servers. One approach is to examine the virtual server's logs.

3.2.1   *Showing logs from a virtual server*

If you need to find out what your virtual server was doing during and after startup, there's a simple solution. AWS allows you to show the server's logs with the help of the Management Console (the web interface you use to start and stop virtual servers). Follow these steps to open your virtual server's logs:

1 Open the EC2 service from the main navigation, and select Instances from the submenu.
2 Select the running virtual server by clicking the row in the table.
3 In the Actions menu, choose Instance Settings > Get System Log.

A window opens and shows you the system logs from your virtual server that would normally be displayed on a physical monitor during startup (see figure 3.15).

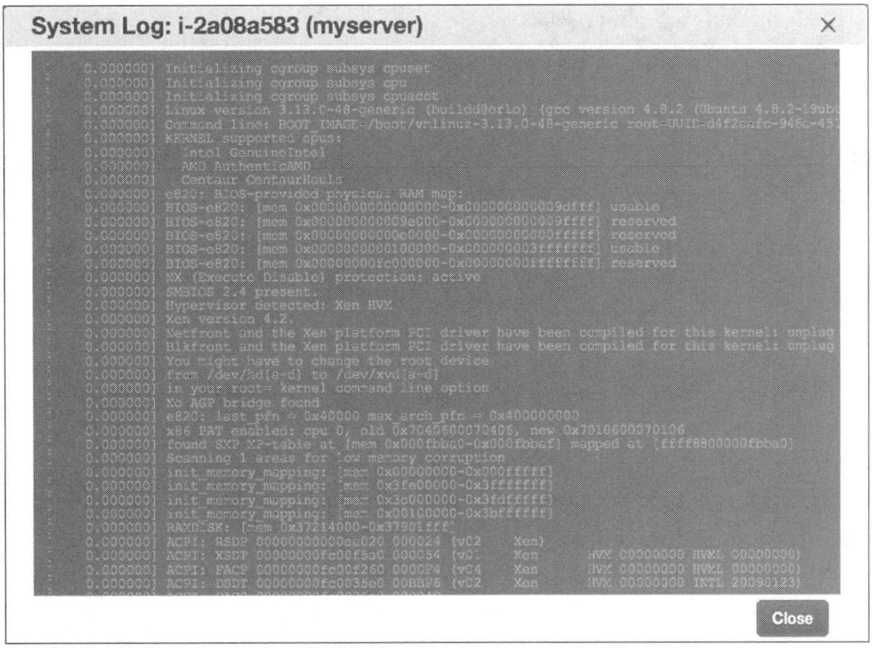

Figure 3.15   Debugging a virtual server with the help of logs

This is a simple and efficient way to access your server's system logs without a SSH connection. Note that it will take several minutes for a log message to appear in the log viewer.

3.2.2 *Monitoring the load of a virtual server*

AWS can help you answer another question: is your virtual server close to its maximum capacity? Follow these steps to open the server's metrics:

1 Open the EC2 service from the main navigation and select Instances from the submenu.
2 Select the running virtual server by clicking the row in the table.
3 Select the Monitoring tab at lower right.
4 Click the Network In chart to dive into the details.

You'll see a graph that shows the virtual server's utilization of incoming networking traffic, similar to figure 3.16. There are metrics for CPU usage, network usage, and disk usage. Unfortunately, there is no metric for memory usage. The metrics are updated every five minutes if you use basic monitoring or every minute if you enable detailed monitoring of your virtual server. Detailed monitoring incurs a cost for some of the instance types.

Metrics and logs will help you monitor and debug your virtual servers. Both tools can help ensure that you're providing high-quality services in a cost-efficient manner.

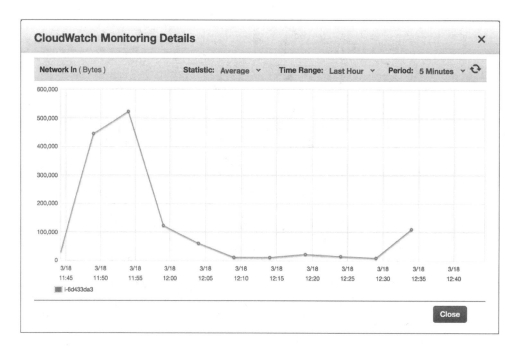

Figure 3.16 Gaining insight into a virtual server's incoming network traffic with the CloudWatch metric

3.3 *Shutting down a virtual server*

To avoid incurring charges, you should always turn off unused virtual servers. You can use the following four actions to control a virtual server's state:

- *Start*—You can always start a stopped virtual server. If you want to create a completely new server, you'll need to launch a virtual server.
- *Stop*—You can always stop a running virtual server. A stopped virtual server isn't billed and can be started later. If you're using network-attached storage, your data persists. A stopped virtual server doesn't incur charges, except for attached resources like network-attached storage.
- *Reboot*—Have you tried turning it off and on again? If you need to reboot your virtual server, this action will help. You won't lose any data when rebooting a virtual server, and all software is still installed after a reboot.
- *Terminate*—Terminating a virtual server means deleting it. You can't start a virtual server that you've already terminated. The virtual server is deleted, together with dependencies like network-attached storage and public and private IP addresses. A terminated virtual server doesn't incur charges.

WARNING The difference between *stopping* and *terminating* a virtual server is important. You can start a stopped virtual server. This isn't possible with a terminated virtual server. If you terminate a virtual server, you delete it.

Figure 3.17 illustrates the difference between stopping and terminating an instance, with the help of a flowchart.

Stopping or terminating unused virtual servers saves money and prevents an unexpected bill from AWS. If you start a virtual server for a short-term task, always create a

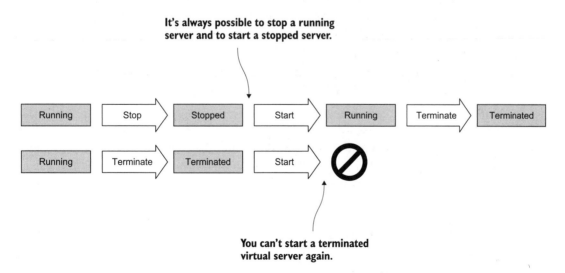

Figure 3.17   Difference between stopping and terminating a virtual server

termination reminder. After you terminate a virtual server, it's no longer available and eventually disappears from the list of virtual servers.

> **Cleaning up**
> Terminate the virtual server named myserver that you started at the beginning of this chapter:
>
> 1 Open the EC2 service from the main navigation and select Instances from the submenu.
> 2 Select the running virtual server by clicking the row in the table.
> 3 In the Actions menu, choose Instance State > Terminate.

3.4 *Changing the size of a virtual server*

It's always possible to change the size of a virtual server. This is an advantage of the cloud and gives you the ability to scale vertically. If you need more computing power, increase the size of the server.

In this section, you'll learn how to change the size of a running virtual server. To begin, follow these steps to start a small virtual server:

1 Open the AWS Management Console and choose the EC2 service.
2 Start the wizard to launch a new virtual server by clicking the Launch Instance button.
3 Select Ubuntu Server 14.04 LTS (HVM) as the AMI for your virtual server.
4 Choose the instance type t2.micro.
5 Click Review and Launch to start the virtual server.
6 Check the summary for the new virtual server and click the Launch button.
7 Choose the option Choose an Existing Key Pair, select the key pair mykey, and click Launch Instances.
8 Switch to the overview of EC2 instances and wait for the new virtual server's state to switch to Running.

You've started a virtual server with the instance type t2.micro. This is one of the smallest virtual servers available on AWS.

Use SSH to connect to your server, as shown in the previous section, and execute `cat /proc/cpuinfo` and `free -m` to gain information about the server's CPU and memory. The output should look similar to this:

```
$ cat /proc/cpuinfo
processor     : 0
vendor_id     : GenuineIntel
cpu family    : 6
model         : 62
model name    : Intel(R) Xeon(R) CPU E5-2670 v2 @ 2.50GHz
stepping      : 4
```

```
microcode    : 0x416
cpu MHz      : 2500.040
cache size   : 25600 KB
[...]

$ free -m
             total      used      free    shared   buffers    cached
Mem:           992       247       744         0         8       191
-/+ buffers/cache:        48       944
Swap:            0         0         0
```

Your virtual server can use a single CPU core and offers 992 MB of memory.

If you need more CPUs, more memory, or more networking capacity, there are many other sizes to choose from. You can even change the virtual server's instance family and version. To increase the size of your virtual server, you first need to stop it:

1. Open the AWS Management Console and choose the EC2 service.
2. Click Instances in the submenu to jump to an overview of your virtual servers.
3. Select your running virtual server from the list by clicking it.
4. Choose Instance State > Stop from the Actions menu.

After waiting for the virtual server to stop, you can change the instance type:

1. Choose Change Instance Type from the Actions menu under Instance Settings. As shown in figure 3.18, a dialog opens in which you can choose the new instance type for your virtual server.
2. Select m3.large for Instance Type.
3. Save your changes by clicking Apply.

You've now changed the size of your virtual server and are ready to start it again.

> **WARNING** Starting a virtual server with instance type m3.large incurs charges. Go to http://aws.amazon.com/ec2/pricing if you want to find out the current on-demand hourly price for an m3.large virtual server.

To do so, select your virtual server and choose Start from the Actions menu under Instance State. Your virtual server starts with more CPUs, more memory, and more networking capabilities. The public and private IP addresses have changed. Grab the new public IP address to reconnect via SSH; you'll find it in the virtual server's details view.

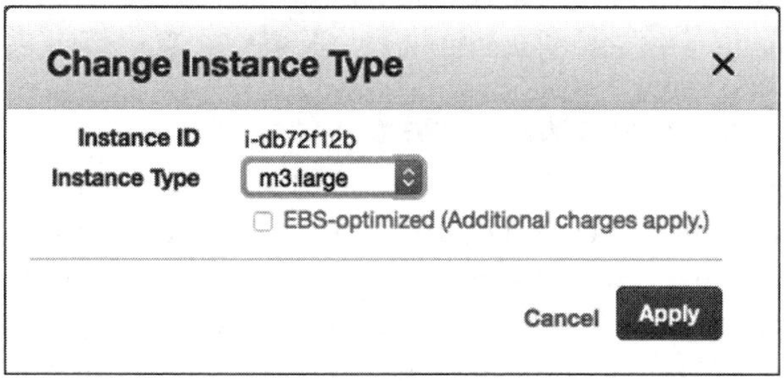

Change Instance Type　✕

Instance ID　i-db72f12b
Instance Type　m3.large
　　　□ EBS-optimized (Additional charges apply.)

Cancel　**Apply**

Figure 3.18   Increase the size of your virtual server by selecting m3.large for Instance Type.

Use SSH to connect to your server, and execute cat /proc/cpuinfo and free -m to gain information about its CPU and memory. The output should look similar to this:

```
$ cat /proc/cpuinfo
processor    : 0
vendor_id    : GenuineIntel
cpu family   : 6
model        : 62
model name   : Intel(R) Xeon(R) CPU E5-2670 v2 @ 2.50GHz
stepping     : 4
microcode    : 0x415
cpu MHz      : 2494.066
cache size   : 25600 KB
[...]

processor    : 1
vendor_id    : GenuineIntel
cpu family   : 6
model        : 62
model name   : Intel(R) Xeon(R) CPU E5-2670 v2 @ 2.50GHz
stepping     : 4
microcode    : 0x415
cpu MHz      : 2494.066
cache size   : 25600 KB
[...]

$ free -m
                 total      used      free    shared   buffers    cached
Mem:              7479       143      7336         0         6        49
-/+ buffers/cache:            87      7392
Swap:                0         0         0
```

Your virtual server can use two CPU cores and offers 7,479 MB of memory. Compare this to a single CPU core and 992 MB of memory before you increased the server's size.

Cleaning up

Terminate the virtual server with instance type m3.large to stop paying for it:

1 Open the EC2 service from the main navigation and select Instances from the submenu.
2 Select the running virtual server by clicking the row in the table.
3 In the Actions menu, choose Instance State > Terminate.

3.5   *Starting a virtual server in another data center*

AWS offers data centers all over the world. To achieve low latency for requests over the internet, it's important to choose the closest data center for the majority of your users. Changing a data center is simple. The Management Console always shows the current data center you're working in, on the right side of the main navigation. So far, you've worked in the data center N. Virginia (US) called us-east-1. To change the data center, click N. Virginia and select Sydney from the menu. Figure 3.19 shows how to jump to the data center in Sydney called ap-southeast-2.

AWS groups its data centers into these regions:

- Asia Pacific, Tokyo (ap-northeast-1)
- Asia Pacific, Singapore (ap-southeast-1)
- Asia Pacific, Sydney (ap-southeast-2)
- EU, Frankfurt (eu-central-1)
- EU, Ireland (eu-west-1)
- South America, Sao Paulo (sa-east-1)
- US East, N. Virginia (us-east-1)
- US West, N. California (us-west-1)
- US West, Oregon (us-west-2)

You can specify the region for most AWS services. The regions are completely independent of each other; data isn't transferred between regions. Typically, a region is a collection of three or more data centers located in the same area. Those data centers are

The region you're working in

Select Asia Pacific (Sydney) as the region to work in.

Figure 3.19 Changing the data center in the Management Console from N. Virginia to Sydney

well connected and offer the ability to build a highly available infrastructure, as you'll discover later in this book. Some AWS services, like the content delivery network (CDN) service and the Domain Name System (DNS) service, act globally on top of these regions and even some additional data centers.

After you change to the EC2 service in the Management Console, you may wonder why no key pair is listed in the EC2 overview. You created a key pair for SSH logins in the region N. Virginia (US). But the regions are independent, so you have to create a new key pair for the Sydney region. Follow these steps (see section 1.2 if you need more details):

1 Open the EC2 service from the main navigation and select Key Pairs from the submenu.
2 Click Create Key Pair, and type in `sydney` as the key pair name.
3 Download and save the key pair.
4 Windows only: Open PuTTYgen and select SSH-2 RSA under Type of Key to Generate. Click Load. Select the sydney.pem file and click Open. Confirm the dialog box. Click Save Private Key.
5 Linux and OS X only: Change the access rights of the file sydney.pem by running `chmod 400 sydney.pem` in the console.

You're ready to start a virtual server in the data center in Sydney. Follow these steps to do so:

1 Open the EC2 service from the main navigation and select Instances from the submenu.
2 Click Launch Instance to start a wizard that will guide you through starting a new virtual server.
3 Select the Amazon Linux AMI (HVM) machine image.
4 Choose t2.micro as the instance type, and click Review and Launch to take the shortcut for starting a new virtual server.
5 Click Edit Security Groups to configure the firewall. Change Security Group Name to webserver and Description to HTTP and SSH. Add a rule of type SSH and another of type HTTP. Allow access to SSH and HTTP from anywhere by defining `0.0.0.0/0` as the source for both rules. Your firewall configuration should look like figure 3.20. Click Review and Launch.
6 Click Launch and select sydney as the existing key pair with which to launch your virtual server.
7 Click View Instances to change to the overview of virtual servers, and wait for your new virtual server to start.

You're finished! A virtual server is running in a data center in Sydney. Let's proceed with installing a web server on it. To do so, you have to connect to your virtual server via SSH. Grab the current public IP address of your virtual server from the details page.

❶ **Change the name and description.**

❷ **Add a rule to allow HTTP requests from anywhere.**

❸ **Click here to proceed.**

Figure 3.20 Configuring the firewall for a web server in Sydney

Open a terminal and type `ssh -i $PathToKey/sydney.pem ec2-user@$PublicIp` with `$PathToKey` replaced by the path to the key file sydney.pem you downloaded and `$PublicIp` replaced by the public IP address from the details of your virtual server. Answer Yes to the security alert regarding the authenticity of the new host.

After establishing a SSH session, you can install a default web server by executing `sudo yum install httpd -y`. To start the web server, type `sudo service httpd start` and press Return to execute the command. Your web browser should show a placeholder site if you open http://$PublicIp·with $PublicIp replaced by the public IP address of your virtual server.

Windows

Find the sydney.ppk file you created after downloading the new key pair and open it by double-clicking. The PuTTY Pageant should appear in the task bar as an icon. Next, start PuTTY and connect to the public IP address from the details of your virtual server. Answer Yes to the security alert regarding the authenticity of the new host, and type in ubuntu as the login name. Press Enter.

NOTE You're using two different operating systems in this chapter. You started with a virtual server based on Ubuntu at the beginning of the chapter. Now you're using Amazon Linux, a distribution based on Red Hat Enterprise Linux. That's why you have to execute different commands to install software. Ubuntu uses apt-get, and Amazon Linux is using yum to do so.

Next, you'll attach a fixed public IP address to the virtual server.

3.6 *Allocating a public IP address*

You've already launched some virtual servers while reading this book. Each virtual server was connected to a public IP address automatically. But every time you launched or stopped a virtual server, the public IP address changed. If you want to host an application under a fixed IP address, this won't work. AWS offers a service called *Elastic IP addresses* for allocating fixed public IP addresses.

You can allocate and associate a public IP address to a virtual web server with the following steps:

1 Open the Management Console and go to the EC2 service.
2 Choose Elastic IPs from the submenu. You'll see an overview of public IP addresses, as shown in figure 3.21.
3 Allocate a public IP address by clicking Allocate New Address.

Now you can associate the public IP address with a virtual server of your choice:

1 Select your public IP address and choose Associate Address from the Actions menu. A dialog similar to figure 3.22 appears.
2 Enter your virtual server's instance ID in the Instance field. Your web server is the only virtual server running at the moment, so you can begin typing i- and use auto-completion to choose the server ID.
3 Click Associate to finish the process.

Your virtual server is now accessible through the public IP address you allocated at the beginning of this section. Point your browser to this IP address, and you should see the placeholder page as you did in section 3.5.

Allocating a public IP address can be useful if you have to make sure the endpoint to your application doesn't change, even if you have to replace the virtual server behind the scenes. For example, assume that virtual server A is running and has an

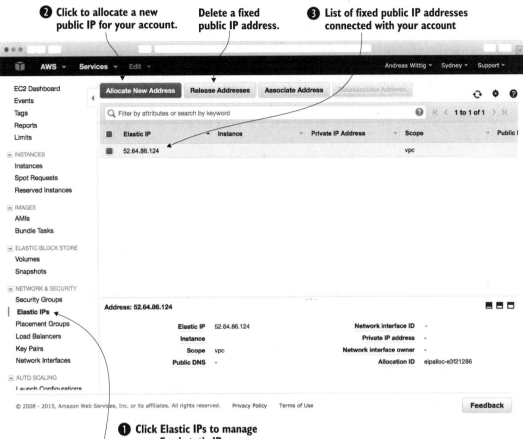

Figure 3.21 Overview of public IP addresses connected to your account in current region

Figure 3.22 Associating a public IP address with your web server

associated Elastic IP address. The following steps let you replace the virtual server with a new one without interruption:

1 Start a new virtual server B to replace running server A.
2 Install and start applications and all dependencies on virtual server B.
3 Disassociate the Elastic IP from virtual server A, and associate it with virtual server B.

Requests using the Elastic IP address will now be routed to virtual server B without interruption.

You can also connect multiple public IP addresses with a virtual server by using multiple network interfaces, as described in the next section. This can be useful if you need to host different applications running on the same port or if you want to use a unique fixed public IP address for different websites.

> **WARNING** IPv4 addresses are rare. To prevent stockpiling Elastic IP addresses, AWS will charge you for Elastic IP addresses that aren't associated with a server. You'll clean up the allocated IP address at the end of the next section.

3.7 Adding an additional network interface to a virtual server

In addition to managing public IP addresses, you can control your virtual server's network interfaces. It's possible to add multiple network interfaces to a virtual server and control the private and public IP addresses associated with those network interfaces. You use an additional network interface to connect a second public IP address to your web server.

Follow these steps to create an additional networking interface for your virtual server (see figure 3.23):

1 Open the Management Console and go to the EC2 service.
2 Select Network Interfaces from the submenu.
3 Click Create Network Interface. A dialog opens.
4 Enter 2nd interface as the description.
5 Choose your virtual server's subnet as the subnet for the new networking interface. You can look this up in your server's details view from the instances overview.
6 Leave Private IP Address empty.
7 Select the Security Groups that have *webserver* in their description.
8 Click Yes, Create.

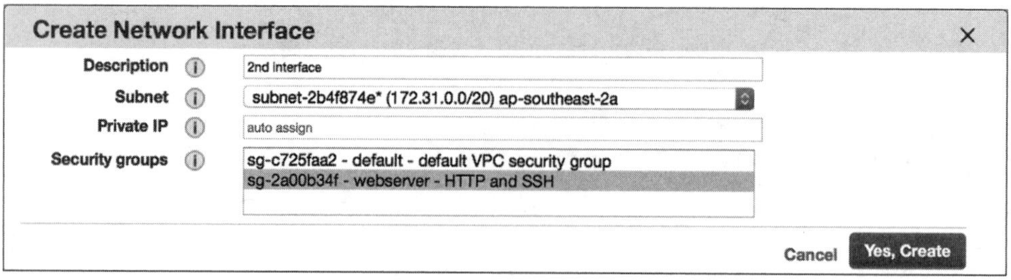

Figure 3.23 Creating an additional networking interface for your virtual server

When the new network interface's state changes to Available, you can attach it to your virtual server. Select the new 2nd Interface network interface, and choose Attach from the menu. A dialog opens, as shown in figure 3.24. Choose the ID of the running virtual server and click Attach.

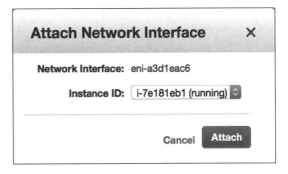

You've attached an additional networking interface to your virtual server. Next, you'll connect an

Figure 3.24   Attaching an additional networking interface to your virtual server

additional public IP address to the additional networking interface. To do so, note the network interface ID of the additional network interface shown in the overview, and follow these steps:

1 Open the Management Console and go to the EC2 service.
2 Choose Elastic IPs from the submenu.
3 Click Allocate New Address to allocate a new public IP address, as you did in section 3.6.
4 Choose Associate Address from the Actions menu, and link it to the additional networking interface you just created by typing in the network interface ID under Network Interface (see figure 3.25).

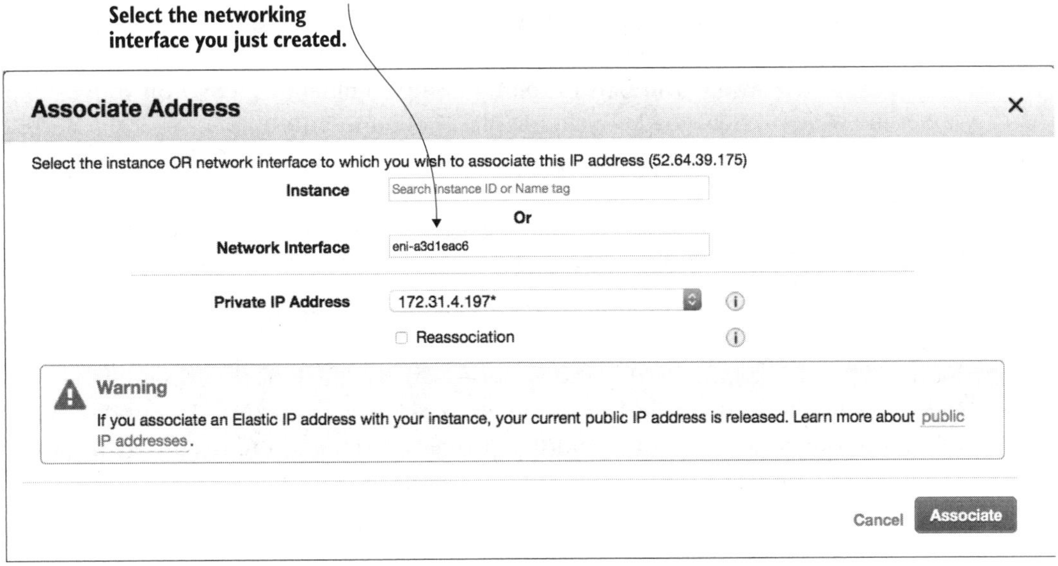

Select the networking interface you just created.

Associate Address   ✕

Select the instance OR network interface to which you wish to associate this IP address (52.64.39.175)

                    Instance   Search Instance ID or Name tag

                                                   Or

        Network Interface   eni-a3d1eac6

        Private IP Address   172.31.4.197*

                                        ☐ Reassociation

⚠ **Warning**
   If you associate an Elastic IP address with your instance, your current public IP address is released. Learn more about public IP addresses.

                                                                          Cancel   **Associate**

Figure 3.25   Associating a public IP address with the additional networking interface

Your virtual server is now reachable under two different public IP addresses. This enables you to serve two different websites, depending on the public IP address. You need to configure the web server to answer requests depending on the public IP address.

After connecting to your virtual server via SSH and insert `ifconfig` into the terminal, you can see your new networking interface attached to the virtual server, as shown in the following code:

```
$ ifconfig
eth0      Link encap:Ethernet  HWaddr 12:C7:53:81:90:86
          inet addr:172.31.1.208  Bcast:172.30.0.255  Mask:255.255.255.0
          inet6 addr: fe80::10c7:53ff:fe81:9086/64 Scope:Link
          UP BROADCAST RUNNING MULTICAST  MTU:1500  Metric:1
          RX packets:62185 errors:0 dropped:0 overruns:0 frame:0
          TX packets:9179 errors:0 dropped:0 overruns:0 carrier:0
          collisions:0 txqueuelen:1000
          RX bytes:89644521 (85.4 MiB)  TX bytes:582899 (569.2 KiB)

eth1      Link encap:Ethernet  HWaddr 12:77:12:53:39:7B
          inet addr:172.31.4.197  Bcast:172.30.0.255  Mask:255.255.255.0
          inet6 addr: fe80::1077:12ff:fe53:397b/64 Scope:Link
          UP BROADCAST RUNNING MULTICAST  MTU:1500  Metric:1
          RX packets:13 errors:0 dropped:0 overruns:0 frame:0
          TX packets:13 errors:0 dropped:0 overruns:0 carrier:0
          collisions:0 txqueuelen:1000
          RX bytes:1256 (1.2 KiB)  TX bytes:1374 (1.3 KiB)
[...]
```

Each network interface is connected to a private and a public IP address. You'll need to configure the web server to deliver different websites depending on the IP address. Your virtual server doesn't know anything about its public IP address, but you can distinguish the requests based on the private IP address.

First you need two websites. Run the following commands via SSH on your virtual server in Sydney to download two simple placeholder websites:

```
$ sudo -s
$ mkdir /var/www/html/a
$ wget -P /var/www/html/a https://raw.githubusercontent.com/AWSinAction/\
code/master/chapter3/a/index.html
$ mkdir /var/www/html/b
$ wget -P /var/www/html/b https://raw.githubusercontent.com/AWSinAction/\
code/master/chapter3/b/index.html
```

Next you need to configure the web server to deliver the websites depending on the called IP address. To do so, add a file named a.conf under /etc/httpd/conf.d with the following content. Change the IP address from 172.31.x.x to the IP address from the `ifconfig` output for the networking interface eth0:

```
<VirtualHost 172.31.x.x:80>
  DocumentRoot /var/www/html/a
</VirtualHost>
```

Repeat the same process for a configuration file named b.conf under /etc/httpd/conf.d with the following content. Change the IP address from 172.31.y.y to the IP address from the ifconfig output for the networking interface eth1:

```
<VirtualHost 172.31.y.y:80>
  DocumentRoot /var/www/html/b
</VirtualHost>
```

To activate the new web server configuration, execute sudo service httpd restart via SSH. Change to the Elastic IP overview in the Management Console. Copy both public IP addresses and open them with your web browser. You should get the answer "Hello A!" or a "Hello B!" depending on the public IP address you're calling. Thus you can deliver two different websites, depending on the public IP address the user is calling. Congrats—you're finished!

> **Cleaning up**
> It's time to clean up your setup:
> 1 Terminate the virtual server.
> 2 Go to Networking Interfaces and select and delete the networking interface.
> 3 Change to Elastic IPs, and select and release the two public IP addresses by clicking Release Addresses from the Actions menu.
>
> That's it. Everything is cleaned up, and you're ready for the next section.

WARNING You switched to the AWS region in Sydney earlier. Now you need to switch back to the region US East (N. Virginia). You can do so by selecting US East (N. Virginia) from the region chooser in the main navigation of the Management Console.

3.8 *Optimizing costs for virtual servers*

Usually you launch virtual servers on demand in the cloud to gain maximum flexibility. You can start and stop an on-demand instance whenever you like, and you're billed for every hour the instance (virtual server) is running. If you want to save money, you have two options: *spot instances* or *reserved instances*. Both help to reduce costs but decrease your flexibility. With a spot instance, you bid for unused capacity in an AWS data center; the price is based on supply and demand. You can use reserved instances if you need a virtual server for a year or longer; you agree to pay for the given time frame and receive a discount in advance. Table 3.2 shows the differences between these options.

Table 3.2 Differences between on-demand, spot, and reserved virtual servers

	On-demand	Reserved	Spot
Price	High	Medium	Low
Flexibility	High	Low	Medium
Reliability	Medium	High	Low

3.8.1   Reserve virtual servers

Reserving a virtual server means to commit to using a specific virtual server in a specific data center. You have to pay for a reserved virtual server whether it's running or not. In return, you benefit from a price reduction of up to 60%. On AWS, you can choose one of the following options if you want to reserve a virtual server:

- No Upfront, 1-year term
- Partial Upfront, 1-year or 3-year term
- All Upfront, 1-year or 3-year term

Table 3.3 shows what this means for a virtual server with 1 CPU, 3.75 GB of memory, and a 4 GB SSD called m3.medium.

Table 3.3   Potential cost savings for a virtual server (m3.medium)

	Monthly cost	Upfront cost	Effective monthly cost	Savings vs. on-demand
On-demand	48.91 USD	0.00 USD	48.91 USD	
No Upfront, 1-year term	35.04 USD	0.00 USD	35.04 USD	28%
Partial Upfront, 1-year term	12.41 USD	211.00 USD	29.99 USD	39%
All Upfront, 1-year term	0.00 USD	353.00 USD	29.42 USD	40%
Partial Upfront, 3-year term	10.95 USD	337.00 USD	20.31 USD	58%
All Upfront, 3-year term	0.00 USD	687.00 USD	19.08 USD	61%

You can trade cost reductions against flexibility by reserving virtual servers on AWS. But there's more. If you own a reservation for a virtual server (a *reserved instance*), the capacity for this virtual server is reserved for you in the public cloud. Why is this important? Suppose demand increases for virtual servers in a data center, perhaps because another data center broke down and many AWS customers have to launch new virtual servers to replace their broken ones. In this rare case, the orders for on-demand virtual servers will pile up, and it may become nearly impossible to start a new virtual server. If you plan to build a highly available setup across multiple data centers, you should also think about reserving the minimum capacity you'll need to keep your applications running. We recommend that you start with on-demand servers and switch to a mix of on-demand and reserved servers later.

3.8.2   Bidding on unused virtual servers

In addition to reserved virtual servers, there's another option for reducing costs: spot instances. With a spot instance, you bid for unused capacity in the AWS cloud. A *spot market* is a market where standardized products are traded for immediate delivery. The price of the products on the market depend on supply and demand. On the AWS spot

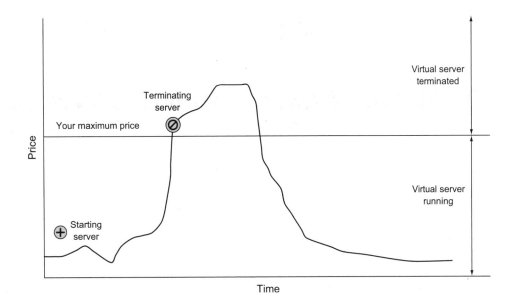

Figure 3.26   Functionality of the spot market for virtual servers

market, the traded products are virtual servers, and they're delivered by starting a virtual server.

Figure 3.26 shows the price chart for a specific instance type for a virtual server. If the current spot price is lower than your maximum price for a specific virtual server in a specific data center, your spot request will be fulfilled, and a virtual server will start. If the current spot price exceeds your bid, your virtual server will be terminated (not stopped) by AWS after two minutes.

The spot price can be more or less flexible depending on the size of the virtual servers and the data center. We've seen a spot price of 10% of the on-demand price and even a spot price greater than the on-demand price. As soon as the spot price exceeds your bid, your server will be terminated within two minutes. You shouldn't use spot instances for tasks like web or mail servers, but you can use them to run asynchronous tasks like analyzing data or encoding media assets. You can even use a spot instance to check for broken links on your website, as you did in section 3.1, because this isn't a time-critical task.

Let's start a new virtual server that uses the price reductions of the spot market. First you have to place your order on the spot market; figure 3.27 shows the starting point for requesting virtual servers. You get there by choosing the EC2 service from the main navigation and selecting Spot Requests from the submenu. Click to open the Pricing History, where you can see the prices for virtual servers; historical prices are available for the different server sizes and different data centers.

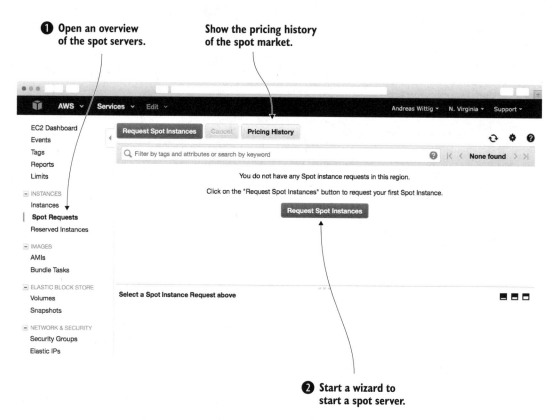

Figure 3.27   Requesting a spot instance

In section 3.1, you started a virtual server. Requesting a spot instance is pretty much the same. Start the wizard by clicking one of the buttons labeled Request Spot Instances. Select Ubuntu Server 14.04 LTS (HVM) as the OS of your virtual server.

You've also seen the step shown in figure 3.28, where you choose the size for your virtual server. You can't start a spot instance with an instance type from the t2 family, so instance types like t2.micro are disabled.

> **WARNING**   Starting a virtual server with instance type m3.medium via spot request incurs charges. The maximum price (bid) is $0.07 per hour in the following example.

Choose the smallest available virtual server class, m3.medium, and click Next: Configure Instance Details.

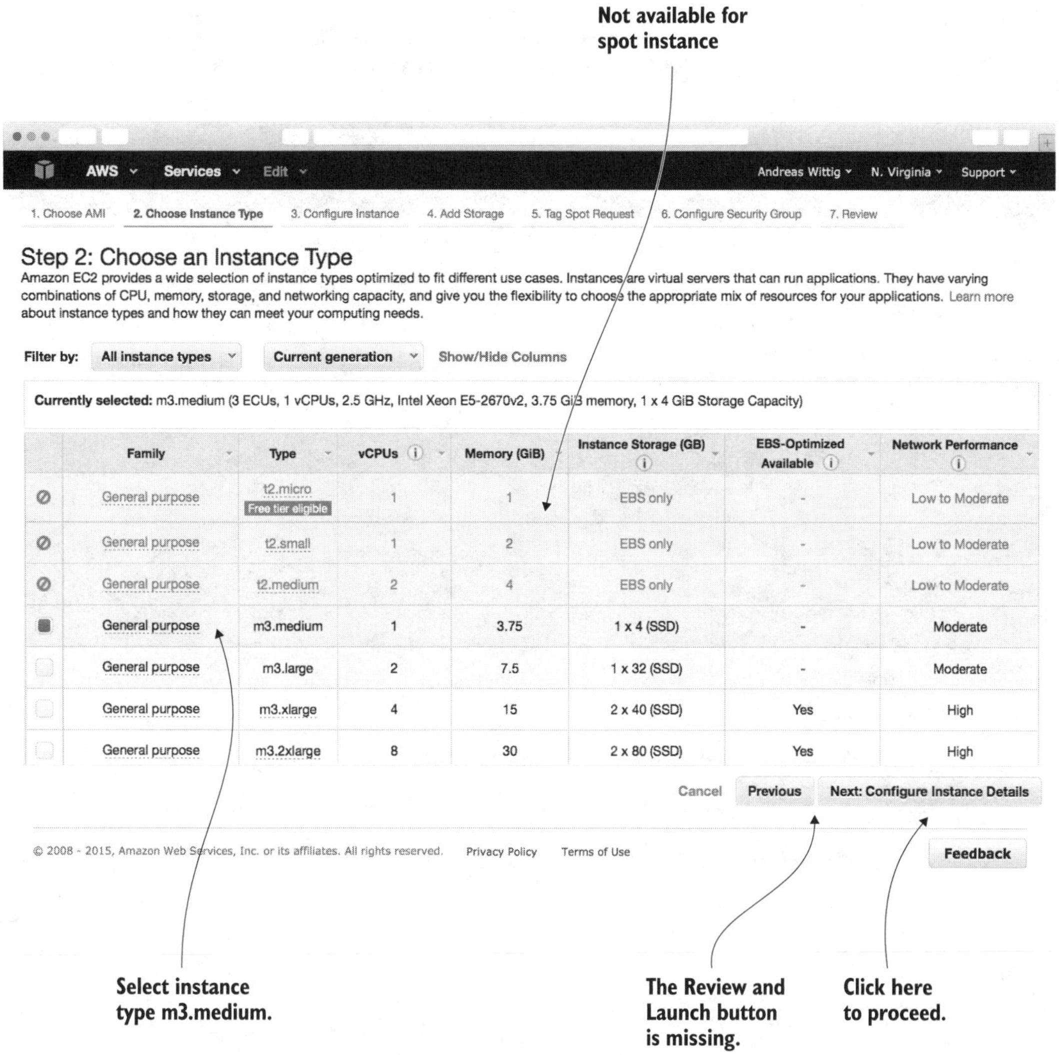

Not available for spot instance

Select instance type m3.medium.

The Review and Launch button is missing.

Click here to proceed.

Figure 3.28   When you're choosing the size of a spot server, AWS greys out instance types that aren't available.

The next step, as shown in figure 3.29, is to configure the details of your virtual server and the spot request. Set the following parameters:

1   Set Number of Instances for the spot request to 1.

2   Choose 0.070 as the Maximum Price for the virtual server. This is the on-demand price for the server size.

3   Select the default Network, with IP address range 172.30.0.0/16.

4   Look at the Current Price section and search for the lowest price. Choose the Subnet with the same description.

Current price for
a virtual server
on the spot market

Maximum price
for your server

No time
restrictions for
a spot request

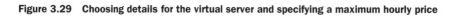

| 1. Choose AMI | 2. Choose Instance Type | **3. Configure Instance** | 4. Add Storage | 5. Tag Spot Request | 6. Configure Security Group | 7. Review |

Step 3: Configure Instance Details

Configure the instance to suit your requirements. You can launch multiple instances from the same AMI, request Spot Instances to take advantage of the lower pricing, assign an access management role to the instance, and more.

Number of instances ⓘ [1]

Purchasing option ⓘ ☑ Request Spot Instances

Current price

us-east-1a	0.0081
us-east-1b	0.452
us-east-1c	0.452
us-east-1e	0.452

Maximum price ⓘ $ [0.070] ◀

Launch group ⓘ [(Optional)]

Request valid from ⓘ Any time Edit

Request valid to ⓘ Any time Edit ◀

Persistent request ⓘ ☐ Persistent request

Network ⓘ [vpc-6b53320e (172.30.0.0/16)] ↻ Create new VPC

Subnet ⓘ [subnet-e16fa6ca(172.30.0.0/24) | us-east-1a] Create new subnet
250 IP Addresses available

Auto-assign Public IP ⓘ [Use subnet setting (Enable)]

IAM role ⓘ [None] ↻ Create new IAM role

Monitoring ⓘ ☐ Enable CloudWatch detailed monitoring
Additional charges apply.

▼ Advanced Details

Cancel   **Previous**   **Review and Launch**   **Next: Add Storage**

Feedback

Keep the default
settings for networking
and access control.

Click here
to proceed.

Figure 3.29   Choosing details for the virtual server and specifying a maximum hourly price

Figure 3.30   Waiting for the spot request to be fulfilled and the virtual server to start

Click Review and Launch to complete the wizard. You'll see a summary of all the settings you made. Click Launch and choose your key pair with the name mykey to request the spot instance.

After you finish the wizard, your request for a virtual server is placed on the market. Clicking View Spot Requests will direct you to the overview of spot requests from which you started. You should see a spot request as shown in figure 3.30. It may take several minutes for your request to be fulfilled. Look at the Status of your request for a virtual server: because the spot market is unpredictable, it's possible for a request to fail. If this happens, repeat the process to create another request, and choose another subnet in which to launch the virtual server.

When the state of your requests flips to Fulfilled, a virtual server is started. You can look at it after switching to Instances via the submenu; you'll find a running or starting instance listed in the overview of virtual servers. You've successfully started a virtual server that is billed as spot instance!

> **Cleaning up**
>
> Terminate the virtual server with instance type m3.medium to stop paying for it:
>
> 1 Open the EC2 service from the main navigation and select Instances from the submenu.
> 2 Select the running virtual server by clicking the row in the table.
> 3 In the Actions menu, choose Instance State > Terminate.
> 4 Switch to the Spot Requests overview. Double-check whether your spot request was canceled. If not, select the spot request and click Cancel.

3.9   *Summary*

- You can choose an OS when starting a virtual server.
- Using logs and metrics can help you to monitor and debug a virtual server.
- Changing the size of your virtual server gives you the flexibility to change the number of CPUs, memory, and storage.
- You can start a virtual server in different regions, consisting of multiple data centers, all over the world.
- Allocating and associating a public IP address to your virtual server gives you the flexibility to replace a virtual server without changing the public IP address.
- You can save on costs by reserving virtual servers or bidding for unused capacity on the virtual server spot market.

Programming
your infrastructure: the
command line, SDKs,
and CloudFormation

This chapter covers

- Understanding the idea of infrastructure as code
- Using the CLI to start a virtual server
- Using the JavaScript SDK for Node.js to start a virtual server
- Using CloudFormation to start a virtual server

Imagine that you want to create room lighting as a service. To switch off the light in a room with software, you need a hardware device like a relay that can break the circuit. This hardware device must have some kind of interface that lets you send it commands like on and off via software. With a relay and an interface, you can offer room lighting as a service. This also applies to virtual server as a service. If you want to start a virtual server via software, you need hardware that can handle and fulfill your request. AWS provides infrastructure that can be controlled via an interface called an *application programming interface (API)*. You can control every part of AWS over the API. Calling the API is possible with SDKs for most programming languages, the command line, and more sophisticated tools.

> ### Not all examples are covered by the Free Tier
> The examples in this chapter are *not* all covered by the Free Tier. A special warning message appears when an example incurs costs. As long as you don't run the other examples longer than a few days, you won't pay anything for them. Keep in mind that this applies only if you created a fresh AWS account for this book and nothing else is going on in your AWS account. Try to complete the examples of the chapter within a few days; you'll clean up your account at the end of each example.

On AWS, everything can be controlled via an API. You interact with AWS by making calls to the REST API using the HTTPS protocol, as figure 4.1 illustrates. Everything is available through the API. You can start a server with a single API call, create 1 TB of storage, or start a Hadoop cluster over the API. By everything, we mean *everything*. You'll need some time to understand the consequences of this. By the time you finish this book, you'll ask why the world wasn't always that easy. Let's look at how the API works.

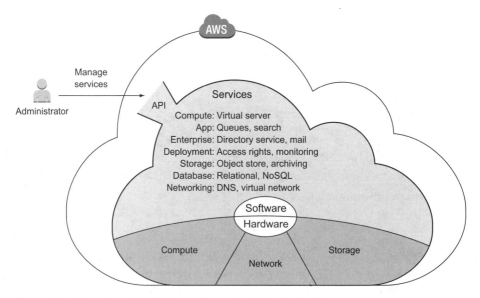

Figure 4.1   Interacting with AWS by making calls to the REST API

To list all the files in the S3 object store, you can send a GET request to the API endpoint:

```
GET / HTTP/1.1
Host: BucketName.s3.amazonaws.com
Authorization: [...]
```

The response will look like this:

```
HTTP/1.1 200 OK
x-amz-id-2: [...]
x-amz-request-id: [...]
Date: Mon, 09 Feb 2015 10:32:16 GMT
Content-Type: application/xml

<?xml version="1.0" encoding="UTF-8"?>
<ListBucketResult xmlns="http://s3.amazonaws.com/doc/2006-03-01/">
[...]
</ListBucketResult>
```

Calling the API directly using plain HTTPS requests is inconvenient. The easy way to talk to AWS is by using the command-line interface or SDKs, as you learn in this chapter. But the API is the foundation of all those tools.

4.1 Infrastructure as code

Infrastructure as code describes the idea of using a high-level programming language to control IT systems. In software development tools like automated tests, code repositories, and build servers are increasing the quality of software engineering. If your infrastructure can be treated as code, you can apply the same techniques to infrastructure code that you do to your application code. In the end, you'll improve the quality of your infrastructure by using automated tests, code repositories, and build servers.

> **WARNING** Don't mix up the terms *infrastructure as code* and *infrastructure as a service (IaaS)!* IaaS means renting servers, storage, and network with a pay-per-use pricing model.

4.1.1 Automation and the DevOps movement

DevOps (Development operations) is an approach driven by software development to bring development and operations closer together. The goal is to deliver rapidly developed software to the customer without a negative impact on quality. Communication and collaboration between development and operations are therefore necessary.

Multiple deploys per day are possible only if your pipeline from code changes to deployment is fully automated. If you commit into the repository, the source code is automatically built and tested against your automated tests. If the build passes the tests, it's automatically installed in your testing environment. Perhaps some integration tests are triggered. After the integration tests have been passed, the change is propagated into production. But this isn't the end of the process; now you need to carefully monitor your system and analyze the logs in real time to ensure that the change was successful.

If your infrastructure is automated, you can spawn a new system for every change introduced to the code repository and run the integration tests isolated from other changes that were pushed to the repository at the same time. Whenever a change is made to the code, a new system is created (servers, databases, networks, and so on) to run the change in isolation.

4.1.2   *Inventing an infrastructure language: JIML*

For the purpose of understanding infrastructure as code in detail, let's invent a new language to describe infrastructure: JSON Infrastructure Markup Language (JIML). Figure 4.2 shows the infrastructure that will be created.

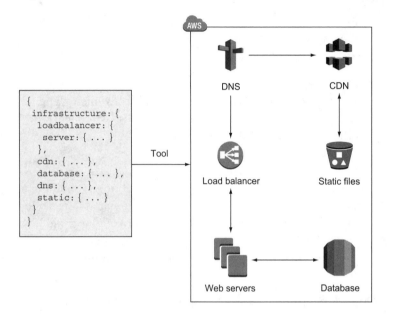

Figure 4.2   From JIML blueprint to infrastructure: infrastructure automation

The infrastructure consists of the following:

- Load balancer (LB)
- Virtual servers
- Database (DB)
- DNS entry
- Content delivery network (CDN)
- Bucket for static files

To reduce issues with syntax, let's say JIML is based on JSON. The following JIML program creates the infrastructure shown in figure 4.2. The $ indicates a reference to an ID.

Listing 4.1   Infrastructure description in JIML

```
{
  "region": "us-east-1",
  "resources": [{
    "type": "loadbalancer",
    "id": "LB",
    "config": {
```

```
      "server": {
        "cpu": 2,
        "ram": 4,
        "os": "ubuntu",
        "waitFor": "$DB"
      },
      "servers": 2
    }
  }, {
    "type": "cdn",
    "id": "CDN",
    "config": {
      "defaultSource": "$LB",
      "sources": [{
        "path": "/static/*",
        "source": "$BUCKET"
      }]
    }
  }, {
    "type": "database",
    "id": "DB",
    "config": {
      "password": "***",
      "engine": "MySQL"
    }
  }, {
    "type": "dns",
    "config": {
      "from": "www.mydomain.com",
      "to": "$CDN"
    }
  }, {
    "type": "bucket",
    "id": "BUCKET"
  }]
}
```

How can this JSON be turned into AWS API calls?

1 Parse the JSON input.

2 The JIML interpreter creates a dependency graph by connecting the resources with their dependencies.

3 The JIML interpreter derives a linear flow of commands from the dependency graph by traversing the tree from the bottom (leaves) to the top (root). The commands are expressed in a pseudo language.

4 The commands in pseudo language are translated into AWS API calls by the JIML runtime.

Let's look at the dependency graph created by the JIML interpreter, shown in figure 4.3.

Traverse the dependency graph from bottom to top and from left to right. The nodes at the bottom have no children: DB ❶ and bucket ❸. Nodes without children have no dependencies. The server ❷ nodes depend on the DB ❶ node. The LB ❹

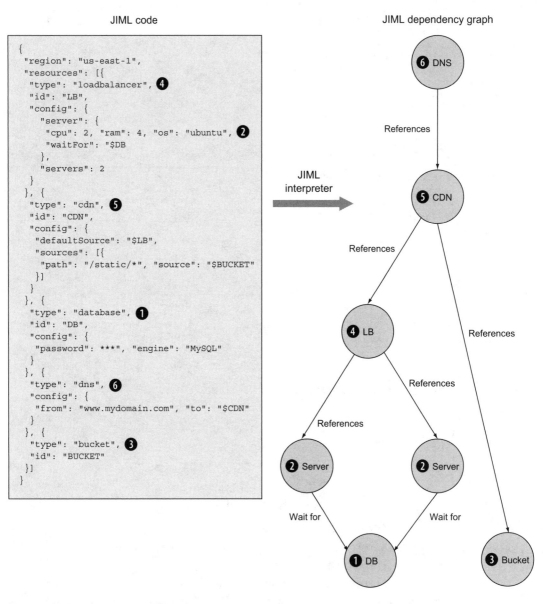

Figure 4.3   The JIML interpreter figures out the order in which resources need to be created.

depends on the server ❷ nodes. The CDN ❺ node depends on the LB ❹ node and the bucket ❸ node. Finally, the DNS ❻ node depends on the CDN node.

The JIML interpreter turns the dependency graph into a linear flow of commands using pseudo language. The pseudo language represents the steps that are needed to create all the resources in the correct order. The nodes at the bottom have no dependencies and are therefore easy to create; that's why they're created first.

Listing 4.2 Linear flow of commands in pseudo language

Create the bucket.   **Create the database.**

```
$DB = database create {"password": "***", "engine": "MySQL"}
$BUCKET = bucket create {}
                                                          Wait for the
await $DB                                                  dependencies.
$SERVER1 = server create {"cpu": 2, "ram": 4, "os": "ubuntu"}
$SERVER2 = server create {"cpu": 2, "ram": 4, "os": "ubuntu"}

await [$SERVER1, $SERVER2]
$LB = loadbalancer create {"servers": [$_SERVER1, $_SERVER2]}

await [$LB, $BUCKET]
$CDN = cdn create {...}                    Create
                                           the CDN.
await $CDN
$DNS = dns create {...}

await $DNS
```

Create the servers. (label pointing to $SERVER1 / $SERVER2 lines)

Create the load balancer. (label pointing to $LB line)

Create the DNS entry. (label pointing to $DNS line)

The last step—translating the commands of the pseudo language into AWS API calls—is skipped. You already learned everything you need to know about infrastructure as code: it's all about dependencies.

Now that you know how important dependencies are to infrastructure as code, let's see how you can use the command line to create infrastructure. The command line is one tool to implement infrastructure as code.

4.2   Using the command-line interface

The AWS command-line interface (CLI) is a convenient way to use AWS from your command line. It runs on Linux, Mac, and Windows and is written in Python. It provides a unified interface for all AWS services. Unless otherwise specified, the output is in JSON format.

You're now going to install and configure the CLI. After that, you can get your hands dirty.

4.2.1   Installing the CLI

How you proceed depends on your OS. If you're having difficulty installing the CLI, consult http://mng.bz/N8L6 for a detailed description of many installation options.

LINUX AND MAC OS X

The CLI requires Python (2.6.5 and greater, 2.7.x and greater, 3.3.x and greater, or 3.4.x and greater) and pip. pip is the recommended tool for installing Python packages. To check your Python version, run python --version in your terminal. If you don't have Python installed or your version is too old, you'll need to find an alternate way to install Python. To find out if you have pip already installed, run pip --version in your terminal. If a version appears, you're fine; otherwise, execute the following to install pip:

```
$ curl "https://bootstrap.pypa.io/get-pip.py" -o "get-pip.py"
$ sudo python get-pip.py
```

Verify your pip installation by running `pip --version` in your terminal again. Now it's time to install the AWS CLI:

```
$ sudo pip install awscli
```

Verify your AWS CLI installation by running `aws --version` in your terminal.

WINDOWS

The following steps guide you through installing the AWS CLI on Windows using the MSI Installer:

1 Download the AWS command-line interface (32-bit or 64-bit) MSI installer from http://aws.amazon.com/cli/.

2 Run the downloaded installer, and install the CLI by going through the installation wizard.

3 Run PowerShell as administrator by searching for the PowerShell entry in the Start menu and choosing Run as Administrator from its context menu.

4 Type `Set-ExecutionPolicy Unrestricted` into PowerShell, and press Enter to execute the command. This allows you to execute the unsigned PowerShell scripts from our examples.

5 Close the PowerShell window; you don't need to work as administrator any longer.

6 Run PowerShell via the PowerShell entry in the Start menu.

7 Verify whether the CLI is working by executing `aws --version` in PowerShell.

4.2.2 Configuring the CLI

To use the CLI, you need to authenticate. Until now, you've used the root AWS account. This account can do everything, good and bad. It's strongly recommended that you not use the AWS root account (you'll learn more about security in chapter 6), so let's create a new user.

To create a new user, open the AWS Management Console at https://console.aws .amazon.com. Click Services in the navigation bar, and click the IAM (AWS Identity and Access Management) service. A page opens as shown in figure 4.4; select Users at left.

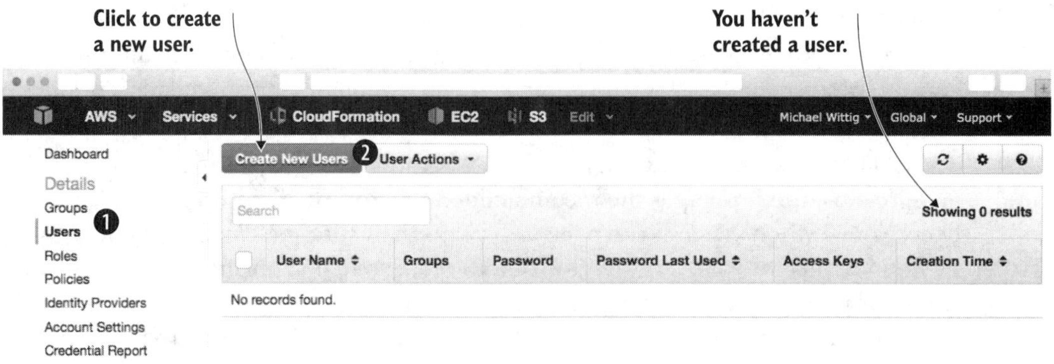

Click to create
a new user.

You haven't
created a user.

Figure 4.4 IAM users (empty)

The user name of the
new user is mycli.

Figure 4.5   Creating an IAM user

Follow these steps to create a new user:

1   Click Create New Users to open the page shown in figure 4.5.
2   Enter mycli as the user name for the first user.
3   Leave the other fields blank, and select Generate an Access Key for Each User.
4   Click the Create button.

The page shown in figure 4.6 opens. Click Show User Security Credentials to display the User Security Credentials box—it's visible only once! You now need to copy the credentials to your CLI configuration. Read on to learn how this works.

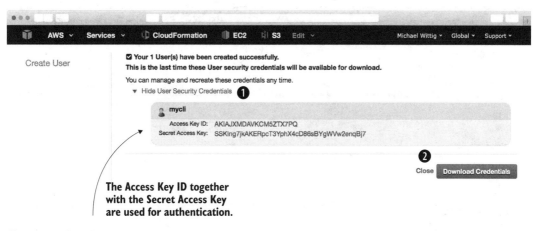

Figure 4.6   Creating an IAM user: showing credentials

Open the terminal on your computer (PowerShell on Windowso or a Bash shell on OS X and Linux, not the AWS Management Console), and run `aws configure`. You're asked for four pieces of information:

- *AWS access key ID*—Copy and paste this value from the User Security Credentials box (your browser window).
- *AWS secret access key*—Copy and paste this value from the User Security Credentials box (your browser window).
- *Default region name*—Enter `us-east-1`.
- *Default output format*—Enter `json`.

In the end, the terminal should look like this:

```
$ aws configure
AWS Access Key ID [None]: AKIAJXMDAVKCM5ZTX7PQ
AWS Secret Access Key [None]: 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
Default region name [None]: us-east-1
Default output format [None]: json
```

The CLI is now configured to authenticate as the user mycli. Switch back to the browser window and click Close to finish the user-creation wizard. The page shown in figure 4.7 opens.

Next you need to deal with authorization to determine what the user mycli is allowed to do. At the moment, the user isn't allowed to do anything (which is the default). Click the mycli user to see the page shown in figure 4.8.

In the Permissions section, in the Managed Policies box, click the Attach Policy button. The page shown in figure 4.9 opens.

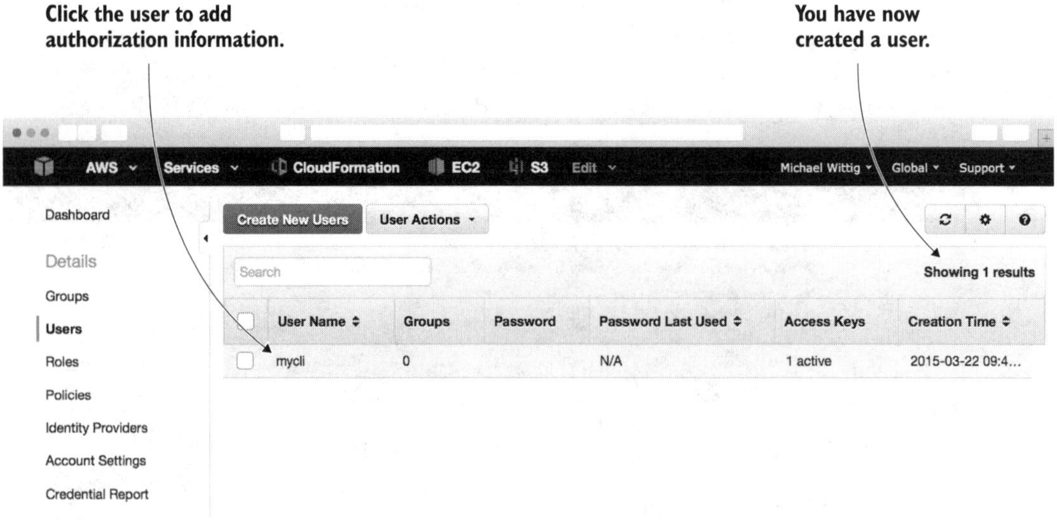

Click the user to add authorization information.

You have now created a user.

Figure 4.7   IAM users

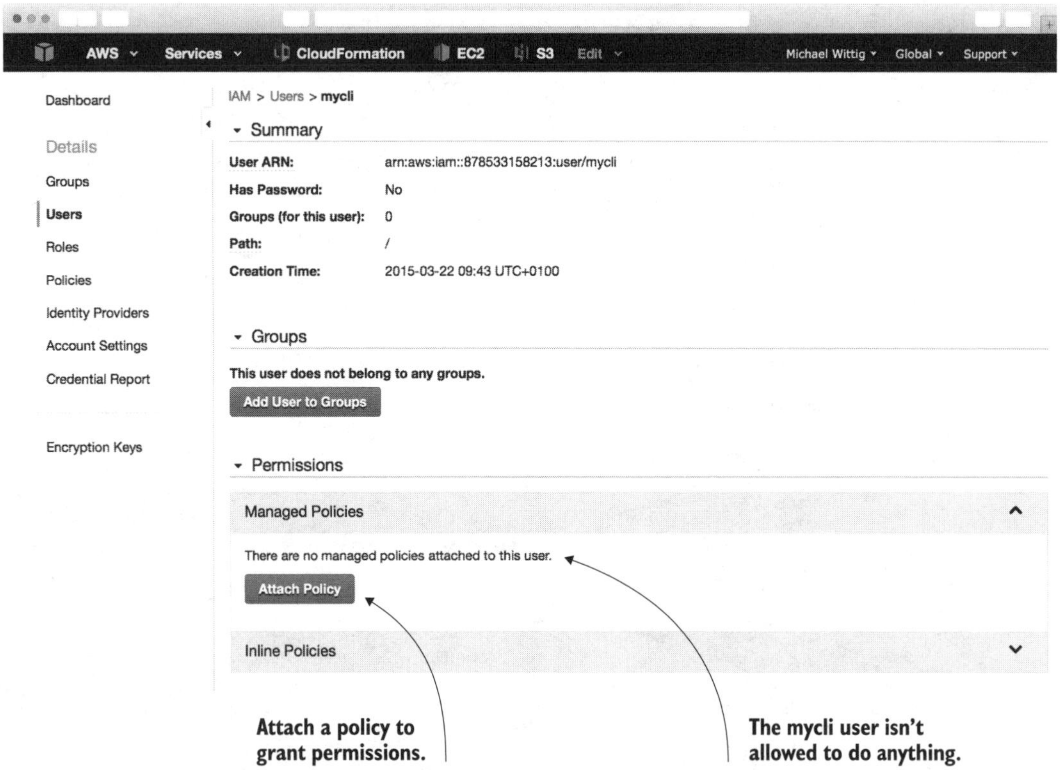

Figure 4.8 IAM user mycli without any permissions

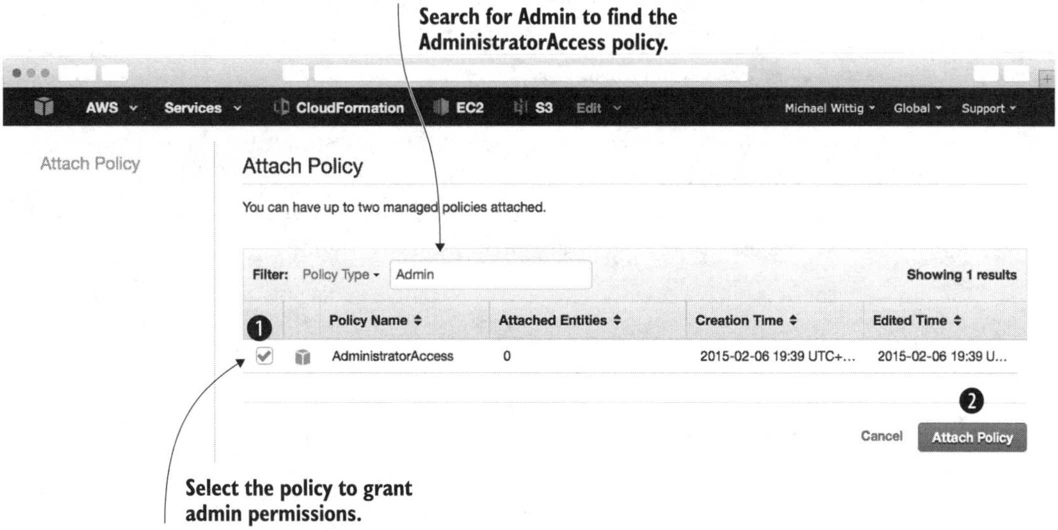

Figure 4.9 Attaching a managed policy to an IAM user

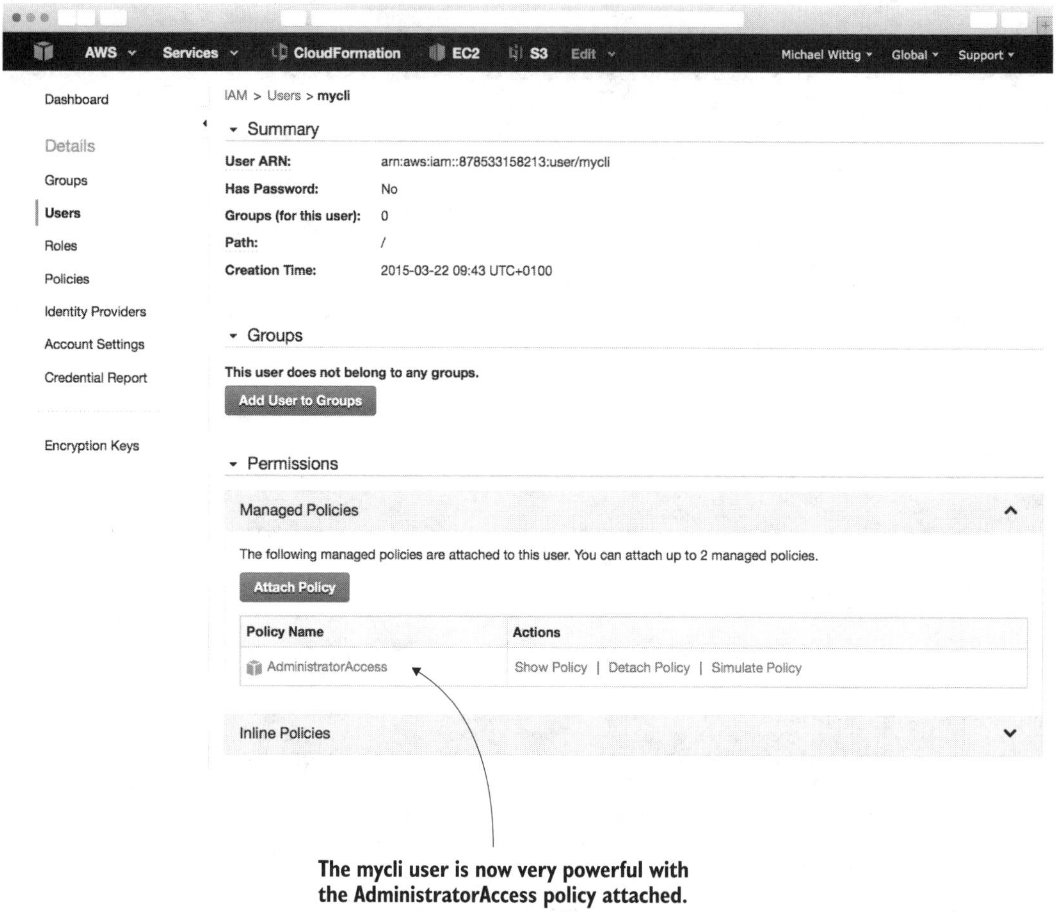

The mycli user is now very powerful with
the AdministratorAccess policy attached.

Figure 4.10   IAM user mycli with admin permissions

Select the policy AdministratorAccess by searching for `Admin`. Click Attach Policy. Now
your mycli user looks like figure 4.10.

It's time to test whether the CLI works. Switch to the terminal window and enter
aws ec2 describe-regions to get a list of all available regions:

```
$ aws ec2 describe-regions
{
  "Regions": [
    {
      "Endpoint": "ec2.eu-central-1.amazonaws.com",
      "RegionName": "eu-central-1"
    },
    {
      "Endpoint": "ec2.sa-east-1.amazonaws.com",
      "RegionName": "sa-east-1"
    },
    [...]
```

```
    {
      "Endpoint": "ec2.ap-southeast-2.amazonaws.com",
      "RegionName": "ap-southeast-2"
    },
    {
      "Endpoint": "ec2.ap-southeast-1.amazonaws.com",
      "RegionName": "ap-southeast-1"
    }
  ]
}
```

It works! You can begin to use the CLI.

4.2.3 Using the CLI

Suppose you want to get a list of all EC2 instances of type t2.micro. Execute aws in your terminal, as shown here:

```
$ aws ec2 describe-instances --filters "Name=instance-type,Values=t2.micro"
{
  "Reservations": []          ◁───┐  Empty list because you
}                                    haven't created an EC2
                                     instance
```

To use the AWS CLI, you need to specify a service and an action. In the previous example, the service is ec2 and the action is describe-instances. You can add options with --key value:

```
$ aws <service> <action> [--key value ...]
```

An important feature of the CLI is the help keyword. You can get help at three levels of detail:

- aws help—Shows all available services
- aws <service> help—Shows all actions available for a certain service
- aws <service> <action> help—Shows all options available for the particular service action

Sometimes you need temporary computing power, like a Linux server to test something via SSH. To do this, you can write a script that creates a virtual server for you. The script will run on your local computer and output how you connect to the server via SSH. After you complete your tests, the script should be able to terminate the virtual server. The script is used like this:

```
$ ./server.sh                                              Waits until started
waiting for i-c033f117 ...          ◁──────┘
i-c033f117 is accepting SSH connections under ec2-54-164-72-62 ...
ssh -i mykey.pem ec2-user@ec2-54-[...]aws.com      ◁───────┐
Press [Enter] key to terminate i-c033f117 ...               SSH connection string
[...]
terminating i-c033f117 ...          ◁─────── Waits until terminated
done.
```

Your server runs until you press the Enter key. When you press Enter, the server is terminated.

The limitations of this solution are as follows:

- It can handle only one server at a time.
- There's a different version for Windows than for Linux and Mac OS X.
- It's a command-line application, not graphical.

Nonetheless, the CLI solution solves the following use cases:

- Creating a virtual server
- Getting the public name of a virtual server to connect via SSH
- Terminating a virtual server if it's no longer needed

Depending on your OS, you'll use either Bash (Linux and Mac OS X) or PowerShell (Windows) to script.

One important feature of the CLI needs explanation before you can begin. The `--query` option uses JMESPath, which is a query language for JSON, to extract data from the result. This can be useful because usually you only need a specific field from the result. Look at the following JSON to see JMESPath in action. This is the result of `aws ec2 describe-images` and shows a list of available AMIs. To start an EC2 instance, you need the `ImageId`, and with JMESPath you can extract that information:

```
{
  "Images": [
    {
      "ImageId": "ami-146e2a7c",
      "State": "available"
    },
    {
      "ImageId": "ami-b66ed3de",
      "State": "available"
    }
  ]
}
```

To extract the first `ImageId`, the path is `Images[0].ImageId`; the result of this query is `"ami-146e2a7c"`. To extract all `State`, the path is `Images[*].State`; the result of this query is `["available", "available"]`. With this short introduction to JMESPath, you're well equipped to extract the data you need.

Where is the code located?

All code can be found in the book's code repository on GitHub: https://github.com/AWSinAction/code. You can download a snapshot of the repository at https://github.com/AWSinAction/code/archive/master.zip.

Linux and Mac OS X can interpret Bash scripts, whereas Windows prefers PowerShell scripts. We've created two versions of the same script.

LINUX AND MAC OS X

You can find the following listing in /chapter4/server.sh in the book's code folder. You can run it either by copying and pasting each line into your terminal or by executing the entire script via chmod +x server.sh && ./server.sh.

Listing 4.3 Creating and terminating a server from the CLI (Bash)

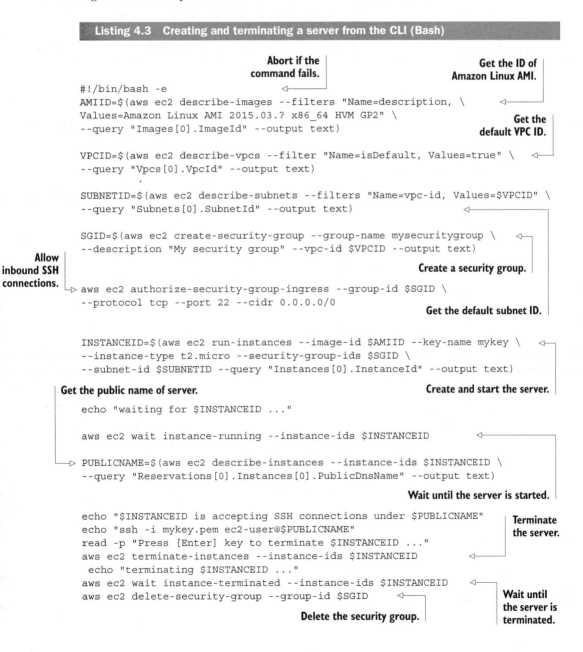

```
#!/bin/bash -e
AMIID=$(aws ec2 describe-images --filters "Name=description, \
Values=Amazon Linux AMI 2015.03.? x86_64 HVM GP2" \
--query "Images[0].ImageId" --output text)

VPCID=$(aws ec2 describe-vpcs --filter "Name=isDefault, Values=true" \
--query "Vpcs[0].VpcId" --output text)

SUBNETID=$(aws ec2 describe-subnets --filters "Name=vpc-id, Values=$VPCID" \
--query "Subnets[0].SubnetId" --output text)

SGID=$(aws ec2 create-security-group --group-name mysecuritygroup \
--description "My security group" --vpc-id $VPCID --output text)

aws ec2 authorize-security-group-ingress --group-id $SGID \
--protocol tcp --port 22 --cidr 0.0.0.0/0


INSTANCEID=$(aws ec2 run-instances --image-id $AMIID --key-name mykey \
--instance-type t2.micro --security-group-ids $SGID \
--subnet-id $SUBNETID --query "Instances[0].InstanceId" --output text)

echo "waiting for $INSTANCEID ..."

aws ec2 wait instance-running --instance-ids $INSTANCEID

PUBLICNAME=$(aws ec2 describe-instances --instance-ids $INSTANCEID \
--query "Reservations[0].Instances[0].PublicDnsName" --output text)


echo "$INSTANCEID is accepting SSH connections under $PUBLICNAME"
echo "ssh -i mykey.pem ec2-user@$PUBLICNAME"
read -p "Press [Enter] key to terminate $INSTANCEID ..."
aws ec2 terminate-instances --instance-ids $INSTANCEID
 echo "terminating $INSTANCEID ..."
aws ec2 wait instance-terminated --instance-ids $INSTANCEID
aws ec2 delete-security-group --group-id $SGID
```

Annotations: Abort if the command fails. · Get the ID of Amazon Linux AMI. · Get the default VPC ID. · Create a security group. · Allow inbound SSH connections. · Get the default subnet ID. · Create and start the server. · Get the public name of server. · Wait until the server is started. · Terminate the server. · Wait until the server is terminated. · Delete the security group.

> **Cleaning up**
>
> Make sure you terminate the server before you go on!

WINDOWS

You can find the following listing in /chapter4/server.ps1 in the book's code folder. Right-click the server.ps1 file and select Run with PowerShell to execute the script.

Listing 4.4   Creating and terminating a server from the CLI (PowerShell)

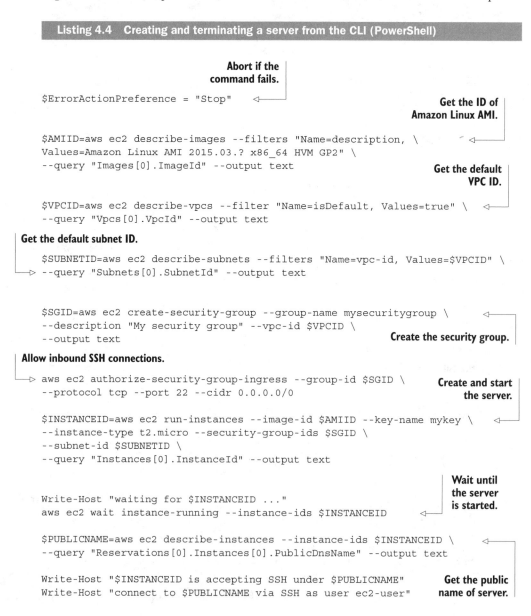

```
$ErrorActionPreference = "Stop"        ⟵  Abort if the
                                           command fails.

                                                              Get the ID of
                                                              Amazon Linux AMI.
$AMIID=aws ec2 describe-images --filters "Name=description, \    ⟵
Values=Amazon Linux AMI 2015.03.? x86_64 HVM GP2" \
--query "Images[0].ImageId" --output text
                                                           Get the default
                                                           VPC ID.
$VPCID=aws ec2 describe-vpcs --filter "Name=isDefault, Values=true" \    ⟵
--query "Vpcs[0].VpcId" --output text
```

Get the default subnet ID.

```
$SUBNETID=aws ec2 describe-subnets --filters "Name=vpc-id, Values=$VPCID" \
⟶  --query "Subnets[0].SubnetId" --output text


$SGID=aws ec2 create-security-group --group-name mysecuritygroup \    ⟵
--description "My security group" --vpc-id $VPCID \
--output text                                        Create the security group.
```

Allow inbound SSH connections.

```
⟶  aws ec2 authorize-security-group-ingress --group-id $SGID \    Create and start
--protocol tcp --port 22 --cidr 0.0.0.0/0                         the server.

$INSTANCEID=aws ec2 run-instances --image-id $AMIID --key-name mykey \   ⟵
--instance-type t2.micro --security-group-ids $SGID \
--subnet-id $SUBNETID \
--query "Instances[0].InstanceId" --output text
                                                                    Wait until
                                                                    the server
                                                                    is started.
Write-Host "waiting for $INSTANCEID ..."
aws ec2 wait instance-running --instance-ids $INSTANCEID        ⟵

$PUBLICNAME=aws ec2 describe-instances --instance-ids $INSTANCEID \    ⟵
--query "Reservations[0].Instances[0].PublicDnsName" --output text

Write-Host "$INSTANCEID is accepting SSH under $PUBLICNAME"      Get the public
Write-Host "connect to $PUBLICNAME via SSH as user ec2-user"    name of server.
```

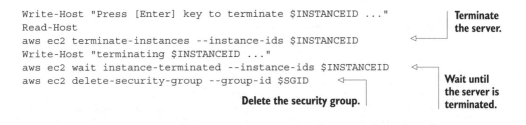

```
Write-Host "Press [Enter] key to terminate $INSTANCEID ..."
Read-Host
aws ec2 terminate-instances --instance-ids $INSTANCEID
Write-Host "terminating $INSTANCEID ..."
aws ec2 wait instance-terminated --instance-ids $INSTANCEID
aws ec2 delete-security-group --group-id $SGID
```

Terminate the server.

Delete the security group.

Wait until the server is terminated.

> **Cleaning up**
>
> Make sure you terminate the server before you go on!

WHY SHOULD YOU SCRIPT?

Why should you script instead of using the graphical AWS Management Console? A script can be reused and will save you time in the long run. You can build new architectures quickly with ready-to-use modules from your former projects. By automating your infrastructure creation, you can also enhance the automation of your deployment pipeline.

Another benefit is that a script is the most accurate documentation you can imagine (even a computer understands it). If you want to reproduce on Monday what you did last Friday, a script is worth its weight in gold. If you're sick and a coworker needs to take care of your tasks, they'll appreciate your scripts.

4.3 *Programming with the SDK*

AWS offers software development kits (SDKs) for a number of programming languages:

- Android
- Browsers (JavaScript)
- iOS
- Java
- .NET

- Node.js (JavaScript)
- PHP
- Python
- Ruby
- Go

An AWS SDK is a convenient way to make calls to the AWS API from your favorite programming language. The SDK takes care of things like authentication, retry on error, HTTPS communication, and JSON (de)serialization. You're free to choose the SDK for your favorite language, but in this book all examples are written in JavaScript and run in the Node.js runtime environment.

> **Installing and getting started with Node.js**
>
> Node.js is a platform to execute JavaScript in an event-driven environment and easily build network applications. To install Node.js, visit https://nodejs.org and download the package that fits your OS. Linux users can also install Node.js via package manager (https://github.com/joyent/node/wiki/Installing-Node.js-via-package-manager).

(continued)

After Node.js is installed, you can verify that everything works by typing `node --version` into your terminal. Your terminal should respond with something similar to `v0.12.*`. Now you're ready to run our JavaScript examples, like the Node Control Center for AWS.

Your Node.js installation comes with a important tool called npm, which is the package manager for Node.js. Verify the installation by running `npm --version` in your terminal.

To run a JavaScript script in Node.js, enter `node script.js` in your terminal. We use Node.js in this book because it's easy to install, it requires no IDE, and the syntax is familiar to most programmers.

Don't be confused by the terms *JavaScript* and *Node.js*. If you want to be precise, JavaScript is the language and Node.js is the execution environment. But don't expect anybody to make that distinction. Node.js is also called *node*.

To understand how the AWS SDK for Node.js (JavaScript) works, let's create a Node.js (JavaScript) application that controls EC2 servers via the AWS SDK.

4.3.1 Controlling virtual servers with SDK: nodecc

The Node Control Center for AWS (nodecc) is an advancement in managing multiple temporary EC2 servers with a text UI written in JavaScript. nodecc has the following features:

- It can handle multiple servers.
- It's written in JavaScript and runs in Node.js, so it's portable across platforms.
- It uses a textual UI.

Figure 4.11 shows what nodecc looks like.

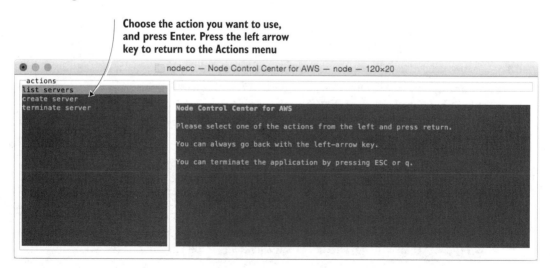

Figure 4.11   Node Control Center for AWS: start screen

You can find the nodecc application at /chapter4/nodecc/ in the book's code folder. Switch to that directory and run npm install in your terminal to install all needed dependencies. To start nodecc, run node index.js. You can always go back with the left arrow key. You can quit the application by pressing Esc or q.

The SDK uses the same settings you created for the CLI, so you're using the mycli user when running nodecc.

4.3.2 How nodecc creates a server

Before you can do anything with nodecc, you need at least one server. To start a server, choose the AMI, as figure 4.12 shows.

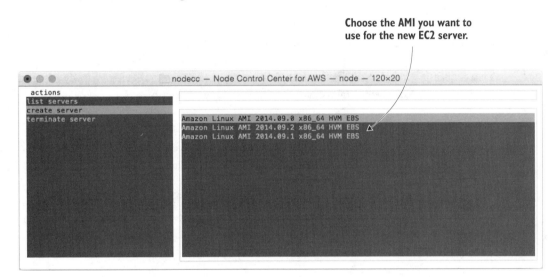

Choose the AMI you want to use for the new EC2 server.

Figure 4.12   nodecc: creating a server (step 1 of 2)

The code that fetches the list of the available AMIs is located at lib/listAMIs.js.

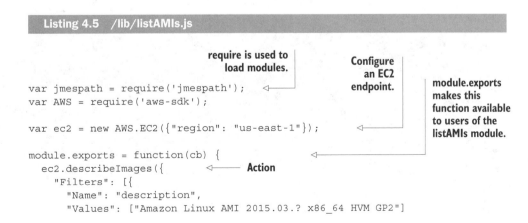

Listing 4.5   /lib/listAMIs.js

require is used to load modules.

Configure an EC2 endpoint.

module.exports makes this function available to users of the listAMIs module.

```
var jmespath = require('jmespath');
var AWS = require('aws-sdk');

var ec2 = new AWS.EC2({"region": "us-east-1"});

module.exports = function(cb) {
  ec2.describeImages({            Action
    "Filters": [{
      "Name": "description",
      "Values": ["Amazon Linux AMI 2015.03.? x86_64 HVM GP2"]
```

```
    }]
  }, function(err, data) {        In case of failure,
    if (err) {          ◄─────┘   err is set.
      cb(err);                                     Otherwise, data
    } else {                          ◄──────────  contains all AMIs.
      var amiIds = jmespath.search(data, 'Images[*].ImageId');
      var descriptions = jmespath.search(data, 'Images[*].Description');
      cb(null, {"amiIds": amiIds, "descriptions": descriptions});
    }
  });
};
```

The code is structured in such a way that each action is implemented in the lib folder. The next step to create a server is to choose the subnet in which the server should be started. You haven't learned about subnets yet, so for now select one randomly; see figure 4.13. The corresponding script is located at `lib/listSubnets.js`.

After you select the subnet, the server is created by `lib/createServer.js`, and you see a Starting screen. Now it's time to find out the public name of the newly created server. Use the left arrow key to switch to the navigation section.

4.3.3   *How nodecc lists servers and shows server details*

One important use case that nodecc must support is showing the public name of a server that you can use to connect via SSH. Because nodecc handles multiple servers, the first step is to select a server, as shown in figure 4.14.

Look at `lib/listServers.js` to see how a list of servers can be retrieved with the AWS SDK. After you select the server, you can display its details; see figure 4.15. You could use the `PublicDnsName` to connect to the instance via SSH. Press the left arrow key to switch back to the navigation section.

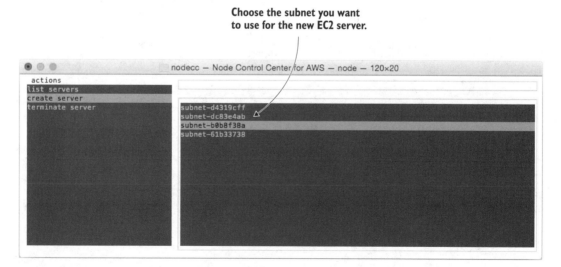

Figure 4.13   nodecc: creating a server (step 2 of 2)

All running servers are listed
by their EC2 instance ID.

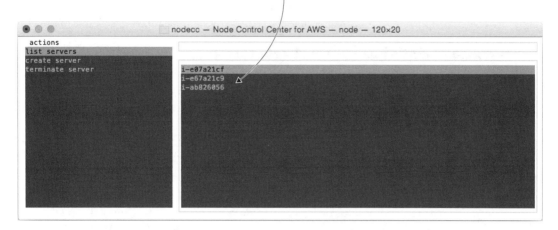

Figure 4.14 nodecc: listing servers

The public name of the
server. Can be used for SSH.

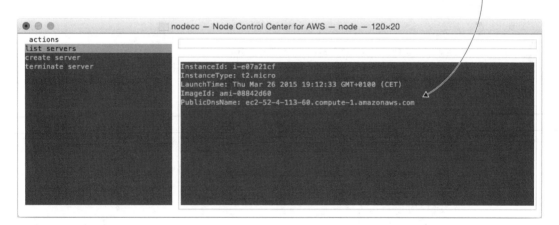

Figure 4.15 nodecc: showing server details

4.3.4 How nodecc terminates a server

To terminate a server, you first have to select it. To list the servers, use lib/
listServers.js again. After the server is selected, lib/terminateServer.js takes
care of termination.

That's nodecc: a text UI program to control temporary EC2 servers. Take some
time to think about what you could create by using your favorite language and the
AWS SDK. Chances are high that you might come up with a new business idea!

Cleaning up

Make sure you terminate all servers before you go on!

4.4   *Using a blueprint to start a virtual server*

Earlier, we talked about JIML to introduce the concept of infrastructure as code. Luckily, AWS already offers a tool that does much better than JIML: AWS CloudFormation. CloudFormation is based on templates, which up to now we've called blueprints.

> **NOTE** We use the term *blueprint* when discussing infrastructure automation in general. Blueprints used for AWS CloudFormation, a configuration management service, are called *templates.*

A *template* is a description of your infrastructure in JSON that can be interpreted by CloudFormation. The idea of describing something rather than listing the necessary actions is called a *descriptive approach.* Descriptive means you tell CloudFormation how your infrastructure should look and how it's connected. You aren't telling CloudFormation what actions are needed to create that infrastructure, and you don't specify the sequence in which the actions need to be executed. Again, it's all about dependencies—but CloudFormation offers you more benefits:

The benefits of CloudFormation are as follows:

- *It's a consistent way to describe infrastructure on AWS.* If you use scripts to create your infrastructure, everyone will solve the same problem differently. This is a hurdle for new developers and operators trying to understand what the code is doing. CloudFormation templates are a clear language to define infrastructure.
- *It can handle dependencies.* Ever tried to register a web server with a load balancer that wasn't yet available? At first glance, you'll miss a lot of dependencies. Trust us: never try to set up complex infrastructure using scripts. You'll end up in dependency hell!
- *It's replicable.* Is your test environment an exact copy of your production environment? Using CloudFormation, you can create two identical infrastructures and keep them in sync.
- *It's customizable.* You can insert custom parameters into CloudFormation to customize your templates as you wish.
- *It's testable.* Your infrastructure is testable if you can create it from a template. Just start a new infrastructure, run your tests, and shut it down again.
- *It's updatable.* CloudFormation supports updates to your infrastructure. It will figure out the parts of the template that have changed and apply those changes as smoothly as possible to your infrastructure.
- *It minimizes human failure.* CloudFormation doesn't get tired—even at 3:00 a.m.

- *It's the documentation for your infrastructure.* A CloudFormation template is a JSON document. You can treat it as code and use a version control system like Git to keep track of the changes.
- *It's free.* Using CloudFormation comes at no additional charge.

We think CloudFormation is one of the most powerful tools available to manage infrastructure on AWS.

4.4.1 Anatomy of a CloudFormation template

A basic CloudFormation template is structured into five parts:

1 *Format version*—The latest template format version is 2010-09-09, and this is currently the only valid value. Specify this; the default is the latest version, which will cause problems if a new format version is introduced in the future.
2 *Description*—What is this template about?
3 *Parameters*—Parameters are used to customize a template with values: for example, domain name, customer ID, and database password.
4 *Resources*—A resource is the smallest block you can describe. Examples are a virtual server, a load balancer, or an elastic IP address.
5 *Outputs*—An output is comparable to a parameter, but the other way around. An output returns something from your template, such as the public name of an EC2 server.

A basic template looks like the following listing.

> **Listing 4.6 CloudFormation template structure**

```
                                    The only valid version
{
  "AWSTemplateFormatVersion": "2010-09-09",   ◁──────┘       What is this
  "Description": "CloudFormation template structure",   ◁───┘ template about?
  "Parameters": {
    [...]              ◁─────── Defines parameters
  },
  "Resources": {
    [...]              ◁─────── Defines resources
  },
  "Outputs": {
    [...]              ◁─────── Defines outputs
  }
}
```

Let's take a closer look at parameters, resources, and outputs.

FORMAT VERSION AND DESCRIPTION

The only valid `AWSTemplateFormatVersion` value at the moment is `"2010-09-09"`. Always specify the format version. If you don't, the latest version is assumed by CloudFormation. As mentioned earlier, this means that if a new format version is introduced in the future, you'll get into serious trouble.

`Description` isn't mandatory, but we encourage you to take some time to document what the template is about. A meaningful description will help you in the future to remember what the template is for. It will also help your coworkers.

PARAMETERS

A parameter has at least a name and a type. We encourage you to add a description as well, as shown in the following listing.

Listing 4.7   CloudFormation parameter structure

```
{
  [...]                        Name of the parameter        This parameter
  "Parameters": {                                           represents a
    "NameOfParameter": {              <──────────           number.
      "Type": "Number",           <──────
      "Description": "This parameter is for demonstration"
      [...]
    }
  },
  [...]
}
```

Valid types are listed in table 4.1.

Table 4.1   CloudFormation parameter types

Type	Description
`String` `CommaDelimitedList`	A string or a list of strings separated by commas
`Number` `List<Number>`	An integer or float or a list of integers or floats
`AWS::EC2::Instance::Id` `List<AWS::EC2::Instance::Id>`	An EC2 instance ID (virtual server) or a list of EC2 instance IDs
`AWS::EC2::Image::Id` `List<AWS::EC2::Image::Id>`	An AMI ID or a list of AMIs
`AWS::EC2::KeyPair::KeyName`	An Amazon EC2 key-pair name
`AWS::EC2::SecurityGroup::Id` `List<AWS::EC2::SecurityGroup::Id>`	A security group ID or a list of security group IDs
`AWS::EC2::Subnet::Id` `List<AWS::EC2::Subnet::Id>`	A subnet ID or a list of subnet IDs
`AWS::EC2::Volume::Id` `List<AWS::EC2::Volume::Id>`	An EBS volume ID (network attached storage) or a list of EBS volume IDs
`AWS::EC2::VPC::Id` `List<AWS::EC2::VPC::Id>`	A VPC ID (virtual private cloud) or a list of VPC IDs
`AWS::Route53::HostedZone::Id` `List<AWS::Route53::HostedZone::Id>`	A DNS zone ID or a list of DNS zone IDs

In addition to using the `Type` and `Description` properties, you can enhance a parameter with the properties listed in table 4.2.

Table 4.2 CloudFormation parameter properties

Property	Description	Example
`Default`	A default value for the parameter	
`NoEcho`	Hides the parameter value in all graphical tools (useful for passwords)	`"NoEcho": true`
`AllowedValues`	Specifies possible values for the parameter	`"AllowedValues": ["1", "2", "3"]`
`AllowedPattern`	More generic than `AllowedValues` because it uses a regular expression	`"AllowedPattern": "[a-zA-Z0-9]*"` allows only a–z, A–Z, and 0–9 with any length
`MinLength,` `MaxLength`	Used in combination with the String type to define minimum and maximum length	
`MinValue,` `MaxValue`	Used in combination with the `Number` type to define lower and upper bounds	

A parameter section of a CloudFormation template could look like this:

```
{
  [...]
  "Parameters": {
    "KeyName": {
      "Description": "Key Pair name",
      "Type": "AWS::EC2::KeyPair::KeyName"          ⟵  Only key names
    },                                                   are allowed.
    "NumberOfServers": {
      "Description": "How many servers do you like?",
      "Type": "Number",
      "Default": "1",
      "MinValue": "1",
      "MaxValue": "5"          ⟵  Prevent massive costs
    },                             with an upper bound.
    "WordPressVersion": {
      "Description": "Which version of WordPress do you want?",
      "Type": "String",
      "AllowedValues": ["4.1.1", "4.0.1"]          ⟵  Restricted to
    }                                                   certain versions
  },
  [...]
}
```

The default is one server. ⟶ (annotation for `"Default": "1"`)

Now you should have a better feel for parameters. If you want to know everything about them, see http://mng.bz/jg7B or follow along in the book and learn by doing.

RESOURCES

A resource has at least a name, a type, and some properties, as shown in the following listing.

Listing 4.8   CloudFormation resources structure

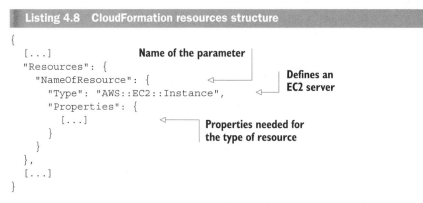

When defining resources, you need to know about the type and the properties of that type. In this book, you'll get to know a lot of resource types and their respective properties. An example of a single EC2 server is shown in the next listing. If you see {"Ref": "NameOfSomething"}, think of it as a placeholder for what's referenced by the name. You can reference parameters and resources to create dependencies.

Listing 4.9   CloudFormation EC2 server resource

```
{
  [...]
  "Resources": {                          Name of the resource
    "Server": {
      "Type": "AWS::EC2::Instance",       Defines an EC2 server
      "Properties": {
        "ImageId": "ami-1ecae776",        Some hard-coded settings
        "InstanceType": "t2.micro",
        "KeyName": {"Ref": "KeyName"},     The settings are defined
        "SubnetId": {"Ref": "Subnet"}      by parameters.
      }
    }
  },
  [...]
}
```

Now you've described the server, but how can you output its public name?

OUTPUTS

A CloudFormation template's output includes at least a name (like parameters and resources) and a value, but we encourage you to add a description as well. You can use outputs to pass data from within your template to the outside (see the following listing).

Listing 4.10   CloudFormation outputs structure

```
{
  [...]
  "Outputs": {
    "NameOfOutput": {                     Name of the output
```

```
      "Value": "1",                                   ⊲——— Value of the output
      "Description": "This output is always 1"
    }
  }
}
```

Static outputs aren't very useful. You'll mostly use values that reference the name of a resource or an attribute of a resource, like its public name, as shown in the next listing.

Listing 4.11 CloudFormation outputs example

```
{
  [...]
  "Outputs": {
    "ServerEC2ID": {
      "Value": {"Ref": "Server"},           ⊲——┤ References the
      "Description": "EC2 ID of the server"       EC2 server
    },
    "PublicName": {
      "Value": {"Fn::GetAtt": ["Server", "PublicDnsName"]},  ⊲──┐ Get the attribute
      "Description": "Public name of the server"                │ PublicDnsName
    }                                                           │ of the EC2 server.
  }
}
```

You'll get to know the most important attributes of Fn::GetAtt later in the book. If you want to know about all of them, see http://mng.bz/q5I4.

Now that we've taken a brief look at the core parts of a CloudFormation template, it's time to make one of your own.

4.4.2 Creating your first template

Suppose you've been asked to provide a virtual server for a developer team. After a few months, the developer team realizes the virtual server needs more CPU power, because the usage pattern has changed. You can handle that request with the CLI and the SDK, but as you learned in section 3.4, before the instance type can be changed, you must stop the instance. The process will be as follows: stop the instance, wait for the instance to stop, change the instance type, start the instance, and wait for the instance to start.

A descriptive approach like that used by CloudFormation is simpler: just change the InstanceType property and update the template. InstanceType can be passed to the template via a parameter. That's it! You can begin creating the template, as shown in the next listing.

Listing 4.12 Template to create an EC2 instance with CloudFormation

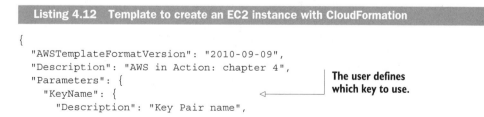

```
{
  "AWSTemplateFormatVersion": "2010-09-09",
  "Description": "AWS in Action: chapter 4",
  "Parameters": {                         ⊲——┤ The user defines
    "KeyName": {                               which key to use.
      "Description": "Key Pair name",
```

You'll learn
about this
in section
6.5.

```
      "Type": "AWS::EC2::KeyPair::KeyName",
      "Default": "mykey"
    },
    "VPC": {
      [...]
    },
    "Subnet": {
      [...]
    },
    "InstanceType": {
      "Description": "Select one of the possible instance types",
      "Type": "String",
      "Default": "t2.micro",
      "AllowedValues": ["t2.micro", "t2.small", "t2.medium"]
    }
  },
  "Resources": {
    "SecurityGroup": {
      "Type": "AWS::EC2::SecurityGroup",
      "Properties": {
        [...]
      }
    },
    "Server": {
      "Type": "AWS::EC2::Instance",
      "Properties": {
        "ImageId": "ami-1ecae776",
        "InstanceType": {"Ref": "InstanceType"},
        "KeyName": {"Ref": "KeyName"},
        "SecurityGroupIds": [{"Ref": "SecurityGroup"}],
        "SubnetId": {"Ref": "Subnet"}
      }
    }
  },
  "Outputs": {
    "PublicName": {
      "Value": {"Fn::GetAtt": ["Server", "PublicDnsName"]},
      "Description": "Public name (connect via SSH as user ec2-user)"
    }
  }
}
```

You'll learn
about this in
section 6.5.

The user defines
the instance type.

You'll learn about
this in section 6.4.

Defines a minimal
EC2 instance

Returns the public name
of the EC2 instance

You can find the full code for the template at /chapter4/server.json in the book's code folder. Please don't worry about VPC, subnets, and security groups at the moment; you'll get to know them in chapter 6.

> ### Where is the template located?
> You can find the template on GitHub. You can download a snapshot of the repository at https://github.com/AWSinAction/code/archive/master.zip. The file we talk about is located at chapter4/server.json. On S3, the same file is located at https://s3.amazonaws.com/awsinaction/chapter4/server.json.

**Click to create a
new infrastructure
from a blueprint.**

**Reload
the page.**

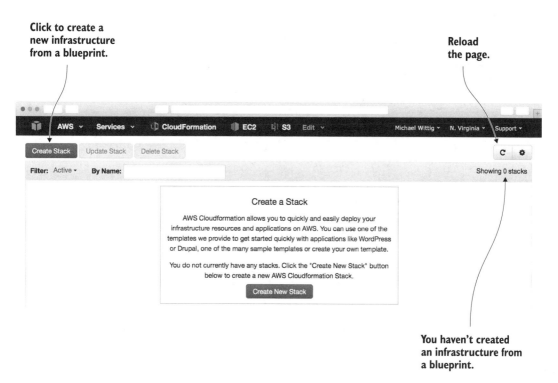

**You haven't created
an infrastructure from
a blueprint.**

Figure 4.16 Overview of CloudFormation stacks

If you create an infrastructure from a template, CloudFormation calls it a *stack*. You can think of *template* versus *stack* much like *class* versus *object*. The template exists only once, whereas many stacks can be created from the same template.

Open the AWS Management Console at https://console.aws.amazon.com. Click Services in the navigation bar, and then click the CloudFormation service. Figure 4.16 shows the initial CloudFormation screen with an overview of all the stacks.

The following steps will guide you through creating your stack:

1. Click the Create Stack button to start a four-step wizard.
2. Give the stack a name like `server1`.
3. Select Specify an Amazon S3 Template URL, and enter `https://s3.amazonaws.com/awsinaction/chapter4/server.json` as shown in figure 4.17.

In the second step, you define parameters:

1. `InstanceType`: Select t2.micro.
2. `KeyName`: Select mykey.
3. `Subnet`: Select the first value in the drop-down list. You'll learn about subnets later.
4. `VPC`: Select the first value in the drop-down list. You'll learn about VPCs later.

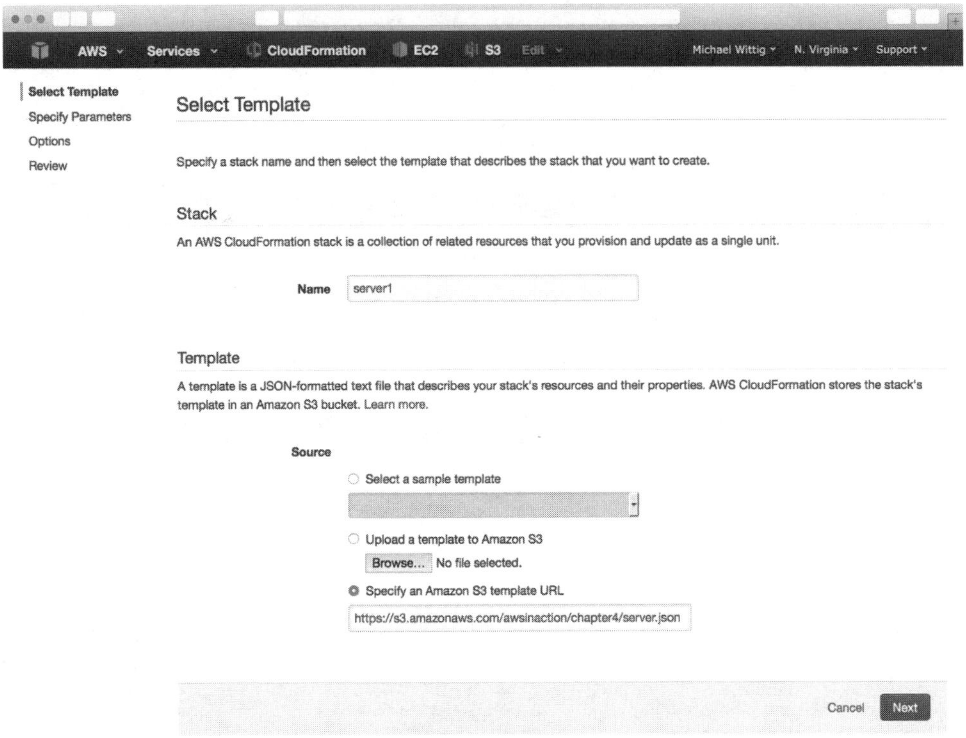

Figure 4.17   Creating a CloudFormation stack: selecting a template (step 1 of 4)

Figure 4.18 shows the parameters step. Click Next after you've chosen a value for every parameter to proceed with the next step.

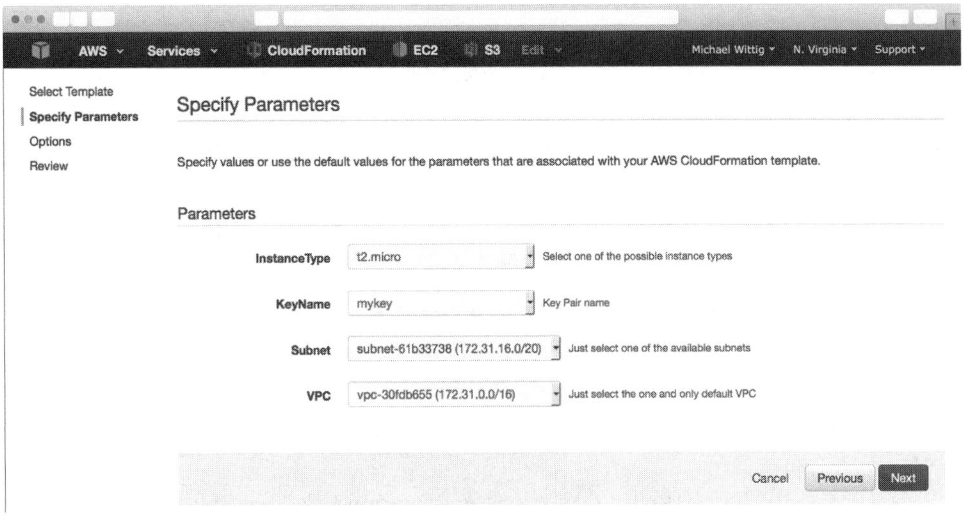

Figure 4.18   Creating a CloudFormation stack: defining parameters (step 2 of 4)

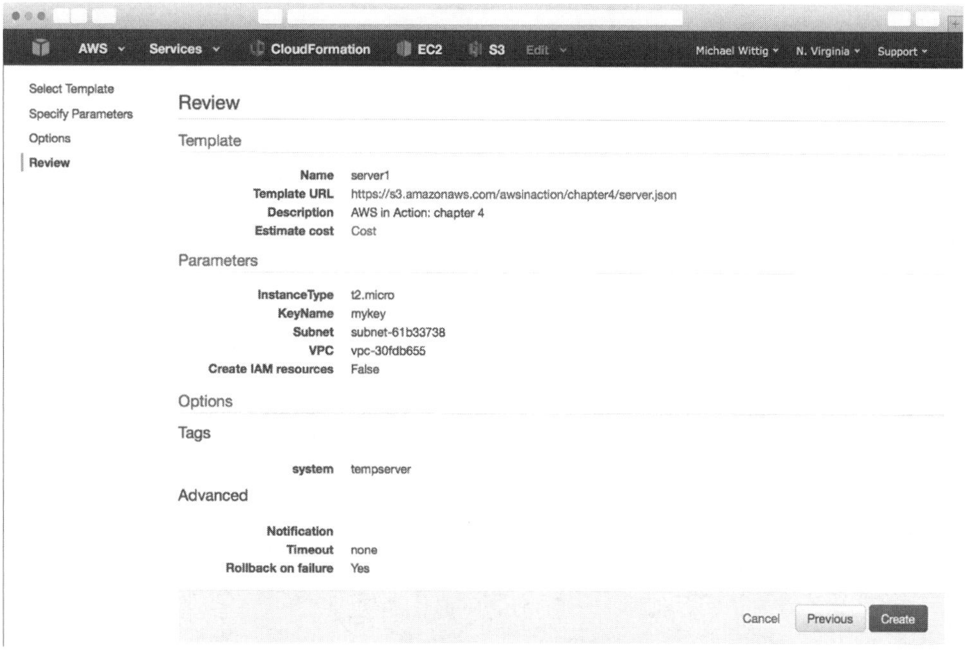

Figure 4.19   Creating a CloudFormation stack: summary (step 4 of 4)

In the third step, you can define tags for the stack. All resources created by the stack will be tagged with these tags automatically. Create a new tag by typing `system` for the Key value and `tempserver` for Value. Click Next. Step 4 displays a summary of the stack, as shown in figure 4.19.

Click Create. The stack is now created. If the process is successful, you'll see the screen shown in figure 4.20. As long as Status is CREATE_IN_PROGRESS, you need to be patient. When Status is CREATE_COMPLETE, select the stack and click the Outputs tab to see the public name of the server.

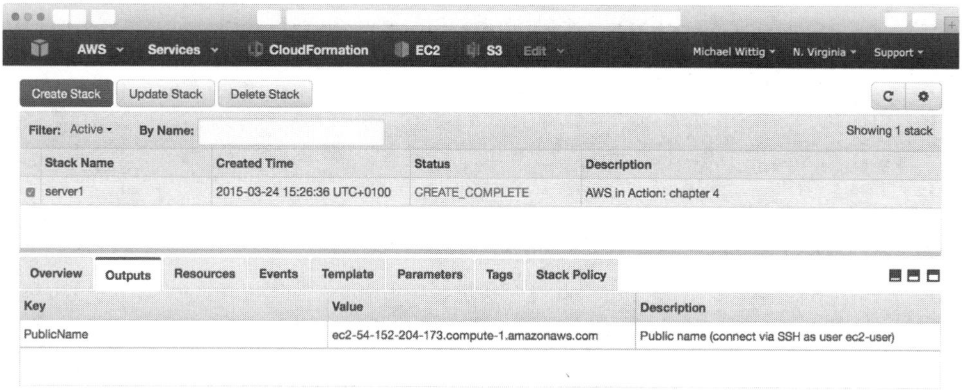

Figure 4.20   The CloudFormation stack has been created.

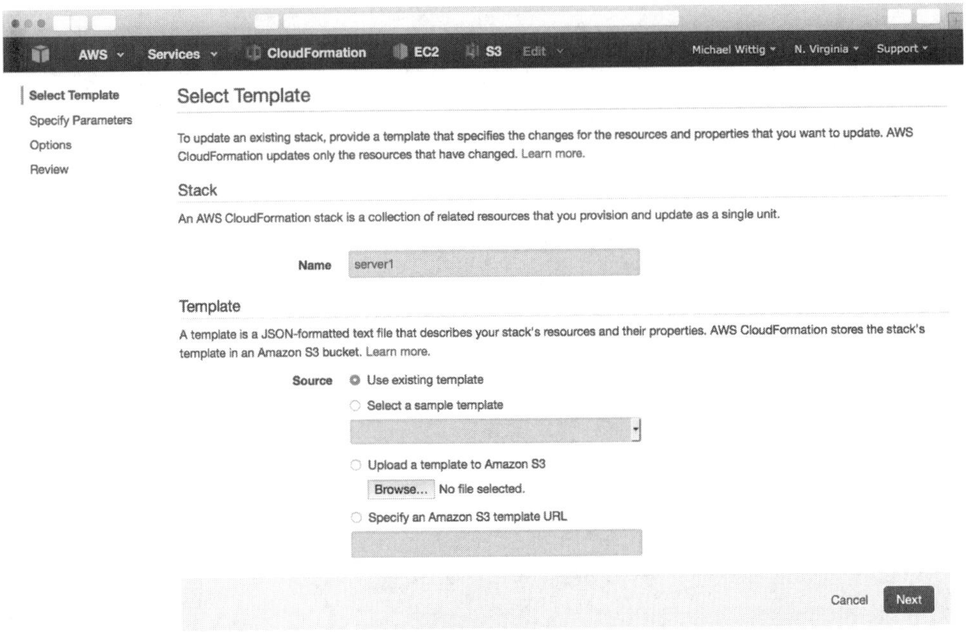

Figure 4.21   Updating the CloudFormation stack: summary (step 1 of 4)

It's time to test the new feature: instance type modification. Select the stack and click the Update Stack button. The wizard that starts is similar to the one you used during stack creation. Figure 4.21 shows the first step of the wizard.

Check that Use Existing Template is selected as the Source. In step 2, you need to change InstanceType: choose t2.small to double or t2.medium to quadruple the computing power of your server.

> **WARNING** Starting a virtual server with instance type t2.small or t2.medium will incur charges. See http://aws.amazon.com/ec2/pricing to find out the current hourly price.

Step 3 is about sophisticated options during the update of the stack. You don't need any of these features now, so skip the step by clicking Next. Step 4 is a summary; click Update. The stack now has Status UPDATE_IN_PROGRESS. After a few minutes, Status should change to UPDATE_COMPLETE. You can select the stack and get the public name by looking at the Outputs tab.

Alternatives to CloudFormation

If you don't want to write plain JSON to create templates for your infrastructure, there are a few alternatives to CloudFormation. Tools like Troposphere, a library written in Python, help you to create CloudFormation templates without having to write JSON. They add another abstraction level on top of CloudFormation to do so.

(continued)

There are also tools that allow you to use infrastructure as code without needing CloudFormation. Terraform and Ansible let you describe your infrastructure as code, for example.

When you changed the parameter, CloudFormation figured out what needed to be done to achieve the end result. That's the power of a descriptive approach: you say what the end result should look like, not how the end result should be achieved.

Cleaning up

Delete the stack by selecting it and clicking the Delete Stack button.

4.5 Summary

- Use the command-line interface (CLI), one of the SDKs, or CloudFormation to automate your infrastructure on AWS.
- Infrastructure as code describes the approach to program the creation and modification of your infrastructure including virtual servers, networking, storage, and more.
- You can use the CLI to automate complex processes in AWS with scripts (Bash and PowerShell).
- You can use SDKs for nine programming languages to embed AWS into your applications and create applications like nodecc.
- CloudFormation uses a descriptive approach in JSON: you only define the end state of your infrastructure, and CloudFormation figures out how this state can be achieved. The major parts of a CloudFormation template are parameters, resources, and outputs.

Automating deployment: CloudFormation, Elastic Beanstalk, and OpsWorks

This chapter covers

- Running a script on server startup to deploy applications
- Deploying common web applications with the help of AWS Elastic Beanstalk
- Deploying multilayer applications with the help of AWS OpsWorks
- Comparing the different deployment services available on AWS

Whether you want to use software from in-house development, open source projects, or commercial vendors, you need to install, update, and configure the application and its dependencies. This process is called *deployment*. In this chapter, you'll learn about three tools for deploying applications to virtual servers on AWS:

- Deploying a VPN solution with the help of AWS CloudFormation and a script started at the end of the boot process.
- Deploying a collaborative text editor with AWS Elastic Beanstalk. The text editor Etherpad is a simple web application and a perfect fit for AWS Elastic Beanstalk, because the Node.js platform is supported by default.
- Deploying an IRC web client and IRC server with AWS OpsWorks. The setup consists of two parts: a Node.js server that delivers the IRC web client and the IRC server itself. The example consists of multiple layers and is perfect for AWS OpsWorks.

We've chosen examples that don't need a storage solution for this chapter, but all three deployment solutions would support delivering an application together with a storage solution. You'll find examples using storage in the next part of the book.

> **Examples are 100% covered by the Free Tier**
> The examples in this chapter are completely covered by the Free Tier. As long as you don't run the examples for longer than a few days, you won't pay anything. Keep in mind that this only applies if you created a fresh AWS account for this book and nothing else is going on in your AWS account. Try to complete the examples of the chapter within a few days; you'll clean up your account at the end of each example.

Which steps are required to deploy a typical web application like WordPress—a widely used blogging platform—to a server?

1 Install an Apache HTTP server, a MySQL database, a PHP runtime environment, a MySQL library for PHP, and an SMTP mail server.
2 Download the WordPress application and unpack the archive on your server.
3 Configure the Apache web server to serve the PHP application.
4 Configure the PHP runtime environment to tweak performance and increase security.
5 Edit the wp-config.php file to configure the WordPress application.
6 Edit the configuration of the SMTP server, and make sure mail can only be sent from the virtual server to avoid misuse from spammers.
7 Start the MySQL, SMTP, and HTTP services.

Steps 1–2 handle installing and updating the executables. These executables are configured in steps 3–6. Step 7 starts the services.

System administrators often perform these steps manually by following how-tos. Deploying applications manually is no longer recommended in a flexible cloud environment. Instead your goal will be to automate these steps with the help of the tools you'll discover next.

5.1   *Deploying applications in a flexible cloud environment*

If you want to use cloud advantages like scaling the number of servers depending on the current load or building a highly available infrastructure, you'll need to start new virtual servers several times a day. On top of that, the number of virtual servers you'll have to supply with updates will grow. The steps required to deploy an application don't change, but as figure 5.1 shows, you need to perform them on multiple servers. Deploying software manually to a growing number of servers becomes impossible over time and has a high risk of human failure. This is why we recommend that you automate the deployment of applications.

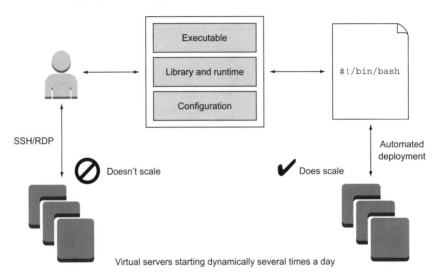

Figure 5.1   Deployment must be automated in a flexible and scalable cloud environment.

The investment in an automated deployment process will pay off in the future by increasing efficiency and decreasing human failures.

5.2   *Running a script on server startup using CloudFormation*

A simple but powerful and flexible way of automating application deployment is to run a script on server startup. To go from a plain OS to a fully installed and configured server, you need to follow these three steps:

1 Start a plain virtual server containing just an OS.
2 Execute a script at the end of the boot process.
3 Install and configure your applications with the help of a script.

First you need to choose an AMI from which to start your virtual server. An AMI bundles the OS and preinstalled software for your virtual server. When you're starting your server from an AMI containing a plain OS without any additional software installed, you need to provision the virtual server at the end of the boot process. Translating the necessary steps to install and configure your application into a script allows you to automate this task. But how do you execute this script automatically after booting your virtual server?

5.2.1 Using user data to run a script on server startup

You can inject a small amount—not more than 16 KB—of data called *user data* into every virtual server. You specify the user data during the creation of a new virtual server. A typical way of using the user data feature is built into most AMIs, such as the Amazon Linux Image and the Ubuntu AMI. Whenever you boot a virtual server based on these AMIs, user data is executed as a shell script at the end of the boot process. The script is executed as user root.

The user data is always accessible from the virtual server with a HTTP GET request to http://169.254.169.254/latest/user-data. The user data behind this URL is only accessible from the virtual server itself. As you'll see in the following example, you can deploy applications of any kind with the help of user data executed as a script.

5.2.2 Deploying OpenSwan as a VPN server to a virtual server

If you're working with a laptop from a coffee house over Wi-Fi, you may want to tunnel your traffic to the internet through a VPN. You'll learn how to deploy a VPN server to a virtual server with the help of user data and a shell script. The VPN solution, called OpenSwan, offers an IPSec-based tunnel that's easy to use with Windows, OS X, and Linux. Figure 5.2 shows the example setup.

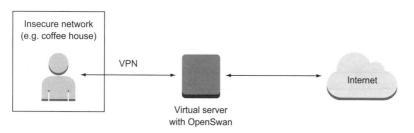

Figure 5.2 Using OpenSwan on a virtual server to tunnel traffic from a personal computer

Open your command line and execute the commands shown in the next listing step by step to start a virtual server and deploy a VPN server on it. We've prepared a Cloud-Formation template that starts the virtual server and its dependencies.

Listing 5.1 Deploying a VPN server to a virtual server: CloudFormation and a shell script

```
$ VpcId=$(aws ec2 describe-vpcs --query Vpcs[0].VpcId --output text)     ⟵

$ SubnetId=$(aws ec2 describe-subnets --filters Name=vpc-id,Values=$VpcId \
  --query Subnets[0].SubnetId --output text)
```

Gets the default VPC

Gets the default subnet

Creates a random shared secret (if openssl doesn't work, create your own random sequence).

Creates a random password (if openssl doesn't work, create your own random sequence).

```
$ SharedSecret=$(openssl rand -base64 30)
```

```
$ Password=$(openssl rand -base64 30)
```

Creates a CloudFormation stack

```
$ aws cloudformation create-stack  --stack-name vpn --template-url \
https://s3.amazonaws.com/awsinaction/chapter5/vpn-cloudformation.json \
--parameters ParameterKey=KeyName,ParameterValue=mykey \
ParameterKey=VPC,ParameterValue=$VpcId \
ParameterKey=Subnet,ParameterValue=$SubnetId \
ParameterKey=IPSecSharedSecret,ParameterValue=$SharedSecret \
ParameterKey=VPNUser,ParameterValue=vpn \
ParameterKey=VPNPassword,ParameterValue=$Password
```

If the status is not COMPLETE, retry in a minute.

```
$ aws cloudformation describe-stacks --stack-name vpn \
--query Stacks[0].Outputs
```

Shortcut for OS X and Linux

You can avoid typing these commands manually at your command line by using the following command to download a bash script and execute it directly on your local machine. The bash script contains the same steps as shown in listing 5.1:

```
$ curl -s https://raw.githubusercontent.com/AWSinAction/\
code/master/chapter5/\
vpn-create-cloudformation-stack.sh | bash -ex
```

The output of the last command should print out the public IP address of the VPN server, a shared secret, the VPN username, and the VPN password. You can use this information to establish a VPN connection from your computer, if you like:

```
[...]
[
  {
    "Description": "Public IP address of the vpn server",
    "OutputKey": "ServerIP",
    "OutputValue": "52.4.68.225"
  },
  {
    "Description": "The shared key for the VPN connection (IPSec)",
    "OutputKey": "IPSecSharedSecret",
    "OutputValue": "sqmvJll/13bD6YqpmsKkPSMs9RrPL8itpr7m5V8g"
  },
  {
    "Description": "The username for the vpn connection",
```

```
    "OutputKey": "VPNUser",
    "OutputValue": "vpn"
  },
  {
    "Description": "The password for the vpn connection",
    "OutputKey": "VPNPassword",
    "OutputValue": "aZQVFufFlUjJkesUfDmMj6DcHrWjuKShyFB/d0lE"
  }
]
```

Let's take a deeper look at the deployment process of the VPN server. You'll dive into the following tasks, which you've used unnoticed so far:

- Starting a virtual server with custom user data and configuring a firewall for the virtual server with AWS CloudFormation
- Executing a shell script at the end of the boot process to install an application and its dependencies with the help of a package manager, and to edit configuration files

USING CLOUDFORMATION TO START A VIRTUAL SERVER WITH USER DATA

You can use CloudFormation to start a virtual server and configure a firewall. The template for the VPN server includes a shell script packed into user data, as shown in listing 5.2.

Fn::Join and Fn::Base64

The CloudFormation template includes two new functions: `Fn::Join` and `Fn::Base64`. With `Fn::Join`, you can join a set of values to make a single value with a specified delimiter:

```
{"Fn::Join": ["delimiter", ["value1", "value2", "value3"]]}
```

The function `Fn::Base64` encodes the input with Base64. You'll need this function because the user data must be encoded in Base64:

```
{"Fn::Base64": "value"}
```

Listing 5.2 Parts of a CloudFormation template to start a virtual server with user data

```
{
  "AWSTemplateFormatVersion": "2010-09-09",
  "Description": "Starts an virtual server (EC2) with OpenSwan [...]",
  "Parameters": {                          ⟵──────┐  Parameters to make
    "KeyName": {                                  │  it possible to reuse
      "Description": "key for SSH access",        │  the template
      "Type": "AWS::EC2::KeyPair::KeyName"
    },
    "VPC": {
```

```
          "Description": "Just select the one and only default VPC.",
          "Type": "AWS::EC2::VPC::Id"
        },
        "Subnet": {
          "Description": "Just select one of the available subnets.",
          "Type": "AWS::EC2::Subnet::Id"
        },
        "IPSecSharedSecret": {
          "Description": "The shared secret key for IPSec.",
          "Type": "String"
        },
        "VPNUser": {
          "Description": "The VPN user.",
          "Type": "String"
        },
        "VPNPassword": {
          "Description": "The VPN password.",
          "Type": "String"
        }
      },
      "Resources": {                                  Describes the
        "EC2Instance": {           ◁─────────────     virtual server
          "Type": "AWS::EC2::Instance",
          "Properties": {
            "InstanceType": "t2.micro",
            "SecurityGroupIds": [{"Ref": "InstanceSecurityGroup"}],
            "KeyName": {"Ref": "KeyName"},
            "ImageId": "ami-1ecae776",                Defines a shell script as user
            "SubnetId": {"Ref": "Subnet"},            data for the virtual server
            "UserData":                  ◁─────────
```
Concatenates and encodes a string value └─▷
```
              {"Fn::Base64": {"Fn::Join": ["", [
                "#!/bin/bash -ex\n",
                "export IPSEC_PSK=", {"Ref": "IPSecSharedSecret"}, "\n",
```
Exports parameters to environment variables to make them available in an external shell script called next ┌─▷
```
                "export VPN_USER=", {"Ref": "VPNUser"}, "\n",
                "export VPN_PASSWORD=", {"Ref": "VPNPassword"}, "\n",
                "export STACK_NAME=", {"Ref": "AWS::StackName"}, "\n",
                "export REGION=", {"Ref": "AWS::Region"}, "\n",
                "curl -s https://…/vpn-setup.sh | bash -ex\n"    ◁──┐
              ]]}}                                                   Fetches the
            },                                                       shell script
            [...]                                                    via HTTP and
          },                                                         executes it
          [...]
        },
        [...]
      },
      "Outputs": {
        [...]
      }
    }
```

Basically, the user data contains a small script to fetch and execute the real script, vpn-setup.sh, which contains all the commands for installing the executables and configuring the services. Doing so frees you from inserting scripts in the unreadable format needed for the JSON CloudFormation template.

INSTALLING AND CONFIGURING A VPN SERVER WITH A SCRIPT

The vpn-setup.sh script shown in listing 5.3 installs packages with the help of the package manager yum and writes some configuration files. You don't have to understand the details of the configuration of the VPN server; you just need to know that this shell script is executed during the boot process to install and configure a VPN server.

> **Listing 5.3 Installing packages and writing configuration files on server startup**

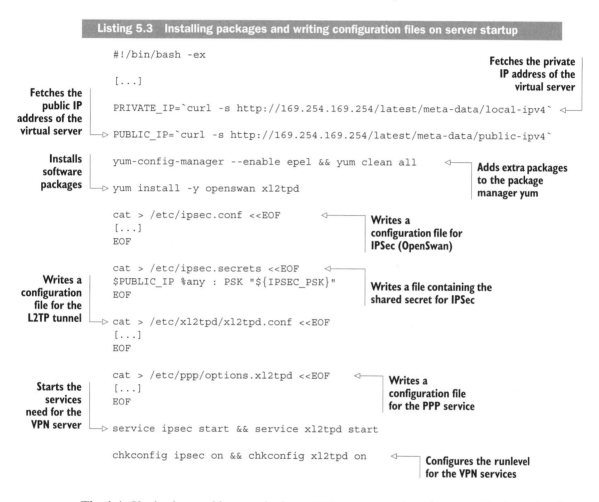

That's it. You've learned how to deploy a VPN server to a virtual server with the help of EC2 user data and a shell script. After you terminate your virtual server, you'll be ready to learn how to deploy a common web application without writing a custom script.

> **Cleaning up**
>
> You've reached the end of the VPN server example. Don't forget to terminate your virtual server and clean up your environment. To do so, enter `aws cloudformation delete-stack --stack-name vpn` at your terminal.

5.2.3   Starting from scratch instead of updating

You've learned how to deploy an application with the help of user data in this section. The script from the user data is executed at the end of the boot process. But how do you update your application with this approach?

You've automated the installation and configuration of software during the boot process of your virtual server, so you can start a new virtual server without any extra effort. If you have to update your application or its dependencies, you can do so with the following steps:

1 Make sure the up-to-date version of your application or software is available through the package repository of your OS, or edit the user data script.
2 Start a new virtual server based on your CloudFormation template and user data script.
3 Test the application deployed to the new virtual server. Proceed with the next step if everything works as it should.
4 Switch your workload to the new virtual server (for example, by updating a DNS record).
5 Terminate the old virtual server, and throw away its unused dependencies.

5.3   Deploying a simple web application with Elastic Beanstalk

It isn't necessary to reinvent the wheel if you have to deploy a common web application. AWS offers a service that can help you to deploy web applications based on PHP, Java, .NET, Ruby, Node.js, Python, Go, and Docker; it's called *AWS Elastic Beanstalk*. With Elastic Beanstalk, you don't have to worry about your OS or virtual servers because it adds another layer of abstraction on top of them.

Elastic Beanstalk lets you handle the following recurring problems:

- Providing a runtime environment for a web application (PHP, Java, and so on)
- Installing and updating a web application automatically
- Configuring a web application and its environment
- Scaling a web application to balance load
- Monitoring and debugging a web application

5.3.1   Components of Elastic Beanstalk

Getting to know the different components of Elastic Beanstalk will help you to understand its functionality. Figure 5.3 shows these elements:

- An *application* is a logical container. It contains versions, environments, and configurations. If you start to use Elastic Beanstalk in a region, you have to create an application first.
- A *version* contains a specific version of your application. To create a new version, you have to upload your executables (packed into an archive) to the service

Amazon S3, which stores static files. A version is basically a pointer to this archive of executables.

- A *configuration template* contains your default configuration. You can manage your application's configuration (such as the port your application listens on) as well as the environment's configuration (such as the size of the virtual server) with your custom configuration template.
- An *environment* is where Elastic Beanstalk executes your application. It consists of a *version* and the *configuration*. You can run multiple environments for one application using the versions and configurations multiple times.

Enough theory for the moment. Let's proceed with deploying a simple web application.

5.3.2 Using Elastic Beanstalk to deploy Etherpad, a Node.js application

Editing a document collaboratively can be painful with the wrong tools. *Etherpad* is an open source online editor that lets you edit a document with many people in real time. You'll deploy this Node.js-based application with the help of Elastic Beanstalk in three steps:

1 Create an application: the logical container.
2 Create a version: a pointer to a specific version of Etherpad.
3 Create an environment: the place where Etherpad will run.

CREATING AN APPLICATION FOR AWS ELASTIC BEANSTALK

Open your command line and execute the following command to create an application for the Elastic Beanstalk service:

```
$ aws elasticbeanstalk create-application --application-name etherpad
```

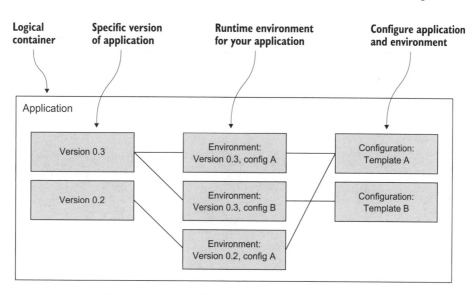

Figure 5.3   An Elastic Beanstalk application consists of versions, configurations, and environments.

You've created a container for all the other components that are necessary to deploy Etherpad with the help of AWS Elastic Beanstalk.

CREATING A VERSION FOR AWS ELASTIC BEANSTALK

You can create a new version of your Etherpad application with the following command:

```
$ aws elasticbeanstalk create-application-version \
--application-name etherpad --version-label 1.5.2 \
--source-bundle S3Bucket=awsinaction,S3Key=chapter5/etherpad.zip
```

For this example, we uploaded a zip archive containing version 1.5.2 of Etherpad. If you want to deploy another application, you can upload your own application to the AWS S3 service for static files.

CREATING AN ENVIRONMENT TO EXECUTE ETHERPAD WITH ELASTIC BEANSTALK

To deploy Etherpad with the help of Elastic Beanstalk, you have to create an environment for Node.js based on Amazon Linux and the version of Etherpad you just created. To get the latest Node.js environment version, called a *solution stack name*, run this command:

```
$ aws elasticbeanstalk list-available-solution-stacks --output text \
--query "SolutionStacks[?contains(@, 'running Node.js')] | [0]"\
64bit Amazon Linux 2015.03 v1.4.6 running Node.js
```

The option `EnvironmentType = SingleInstance` launches a single virtual server without the ability to scale and load-balance automatically. Replace `$SolutionStackName` with the output from the previous command:

```
$ aws elasticbeanstalk create-environment --environment-name etherpad \
--application-name etherpad \
--option-settings Namespace=aws:elasticbeanstalk:environment,\
OptionName=EnvironmentType,Value=SingleInstance \
--solution-stack-name "$SolutionStackName" \
--version-label 1.5.2
```

HAVING FUN WITH ETHERPAD

You've created an environment for Etherpad. It will take several minutes before you can point your browser to your Etherpad installation. The following command helps you track the state of your Etherpad environment:

```
$ aws elasticbeanstalk describe-environments --environment-names etherpad
```

If Status turns to Ready and Health turns to Green, you're ready to create your first Etherpad document. The output of the `describe` command should look similar to the following example.

Listing 5.4   Describing the status of the Elastic Beanstalk environment

```
{
  "Environments": [{
    "ApplicationName": "etherpad",
    "EnvironmentName": "etherpad",
    "VersionLabel": "1",                          Wait until Status
    "Status": "Ready",          ◄───────────────  turns to Ready.
    "EnvironmentId": "e-pwbfmgrsjp",
    "EndpointURL": "23.23.223.115",
    "SolutionStackName": "64bit Amazon Linux 2015.03 v1.4.6 running Node.js",
    "CNAME": "etherpad-cxzshvfjzu.elasticbeanstalk.com",    ◄─
    "Health": "Green",      ◄─                              DNS record for the
    "Tier": {                                               environment (for
      "Version": " ",         Wait until Health             example, to open
      "Type": "Standard",     turns to Green.               with a browser)
      "Name": "WebServer"
    },
    "DateUpdated": "2015-04-07T08:45:07.658Z",
    "DateCreated": "2015-04-07T08:40:21.698Z"
  }]
}
```

You've deployed a Node.js web application to AWS with three commands. Point your browser to the URL shown in CNAME and open a new document by typing in a name for it and clicking the OK button. Figure 5.4 shows an Etherpad document in action.

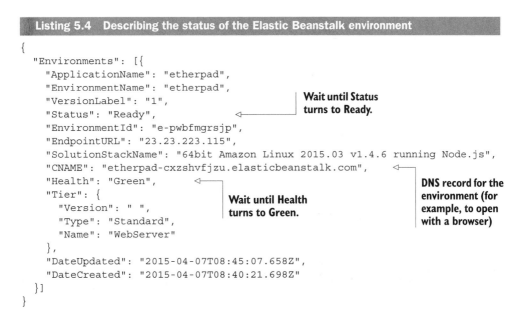

Figure 5.4   Online text editor Etherpad in action

EXPLORING ELASTIC BEANSTALK WITH THE MANAGEMENT CONSOLE

You've deployed Etherpad with the help of Elastic Beanstalk and the AWS command-line interface (CLI) by creating an application, a version, and an environment. You can also control the Elastic Beanstalk service with the help of the Management Console, a web-based user interface:

1 Open the AWS Management Console at https://console.aws.amazon.com.
2 Click Services in the navigation bar, and click the Elastic Beanstalk service.
3 Click the etherpad environment, represented by a green box. An overview of the Etherpad application is shown, as in figure 5.5.

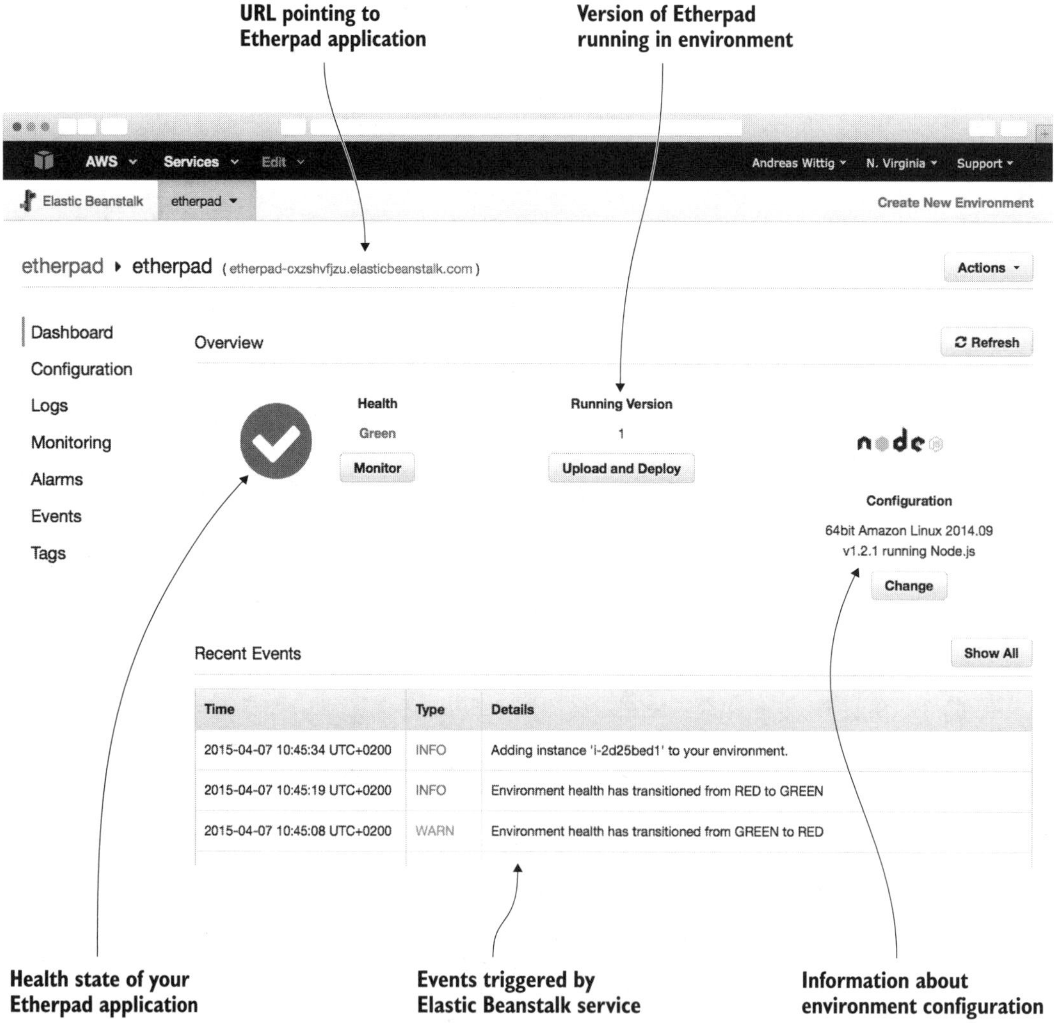

URL pointing to
Etherpad application

Version of Etherpad
running in environment

Health state of your
Etherpad application

Events triggered by
Elastic Beanstalk service

Information about
environment configuration

Figure 5.5   Overview of AWS Elastic Beanstalk environment running Etherpad

You can also fetch the log messages from your application with the help of Elastic Beanstalk. Download the latest log messages with the following steps:

1   Choose Logs from the submenu. You'll see a screen like that shown in figure 5.6.
2   Click Request Logs, and choose Last 100 Lines.
3   After a few seconds, a new entry will appear in the table. Click Download to download the log file to your computer.

> ## Cleaning up
>
> Now that you've successfully deployed Etherpad with the help of AWS Elastic Beanstalk and learned about the service's different components, it's time to clean up. Run the following command to terminate the Etherpad environment:
>
> ```
> $ aws elasticbeanstalk terminate-environment --environment-name etherpad
> ```
>
> You can check the state of the environment by executing the following command:
>
> ```
> $ aws elasticbeanstalk describe-environments --environment-names etherpad
> ```
>
> Wait until Status has changed to Terminated, and then proceed with the following command:
>
> ```
> $ aws elasticbeanstalk delete-application --application-name etherpad
> ```
>
> That's it. You've terminated the virtual server providing the environment for Etherpad and deleted all components of Elastic Beanstalk.

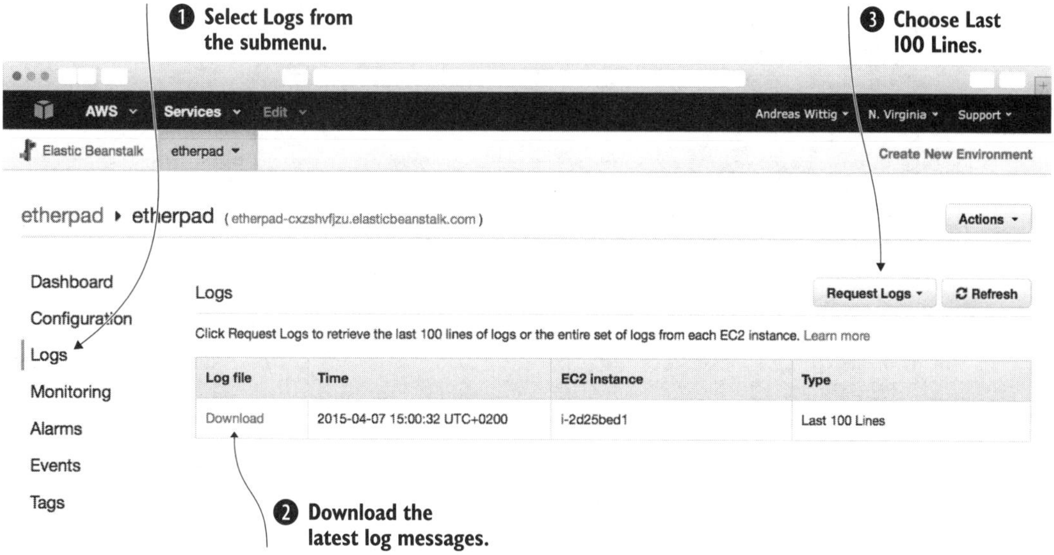

Figure 5.6   Downloading logs from a Node.js application via AWS Elastic Beanstalk

5.4   *Deploying a multilayer application with OpsWorks*

Deploying a basic web application with the help of Elastic Beanstalk is convenient. But if you have to deploy a more complex application consisting of different services— also called *layers*—you'll reach the limits of Elastic Beanstalk. In this section, you'll learn about AWS OpsWorks, a free service offered by AWS that can help you to deploy a multilayer application.

OpsWorks helps you control AWS resources like virtual servers, load balancers, and databases and lets you deploy applications. The service offers some standard layers with the following runtimes:

- HAProxy (load balancer)
- PHP app server
- MySQL (database)
- Rails app server (Ruby on Rails)
- Java app server (Tomcat server)
- Memcached (in-memory cache)
- Static web server
- AWS Flow (Ruby)
- Ganglia (monitoring)

You can also add a custom layer to deploy anything you want. The deployment is controlled with the help of *Chef*, a configuration-management tool. Chef uses *recipes* organized in *cookbooks* to deploy applications to any kind of system. You can adopt the standard recipes or create your own.

About Chef

Chef is a configuration-management tool like Puppet, SaltStack, and Ansible. Chef transforms templates (recipes) written in a domain-specific language (DSL) into actions, to configure and deploy applications. A recipe can include packages to install, services to run, or configuration files to write, for example. Related recipes can be combined into cookbooks. Chef analyzes the status quo and changes resources where necessary to reach the described state from the recipe.

You can reuse cookbooks and recipes from others with the help of Chef. The community publishes a variety of cookbooks and recipes at https://supermarket.chef.io under open source licenses.

Chef can be run in solo or client/server mode. It acts as a fleet-management tool in client/server mode. This can help if you have to manage a distributed system consisting of many virtual servers. In solo mode, you can execute recipes on a single virtual server. AWS OpsWorks uses solo mode integrated in its own fleet management without needing to configure and operate a setup in client/server mode.

In addition to letting you deploy applications, OpsWorks helps you to scale, monitor and update your virtual servers running beneath the different layers.

5.4.1   *Components of OpsWorks*

Getting to know the different components of OpsWorks will help you understand its functionality. Figure 5.7 shows these elements:

- A *stack* is a container for all other components of OpsWorks. You can create one or more stacks and add one or more layers to each stack. You could use different stacks to separate the production environment from the testing environment, for example. Or you could use different stacks to separate different applications.
- A *layer* belongs to a stack. A layer represents an application; you can also call it a service. OpsWorks offers predefined layers for standard web applications like PHP and Java, but you're free to use a custom stack for any application you can think of. A layer is responsible for configuring and deploying software to virtual servers. You can add one or multiple virtual servers to a layer. The virtual servers are called *instances* in this context.
- An *instance* is the representation for a virtual server. You can launch one or multiple instances for each layer. You can use different versions of Amazon Linux and Ubuntu or a custom AMI as a basis for the instances, and you can specify rules for launching and terminating instances based on load or timeframes for scaling.
- An *app* is the software you want to deploy. OpsWorks deploys your app to a suitable layer automatically. You can fetch apps from a Git or Subversion repository or as archives via HTTP. OpsWorks helps you to install and update your apps onto one or multiple instances.

Let's look at how to deploy a multilayer application with the help of OpsWorks.

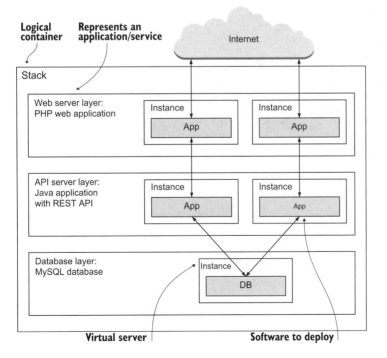

Figure 5.7 Stacks, layers, instances, and apps are the main components of OpsWorks.

5.4.2   *Using OpsWorks to deploy an IRC chat application*

Internet Relay Chat (IRC) is still a popular means of communication. In this section, you'll deploy *kiwiIRC*, a web-based IRC client, and your own IRC server. Figure 5.8 shows the setup of a distributed system consisting of a web application delivering the IRC client and an IRC server.

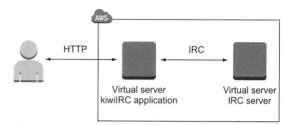

kiwiIRC is an open source web application written in JavaScript for Node.js. The following steps are necessary to deploy a two-layer application with the help of OpsWorks:

Figure 5.8   Building your own IRC infrastructure consisting of a web application and an IRC server

1 Create a stack, the container for all other components.
2 Create a Node.js layer for kiwiIRC.
3 Create a custom layer for the IRC server.
4 Create an app to deploy kiwiIRC to the Node.js layer.
5 Add an instance for each layer.

You'll learn how to handle these steps with the Management Console. You can also control OpsWorks from the command line, as you did Elastic Beanstalk, or with CloudFormation.

CREATING A NEW OPSWORKS STACK

Open the Management Console at https://console.aws.amazon.com/opsworks, and create a new stack. Figure 5.9 illustrates the necessary steps:

1 Click Add Stack under Select Stack or Add Your First Stack.
2 For Name, type in `irc`.
3 For Region, choose US East (N. Virginia).
4 The default VPC is the only one available. Select it.
5 For Default Subnet, select us-east-1a.
6 For Default Operating System, choose Ubuntu 14.04 LTS.
7 For Default Root Device Type, select EBS Backed.
8 For IAM Role, choose New IAM Role. Doing so automatically creates the necessary dependency.
9 Select your SSH key, mykey, for Default SSH Key.
10 For Default IAM Instance Profile, choose New IAM Instance Profile. Doing so automatically creates the necessary dependency.
11 For Hostname Theme, choose Layer Dependent. Your virtual servers will be named depending on their layer.
12 Click Add Stack to create the stack.

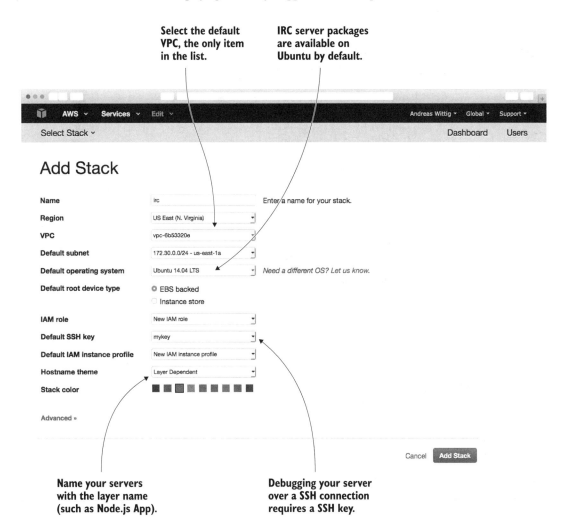

Figure 5.9 Creating a new stack with OpsWorks

You're redirected to an overview of your irc stack. Everything is ready for you to create the first layer.

CREATING A NODE.JS LAYER FOR AN OPSWORKS STACK

kiwiIRC is a Node.js application, so you need to create a Node.js layer for the irc stack. Follow these steps to do so:

1 Select Layers from the submenu.
2 Click the Add Layer button.
3 For Layer Type, select Node.js App Server, as shown in figure 5.10.
4 Select the latest 0.10.x version of Node.js.
5 Click Add Layer.

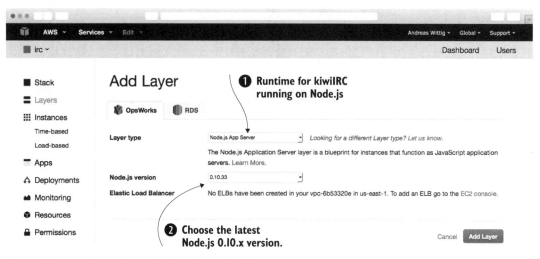

Figure 5.10   Creating a layer with Node.js for kiwiIRC

You've created a Node.js layer. Now you need to repeat these steps to add another layer and deploy your own IRC server.

CREATING A CUSTOM LAYER FOR AN OPSWORKS STACK

An IRC server isn't a typical web application, so the default layer types are out of the question. You'll use a custom layer to deploy an IRC server. The Ubuntu package repository includes various IRC server implementations; you'll use the ircd-ircu package. Follow these steps to create a custom stack for the IRC server:

1   Select Layers from the submenu.
2   Click Add Layer.
3   For Layer Type, select Custom, as shown in figure 5.11.
4   For Name and for Short Name, type in irc-server.
5   Click Add Layer.

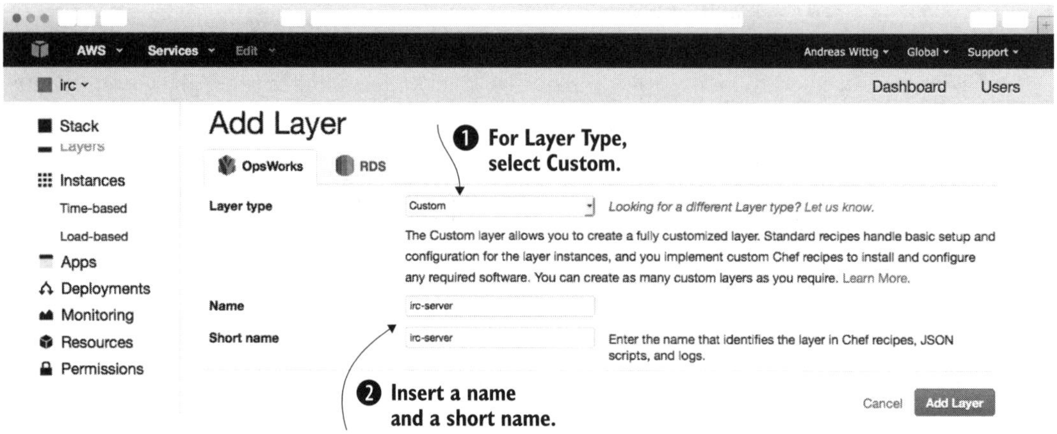

Figure 5.11   Creating a custom layer to deploy an IRC server

You've created a custom layer.

The IRC server needs to be reachable through port 6667. To allow access to this port, you need to define a custom firewall. Execute the commands shown in listing 5.5 to create a custom firewall for your IRC server.

Shortcut for OS X and Linux

You can avoid typing these commands manually to your command line by using the following command to download a bash script and execute it directly on your local machine. The bash script contains the same steps as shown in listing 5.5:

```
$ curl -s https://raw.githubusercontent.com/AWSinAction/\
code/master/chapter5/irc-create-cloudformation-stack.sh \
| bash -ex
```

Listing 5.5   Creating a custom firewall with the help of CloudFormation

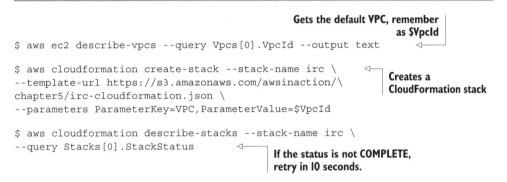

```
                                          Gets the default VPC, remember
                                                          as $VpcId

$ aws ec2 describe-vpcs --query Vpcs[0].VpcId --output text   ◁────┘

$ aws cloudformation create-stack --stack-name irc \      ◁──┐ Creates a
--template-url https://s3.amazonaws.com/awsinaction/\          CloudFormation stack
chapter5/irc-cloudformation.json \
--parameters ParameterKey=VPC,ParameterValue=$VpcId

$ aws cloudformation describe-stacks --stack-name irc \
--query Stacks[0].StackStatus        ◁──┐ If the status is not COMPLETE,
                                          retry in 10 seconds.
```

Next you need to attach this custom firewall configuration to the custom OpsWorks layer. Follow these steps:

1 Select Layers from the submenu.
2 Open the irc-server layer by clicking it.
3 Change to the Security tab and click Edit.
4 For Custom Security Groups, select the security group that starts with irc, as shown in figure 5.12.
5 Click Save.

You need to configure one last thing for the IRC server layer: the layer recipes to deploy an IRC server. Follow these steps to do so:

1 Select Layers from the submenu.
2 Open the irc-server layer by clicking it.
3 Change to the Recipes tab and click Edit.
4 For OS Packages, add the package ircd-ircu, as shown in figure 5.13.
5 Click the + button and then the Save button.

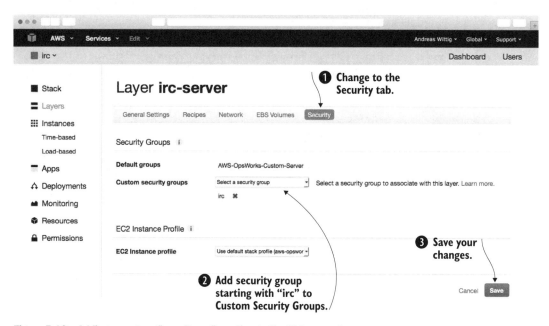

Figure 5.12   Adding a custom firewall configuration to the IRC server layer

Figure 5.13   Adding an IRC package to a custom layer

You've successfully created and configured a custom layer to deploy the IRC server. Next you'll add the kiwiIRC web application as an app to OpsWorks.

ADDING AN APP TO THE NODE.JS LAYER

OpsWorks can deploy apps to a default layer. You've already created a Node.js layer. With the following steps, you'll add an app to this layer:

1 Select Apps from the submenu.
2 Click the Add an App button.
3 For Name, type in `kiwiIRC`.
4 For Type, select Node.js.
5 For Repository Type, select Git, and type in `https://github.com/AWSinAction/KiwiIRC.git` for Repository URL, as shown in figure 5.14.
6 Click the Add App button.

Your first OpsWorks stack is now fully configured. Only one thing is missing: you need to start some instances.

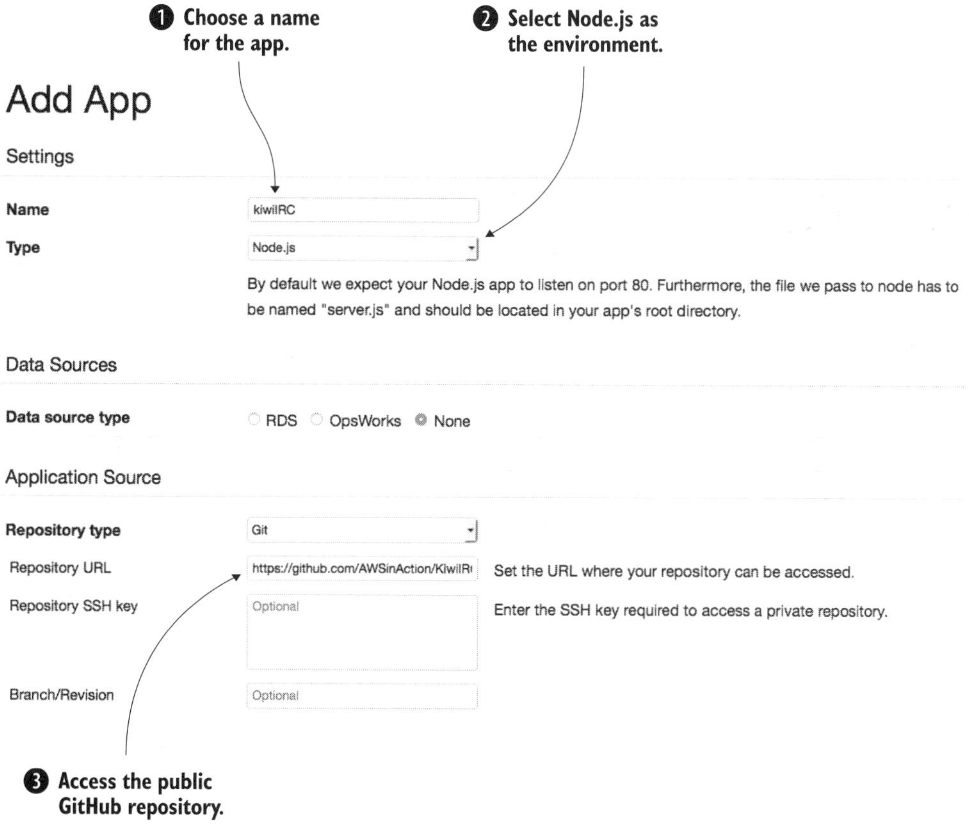

Figure 5.14   Adding kiwiIRC, a Node.js app, to OpsWorks

ADDING INSTANCES TO RUN THE IRC CLIENT AND SERVER

Adding two instances will bring the kiwiIRC client and the IRC server into being. Adding a new instance to a layer is easy—follow these steps:

1   Select Instances from the submenu.
2   Click the Add an Instance button on the Node.js App Server layer.
3   For Size, select t2.micro, the smallest and cheapest virtual server, as shown in figure 5.15.
4   Click Add Instance.

You've added an instance to the Node.js App Server layer. Repeat these steps for the irc-server layer as well.

The overview of instances should be similar to figure 5.16. To start the instances, click Start for both.

It will take some time for the virtual servers to boot and the deployment to run. It's a good time to get some coffee or tea.

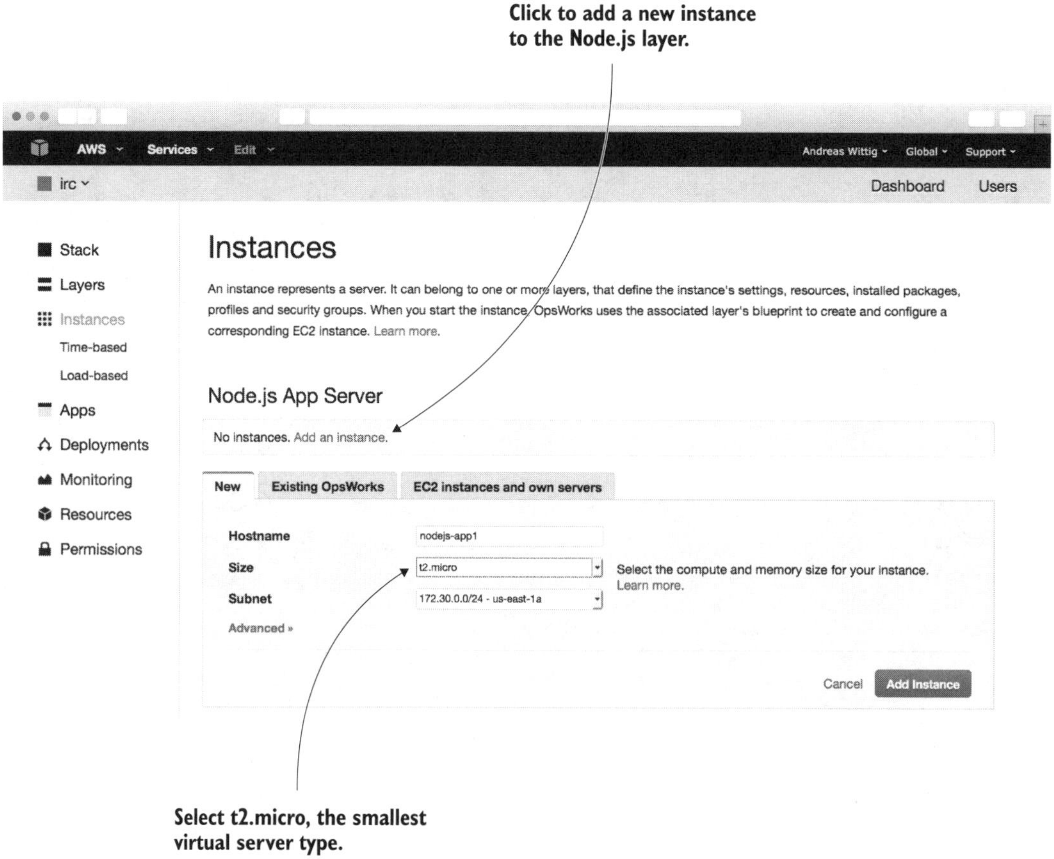

Figure 5.15   Adding a new instance to the Node.js layer

Figure 5.16   Starting the instances for the IRC web client and server

HAVING FUN WITH KIWIIRC

Be patient until the status of both instances changes to Online, as shown in figure 5.17. You can now open kiwiIRC in your browser by following these steps:

1   Keep in mind the public IP address of the instance irc-server1. You'll need it to connect to your IRC server later.

2   Click the public IP address of the nodejs-app1 instance to open the kiwiIRC web application in a new tab of your browser.

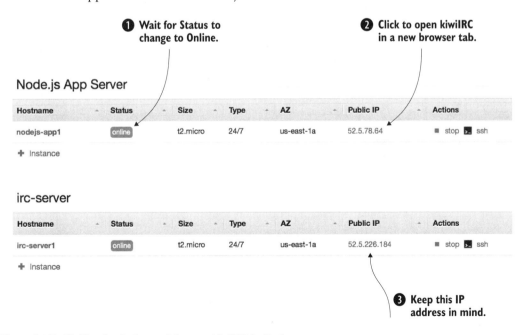

Figure 5.17   Waiting for deployment to open kiwiIRC in the browser

The kiwiIRC application should load in your browser, and you should see a login screen like the one shown in figure 5.18. Follow these steps to log in to your IRC server with the kiwiIRC web client:

1 Type in a nickname.
2 For Channel, type in #awsinaction.
3 Open the details of the connection by clicking Server and Network.
4 Type the IP address of irc-server1 into the Server field.
5 For Port, type in 6667.
6 Disable SSL.
7 Click Start, and wait a few seconds.

Congratulations! You've deployed a web-based IRC client and an IRC server with the help of AWS OpsWorks.

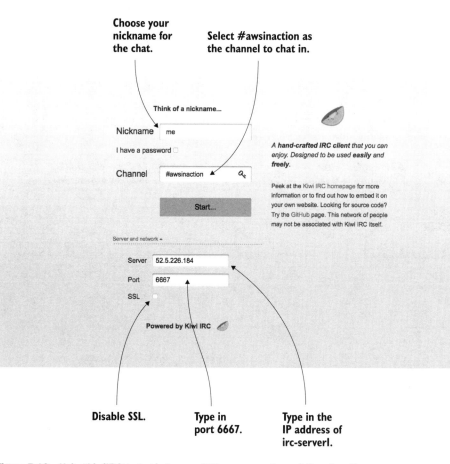

Figure 5.18   Using kiwiIRC to log in to your IRC server on channel #awsinaction

Cleaning up

It's time to clean up. Follow these steps to avoid unintentional costs:

1 Open the OpsWorks service with the Management Console.
2 Select the irc stack by clicking it.
3 Select Instances from the submenu.
4 Stop both instances and wait until Status is Stopped for both.
5 Delete both instances, and wait until they disappear from the overview.
6 Select Apps from the submenu.
7 Delete the kiwiIRC app.
8 Select Stack from the submenu.
9 Click the Delete Stack button, and confirm the deletion.
10 Execute `aws cloudformation delete-stack --stack-name irc` from your terminal.

5.5 Comparing deployment tools

You have deployed applications in three ways in this chapter:

- Using AWS CloudFormation to run a script on server startup
- Using AWS Elastic Beanstalk to deploy a common web application
- Using AWS OpsWorks to deploy a multilayer application

In this section, we'll discuss the differences between these solutions.

5.5.1 Classifying the deployment tools

Figure 5.19 classifies the three AWS deployment options. The effort required to deploy an application with the help of AWS Elastic Beanstalk is low. To benefit from this, your application has to fit into the conventions of Elastic Beanstalk. For example, the application must run in one of the standardized runtime environments. If you're using OpsWorks, you'll have more freedom to adapt the service to the needs of your application. For example, you can deploy different layers that depend on each other, or you can use a custom layer to deploy any application with the help of a Chef recipe; this takes extra effort but gives you additional freedom. On the other end of the spectrum, you'll find CloudFormation and deploying applications with the help of a script running at the end of the boot process. You can deploy any application with the help of CloudFormation. The disadvantage of this approach is that you have to do more work because you don't use standard tooling.

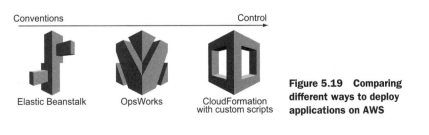

Conventions   Control

Elastic Beanstalk   OpsWorks   CloudFormation with custom scripts

Figure 5.19 Comparing different ways to deploy applications on AWS

5.5.2 Comparing the deployment services

The previous classification can help you decide the best fit to deploy an application. The comparison in table 5.1 highlights other important considerations.

Table 5.1   Differences between using CloudFormation with a script on server startup, Elastic Beanstalk, and OpsWorks

	CloudFormation with a script on server startup	Elastic Beanstalk	OpsWorks
Configuration-management tool	All available tools	Proprietary	Chef
Supported platforms	Any	<ul><li>PHP</li><li>Node.js</li><li>IIS</li><li>Java/Tomcat</li><li>Python</li><li>Ruby</li><li>Docker</li></ul>	<ul><li>Ruby on Rails</li><li>Node.js</li><li>PHP</li><li>Java/Tomcat</li><li>Custom/any</li></ul>
Supported deployment artifacts	Any	Zip archive on Amazon S3	Git, SVN, archive (such as Zip)
Common use case	Complex and nonstandard environments	Common web application	Micro-services environment
Update without downtime	Possible	Yes	Yes
Vendor lock-in effect	Medium	High	Medium

Many other options are available for deploying applications on AWS, from open source software to third-party services. Our advice is to use one of the AWS deployment services because they're well integrated into many other AWS services. We recommend that you use CloudFormation with user data to deploy applications because it's a flexible approach. It is also possible to manage Elastic Beanstalk and Ops Works with the help of CloudFormation.

An automated deployment process will help you to iterate and innovate more quickly. You'll deploy new versions of your applications more often. To avoid service interruptions, you need to think about testing changes to software and infrastructure in an automated way and being able to roll back to a previous version quickly if necessary.

5.6   Summary

- It isn't advisable to deploy applications to virtual servers manually because virtual servers pop up more often in a dynamic cloud environment.
- AWS offers different tools that can help you deploy applications onto virtual servers. Using one of these tools prevents you from reinventing the wheel.

- You can throw away a server to update an application if you've automated your deployment process.
- Injecting Bash or PowerShell scripts into a virtual server during startup allows you to initialize servers individually—for example, for installing software or configuring services.
- OpsWorks is good for deploying multilayer applications with the help of Chef.
- Elastic Beanstalk is best suited for deploying common web applications.
- CloudFormation gives you the most control when you're deploying more complex applications.

Securing
your system: IAM,
security groups, and VPC

6

This chapter covers

- Keeping your software up to date
- Controlling access to your AWS account with users and roles
- Keeping your traffic under control with security groups
- Using CloudFormation to create a private network
- Who is responsible for security?

If security is a wall, you'll need a lot of bricks to build that wall. This chapter focuses on the four most important bricks to secure your systems on AWS:

- *Installing software updates*—New security vulnerabilities are found in software every day. Software vendors release updates to fix those vulnerabilities. It's your job to install those updates as quickly as possible after they're released. Otherwise, your system will be an easy victim for hackers.

- *Restricting access to your AWS account*—This becomes even more important if you aren't the only one accessing your AWS account (if coworkers and scripts are also accessing it). A script with a bug can easily terminate all your EC2 instances instead of the one you intended. Granting least permissions is key to securing your AWS resources from accidental or intended disastrous actions.
- *Controlling network traffic to and from your EC2 instances*—You only want ports to be accessible if they must be. If you run a web server, the only ports you need to open to the outside world are port 80 for HTTP traffic and 443 for HTTPS traffic. Close down all the other ports!
- *Creating a private network in AWS*—You can create subnets that aren't reachable from the internet. And if they're not reachable, nobody can access them. Nobody? You'll learn how you can get access to them while preventing others from doing so.

> **Examples are 100% covered by the Free Tier**
>
> The examples in this chapter are completely covered by the Free Tier. As long as you don't run the examples for longer than a few days, you won't pay anything. Keep in mind that this only applies if you created a fresh AWS account for this book and nothing else is going on in your AWS account. Try to complete the examples of the chapter within a few days; you'll clean up your account at the end of each example.

One important brick is missing: securing your self-developed applications. You need to check user input and allow only the necessary characters, don't save passwords in plain text, use SSL to encrypt traffic between your servers and your users, and so on.

> **Chapter requirements**
>
> To fully understand this chapter, you should be familiar with the following concepts:
>
> - Subnet
> - Route table
> - Access control list (ACL)
> - Gateway
> - Firewall
> - Port
> - Access management
> - Basics of the Internet Protocol (IP), including IP addresses

6.1   Who's responsible for security?

AWS is a shared-responsibility environment, meaning responsibility is shared between AWS and you. AWS is responsible for the following:

- Protecting the network through automated monitoring systems and robust internet access to prevent Distributed Denial of Service (DDoS) attacks
- Performing background checks on employees who have access to sensitive areas

- Decommissioning storage devices by physically destroying them after end of life
- Ensuring physical and environmental security of data centers, including fire protection and security staff

The security standards are reviewed by third parties; you can find an up-to-date overview at http://aws.amazon.com/compliance/.

What are your responsibilities?

- Encrypting network traffic to prevent attackers from reading or manipulating data (for example, HTTPS)
- Configuring a firewall for your virtual private network that controls incoming and outgoing traffic with security groups and ACLs
- Managing patches for the OS and additional software on virtual servers
- Implementing access management that restricts access to AWS resources like S3 and EC2 to a minimum with IAM

Security in the cloud involves an interaction between AWS and you, the customer. If you play by the rules, you can achieve high security standards in the cloud.

6.2   Keeping your software up to date

Not a week goes by without the release of important updates to fix security vulnerabilities. Sometimes your OS is affected; or software libraries like OpenSSL; or environments like Java, Apache, and PHP; or applications like WordPress. If a security update is released, you must install it quickly, because the exploit may have been released with the update or because everyone can look at the source code to reconstruct the vulnerability. You should have a working plan for how to apply updates to all running servers as quickly as possible.

6.2.1   Checking for security updates

If you log in to an Amazon Linux EC2 instance via SSH, you'll see the following message of the day:

```
$ ssh ec2-user@ec2-52-6-25-163.compute-1.amazonaws.com
Last login: Sun Apr 19 07:08:08 2015 from [...]

   __|  __|_  )
   _|  (     /   Amazon Linux AMI
   ___|\___|___|
```

```
https://aws.amazon.com/[...]/2015.03-release-notes/
4 package(s) needed for security, out of 28 available   ◁──┘
Run "sudo yum update" to apply all updates.
```

4 security updates are available.

This example shows that four security updates are available; this number will vary when you look for updates. AWS won't apply updates for you on your EC2 instances—you're responsible for doing so.

You can use the `yum` package manager to handle updates on Amazon Linux. Run
`yum --security check-update` to see which packages require a security update:

The output will be different when you run the command.

```
$ yum --security check-update    ◄──┘
4 package(s) needed for security, out of 28 available

[...]
openssl.x86_64          1:1.0.1k-1.84.amzn1    amzn-updates   ◄──┘
[...]
unzip.x86_64            6.0-2.9.amzn1          amzn-updates   ◄─
[...]
```

OpenSSL is a library for SSL encryption.

unzip can (de)compress files.

We encourage you to follow the Amazon Linux AMI Security Center at https://
alas.aws.amazon.com to receive security bulletins affecting Amazon Linux. Whenever
a new security update is released, you should check whether you're affected.

When dealing with security updates, you may face either of these two situations:

- When the server starts the first time, many security updates need to be installed
  in order for the server to be up to date.
- New security updates are released when your server is running, and you need to
  install these updates while the server is running.

Let's look how to handle these situations.

6.2.2 Installing security updates on server startup

If you create your EC2 instances with CloudFormation templates, you have three
options for installing security updates on startup:

- *Install all updates on server start.* Include `yum -y update` in your user-data script.
- *Install only security updates on server start.* Include `yum -y --security update` in
  your user-data script.
- *Define the package versions explicitly.* Install updates identified by a version number.

The first two options can be easily included in the user data of your EC2 instance. You
install all updates as follows:

```
[...]
"Server": {
  "Type": "AWS::EC2::Instance",
  "Properties": {
    [...]
    "UserData": {"Fn::Base64": {"Fn::Join": ["", [
      "#!/bin/bash -ex\n",
      "yum -y update\n"          ◄─
    ]]}}                                    Installs all updates
  }                                         on server start
}
[...]
```

To install only security updates, do the following:

```
[...]
"Server": {
  "Type": "AWS::EC2::Instance",
  "Properties": {
    [...]
    "UserData": {"Fn::Base64": {"Fn::Join": ["", [
      "#!/bin/bash -ex\n",
      "yum -y --security update\n"      ◁─┐
    ]]}}                                    │  Installs only security
  }                                         │  updates on server start
}
[...]
```

The problem with installing all updates is that your system becomes unpredictable. If your server was started last week, all updates were applied that were available last week. But in the meantime, new updates have been released. If you start a new server today and install all updates, you'll end up with a different server than the server from last week. *Different* can mean that for some reason it's not working anymore. That's why we encourage you to explicitly define the updates you want to install. To install security updates with an explicit version, you can use the yum update-to command. yum update-to updates a package to an explicit version instead of the latest:

```
                                          ┌─ Updates openssl to
                                          │  version I.0.Ik-I.84.amznI
yum update-to openssl-1.0.1k-1.84.amzn1 \  ◁─┘
unzip-6.0-2.9.amzn1      ◁─┐
                          │  Updates unzip to
                          │  version 6.0-2.9.amznI
```

Using a CloudFormation template to describe an EC2 instance with explicitly defined updates looks like this:

```
[...]
"Server": {
  "Type": "AWS::EC2::Instance",
  "Properties": {
    [...]
    "UserData": {"Fn::Base64": {"Fn::Join": ["", [
      "#!/bin/bash -ex\n",
      "yum -y update-to openssl-1.0.1k-1.84.amzn1 unzip-6.0-2.9.amzn1\n"
    ]]}}
  }
}
[...]
```

The same approach works for non-security-related package updates. Whenever a new security update is released, you should check whether you're affected and modify the user data to keep new systems secure.

6.2.3 *Installing security updates on running servers*

From time to time, you must install security updates on all your running servers. You could manually log in to all your servers using SSH and run yum -y --security update or yum update-to [...], but if you have many servers or the number of servers grows, this can be annoying. One way to automate this task is to use a small script that gets a list of your servers and executes yum in all of them. The following listing shows how this can be done in Bash. You can find the code in /chapter6/update.sh in the book's code folder.

> **Listing 6.1 Installing security updates on all running EC2 instances**

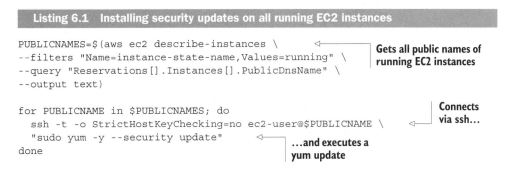

```
PUBLICNAMES=$(aws ec2 describe-instances \          ◁————────┐  Gets all public names of
--filters "Name=instance-state-name,Values=running" \        │  running EC2 instances
--query "Reservations[].Instances[].PublicDnsName" \
--output text)

                                                          ┌── Connects
for PUBLICNAME in $PUBLICNAMES; do                        │   via ssh...
  ssh -t -o StrictHostKeyChecking=no ec2-user@$PUBLICNAME \  ◁──┘
  "sudo yum -y --security update"      ◁──┐
done                                      │ ...and executes a
                                            yum update
```

Now you can quickly apply updates to all of your running servers.

Some security updates require you to reboot the virtual server—for example, if you need to patch the kernel of your virtual servers running on Linux. You can automate the reboot of the servers or switch to an updated AMI and start new virtual servers instead. For example, a new AMI of Amazon Linux is released four times a year.

6.3 *Securing your AWS account*

Securing your AWS account is critical. If someone gets access to your AWS account, they can steal your data, destroy everything (data, backups, servers), or steal your identity to do bad stuff. Figure 6.1 shows an AWS account. Each AWS account comes with a root user. In this book's example, you're using the root user when you use the Management Console; if you use the CLI, you're using the mycli user that you created in section 4.2. In addition to the root user, an AWS account is a basket for all the resources you own: EC2 instances, CloudFormation stacks, IAM users, and so on.

To access your AWS account, an attacker must be able to authenticate with your account. There are three ways to do so: using the root user, using a normal user, or authenticating as an AWS resource like an EC2 instance. To authenticate as a (root) user, the attacker needs the password or the access key. To authenticate as an AWS resource like an EC2 server, the attacker needs to send API/CLI requests from that EC2 instance.

In this section, you'll begin protecting your root user with multifactor authentication (MFA). Then you'll stop using the root user, create a new user for daily operations, and learn to grant least permissions to a role.

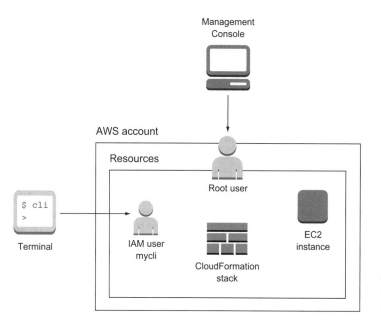

Figure 6.1 An AWS account contains all the AWS resources and comes with a root user by default.

6.3.1 Securing your AWS account's root user

We advise you to enable multifactor authentication (MFA) for your root user if you're going to use AWS in production. After MFA is activated, you need a password and a temporary token to log in as the root user. Thus an attacker needs not only your password, but also your MFA device.

Follow these steps to enable MFA, as shown in figure 6.2:

1 Click your name in the navigation bar at the top of the Management Console.
2 Click Security Credentials.
3 A pop-up may show up the first time. You need to select: Continue to Security Credentials.
4 Install a MFA app on your smartphone (such as Google Authenticator).
5 Expand the Multi-Factor Authentication (MFA) section.
6 Click Activate MFA.
7 Follow the instructions in the wizard. Use the MFA app on your smartphone to scan the QR code that is displayed.

If you're using your smartphone as a virtual MFA device, it's a good idea not to log in to the Management Console from your smartphone or to store the root user's password on the phone. Keep the MFA token separate from your password.

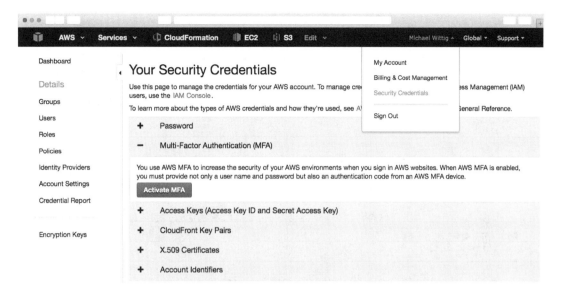

Figure 6.2   Protect your root user with multifactor authentication (MFA).

6.3.2   Identity and Access Management service

The Identity and Access Management (IAM) service provides everything needed for authentication and authorization with the AWS API. Every request you make to the AWS API goes through IAM to check whether the request is allowed. IAM controls who (authentication) can do what (authorization) in your AWS account: who's allowed to create EC2 instances? Is the user allowed to terminate a specific EC2 instance?

Authentication with IAM is done with users or roles, whereas authorization is done by policies. How do users and roles differ? Table 6.1 shows the differences. Roles authenticate an EC2 instance; a user should be used for everything else.

Table 6.1   Differences between root user, IAM user, and IAM role

	Root user	IAM user	IAM role
Can have a password	Always	Yes	No
Can have an access key	Yes (not recommended)	Yes	No
Can belong to a group	No	Yes	No
Can be associated with an EC2 instance	No	No	Yes

IAM users and IAM roles use policies for authorization. Let's look at policies first as we continue with users and roles. Keep in mind that users and roles can't do anything until you allow certain actions with a policy.

6.3.3   *Policies for authorization*

A policy is defined in JSON and contains one or more statements. A statement can either allow or deny specific actions on specific resources. You can find an overview of all the actions available for EC2 resources at http://mng.bz/WQ3D. The wildcard character * can be used to create more generic statements.

The following policy has one statement that allows every action for the EC2 service for all resources:

```
{
  "Version": "2012-10-17",        ◁──  Specifies 2012-10-17 to
  "Statement": [{                      lock down the version
    "Sid": "1",
    "Effect": "Allow",     ◁──  Allows (the other option is Deny) ...
    "Action": ["ec2:*"],   ◁──  ... every EC2 action (wildcard *) ...
    "Resource": ["*"]      ◁──  ... and every resource
  }]
}
```

If you have multiple statements that apply to the same action, Deny overrides Allow. The following policy allows all EC2 actions except terminating instances:

```
{
  "Version": "2012-10-17",
  "Statement": [{
    "Sid": "1",
    "Effect": "Allow",
    "Action": ["ec2:*"],
    "Resource": ["*"]
  }, {
    "Sid": "2",
    "Effect": "Deny",     ◁──  Denies ...
    "Action": ["ec2:TerminateInstances"],   ◁──  ... termination of EC2 instances
    "Resource": ["*"]
  }]
}
```

The following policy denies all EC2 actions. The ec2:TerminateInstances statement isn't crucial, because Deny overrides Allow. When you deny an action, you can't allow that action with another statement:

```
{
  "Version": "2012-10-17",
  "Statement": [{
    "Sid": "1",
    "Effect": "Deny",
    "Action": ["ec2:*"],    ◁──  Denies every EC2 action
    "Resource": ["*"]
  }, {
    "Sid": "2",
    "Effect": "Allow",
    "Action": ["ec2:TerminateInstances"],   ◁──  Allow isn't crucial; Deny overrides Allow.
    "Resource": ["*"]
  }]
}
```

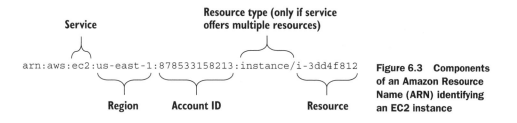

Figure 6.3 Components of an Amazon Resource Name (ARN) identifying an EC2 instance

So far, the `Resource` part has been `["*"]` for every resource. Resources in AWS have an Amazon Resource Name (ARN); figure 6.3 shows the ARN of an EC2 instance.

To find out the account ID, you can use the CLI:

```
$ aws iam get-user --query "User.Arn" --output text
arn:aws:iam::878533158213:user/mycli
```

Account ID has 12 digits (878533158213)

If you know your account ID, you can use ARNs to allow access to specific resources of a service:

```
{
  "Version": "2012-10-17",
  "Statement": [{
    "Sid": "2",
    "Effect": "Allow",
    "Action": ["ec2:TerminateInstances"],
    "Resource": ["arn:aws:ec2:us-east-1:878533158213:instance/i-3dd4f812"]
  }]
}
```

There are two types of policies:

- *Managed policy*—If you want to create policies that can be reused in your account, a managed policy is what you're looking for. There are two types of managed policies:
  - *AWS managed policy*—A policy that is maintained by AWS. There are policies that grant admin rights, read-only rights, and so on.
  - *Customer managed*—Could be a policy that represents the roles in your organization.
- *Inline policy*—A policy that belongs to a certain IAM role, user, or group. The inline policy can't exist without the IAM role, the user, or the group.

With CloudFormation, it's easy to maintain inline policies; that's why we use inline policies most of the time in this book. One exception is the mycli user: this user has the AWS managed policy `AdministratorAccess` attached.

6.3.4 Users for authentication, and groups to organize users

A user can authenticate with either a password or an access key. When you log in to the Management Console, you're authenticating with your password. When you use the CLI from your computer, you use an access key to authenticate as the mycli user.

You're using the root user at the moment to log in to the Management Console. Because using least permissions is always a good idea, you'll create a new user for the Management Console. To make things easier if you want to add users in the future, you'll first create a group for all admin users. A group can't be used to authenticate, but it centralizes authorization. If you want to stop your admin users from terminating EC2 servers, you only need to change the policy for the group instead of changing it for all admin users. A user can be the member of none, one, or multiple groups.

It's easy to create groups and users with the CLI. Replace `$Password` with a secure password:

```
$ aws iam create-group --group-name "admin"
$ aws iam attach-group-policy --group-name "admin" \
--policy-arn "arn:aws:iam::aws:policy/AdministratorAccess"
$ aws iam create-user --user-name "myuser"
$ aws iam add-user-to-group --group-name "admin" --user-name "myuser"
$ aws iam create-login-profile --user-name "myuser" --password "$Password"
```

The user myuser is ready to be used. But you must use a different URL to access the Management Console if you aren't using the root user: https://$accountId.signin .aws.amazon.com/console. Replace `$accountId` with the account ID that you extracted earlier with the `aws iam get-user` call.

Enabling MFA for IAM users

We encourage you to enable MFA for all users as well. If possible, don't use the same MFA device for your root user and everyday users. You can buy hardware MFA devices for $13 from AWS partners like Gemalto. To enable MFA for your users, follow these steps:

1 Open the IAM service in the Management Console.
2 Choose Users at left.
3 Select the myuser user.
4 Click the Manage MFA Device button in the Sign-In Credentials section at the bottom of the page. The wizard is the same as for the root user.

You should have MFA activated for all users who have a password—users who can be used with the Management Console.

WARNING Stop using the root user from now on. Always use myuser and the new link to the Management Console.

WARNING You should never copy a user's access key to an EC2 instance; use IAM roles instead! Don't store security credentials in your source code. And never ever check them into your Git or SVN repository. Try to use IAM roles instead whenever possible.

6.3.5 *Roles for authentication of AWS resources*

An IAM role can be used to authenticate AWS resources like virtual servers. You can attach no roles, one role, or multiple roles to an EC2 instance. Each AWS API request from an AWS resource (like an EC2 instance) will authenticate with the roles attached. If the AWS resource has one role or multiple roles attached, IAM will check all policies attached to those roles to determine whether the request is allowed. By default, EC2 instances have no role and therefore aren't allowed to make any calls to the AWS API.

Do you remember the temporary EC2 instances from chapter 4? It appeared that temporary servers weren't terminated—people forget to do so. A lot of money was wasted because of that. You'll now create an EC2 instance that stops itself after a while. The at command stops the instance after a 5-minute delay:

```
echo "aws ec2 stop-instances --instance-ids i-3dd4f812" | at now + 5 minutes
```

The EC2 instance needs permission to stop itself. You can use an inline policy to allow this. The following listing shows how you define a role as a resource in CloudFormation:

```
"Role": {
  "Type": "AWS::IAM::Role",
  "Properties": {
    "AssumeRolePolicyDocument": {          <-- Magic: copy and paste
      "Version": "2012-10-17",
      "Statement": [{
        "Effect": "Allow",
        "Principal": {
          "Service": ["ec2.amazonaws.com"]
        },
        "Action": ["sts:AssumeRole"]
      }]
    },
    "Path": "/",                           Policies begin
    "Policies": [{
      "PolicyName": "ec2",
      "PolicyDocument": {                  <-- Policy definition
        "Version": "2012-10-17",
        "Statement": [{
          "Sid": "Stmt1425388787000",
          "Effect": "Allow",
          "Action": ["ec2:StopInstances"],   Creates EC2 instance after role: can't {"Ref"} an instance ID!
          "Resource": ["*"],               <--
          "Condition": {                   Condition can solve the problem: only allow if tagged with the stack ID
            "StringEquals": {"ec2:ResourceTag/aws:cloudformation:stack-id":
            {"Ref": "AWS::StackId"}}
          }
        }]
      }
    }]
  }
}
```

To attach an inline role to an instance, you must first create an instance profile:

```
"InstanceProfile": {
  "Type": "AWS::IAM::InstanceProfile",
  "Properties": {
    "Path": "/",
    "Roles": [{"Ref": "Role"}]
  }
}
```

Now you can combine the role with the EC2 instance:

```
"Server": {
  "Type": "AWS::EC2::Instance",
  "Properties": {
    "IamInstanceProfile": {"Ref": "InstanceProfile"},
    [...],
    "UserData": {"Fn::Base64": {"Fn::Join": ["", [
      "#!/bin/bash -ex\n",
      "INSTANCEID=`curl -s ",
      "http://169.254.169.254/latest/meta-data/instance-id`\n",
      "echo \"aws --region us-east-1 ec2 stop-instances ",
      "--instance-ids $INSTANCEID\" | at now + 5 minutes\n"
    ]]}}
  }
}
```

Create the CloudFormation stack with the template located at https://s3.amazonaws .com/awsinaction/chapter6/server.json. You can specify the lifetime of the server via a parameter. Wait until the lifetime is reached and see if your instance is stopped. The lifetime begins when the server is fully started and booted.

> **Cleaning up**
> Don't forget to delete your stack after you finish this section to clean up all used resources. Otherwise you'll likely be charged for the resources you use.

6.4   *Controlling network traffic to and from your virtual server*

You only want traffic to enter or leave your EC2 instance that has to do so. With a firewall, you can control ingoing (also called inbound or ingress) and outgoing (also called outbound or egress) traffic. If you run a web server, the only ports you need to open to the outside world are port 80 for HTTP traffic and 443 for HTTPS traffic. All other ports should be closed down. Only open ports that must be open, just as you grant least permissions with IAM. If you have a strict firewall, you shut down a lot of possible security holes. You can also prevent the accidental sending of mail to customers from a test system by not opening outgoing SMTP connections for test systems.

Before network traffic can enter or leave your EC2 instance, it goes through a firewall provided by AWS. The firewall inspects the network traffic and uses rules to decide whether the traffic is allowed or denied.

IP vs. IP address

The abbreviation IP is used for Internet Protocol, whereas an IP address is something like 84.186.116.47.

Figure 6.4 shows how an SSH request from a source IP address 10.0.0.10 is inspected by the firewall and received by the destination IP address 10.10.0.20. In this case, the firewall allows the request because there's a rule that allows TCP traffic on port 22 between the source and the destination.

Source vs. destination

Inbound security-group rules filter based on the source of the network traffic. The source is either an IP address or a security group. Thus you can allow inbound traffic only from specific source IP address ranges.

Outbound security-group rules filter based on the destination of the network traffic. The destination is either an IP address or a security group. You can allow outbound traffic to only specific destination IP address ranges.

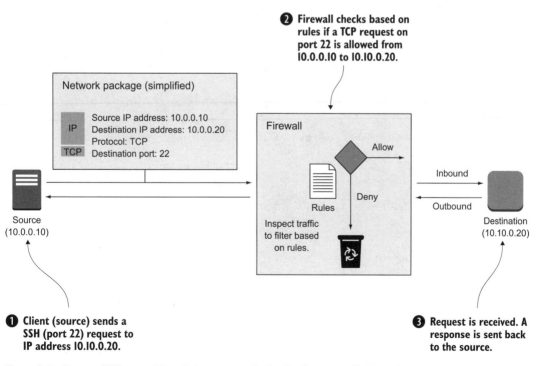

❷ Firewall checks based on rules if a TCP request on port 22 is allowed from 10.0.0.10 to 10.10.0.20.

Network package (simplified)

IP Source IP address: 10.0.0.10
Destination IP address: 10.0.0.20
Protocol: TCP
TCP Destination port: 22

Firewall

Allow

Inbound

Rules

Deny

Outbound

Inspect traffic to filter based on rules.

Source (10.0.0.10)

Destination (10.10.0.20)

❶ Client (source) sends a SSH (port 22) request to IP address 10.10.0.20.

❸ Request is received. A response is sent back to the source.

Figure 6.4   How an SSH request travels from source to destination, controlled by a firewall

AWS is responsible for the firewall, but you're responsible for the rules. By default, all inbound traffic is denied and all outbound traffic is allowed. You can then begin to allow inbound traffic. If you add rules for outgoing traffic, the default will switch from allow all to deny all, and only the exceptions you add will be allowed.

6.4.1 Controlling traffic to virtual servers with security groups

A security group can be associated with AWS resources like EC2 instances. It's common for EC2 instances to have more than one security group associated with them and for the same security group to be associated with many EC2 instances.

A security group follows a set of rules. A rule can allow network traffic based on the following:

- Direction (inbound or outbound)
- IP protocol (TCP, UDP, ICMP)
- Source/destination IP address
- Port
- Source/destination security group (works only in AWS)

You can define rules that allow all traffic to enter and leave your server; AWS won't prevent you from doing so. But it's good practice to define your rules so they're as restrictive as possible.

A security group resource in CloudFormation is of type AWS::EC2::SecurityGroup. The following listing is in /chapter6/firewall1.json in the book's code folder: the template describes an empty security group associated with a single EC2 instance.

Listing 6.2   Empty security group associated with a single EC2 instance

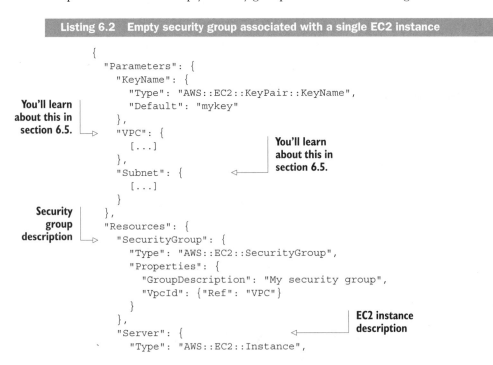

```json
{
  "Parameters": {
    "KeyName": {
      "Type": "AWS::EC2::KeyPair::KeyName",
      "Default": "mykey"
    },
    "VPC": {
      [...]
    },
    "Subnet": {
      [...]
    }
  },
  "Resources": {
    "SecurityGroup": {
      "Type": "AWS::EC2::SecurityGroup",
      "Properties": {
        "GroupDescription": "My security group",
        "VpcId": {"Ref": "VPC"}
      }
    },
    "Server": {
      "Type": "AWS::EC2::Instance",
```

You'll learn about this in section 6.5.

You'll learn about this in section 6.5.

Security group description

EC2 instance description

```
                          "Properties": {
Associates a                "ImageId": "ami-1ecae776",
security group              "InstanceType": "t2.micro",
with an EC2                 "KeyName": {"Ref": "KeyName"},
instance by Ref  └─▷       "SecurityGroupIds": [{"Ref": "SecurityGroup"}],
                           "SubnetId": {"Ref": "Subnet"}
                          }
                        }
                      }
                    }
```

To explore security groups, you can try the CloudFormation template located at https://s3.amazonaws.com/awsinaction/chapter6/firewall1.json. Create a stack based on that template, and then copy the `PublicName` from the stack output.

6.4.2 Allowing ICMP traffic

If you want to ping an EC2 instance from your computer, you must allow inbound Internet Control Message Protocol (ICMP) traffic. By default, all inbound traffic is blocked. Try `ping $PublicName` to make sure `ping` isn't working:

```
$ ping ec2-52-5-109-147.compute-1.amazonaws.com
PING ec2-52-5-109-147.compute-1.amazonaws.com (52.5.109.147): 56 data bytes
Request timeout for icmp_seq 0
Request timeout for icmp_seq 1
[...]
```

You need to add a rule to the security group that allows inbound traffic, where the protocol equals ICMP. The following listing can be found at `/chapter6/firewall2.json` in the book's code folder.

Listing 6.3   Security group that allows ICMP

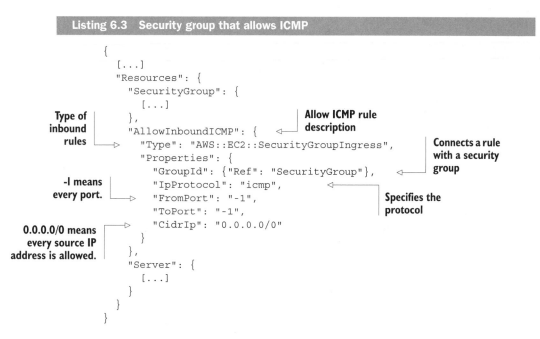

Update the CloudFormation stack with the template located at https://s3.amazonaws
.com/awsinaction/chapter6/firewall2.json, and retry the `ping` command. It should
now look like this:

```
$ ping ec2-52-5-109-147.compute-1.amazonaws.com
PING ec2-52-5-109-147.compute-1.amazonaws.com (52.5.109.147): 56 data bytes
64 bytes from 52.5.109.147: icmp_seq=0 ttl=49 time=112.222 ms
64 bytes from 52.5.109.147: icmp_seq=1 ttl=49 time=121.893 ms
[...]
round-trip min/avg/max/stddev = 112.222/117.058/121.893/4.835 ms
```

Everyone's inbound ICMP traffic (every source IP address) is now allowed to reach the
EC2 instance.

6.4.3   Allowing SSH traffic

Once you can ping your EC2 instance, you want to log in to your server via SSH. To do
so, you must create a rule to allow inbound TCP requests on port 22.

Listing 6.4   **Security group that allows SSH**

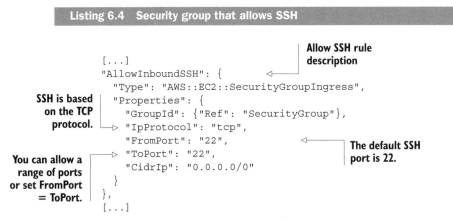

Update the CloudFormation stack with the template located at https://s3.amazonaws
.com/awsinaction/chapter6/firewall3.json. You can now log in to your server using
SSH. Keep in mind that you still need the correct private key. The firewall only controls the network layer; it doesn't replace key-based or password-based authentication.

6.4.4   Allowing SSH traffic from a source IP address

So far, you're allowing inbound traffic on port 22 (SSH) from every source IP address.
You can restrict access to only your IP address.

Hard-coding the public IP address into the template isn't a good solution because
this changes from time to time. But you already know the solution: parameters. You
need to add a parameter that holds your current public IP address, and you need to
modify the `AllowInboundSSH` rule. You can find the following listing in /chapter6/
`firewall4.json` in the book's code folder.

Listing 6.5　Security group that allows SSH only from specific IP address

```
[...]
"Parameters": {
  [...]
  "IpForSSH": {                    ◄───┐   Public IP address
    "Description": "Your public IP address to allow SSH access",   parameter
    "Type": "String"
  }
},
"Resources": {
  "AllowInboundSSH": {
    "Type": "AWS::EC2::SecurityGroupIngress",
    "Properties": {
      "GroupId": {"Ref": "SecurityGroup"},
      "IpProtocol": "tcp",
      "FromPort": "22",
      "ToPort": "22",
      "CidrIp": {"Fn::Join": ["", [{"Ref": "IpForSSH"}, "/32"]]}   ◄───┐
    }                                                      Uses $IpForSSH/32
  },                                                            as a value
  [...]
}
```

What's the difference between public and private IP addresses?

On my local network, I'm using private IP addresses that start with 192.168.0.*. My laptop uses 192.168.0.10, and my iPad uses 192.168.0.20. But if I access the internet, I have the same public IP (such as 79.241.98.155) for my laptop and iPad. That's because only my internet gateway (the box that connects to the internet) has a public IP address, and all requests are redirected by the gateway (if you want to dive deep into this, search for *network address translation*). Your local network doesn't know about this public IP address. My laptop and iPad only know that the internet gateway is reachable under 192.168.0.1 on the private network.

To find out your public IP address, visit http://api.ipify.org. For most of us, our public IP address changes from time to time, usually when we reconnect to the internet (which happens every 24 hours in my case).

Update the CloudFormation stack with the template located at https://s3.amazonaws .com/awsinaction/chapter6/firewall4.json. Type in your public IP address $IPForSSH when asked for parameters. Now only your IP address can open SSH connections to your EC2 instance.

Classless Inter-Domain Routing (CIDR)

You may wonder what /32 means in listing 6.5. To understand what's going on, you need to switch your brain into binary mode. An IP address is 4 bytes or 32 bits long. The /32 defines how many bits (32, in this case) should be used to form a range of addresses. If you want to define the exact IP address that's allowed, you must use all 32 bits.

> **(continued)**
> But sometimes it makes sense to define a range of allowed IP addresses. For example, you can use `10.0.0.0/8` to create a range between 10.0.0.0 and 10.255.255.255, `10.0.0.0/16` to create a range between 10.0.0.0 and 10.0.255.255, or `10.0.0.0/24` to create a range between 10.0.0.0 and 10.0.0.255. You aren't required to use the binary boundaries (8, 16, 24, 32), but they're easier for most people to understand. You already used `0.0.0.0/0` to create a range that contains every possible IP address.

Now you can control network traffic that comes from outside AWS or goes outside AWS by filtering based on protocol, port, and source IP address.

6.4.5   *Allowing SSH traffic from a source security group*

If you want to control traffic from one AWS resource (like an EC2 instance) to another, security groups are powerful. You can control network traffic based on whether the source or destination belongs to a specific security group. For example, you can define that a MySQL database can only be accessed if the traffic comes from your web servers, or that only your web cache servers are allowed to access the web servers. Because of the elastic nature of the cloud, you'll likely deal with a dynamic number of servers, so rules based on source IP addresses are difficult to maintain. This becomes easy if your rules are based on source security groups.

To explore the power of rules based on a source security group, let's look at the concept of a *bastion host* for SSH access (some people call it a *jump box*). The trick is that only one server, the bastion host, can be accessed via SSH from the internet (it should be restricted to a specific source IP address). All other servers can only be reached via SSH from the bastion host. This approach has two advantages:

- You have only one entry point into your system, and that entry point does nothing but SSH. The chances of this box being hacked are small.
- If one of your web servers, mail servers, FTP servers, and so on, is hacked, the attacker can't jump from that server to all the other servers.

To implement the concept of a bastion host, you must follow these two rules:

- Allow SSH access to the bastion host from 0.0.0.0/0 or a specific source address.
- Allow SSH access to all other servers only if the traffic source is the bastion host.

Figure 6.5 shows a bastion host with two servers that are only reachable via SSH from the bastion host.

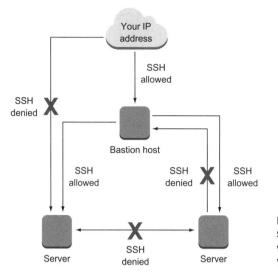

Figure 6.5   The bastion host is the only SSH access point to the system from which you can reach all the other servers via SSH (realized with security groups).

The following listing shows the SSH rule that allows traffic from a specific source security group.

Listing 6.6   Security group that allows SSH from bastion host

```
[...]
"SecurityGroupPrivate": {                    <--------- New security group
  "Type": "AWS::EC2::SecurityGroup",
  "Properties": {
    "GroupDescription": "My security group",
    "VpcId": {"Ref": "VPC"}
  }
},
"AllowPrivateInboundSSH": {
  "Type": "AWS::EC2::SecurityGroupIngress",
  "Properties": {
    "GroupId": {"Ref": "SecurityGroupPrivate"},
    "IpProtocol": "tcp",
    "FromPort": "22",                              Allow only if the
    "ToPort": "22",                                source is the other
    "SourceSecurityGroupId": {"Ref": "SecurityGroup"}   <--| security group.
  }
},
[...]
```

Update the CloudFormation stack with the template located at https://s3.amazonaws
.com/awsinaction/chapter6/firewall5.json. If the update is completed, the stack
shows three outputs:

- `BastionHostPublicName`—Use the bastion host to connect via SSH from your
  computer.

- `Server1PublicName`—You can connect to this server only from the bastion host.
- `Server2PublicName`—You can connect to this server only from the bastion host.

Now connect to `BastionHostPublicName` via SSH using `ssh -i $PathToKey/mykey.pem -A ec2-user@$BastionHostPublicName`. Replace `$PathToKey` with the path to your SSH key and `$BastionHostPublicName` with the public name of the bastion host. The `-A` option is important to enable `AgentForwarding`; agent forwarding lets you authenticate with the same key you used to log in to the bastion host for further SSH logins initiated from the bastion host.

Execute the following command to add your key to the SSH agent. Replace `$Path-ToKey` with the path to the SSH key:

```
ssh-add $PathToKey/mykey.pem
```

6.4.6 *Agent forwarding with PuTTY*

To make agent forwarding work with PuTTY, you need to make sure your key is loaded to PuTTY Pageant by double-clicking the private key file. You must also enable Connection > SSH > Auth > Allow Agent Forwarding, as shown in figure 6.6.

Enable agent forwarding.

Figure 6.6 Allow agent forwarding with PuTTY.

From the bastion host, you can then continue to log in to `$Server1PublicName` or `$Server2PublicName`:

> **Log in to the bastion host.**

```
[computer]$ ssh -i mykey.pem -A ec2-user@ec2-52-4-234-102.[...].com   ◁─┘
Last login: Sat Apr 11 11:28:31 2015 from [...]
[...]
[bastionh]$ ssh ec2-52-4-125-194.compute-1.amazonaws.com   ◁─┐
Last login: Sat Apr 11 11:28:43 2015 from [...]              │
[...]                                                         │
```

> **Log in to $Server1PublicName from the bastion host.**

The bastion host can be used to add a layer of security to your system. If one of your servers is compromised, an attacker can't jump to other servers in your system. This reduces the potential damage an attacker can inflict. It's important that the bastion host does nothing but SSH, to reduce the chance of it becoming a security risk. We use the bastion-host pattern frequently to protect our clients.

> **Cleaning up**
>
> Don't forget to delete your stack after you finish this section to clean up all used resources. Otherwise you'll likely be charged for the resources you use.

6.5 Creating a private network in the cloud: Virtual Private Cloud (VPC)

By creating a Virtual Private Cloud (VPC), you get your own private network on AWS. *Private* means you can use the address ranges 10.0.0.0/8, 172.16.0.0/12, or 192.168.0.0/16 to design a network that isn't necessarily connected to the public internet. You can create subnets, route tables, access control lists (ACLs), and gateways to the internet or a VPN endpoint.

A subnet allows you to separate concerns. Create a new subnet for your databases, web servers, caching servers, or application servers, or whenever you can separate two systems. Another rule of thumb is that you should have at least two subnets: public and private. A public subnet has a route to the internet; a private subnet doesn't. Your web servers should be in the public subnet, and your database resides in the private subnet.

For the purpose of understanding how a VPC works, you'll create a VPC to host an enterprise web application. You'll re-implement the bastion host concept from the previous section by creating a public subnet that contains only the bastion host server. You'll also create a private subnet for your web servers and one public subnet for your web caches. The web caches absorb most of the traffic by responding with the latest version of the page they have in their cache, and they redirect traffic to the private web servers. You can't access a web server directly over the internet—only through the web caches.

The VPC uses the address space 10.0.0.0/16. To separate concerns, you'll create two public subnets and one private subnet in the VPC:

- 10.0.1.0/24 public SSH bastion host subnet
- 10.0.2.0/24 public Varnish web cache subnet
- 10.0.3.0/24 private Apache web server subnet

What does 10.0.0.0/16 mean?

10.0.0.0/16 represents all IP addresses between 10.0.0.0 and 10.0.255.255. It's using CIDR notation (explained earlier in the chapter).

Network ACLs restrict traffic that goes from one subnet to another like a firewall. The SSH bastion host from section 6.4 can be implemented with these ACLs:

- SSH from 0.0.0.0/0 to 10.0.1.0/24 is allowed.
- SSH from 10.0.1.0/24 to 10.0.2.0/24 is allowed.
- SSH from 10.0.1.0/24 to 10.0.3.0/24 is allowed.

To allow traffic to the Varnish web cache and the HTTP servers, additional ACLs are required:

- HTTP from 0.0.0.0/0 to 10.0.2.0/24 is allowed.
- HTTP from 10.0.2.0/24 to 10.0.3.0/24 is allowed.

Figure 6.7 shows the architecture of the VPC.

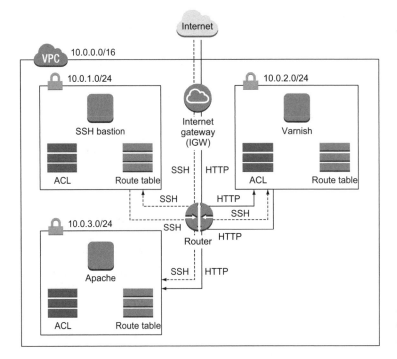

Figure 6.7   VPC with three subnets to secure a web application

You'll use CloudFormation to describe the VPC with its subnets. The template is split into smaller parts to make it easier to read in the book. As usual, you'll find the code in the book's code repository on GitHub: https://github.com/AWSinAction/code. The template is located at /chapter6/vpc.json.

6.5.1 Creating the VPC and an internet gateway (IGW)

The first resources in the template are the VPC and the internet gateway (IGW). The IGW will translate the public IP addresses of your virtual servers to their private IP addresses using network address translation (NAT). All public IP addresses used in the VPC are controlled by this IGW:

```
"VPC": {
  "Type": "AWS::EC2::VPC",
  "Properties": {
    "CidrBlock": "10.0.0.0/16",        ⟵——— Address space
    "EnableDnsHostnames": "true"
  }
},                                          Accesses the internet and NAT
"InternetGateway": {               ⟵——— for public IP addresses via IGW
  "Type": "AWS::EC2::InternetGateway",
  "Properties": {
    [...]
  }
},                                          Attaches the
"VPCGatewayAttachment": {        ⟵——— gateway to the VPC
  "Type": "AWS::EC2::VPCGatewayAttachment",
  "Properties": {
    "VpcId": {"Ref": "VPC"},
    "InternetGatewayId": {"Ref": "InternetGateway"}
  }
},
```

Next you'll define the subnet for the bastion host.

6.5.2 Defining the public bastion host subnet

The bastion host subnet will only run a single machine to secure SSH access:

```
"SubnetPublicSSHBastion": {           You'll learn about
  "Type": "AWS::EC2::Subnet",         this in chapter II.
  "Properties": {
    "AvailabilityZone": "us-east-1a",   ⟵        Address
    "CidrBlock": "10.0.1.0/24",       ⟵          space
    "VpcId": {"Ref": "VPC"}
  }
},
"RouteTablePublicSSHBastion": {   ⟵——— Route table
  "Type": "AWS::EC2::RouteTable",
  "Properties": {
    "VpcId": {"Ref": "VPC"}
  }
},                                          Associates the
                                            route table with
                                            the subnet
"RouteTableAssociationPublicSSHBastion": {   ⟵
```

```
      "Type": "AWS::EC2::SubnetRouteTableAssociation",
      "Properties": {
        "SubnetId": {"Ref": "SubnetPublicSSHBastion"},
        "RouteTableId": {"Ref": "RouteTablePublicSSHBastion"}
      }
    },
    "RoutePublicSSHBastionToInternet": {
      "Type": "AWS::EC2::Route",
      "Properties": {
        "RouteTableId": {"Ref": "RouteTablePublicSSHBastion"},
        "DestinationCidrBlock": "0.0.0.0/0",          ◁─── Routes everything
        "GatewayId": {"Ref": "InternetGateway"}             (0.0.0.0/0) to the IGW
      },
      "DependsOn": "VPCGatewayAttachment"
    },
    "NetworkAclPublicSSHBastion": {       ◁─── ACL
      "Type": "AWS::EC2::NetworkAcl",
      "Properties": {
        "VpcId": {"Ref": "VPC"}
      }
    },
    "SubnetNetworkAclAssociationPublicSSHBastion": {    ◁─── Associates the ACL
      "Type": "AWS::EC2::SubnetNetworkAclAssociation",        with the subnet
      "Properties": {
        "SubnetId": {"Ref": "SubnetPublicSSHBastion"},
        "NetworkAclId": {"Ref": "NetworkAclPublicSSHBastion"}
      }
    },
```

The definition of the ACL follows:

```
    "NetworkAclEntryInPublicSSHBastionSSH": {     ◁─── Allows inbound SSH
      "Type": "AWS::EC2::NetworkAclEntry",             from everywhere
      "Properties": {
        "NetworkAclId": {"Ref": "NetworkAclPublicSSHBastion"},
        "RuleNumber": "100",
        "Protocol": "6",
        "PortRange": {
          "From": "22",
          "To": "22"
        },
        "RuleAction": "allow",
        "Egress": "false",           ◁─── Inbound
        "CidrBlock": "0.0.0.0/0"
      }
    },                                             Ephemeral ports used
    "NetworkAclEntryInPublicSSHBastionEphemeralPorts": {  ◁─── for short-lived TCP/IP
      "Type": "AWS::EC2::NetworkAclEntry",                     connections
      "Properties": {
        "NetworkAclId": {"Ref": "NetworkAclPublicSSHBastion"},
        "RuleNumber": "200",
        "Protocol": "6",
        "PortRange": {
          "From": "1024",
          "To": "65535"
```

```
      },
      "RuleAction": "allow",
      "Egress": "false",
      "CidrBlock": "10.0.0.0/16"
    }
  },
  "NetworkAclEntryOutPublicSSHBastionSSH": {          <──┐ Allows outbound
    "Type": "AWS::EC2::NetworkAclEntry",                   SSH to VPC
    "Properties": {
      "NetworkAclId": {"Ref": "NetworkAclPublicSSHBastion"},
      "RuleNumber": "100",
      "Protocol": "6",
      "PortRange": {
        "From": "22",
        "To": "22"
      },
      "RuleAction": "allow",
      "Egress": "true",              <──── Outbound
      "CidrBlock": "10.0.0.0/16"
    }
  },
  "NetworkAclEntryOutPublicSSHBastionEphemeralPorts": {    <──┐ Ephemeral
    "Type": "AWS::EC2::NetworkAclEntry",                        ports
    "Properties": {
      "NetworkAclId": {"Ref": "NetworkAclPublicSSHBastion"},
      "RuleNumber": "200",
      "Protocol": "6",
      "PortRange": {
        "From": "1024",
        "To": "65535"
      },
      "RuleAction": "allow",
      "Egress": "true",
      "CidrBlock": "0.0.0.0/0"
    }
  },
```

There's an important difference between security groups and ACLs: security groups are stateful, but ACLs aren't. If you allow an inbound port on a security group, the outbound response that belongs to a request on the inbound port is allowed as well. A security group rule will work as you expect it to. If you open inbound port 22 on a security group, you can connect via SSH.

That's not true for ACLs. If you open inbound port 22 on an ACL for your subnet, you can't connect via SSH. In addition, you need to allow outbound ephemeral ports because sshd (SSH daemon) accepts connections on port 22 but uses an ephemeral port for communication with the client. Ephemeral ports are selected from the range starting at 1024 and ending at 65535.

If you want to make a SSH connection from within your subnet, you have to open outbound port 22 and inbound ephemeral ports as well. If you aren't familiar with all this, you should go with security groups and allow everything on the ACL level.

6.5.3   Adding the private Apache web server subnet

The subnet for the Varnish web cache is similar to the bastion host subnet because it's also a public subnet; that's why we'll skip it. You'll continue with the private subnet for the Apache web server:

```
"SubnetPrivateApache": {
  "Type": "AWS::EC2::Subnet",
  "Properties": {
    "AvailabilityZone": "us-east-1a",
    "CidrBlock": "10.0.3.0/24",                    ◄──── Address
    "VpcId": {"Ref": "VPC"}                              space
  }
},
"RouteTablePrivateApache": {           ◄──── No route to
  "Type": "AWS::EC2::RouteTable",            the IGW
  "Properties": {
    "VpcId": {"Ref": "VPC"}
  }
},
"RouteTableAssociationPrivateApache": {
  "Type": "AWS::EC2::SubnetRouteTableAssociation",
  "Properties": {
    "SubnetId": {"Ref": "SubnetPrivateApache"},
    "RouteTableId": {"Ref": "RouteTablePrivateApache"}
  }
},
```

The only difference between a public and a private subnet is that a private subnet doesn't have a route to the IGW. Traffic between subnets of a VPC is always routed by default. You can't remove the routes between the subnets. If you want to prevent traffic between subnets in a VPC, you need to use ACLs attached to the subnets.

6.5.4   Launching servers in the subnets

Your subnets are ready and you can continue with the EC2 instances. First you describe the bastion host:

```
"BastionHost": {
  "Type": "AWS::EC2::Instance",
  "Properties": {
    "ImageId": "ami-1ecae776",
    "InstanceType": "t2.micro",
    "KeyName": {"Ref": "KeyName"},          Assigns a public
    "NetworkInterfaces": [{                     IP address
      "AssociatePublicIpAddress": "true",   ◄──────────────┘
      "DeleteOnTermination": "true",                        Launches in
      "SubnetId": {"Ref": "SubnetPublicSSHBastion"},  ◄──── the bastion
      "DeviceIndex": "0",                                   host subnet
      "GroupSet": [{"Ref": "SecurityGroup"}]   ◄──────┐
    }]                                            This security group
  }                                               allows everything.
},
```

The Varnish server looks similar. But again, the private Apache web server differs in configuration:

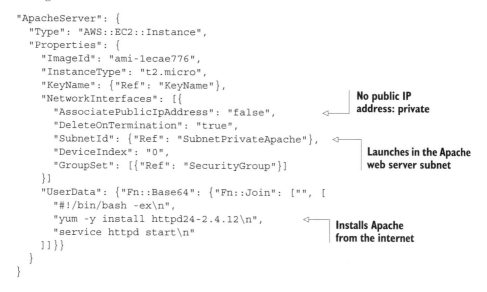

```
"ApacheServer": {
  "Type": "AWS::EC2::Instance",
  "Properties": {
    "ImageId": "ami-1ecae776",
    "InstanceType": "t2.micro",
    "KeyName": {"Ref": "KeyName"},
    "NetworkInterfaces": [{
      "AssociatePublicIpAddress": "false",          ⟵ No public IP
      "DeleteOnTermination": "true",                     address: private
      "SubnetId": {"Ref": "SubnetPrivateApache"},   ⟵
      "DeviceIndex": "0",                               Launches in the Apache
      "GroupSet": [{"Ref": "SecurityGroup"}]           web server subnet
    }]
    "UserData": {"Fn::Base64": {"Fn::Join": ["", [
      "#!/bin/bash -ex\n",
      "yum -y install httpd24-2.4.12\n",           ⟵ Installs Apache
      "service httpd start\n"                           from the internet
    ]]}}
  }
}
```

You're now in serious trouble: installing Apache won't work because your private subnet has no route to the internet.

6.5.5 *Accessing the internet from private subnets via a NAT server*

Public subnets have a route to the internet gateway. You can use a similar mechanism to provide internet access for private subnets without having a direct route to the internet: use a NAT server in a public subnet, and create a route from your private subnet to the NAT server. A NAT server is a virtual server that handles network address translation. Internet traffic from your private subnet will access the internet from the public IP address of the NAT server.

> **WARNING** Traffic from your EC2 instances to other AWS services that are accessed via the API (Object Store S3, NoSQL database DynamoDB) will go through the NAT instance. This can quickly become a major bottleneck. If your EC2 instances need to communicate heavily with the internet, the NAT instance is most likely not a good idea. Consider launching these instances in a public subnet instead.

To keep concerns separated, you'll create a new subnet for the NAT server. AWS provides an image (AMI) for a virtual server that has the configuration done for you:

```
"SubnetPublicNAT": {
  "Type": "AWS::EC2::Subnet",
  "Properties": {
    "AvailabilityZone": "us-east-1a",          10.0.0.0/24 is
    "CidrBlock": "10.0.0.0/24",            ⟵   the NAT subnet.
    "VpcId": {"Ref": "VPC"}
```

```
    }
  },
  "RouteTablePublicNAT": {
    "Type": "AWS::EC2::RouteTable",
    "Properties": {
      "VpcId": {"Ref": "VPC"}
    }
  },
  [...]
  "RoutePublicNATToInternet": {
    "Type": "AWS::EC2::Route",
    "Properties": {
      "RouteTableId": {"Ref": "RouteTablePublicNAT"},
      "DestinationCidrBlock": "0.0.0.0/0",
      "GatewayId": {"Ref": "InternetGateway"}
    },
    "DependsOn": "VPCGatewayAttachment"
  },
  [...]
  "NatServer": {
    "Type": "AWS::EC2::Instance",
    "Properties": {
      "ImageId": "ami-303b1458",
      "InstanceType": "t2.micro",
      "KeyName": {"Ref": "KeyName"},
      "NetworkInterfaces": [{
        "AssociatePublicIpAddress": "true",
        "DeleteOnTermination": "true",
        "SubnetId": {"Ref": "SubnetPublicNAT"},
        "DeviceIndex": "0",
        "GroupSet": [{"Ref": "SecurityGroup"}]
      }],
      "SourceDestCheck": "false"
    }
  },
  [...]
  "RoutePrivateApacheToInternet": {
    "Type": "AWS::EC2::Route",
    "Properties": {
      "RouteTableId": {"Ref": "RouteTablePrivateApache"},
      "DestinationCidrBlock": "0.0.0.0/0",
      "InstanceId": {"Ref": "NatServer"}
    }
  },
```

> The NAT subnet is public with a route to the internet.

> AWS provides a configured image for NAT instances.

> Public IP address that will be the source of all traffic from private subnets to the internet

> By default, an instance must be the source or destination of any traffic it sends or receives. Disable it for NAT instances.

> Route from the Apache subnet to the NAT instance

Now you're ready to create the CloudFormation stack with the template located at https://s3.amazonaws.com/awsinaction/chapter6/vpc.json. Once you've done so, copy the VarnishServerPublicName output and open it in your browser. You'll see an Apache test page that was cached by Varnish.

Cleaning up

Don't forget to delete your stack after finishing this section, to clean up all used resources. Otherwise you'll likely be charged for the resources you use.

6.6   *Summary*

- AWS is a shared-responsibility environment in which security can be achieved only if you and AWS work together. You're responsible for securely configuring your AWS resources and your software running on EC2 instances while AWS protects buildings and host systems.
- Keeping your software up to date is key and can be automated.
- The Identity and Access Management (IAM) service provides everything needed for authentication and authorization with the AWS API. Every request you make to the AWS API goes through IAM to check whether the request is allowed. IAM controls who can do what in your AWS account. Grant least permissions to your users and roles to protect your AWS account.
- Traffic to or from AWS resources like EC2 instances can be filtered based on protocol, port, and source or destination with the help of security groups.
- A bastion host is a well-defined, single point of access to your system. It can be used to secure SSH access to your servers. Implementation can be done with security groups or ACLs.
- A VPC is a private network in AWS where you have full control. With VPCs, you can control routing, subnets, ACLs, and gateways to the internet or your company network via VPN.
- You should separate concerns in your network to reduce potential damage if, for example, one of your subnets is hacked. Keep every system in a private subnet that doesn't need to be accessed from the public internet, to reduce your attackable surface.

Part 3

Storing data in the cloud

Suppose there's a guy named Singleton in your office who knows all about the file server. If Singleton is out of the office, no one else can maintain the file server. When Singleton goes on vacation, the file server crashes—no one knows where the backup is located, and the boss needs the document now or the company will lose a lot of money. If Singleton had stored his knowledge in a database, coworkers could look up the information. But because the knowledge and Singleton are tidily coupled, the data is unavailable.

Now imagine a server with important files located on a hard disk. As long as the server is up and running, everything is fine. But things fail all the time—and so will the server, eventually. If a user uploads a document on your website, where is it stored? Chances are high that the document is persisted to hard disk on the server. Suppose the document is uploaded to your website but persisted as an object in an independent object store: if the server fails, the document is still available. If you need two servers to handle the load on your website, they both have access to that document because it isn't coupled to a single server. If you separate your state from your server, your system can become fault-tolerant and elastic. Highly specialized solutions like object stores and databases can persist your state.

Chapter 7 introduces S3, a service offering object storage. You'll learn how to integrate the object store into your applications to implement a stateless server. Chapter 8 discusses block-level storage for virtual servers offered by AWS and how to operate legacy software on block-level storage. Chapter 9 introduces RDS, a service offering you managed relational database systems like PostgreSQL, MySQL, Oracle, and Microsoft SQL server. If your applications use such a relational database system, this is an easy way to implement a stateless server architecture. Chapter 10 introduces DynamoDB, a service that offers a NoSQL database; you can integrate this NoSQL database into your applications to implement a stateless server.

Storing your objects: S3 and Glacier

7

This chapter covers

- Transferring files to S3 with the help of the terminal
- Integrating S3 into your applications with SDKs
- Hosting a static website with S3
- Diving into the internals of the S3 object store

You can store images, videos, documents, and executables with the help of an object store. You'll learn about the concept of an object store in this chapter. In addition, we'll introduce a managed service on AWS offering an object store: Amazon S3. You'll also learn about Amazon Glacier, a backup and archiving store.

Not all examples are covered by the Free Tier

The examples in this chapter are not all covered by the Free Tier. A special warning message appears when an example incurs costs. As long as you don't run all other examples longer than a few days, you won't pay anything for them. Keep in mind that this applies only if you created a fresh AWS account for this book and nothing else is going on in your AWS account. Try to complete the examples of the chapter within a few days; you'll clean up your account at the end of each example.

7.1   Concept of an object store

Back in the old days, data was managed as files in a hierarchy consisting of folders and files. The file was the representation of the data. In an *object store*, data is stored as objects. Each object consists of a globally unique identifier, some metadata, and the data itself, as figure 7.1 illustrates. An object's *globally unique identifier* is also known as its *key*; addressing the object from different devices and machines in a distributed system is possible with the globally unique identifier.

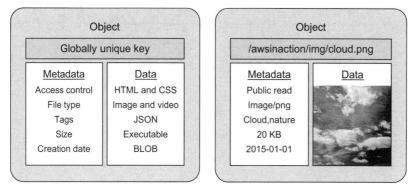

Figure 7.1   Objects stored in an object store have three parts: a unique ID, metadata describing the content, and the content itself (such as an image).

The separation of metadata and data allows clients to work only with the metadata for managing and querying data. You only have to load the data if you really need it. Metadata is also used to store access-control information and for other management tasks.

7.2   Amazon S3

The Amazon S3 object store is one of the oldest services on AWS. Amazon S3 is an acronym for Amazon Simple Storage Service. It's a typical web service that lets you store and retrieve data via an API reachable over HTTPS.

The service offers unlimited storage space and stores your data in a highly available and durable way. You can store any kind of data, such as images, documents, and binaries, as long as the size of a single object doesn't exceed 5 TB. You have to pay for every GB you store in S3, and you also incur minor costs for every request and transferred data. As figure 7.2 shows, you can access S3 via HTTPS using the Management Console, the command-line interface (CLI), SDKs, and third-party tools, to upload and download objects.

Figure 7.2   Uploading and downloading an object to S3 via HTTPS

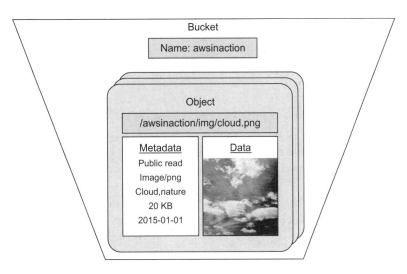

Figure 7.3 S3 uses buckets with a globally unique name to group objects.

S3 uses *buckets* to group objects. A bucket is a container for objects. You can create up to 100 buckets, each of which has a globally unique name. By *unique* we really mean unique—you have to choose a bucket name that isn't used by any other AWS customer in any other region, so we advise you to prefix the buckets with your domain name (such as com.mydomain.*) or your company name. Figure 7.3 shows the concept.

Typical use cases are as follows:

- Backing up and restoring files with S3 and the help of the AWS CLI
- Archiving objects with Amazon Glacier to save money compared to Amazon S3
- Integrating Amazon S3 into applications with the help of the AWS SDKs to store and fetch objects such as images
- Hosting static web content that can be viewed by anyone with the help of S3

7.3 *Backing up your data*

Critical data needs to be backed up to avoid loss. Depending on your requirements, you may need to back up data on multiple devices and/or at an offsite location. You can store any data in the form of objects to S3, so you can use S3 as a backup space.

In this section, you'll learn how to use the AWS CLI to upload and download data to and from S3. This approach isn't limited to the use case of an offsite backup; you can use it in many other scenarios as well.

First you need to create a bucket for your data on S3. As we mentioned earlier, the name of the bucket must be unique among all other S3 buckets, even those in other regions and those of other AWS customers. Run the following command in the terminal, replacing $YourName with your name:

```
$ aws s3 mb s3://awsinaction-$YourName
```

Your command should look similar to this one:

```
$ aws s3 mb s3://awsinaction-awittig
```

If your bucket name conflicts with an existing bucket, you'll get an error like this one:

```
A client error (BucketAlreadyExists) [...]
```

In this case, you'll need to use a different `$YourName`.

Everything is ready to upload your data. Choose a folder you'd like to back up, such as your Desktop folder. Try to choose a folder with a total size of less than 1 GB with less than 1000 files in it, to avoid long waiting times and exceeding the Free Tier. The following command uploads the data from your local folder to your S3 bucket. Replace `$Path` with the path to your folder and `$YourName` with your name. `sync` compares your folder with the /backup folder in your S3 bucket and uploads only new or changed files:

```
$ aws s3 sync $Path s3://awsinaction-$YourName/backup
```

Your command should look similar to this one:

```
$ aws s3 sync /Users/andreas/Desktop s3://awsinaction-awittig/backup
```

Depending on the size of your folder and the speed of your internet connection, the upload can take some time.

After uploading your folder to your S3 bucket to back it up, you can test the restore process. Execute the following command in your terminal, replacing `$Path` with a folder you'd like to use for the restore (don't use the folder you backed up) and `$YourName` with your name. Your Downloads folder would be a good place to test the restore process:

```
$ aws s3 cp --recursive s3://awsinaction-$YourName/backup $Path
```

Your command should look similar to this one:

```
$ aws s3 cp --recursive s3://awsinaction-awittig/backup/ \
/Users/andreas/Downloads/restore
```

Again, depending on the size of your folder and the speed of your internet connection, the download may take a while.

Versioning for objects

By default, S3 versioning is disabled for every bucket. Suppose you use the following steps to upload two objects:

1 Add an object with key *A* and data *1*.
2 Add an object with key *A* and data *2*.

If you download, also known as *get*, the object with key *A*, you'll download data *2*. The old data *1* doesn't exist anymore.

(continued)

You can change this behavior by turning on *versioning* for a bucket. The following command activates versioning for your bucket. Replace $YourName with your name:

```
$ aws s3api put-bucket-versioning --bucket awsinaction-$YourName \
--versioning-configuration Status=Enabled
```

If you repeat the previous steps, the first version of object *A* consisting of data *1* will be accessible even after you add an object with key *A* and data *2*. The following command retrieves all objects and versions:

```
$ aws s3api list-object-versions --bucket awsinaction-$YourName
```

You can now download all versions of an object.

Versioning can be useful in backup and archiving scenarios. Keep in mind that the size of the bucket you'll have to pay for will grow with every new version.

You no longer need to worry about losing data. S3 is designed for 99.999999999% durability of objects over a year.

Cleaning up

Execute the following command to remove the S3 bucket containing all the objects from your backup. You'll have to replace $YourName with your name to select the right bucket. rb removes the bucket; the force option triggers a delete for every object in the bucket before the bucket itself is deleted:

```
$ aws s3 rb --force s3://awsinaction-$YourName
```

Your command should look similar to this one:

```
$ aws s3 rb --force s3://awsinaction-awittig
```

You're finished—you've uploaded and downloaded files to S3 with the help of the CLI.

Removing bucket causes BucketNotEmpty error

If you turn on versioning for your bucket, removing the bucket will cause a Bucket-NotEmpty error. Use the Management Console to delete the bucket in this case:

1 Open the Management Console with your browser.
2 Go to the S3 service with the help of the main navigation.
3 Select your bucket.
4 Execute the Delete Bucket action from the Actions submenu.

7.4   Archiving objects to optimize costs

You used S3 to back up your data in the previous section. If you want to reduce the cost of backup storage, you should consider another AWS service: *Amazon Glacier.* The price of storing data with Glacier is about a third of what you pay to store data with S3. But what's the catch? Table 7.1 shows the differences between S3 and Glacier.

Table 7.1   Differences between storing data with S3 and Glacier

	S3	Glacier
Cost per GB	$0.03 USD	$0.01 USD
Accessibility	Immediate upon request	3–5 hours after request
Durability	Designed annual durability of 99.999999999%	Designed annual durability of 99.999999999%

You can use Glacier as a standalone service accessible via HTTPS or use the integration into S3, as you will in the following example.

7.4.1   Creating an S3 bucket for use with Glacier

In this section, you'll learn how to use the S3 integration of Glacier to reduce the cost of storing data. This can be helpful if you're doing an offsite backup, as in the previous section. First you need to create a new S3 bucket:

1 Open the Management Console at https://console.aws.amazon.com.
2 Move to the S3 service with the help of the main menu.
3 Click the Create Bucket button.
4 Type in a unique name for your bucket and choose US Standard as the bucket region, as shown in figure 7.4.
5 Click the Create button.

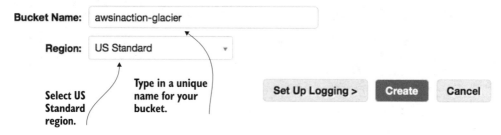

Figure 7.4   Creating an S3 bucket via the Management Console

7.4.2 Adding a lifecycle rule to a bucket

You can add one or multiple *lifecycle rules* to a bucket to manage the life of your objects. A lifecycle rule can be used to *archive* or *delete* objects after a given number of days. Archiving an object with the help of a lifecycle rule moves it from S3 to Glacier.

To add a lifecycle rule that moves objects to Glacier, follow these steps:

1 Open the S3 service with the Management Console.
2 Open your bucket's properties by clicking the magnifier next to the bucket's line, as shown in figure 7.5.
3 The properties are shown at right. Click the Lifecycle section.
4 Click the Add Rule button.

WARNING Using Glacier is not covered by the Free Tier. The example will incur a very low cost. Go to https://aws.amazon.com/glacier/pricing if you want to find out the current pricing.

A wizard starts that will guide you through the process of creating a new lifecycle rule for your bucket. The first step is to choose the target for your lifecycle rule. Choose the Whole Bucket option, as shown in figure 7.6, and click Configure Rule to proceed with the next step.

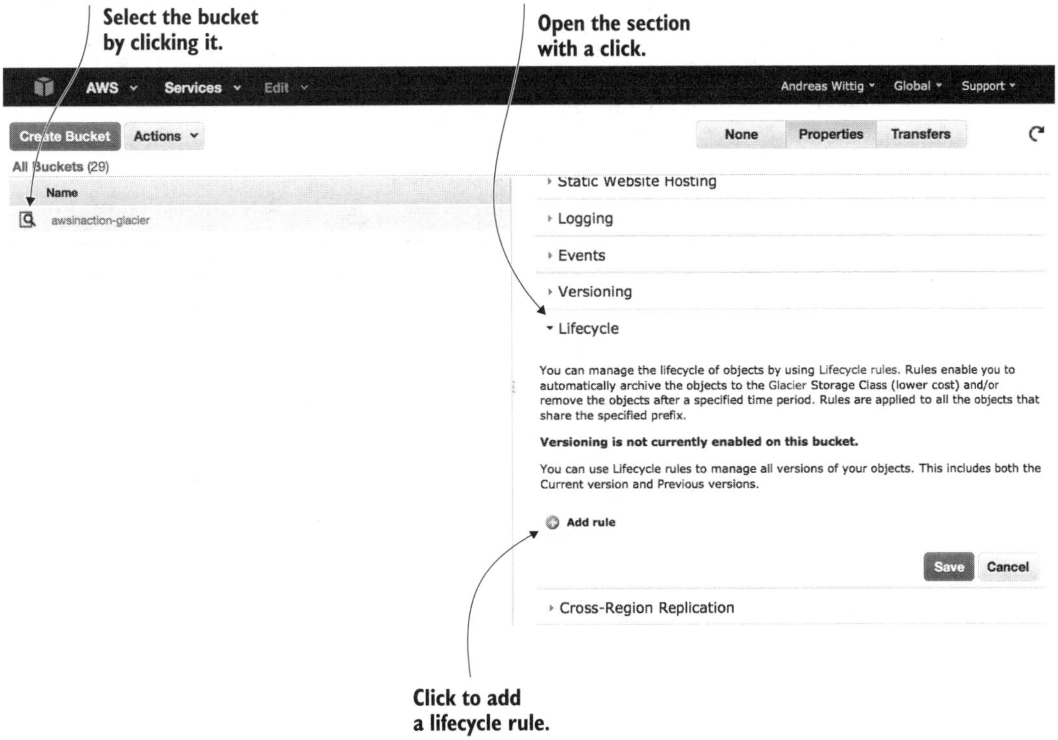

Figure 7.5   Adding a lifecycle rule to move objects to Glacier automatically

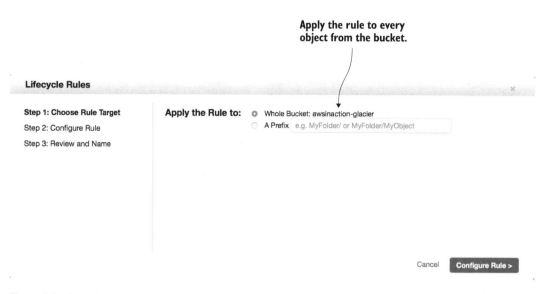

Figure 7.6 Choosing the target for the lifecycle rule

The next step configures the lifecycle rule. For Action on Objects, select Archive Only to move objects from S3 to Glacier with this rule. To trigger the lifecycle rule as quickly as possible after an object is created, choose 0 days as the time lag for the rule, as shown in figure 7.7. Click Review to proceed with the last step of the wizard.

One more thing: name your lifecycle rule as shown in figure 7.8, and review the rule's details. If everything is fine, click the Create and Activate Rule button.

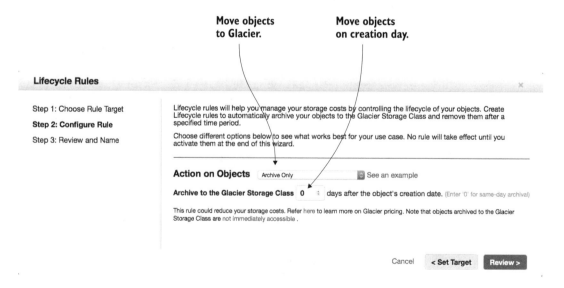

Figure 7.7 Editing the rule to move objects to Glacier the same day they're created

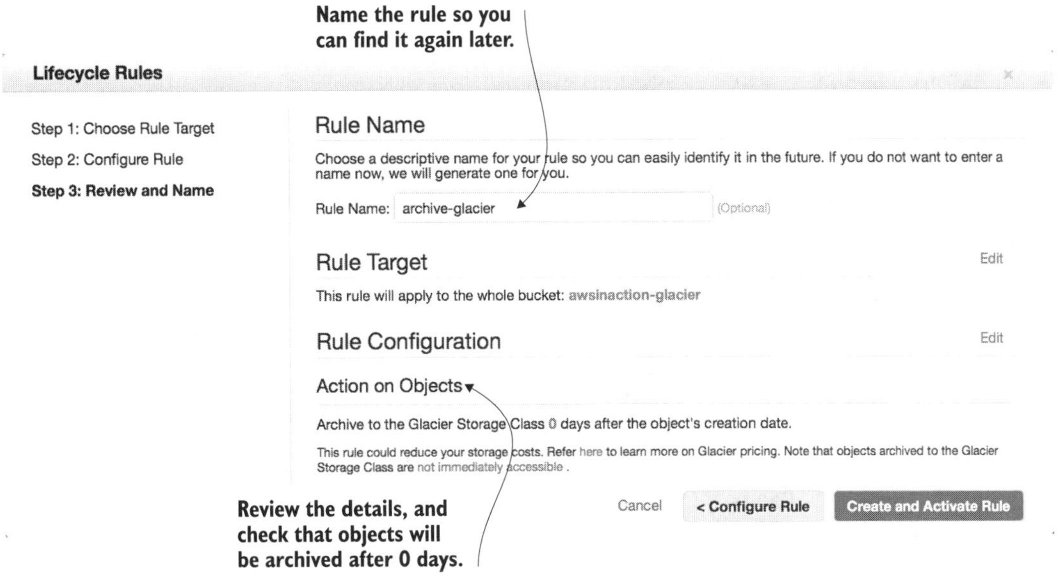

Name the rule so you can find it again later.

Lifecycle Rules

Step 1: Choose Rule Target

Step 2: Configure Rule

Step 3: Review and Name

Rule Name

Choose a descriptive name for your rule so you can easily identify it in the future. If you do not want to enter a name now, we will generate one for you.

Rule Name: archive-glacier (Optional)

Rule Target   Edit

This rule will apply to the whole bucket: awsinaction-glacier

Rule Configuration   Edit

Action on Objects ▾

Archive to the Glacier Storage Class 0 days after the object's creation date.

This rule could reduce your storage costs. Refer here to learn more on Glacier pricing. Note that objects archived to the Glacier Storage Class are not immediately accessible .

Review the details, and check that objects will be archived after 0 days.

Cancel   < Configure Rule   Create and Activate Rule

Figure 7.8   Naming and reviewing the lifecycle rule for an S3 bucket

7.4.3   Experimenting with Glacier and your lifecycle rule

You've successfully created a lifecycle rule that will automatically move all objects from the bucket to Glacier.

> **NOTE**   It will take up to 24 hours for the lifecycle rule to move your objects to Glacier. The restore process from Glacier to S3 will take 3 to 5 hours, so feel free to go on reading without executing the steps from the example yourself.

You can open your bucket by clicking the bucket name. To upload files, click Upload in the Management Console. In figure 7.9, we've uploaded three files to S3. By default, all files are stored with storage class Standard, which means they're stored in S3.

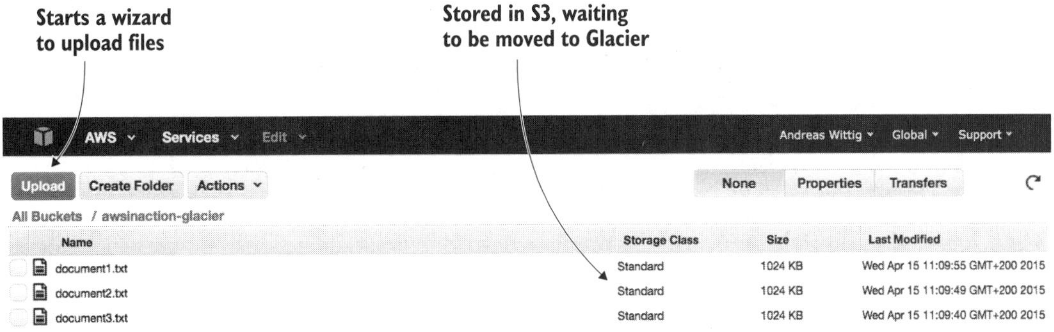

Starts a wizard to upload files

Stored in S3, waiting to be moved to Glacier

AWS ˅   Services ˅   Edit ˅   Andreas Wittig ˅   Global ˅   Support ˅

Upload   Create Folder   Actions ˅   None   Properties   Transfers   ↻

All Buckets / awsinaction-glacier

Name	Storage Class	Size	Last Modified
document1.txt	Standard	1024 KB	Wed Apr 15 11:09:55 GMT+200 2015
document2.txt	Standard	1024 KB	Wed Apr 15 11:09:49 GMT+200 2015
document3.txt	Standard	1024 KB	Wed Apr 15 11:09:40 GMT+200 2015

Figure 7.9   The lifecycle rule will move objects to Glacier after a few hours.

The lifecycle rule will move the created objects to Glacier. But even though the chosen time gap is 0 days, the move will take up to 24 hours. After your objects have moved to Glacier, the storage class will switch to Glacier.

You can't directly download files stored in Glacier, but you can trigger a restore of an object from Glacier to S3. Follow these steps to trigger a restore with the help of the Management Console:

1 Open the S3 bucket.
2 Select the object you want to restore from Glacier to S3 by clicking it.
3 Choose Actions > Initiate Restore.
4 A dialog appears in which you choose the number of days the object will be available via S3 after the restore from Glacier, as shown in figure 7.10.
5 Click OK to initiate the restore.

Restoring an object usually takes 3 to 5 hours. After the restore is complete, you can download the object.

Cleaning up

Delete your bucket after you finish the Glacier example. You can do this with the help of the Management Console by following these steps:

1 Open the S3 service with the Management Console.
2 Open the properties of your bucket by clicking the magnifier symbol at the beginning of the bucket's line.
3 Choose Actions > Delete.
4 Click OK to confirm the deletion.

You've learned how to use S3 with the help of the CLI and the Management Console. Next we'll show you how to integrate S3 into your applications with the help of SDKs.

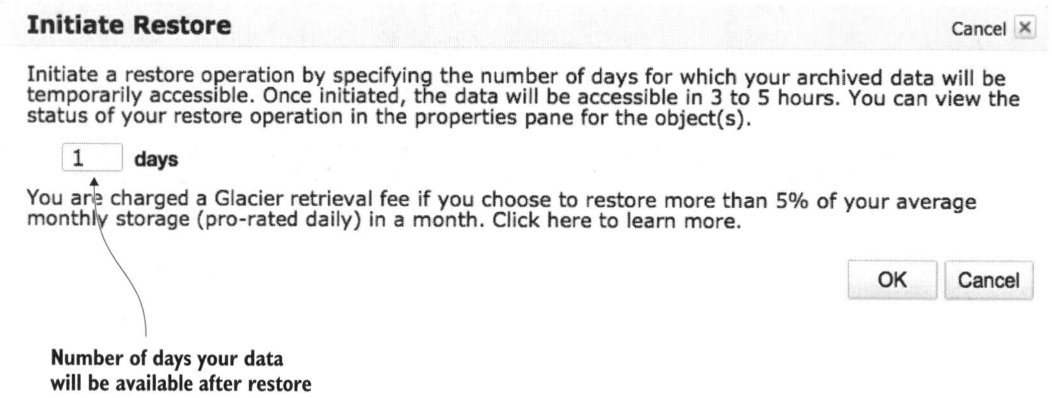

Initiate Restore   Cancel ✕

Initiate a restore operation by specifying the number of days for which your archived data will be temporarily accessible. Once initiated, the data will be accessible in 3 to 5 hours. You can view the status of your restore operation in the properties pane for the object(s).

| 1 | days

You are charged a Glacier retrieval fee if you choose to restore more than 5% of your average monthly storage (pro-rated daily) in a month. Click here to learn more.

OK   Cancel

**Number of days your data
will be available after restore**

Figure 7.10   A restore from Glacier to S3 is simple but takes 3–5 hours.

7.5   *Storing objects programmatically*

S3 is accessible over an API via HTTPS. This enables you to integrate S3 into your applications by making requests to the API programmatically. If you're using a common programming language like Java, JavaScript, PHP, Python, Ruby, or .NET, you can use a primary SDK offered by AWS for free. You can execute the following operations with the help of a SDK directly from your application:

- Listing buckets and their objects
- Creating, removing, updating, and deleting (CRUD) objects and buckets
- Managing access to and the cycle of objects

You can integrate S3 into your application in the following use cases, for example:

- *Allow a user to upload a profile picture.* Store the image in S3 and make it publicly accessible. Integrate the image into your website via HTTPS.
- *Generate monthly reports (such as PDFs) and make them accessible to users.* Create the documents and upload them to S3. If users want to download documents, fetch them from S3.
- *Share data between different applications.* You can access documents from different applications. For example, application A can write an object with the latest information about sales, and application B can download the document and analyze the data.

Integrating S3 into an application is a way to implement the concept of a *stateless server.* In this section, you'll dive into a simple web application called Simple S3 Gallery. The web application is built on top of Node.js and uses the AWS SDK for JavaScript and Node.js. You can easily transfer what you learn from this example to SDKs for other programming languages; the concepts are the same. Simple S3 Gallery allows you to upload images to S3 and shows all the images you've already uploaded. Figure 7.11 shows Simple S3 Gallery in action. Let's set up S3 to start your own gallery.

Simple S3 Gallery

Upload

Browse... No file selected.

Upload

Images

Figure 7.11   The Simple S3 Gallery app lets you upload images to an S3 bucket and then download them from the bucket for display.

7.5.1   *Setting up an S3 bucket*

To begin, you need to set up an empty bucket. Execute the following command, replacing $YourName with your name or nickname:

```
$ aws s3 mb s3://awsinaction-sdk-$YourName
```

Your bucket is ready to go. Installing the web application is the next step.

7.5.2   *Installing a web application that uses S3*

You can find the Simple S3 Gallery application in /chapter7/gallery/ in the book's code folder. Switch to that directory, and run npm install in your terminal to install all needed dependencies.

To start the web application, run the following command. Replace $YourName with your name; the name of the S3 bucket is passed to the web application:

```
$ node server.js awsinaction-sdk-$YourName
```

> **Where is the code located?**
>
> You can find all the code in the book's code repository on GitHub: https://github.com/AWSinAction/code. You can download a snapshot of the repository at https://github.com/AWSinAction/code/archive/master.zip.

After you start the server, you can open the gallery application. To do so, open http://localhost:8080 with your browser. Try uploading a few images.

7.5.3   *Reviewing code access: S3 with SDK*

You've seen Simple S3 Gallery upload and show images from S3. Inspecting parts of the code will help you to understand how you can integrate S3 into your own applications. It's not a problem if you don't follow all the details of the programming language (JavaScript) and the Node.js platform; we want you to get an idea of how to use S3 via SDKs.

UPLOADING AN IMAGE TO S3

You can upload an image to S3 with the putObject() function of the S3 service from the SDK. Your application will connect to the S3 service and transfer the image via HTTPS. The following listing shows how to do so.

Listing 7.1   Uploading an image with the AWS SDK for S3

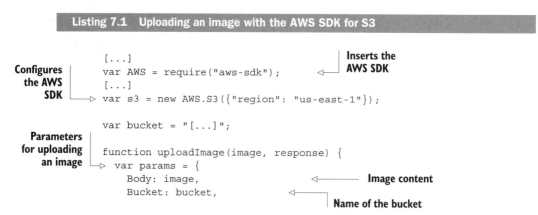

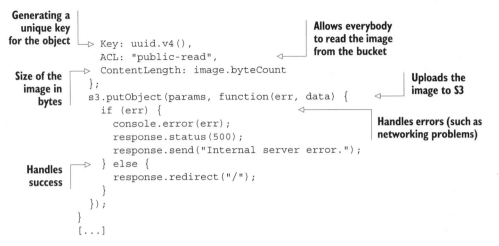

The AWS SDK takes care of sending all the necessary HTTPS requests to the S3 API in the background.

LISTING ALL THE IMAGES IN THE S3 BUCKET

To display a list of images, the application needs to list all the objects in your bucket. This can be done with the `listObjects()` function of the S3 service. The next listing shows the implementation of the corresponding function in the server.js JavaScript file, acting as a web server.

Listing 7.2 Retrieving all the image locations from the S3 bucket

```
[...]
var bucket = "[...]";

function listImages(response) {
  var params = {
    Bucket: bucket
  };
  s3.listObjects(params, function(err, data) {
    if (err) {
      console.error(err);
      response.status(500);
      response.send("Internal server error.");
    } else {
      var stream = mu.compileAndRender("index.html",
        {
          Objects: data.Contents,
          Bucket: bucket
        }
      );
      stream.pipe(response);
    }
  });
}
```

Defines parameters for the list-objects operation

Calls the list-objects operation

The resulting data contains the objects from the bucket list.

Listing the objects returns all the images from the bucket, but the list doesn't include the image content. During the uploading process, the access rights to the images are set to public read. This means anyone can download the images with the bucket name and a random key directly from S3. The following listing shows an excerpt of the index.html template, which is rendered on request. The `Objects` variable contains all the objects from the bucket.

Listing 7.3   Template to render the data as HTML

```
[...]
<h2>Images</h2>
{{#Objects}}                          ◁─── Iterates over
  <p>                                       all objects
    <img src="https://s3.amazonaws.com/{{Bucket}}/{{Key}}"/>
  </p>
{{/Objects}}
[...]
```

Puts together the URL to fetch an image from the bucket

You've now seen the three important parts of the Simple S3 Gallery integration with S3: uploading an image, listing all images, and downloading an image.

Cleaning up

Don't forget to clean up and delete the S3 bucket used in the example. Use the following command, replacing $YourName with your name:

```
$ aws s3 rb --force s3://awsinaction-sdk-$YourName
```

You've learned how to use S3 with the help of the AWS SDK for JavaScript and Node.js. Using the AWS SDK for other programming languages is similar.

7.6   *Using S3 for static web hosting*

You can host a static website with S3 and deliver static content like HTML, CSS, images (such as PNG and JPG), audio, and videos. You can't execute server-side scripts like PHP or JSP, but it's possible to deliver client-side scripts (such as JavaScript) from S3.

Increasing speed by using a CDN

Using a content-delivery network (CDN) helps reduce the load time for static web content. A CDN distributes static content like HTML, CSS, and images to servers all around the world. If a user sends out a request for some static content, the CDN serves that request from the nearest available server with the lowest latency.

Amazon S3 isn't a CDN, but you can easily use S3 as the back end for the CDN service of AWS: Amazon CloudFront. See the CloudFront documentation at http://mng.bz/Kctu if you want to set this up; we won't cover it in this book.

In addition, S3 offers the following features for hosting a static website:

- Define a custom index document and error documents.
- Define redirects for all or specific requests.
- Set up a custom domain for S3 bucket.

7.6.1 Creating a bucket and uploading a static website

First you need to create a new S3 bucket. To do so, open your terminal and execute the following command. Replace `$BucketName` with your own bucket name. As we've mentioned, the bucket name has to be globally unique, so it's a good idea to use your domain name as the bucket name (for example, static.yourdomain.com). If you want to redirect your domain name to S3, it's even mandatory that you use your entire domain name as the bucket name:

```
$ aws s3 mb s3://$BucketName
```

The bucket is empty; you'll place a HTML document in it next. We've prepared a placeholder HTML file. Download it to your local machine from the following URL:

```
https://raw.githubusercontent.com/AWSinAction/
➡ code/master/chapter7/helloworld.html
```

You can now upload the file to S3. Execute the following command to do so, replacing `$PathToPlacerholder` with the path to the HTML file you downloaded in the previous step and `$BucketName` with the name of your bucket:

```
$ aws s3 cp $PathToPlaceholder/helloworld.html \
s3://$BucketName/helloworld.html
```

You've now created a bucket and uploaded an HTML document called helloworld .html. You need to configure the bucket next.

7.6.2 Configuring a bucket for static web hosting

By default, only you, the owner, can access files from your S3 bucket. You want to use S3 to deliver your static website, so you'll need to allow everyone to view or download the documents included in your bucket. A *bucket policy* will help you control access to bucket objects globally. You already know about IAM policies from chapter 6: an IAM policy is defined in JSON and contains one or more statements, and a statement can either allow or deny specific actions on specific resources. A bucket policy is similar to an IAM policy.

Download our bucket policy from the following URL:

```
https://raw.githubusercontent.com/AWSinAction/code/
➡ master/chapter7/bucketpolicy.json
```

You need to edit the bucketpolicy.json file next. The following listing explains the policy. Open the file with the editor of your choice, and replace $BucketName with the name of your bucket.

Listing 7.4   Bucket policy allowing read-only access to every object in a bucket

```
{
  "Version":"2012-10-17",
  "Statement":[
    {
      "Sid":"AddPerm",
      "Effect":"Allow",            ◁─── Allows access ...
      "Principal": "*",            ◁─── ... for anyone ...
      "Action":["s3:GetObject"],   ◁─── ... to download objects ...
      "Resource":["arn:aws:s3:::$BucketName/*"]   ◁─── ... from your bucket
    }
  ]
}
```

You can add the bucket policy to your bucket with the following command. Replace $BucketName with the name of your bucket and $PathToPolicy with the path to the bucketpolicy.json file:

```
$ aws s3api put-bucket-policy --bucket $BucketName \
--policy file://$PathToPolicy/bucketpolicy.json
```

Every object in the bucket can now be downloaded by anyone. You need to enable and configure the static web-hosting feature of S3 next. To do so, execute the following command, replacing $BucketName with the name of your bucket:

```
$ aws s3 website s3://$BucketName --index-document helloworld.html
```

Your bucket is now configured to deliver a static website. The HTML document helloworld.html is used as index page. You'll learn how to access your website next.

7.6.3   *Accessing a website hosted on S3*

You can now access your static website with a browser. To do so, you need to choose the right endpoint. The endpoints for S3 static web hosting depend on your bucket's region:

```
$BucketName.s3-website-$Region.amazonaws.com
```

Your bucket was created in the default region us-east-1, so enter $BucketName to put together the endpoint for your bucket, and replace $Region with us-east-1:

```
$BucketName.s3-website-us-east-1.amazonaws.com
```

Open this URL with your browser, and you should be welcomed by a Hello World website.

Linking a custom domain to an S3 bucket

If you want to avoid hosting static content under a domain like awsinaction.s3-website-us-east-1.amazonaws.com, you can link a custom domain to an S3 bucket. All you have to do is to add a CNAME record for your domain, pointing to the bucket's S3 endpoint.

The CNAME record will only work if you comply with the following requirements:

- Your bucket name must match the CNAME record name. For example, if you want to create a CNAME for static.yourdomain.com, your bucket name must be static.yourdomain.com as well.
- CNAME records won't work for the primary domain name. You need to use a subdomain for CNAMEs like *static* or *www*, for example. If you want to link a primary domain name to an S3 bucket, you need to use the Route 53 DNS service from AWS.

Cleaning up

Don't forget to clean up your bucket after you finish the example. To do so, execute the following command, replacing `$BucketName` with the name of your bucket:

```
$ aws s3 rb --force s3://$BucketName
```

7.7 Internals of the object store

It's valuable to know about some internals of the S3 object store when using the service via the CLI or integrating it into your applications. A big difference between S3 and many other approaches to object stores is the fact that they're *eventually consistent*. If you don't consider this, you'll observe strange behavior if you try to read objects immediately after you update them. Another challenge is creating object keys that offer maximum I/O performance on S3. You'll learn more about both topics next.

7.7.1 Ensuring data consistency

If you're creating, updating, or deleting an object on S3, this operation is *atomic*. This means if you're reading an object after a create, an update, or a delete, you'll never get corrupted or partial data. But it's possible that a read will return the old data for a while.

S3 provides *eventual consistency*. If you upload a new version of an existing object to S3 and your request is successful, your data is safely stored. But downloading the updated object immediately can return the *old* version, as shown in figure 7.12. If you retry downloading the object, after a while the new version will be available.

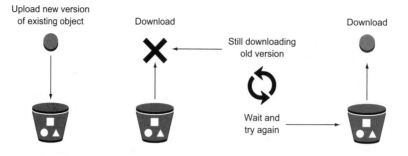

Figure 7.12   Eventual consistency: if you update an object and try to read it, the object may contain the old version. After some time passes, the latest version is available.

Read requests after uploading a new object will be consistent if you use the s3-external-1.amazonaws.com endpoint to access your S3 bucket in US Standard; the same is true for buckets in regions other than US Standard. But read requests after an update or delete will be eventually consistent.

7.7.2   Choosing the right keys

Naming variables or files is one of the most difficult tasks in IT. This is especially true for choosing the right keys for objects you want to store in S3. In S3, keys are stored in alphabetical order in an index. The key name determines which partition the key is stored in. If your keys begin with the same characters, the maximum I/O performance of your S3 bucket will be limited. Instead, you should choose keys for your objects that begin with different characters. As figure 7.13 shows, this will give you maximum I/O performance.

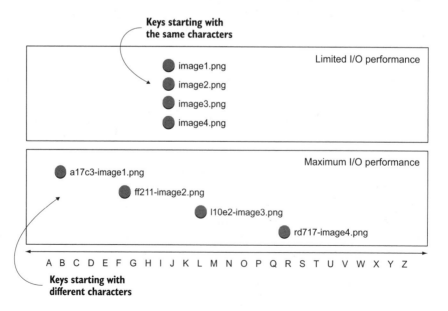

Figure 7.13   To improve I/O performance with S3, don't use keys that start with the same characters.

Using a slash (/) in the key name acts like creating a folder for your object. If you create an object with the key `folder/object.png`, the folder will become visible as *folder* if you're browsing your bucket with a GUI like the Management Console, for example. But technically, the key of the object still is `folder/object.png`.

Suppose you need to store images that were uploaded by different users. You come up with the following naming schema for your object keys:

```
$ImageId.png
```

`$ImageId` is an ascending numerical ID. A list of your objects might look like this:

```
/image1.png
/image2.png
/image3.png
/image4.png
```

The object keys are in alphabetical order, and your maximum throughput with S3 won't be optimal. You can fix this by adding a hash prefix to each object. For example, you can use the MD5 hash of the original key name and prepend it to the key:

```
/a17c3-image1.png
/ff211-image2.png
/l10e2-image3.png
/rd717-image4.png
```

This will help distribute your keys across partitions and increase the I/O performance of S3. Knowing about the internals of S3 helps you to optimize your usage.

7.8 Summary

- An object consists of a unique identifier, metadata to describe and manage the object, and the content itself. You can save images, documents, executables, or any other content as an object in an object store.
- Amazon S3 is an object store accessible only via HTTPS. You can upload, manage, and download objects with the CLI, SDKs, or the Management Console.
- Integrating S3 into your applications will help you implement the concept of a stateless server because you don't have to store objects locally on the server.
- You can define a lifecycle for your objects that will move the objects from Amazon S3 to Amazon Glacier, a special service to archive data that you don't need to access frequently. Doing so reduces your cost for storing data.
- S3 is an eventually consistent object store. You have to consider this if you integrate it into your applications and processes to avoid unpleasant surprises.

Storing your data on hard drives: EBS and instance store

This chapter covers

- Attaching network storage to your EC2 instance
- Using the instance store of your EC2 instance
- Backing up your block-level storage
- Testing and tweaking the performance of your block-level storage
- Instance storage versus network-attached storage

Block-level storage with a disk file system (FAT32, NTFS, ext3, ext4, XFS, and so on) can be used to store files as you do on a personal computer. A block is a sequence of bytes and the smallest addressable unit. The OS is the intermediary between the application that wants to access files and the underlying file system and block-level storage. The disk file system manages where (at what block address) your files are persisted on the underlying block-level storage. You can use block-level storage only in combination with an EC2 instance where the OS runs.

The OS provides access to block-level storage via open, write, and read system calls. The simplified flow of a read request goes like this:

1 An application wants to read the file `/path/to/file.txt` and makes a read system call.
2 The OS forwards the read request to the file system.
3 The file system translates `/path/to/file.txt` to the block on the disk where the data is stored.

Applications like databases that read or write files by using system calls must have access to block-level storage for persistence. You can't tell a MySQL database to store its files in an object store because MySQL uses system calls to access files.

> ### Not all examples are covered by the Free Tier
> The examples in this chapter are not all covered by the Free Tier. A special warning message appears when an example incurs costs. As long as you don't run all other examples longer than a few days, you won't pay anything for them. Keep in mind that this applies only if you created a fresh AWS account for this book and nothing else is going on in your AWS account. Try to complete the examples of the chapter within a few days; you'll clean up your account at the end of each example.

AWS provides two kinds of block-level storage: network-attached storage (NAS) and instance storage. NAS is (like iSCSI) attached to your EC2 instance via a network connection, whereas instance storage is a normal hard disk that the host system provides to your EC2 instance. NAS is the best choice for most problems because it provides 99.999% availability of your data. Instance storage is interesting if you're optimizing for performance. The next three sections will introduce and compare the two block-level storage solutions by connecting block-level storage with an EC2 instance, doing performance tests, and exploring how to back up the data. After that, you'll set up a shared file system using instance storage and NAS.

8.1 Network-attached storage

Elastic Block Store (EBS) provides network-attached, block-level storage with 99.999% availability. Figure 8.1 shows how you can use EBS volumes with EC2 instances.

EBS volumes

- Aren't part of your EC2 instances; they're attached to your EC2 instance via a network connection. If you terminate your EC2 instance, the EBS volumes remain.
- Can be attached to no EC2 instances or one EC2 instance at a time.

EC2 instance   EBS volume

Figure 8.1 EBS volumes are independent resources but can only be used when attached to an EC2 instance.

- Can be used like normal hard disks.
- Are comparable to RAID1: your data is saved to multiple disks in the background.

WARNING You can't attach the same EBS volume to multiple servers!

8.1.1 Creating an EBS volume and attaching it to your server

The following example demonstrates how to create an EBS volume and attach it to an EC2 instance with the help of CloudFormation:

```
"Server": {
  "Type": "AWS::EC2::Instance",
  "Properties": {
    [...]
  }
},
"Volume": {                                      EBS volume
  "Type":"AWS::EC2::Volume",         ◁─┘ description
  "Properties": {
    "AvailabilityZone": {"Fn::GetAtt": ["Server", "AvailabilityZone"]},
    "Size": "5",
    "VolumeType": "gp2"              ◁───── SSD backed
  }
},
"VolumeAttachment": {                            Attach EBS volume
  "Type": "AWS::EC2::VolumeAttachment",   ◁─┘ to server
  "Properties": {
    "Device": "/dev/xvdf",
    "InstanceId": {"Ref": "Server"},
    "VolumeId": {"Ref": "Volume"}
  }
}
}
```

5 GB capacity ⌎→ points to `"Size": "5",`

Device name ⌎→ points to `"Device": "/dev/xvdf",`

An EBS volume is a standalone resource. This means your EBS volume can exist without an EC2 server, but you need an EC2 server to use the EBS volume.

8.1.2 Using Elastic Block Store

To help you explore EBS, we've prepared a CloudFormation template located at https://s3.amazonaws.com/awsinaction/chapter8/ebs.json. Create a stack based on that template, and set the `AttachVolume` parameter to yes. Then, copy the `Public-Name` output and connect via SSH.

You can see the attached EBS volumes with the help of `fdisk`. Usually, EBS volumes can be found at /dev/xvdf to /dev/xvdp. The root volume (/dev/xvda) is an exception—it's based on the AMI you choose when you launch the EC2 instance and contains everything needed to boot the instance (your OS files):

```
$ sudo fdisk -l
Disk /dev/xvda: 8589 MB [...]           Root volume (your
Units = sectors of 1 * 512 = 512 bytes   ◁─┘ OS lives here)
Sector size (logical/physical): 512 bytes / 512 bytes
```

```
I/O size (minimum/optimal): 512 bytes / 512 bytes
Disk label type: gpt


#          Start        End    Size  Type            Name
  1         4096   16777182      8G  Linux filesyste Linux
128         2048       4095      1M  BIOS boot parti BIOS Boot Partition

Disk /dev/xvdf: 5368 MB [...]        ◁────── Attached EBS volume
Units = sectors of 1 * 512 = 512 bytes
Sector size (logical/physical): 512 bytes / 512 bytes
I/O size (minimum/optimal): 512 bytes / 512 bytes
```

The first time you use a newly created EBS volume, you must create a file system. You could also create partitions, but in this case the volume size is only 5 GB, so you probably don't want to split it up further. It's also best practice to not use partitions with EBS volumes. Create volumes with the size you need; if you need two separate "partitions," create two volumes. In Linux, you can create a file system with the help of mkfs. The following example creates an ext4 file system:

```
$ sudo mkfs -t ext4 /dev/xvdf
mke2fs 1.42.12 (29-Aug-2014)
Creating filesystem with 1310720 4k blocks and 327680 inodes
Filesystem UUID: e9c74e8b-6e10-4243-9756-047ceaf22abc
Superblock backups stored on blocks:
  32768, 98304, 163840, 229376, 294912, 819200, 884736

Allocating group tables: done
Writing inode tables: done
Creating journal (32768 blocks): done
Writing superblocks and filesystem accounting information: done
```

After the file system has been created, you can mount the device:

```
$ sudo mkdir /mnt/volume/
$ sudo mount /dev/xvdf /mnt/volume/
```

To see mounted volumes, use df -h:

```
$ df -h
Filesystem  Size  Used Avail Use% Mounted on        │ Root volume (your
/dev/xvda1  7.8G  1.1G  6.6G  14% /          ◁──────┘ OS lives here)
devtmpfs    490M   60K  490M   1% /dev
tmpfs       499M     0  499M   0% /dev/shm
/dev/xvdf   4.8G   10M  4.6G   1% /mnt/volume    ◁────── EBS volume
```

EBS volumes have one big advantage: they aren't part of the EC2 instance; they're independent resources. To see how an EBS volume is independent of the server, you'll now save a file to the volume and then unmount and detach the volume:

```
$ sudo touch /mnt/volume/testfile    ◁───┐ Creates testfile
$ sudo umount /mnt/volume/                │ in /mnt/volume/
```

Update the CloudFormation stack, and change the AttachVolume parameter to no. This will detach the EBS volume from the EC2 instance. After the update is completed, only your root device is left:

```
$ sudo fdisk -l
Disk /dev/xvda: 8589 MB, 8589934592 bytes, 16777216 sectors
Units = sectors of 1 * 512 = 512 bytes
Sector size (logical/physical): 512 bytes / 512 bytes
I/O size (minimum/optimal): 512 bytes / 512 bytes
Disk label type: gpt


#         Start         End    Size  Type            Name
  1        4096    16777182     8G   Linux filesyste Linux
128        2048        4095     1M   BIOS boot parti BIOS Boot Partition
```

The testfile in /mnt/volume/ is also gone:

```
$ ls /mnt/volume/testfile
ls: cannot access /mnt/volume/testfile: No such file or directory
```

Now you'll attach the EBS volume again. Update the CloudFormation stack, and change the AttachVolume parameter to yes. After the update is completed, /dev/xvdf is again available:

```
$ sudo mount /dev/xvdf /mnt/volume/
$ ls /mnt/volume/testfile        ◁——————  Checks whether testfile
/mnt/volume/testfile                       is still in /mnt/volume/
```

Voilà: the file testfile that you created in /mnt/volume/ is still there.

8.1.3 Tweaking performance

Performance testing of hard disks is divided between read and write tests. Many tools are available. One of the simpler tools is dd, which can perform block-level reads and writes between a source if=/path/to/source and a destination of=/path/to/destination:

```
                $ sudo dd if=/dev/zero of=/mnt/volume/tempfile bs=1M count=1024 \   ◁—┐
                    conv=fdatasync,notrunc
  63.2 MB/s                1024+0 records in                      Writes I MB I,024 times
    write                  1024+0 records out
performance  └▷ 1073741824 bytes (1.1 GB) copied, 16.9858 s, 63.2 MB/s

   Flushes   ┌▷ $ echo 3 | sudo tee /proc/sys/vm/drop_caches
    caches   │
                $ sudo dd if=/mnt/volume/tempfile of=/dev/null bs=1M count=1024    ◁—┐
                1024+0 records in                         Reads I MB I,024 times
                1024+0 records out
                1073741824 bytes (1.1 GB) copied, 16.3157 s, 65.8 MB/s  ◁—┐
                                                                    65.8 MB/s read
                                                                    performance
```

Keep in mind that depending on your actual workload, performance can vary. The example assumes that the file size is 1 MB. If you're hosting websites, you'll most likely deal with lots of small files instead.

But EBS performance is a bit more complicated. Performance depends on the EC2 instance type and the EBS volume type. Table 8.1 gives an overview of EC2 instance types that are EBS-optimized by default or can be optimized for an additional hourly charge. Input/output operations per second (IOPS) are measured using 16 KB I/O size. Performance depends heavily on your workload: read versus write, and the size of your I/O operations. These numbers are illustrations, and your mileage may vary.

Table 8.1   What performance can be expected from EBS optimized instance types?

Use case	Instance type	Max bandwidth (MiB/s)	Max IOPS	EBS optimized by default?
General purpose	m3.xlarge–c4.large	60–120	4,000–8,000	No
Compute optimized	c3.xlarge–3.4xlarge	60–240	4,000–16,000	No
Compute optimized	c4.large–c4.8xlarge	60–480	4,000–32,000	Yes
Memory optimized	r3.xlarge–r3.4xlarge	60–240	4,000–16,000	No
Storage optimized	i2.xlarge–i2.4xlarge	60–240	4,000–16,000	No
Storage optimized	d2.xlarge–d2.8xlarge	90–480	6,000–32,000	Yes

Depending on your storage workload, you must choose an EC2 instance that can deliver the bandwidth you require. Additionally, your EBS volume must be able to saturate the bandwidth. Table 8.2 shows the different EBS volume types available and how they perform.

Table 8.2   How EBS volume types differ

EBS volume type	Size	Maximum throughput MiB/s	IOPS	IOPS burst	Price
Magnetic	1 GiB–1 TiB	40–90	100	Hundreds	$
General purpose (SSD)	1 GiB–16 TiB	160	3 per GiB (up to 10,000)	3,000	$$
Provisioned IOPS (SSD)	4 GiB–16 TiB	320	As much as you provision (up to 30 per GiB or 20,000)	-	$$$

EBS volumes are charged for based on the size of the volume, no matter how much you use of that size. If you provision a 100 GiB volume, you pay for 100 GiB even if you have no data on the volume. If you use magnetic volumes, you must also pay for every I/O operation you perform. A provisioned IOPS (SSD) volume is additionally charged

> **GiB and TiB**
>
> The terms *gibibyte* (GiB) and *tebibyte* (TiB) aren't used often; you're probably more familiar with gigabyte and terabyte. But AWS uses them in some places. Here's what they mean:
>
> - 1 GiB = 2^30 bytes = 1,073,741,824 bytes
> - 1 GiB is ~ 1.074 GB
> - 1 GB = 10^9 bytes = 1,000,000,000 bytes

for based on the provisioned IOPS. Use the AWS Simple Monthly Calculator at http://aws.amazon.com/calculator to determine how much your storage setup will cost.

We advise you to use general-purpose (SSD) volumes as the default. If your workload requires more IOPS, then go with provisioned IOPS (SSD). You can attach multiple EBS volumes to a single instance to increase overall capacity or for additional performance.

You can increase performance by combining two (or more) volumes together in a software RAID0, also called *striping*. RAID0 means that if you have two disks, your data is distributed over those two disks, but data resides only on one disk. A software RAID can be created with mdadm in Linux.

8.1.4   Backing up your data

EBS volumes offer 99.999% availability, but you should still create backups from time to time. Fortunately, EBS offers an optimized, easy-to-use way of backing up EBS volumes with EBS snapshots. A *snapshot* is a block-level incremental backup that is saved on S3. If your volume is 5 GB in size and you use 1 GB of data, your first snapshot will be around 1 GB in size. After the first snapshot is created, only the changes will be saved to S3 to reduce the size of the backup. EBS snapshots are charged for based on how many gigabytes you use.

You'll now create a snapshot with the help of the CLI. Before you can do so, you need to know the EBS volume ID. You can find it as the VolumeId output of the Cloud-Formation stack or by running the following:

```
$ aws --region us-east-1 ec2 describe-volumes \
--filters "Name=size,Values=5"  --query "Volumes[].VolumeId" \
--output text
vol-fd3c0aba          ⟵── Your $VolumeId
```

With the volume ID, you can go on to create a snapshot: **Replace with your $VolumeId**

```
$ aws --region us-east-1 ec2 create-snapshot --volume-id $VolumeId  ⟵┘
{
  "Description": null,
  "Encrypted": false,
  "VolumeId": "vol-fd3c0aba",
  "State": "pending",      ⟵──── Status of your
  "VolumeSize": 5,                snapshot
```

```
  "Progress": null,
  "StartTime": "2015-05-04T08:28:18.000Z",
  "SnapshotId": "snap-cde01a8c",          ◁──────── Your $SnapshotId
  "OwnerId": "878533158213"
}
```

Creating a snapshot can take some time, depending on how big your volume is and how many blocks have changed since the last backup. You can see the status of the snapshot by running the following:

```
$ aws --region us-east-1 ec2 describe-snapshots --snapshot-ids $SnapshotId  ◁──┐
{                                                                    Replace with your
  "Snapshots": [                                                          $SnapshotId
    {
      "Description": null,
      "Encrypted": false,
      "VolumeId": "vol-fd3c0aba",
      "State": "completed",          ◁──────── A value of completed means
      "VolumeSize": 5,                          the snapshot is finished.
      "Progress": "100%",
      "StartTime": "2015-05-04T08:28:18.000Z",
      "SnapshotId": "snap-cde01a8c",
      "OwnerId": "878533158213"
    }
  ]
}
```

Progress of your snapshot (annotation pointing to "Progress": "100%",)

Creating a snapshot of an attached, mounted volume is possible but can cause problems with writes that aren't flushed to disk. If you must create a snapshot while the volume is in use, you can do so safely as follows:

1 Freeze all writes by running `fsfreeze -f /mnt/volume/` on the server.
2 Create a snapshot.
3 Resume writes by running `fsfreeze -u /mnt/volume/` on the server.
4 Wait until the snapshot is completed.

You must only freeze when snapshot creation is requested. You must not freeze until the snapshot is completed.

To restore a snapshot, you must create a new EBS volume based on that snapshot. When you launch an EC2 instance from an AMI, AWS creates a new EBS volume (root volume) based on a snapshot (an AMI is a snapshot).

Cleaning up

Don't forget to delete the snapshot:

```
$ aws --region us-east-1 ec2 delete-snapshot --snapshot-id $SnapshotId
```

Also delete your stack after you finish this section to clean up all used resources. Otherwise, you'll likely be charged for the resources you use.

8.2   *Instance stores*

An instance store provides block-level storage like a normal hard disk. Figure 8.2 shows that the instance store is part of an EC2 instance and available only if your instance is running; it won't persist your data if you stop or terminate the instance. Therefore you don't pay separately for an instance store; instance store charges are included in the EC2 instance price.

In comparison to an EBS volume, which is attached via network to your virtual server, an instance store is included in the virtual server and can't exist without the virtual server.

Don't use an instance store for data that must not be lost; use it for caching, temporary processing, or applications that replicate data to several servers as some databases do. If you want to set up your favorite NoSQL database, chances are high that data replication is handled by the application and you can use an instance store to get the highest available I/O performance.

> **WARNING**   If you stop or terminate your EC2 instance, the instance store is lost. *Lost* means all data is destroyed and can't be restored!

AWS offers SSD and HDD instance stores from 4 GB up to 48 TB. Table 8.3 shows all EC2 instance families with instance stores.

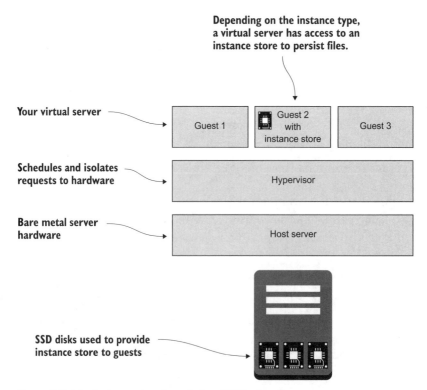

Figure 8.2   The instance store is part of an EC2 instance.

Table 8.3   Instance families with instance stores

Use case	Instance type	Instance store type	Instance store size in GB
General purpose	m3.medium–m3.2xlarge	SSD	1 × 4–2 × 80
Compute optimized	c3.large–c3.8xlarge	SSD	2 × 16–2 × 320
Memory optimized	r3.large–r3.8xlarge	SSD	1 × 32–2 × 320
Storage optimized	i2.xlarge–i2.8xlarge	SSD	1 × 800–8 × 800
Storage optimized	d2.xlarge–d2.8xlarge	HDD	3 × 2,000–24 × 2,000

If you want to launch an EC2 instance with an instance store manually, open the Management Console and start the Launch Instance wizard as you did in section 3.1.1:

WARNING   Starting a virtual server with instance type m3.medium will incur charges. See http://aws.amazon.com/ec2/pricing if you want to find out the current hourly price.

- Go through steps 1 to 3: choose an AMI, choose the m3.medium instance type, and configure the instance details.
- In step 4, configure an instance store as shown in figure 8.3:
  1 Click the Add New Volume button.
  2 Select Instance Store 0.
  3 Set the device name to /dev/sdb.
- Complete steps 5 to 7: tag the instance, configure a security group, and review the instance launch.

The instance store can now be used by your EC2 instance.

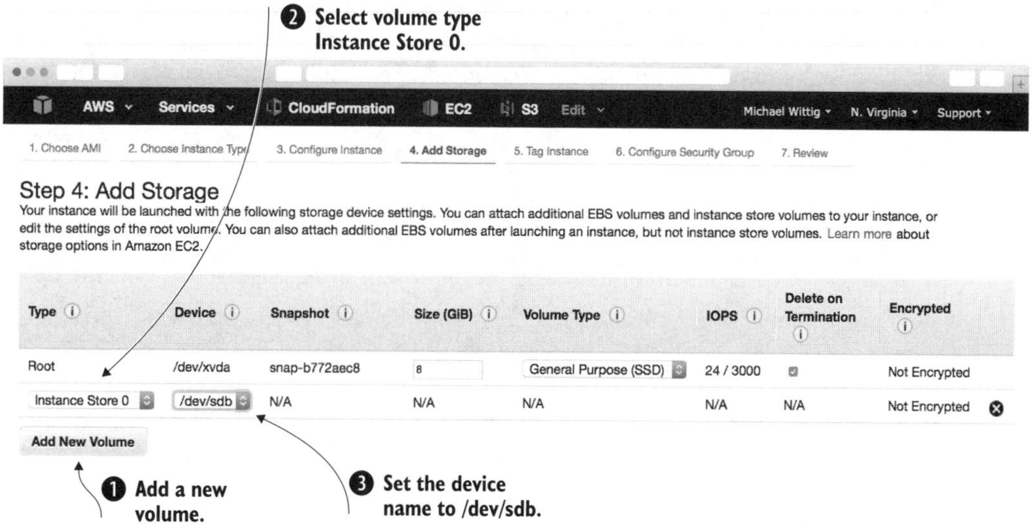

Figure 8.3   Adding an instance store volume during manual EC2 instance launch

Listing 8.1 demonstrates how to use an instance store with the help of CloudFormation. If you launch an EC2 instance from an EBS-backed root volume (which is the default), you must define a `BlockDeviceMappings` to map EBS and instance store volumes to device names. Compared to the EBS template snippet, an instance store isn't a stand-alone resource like an EBS volume; the instance store is part of your EC2 instance: Depending on the instance type, you'll have zero, one, or multiple instance store volumes for mapping.

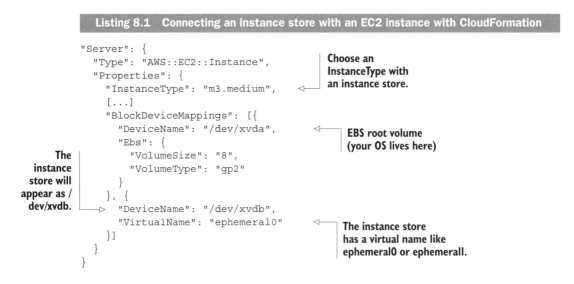

Listing 8.1   Connecting an instance store with an EC2 instance with CloudFormation

```
"Server": {
  "Type": "AWS::EC2::Instance",         Choose an
  "Properties": {                        InstanceType with
    "InstanceType": "m3.medium",         an instance store.
    [...]
    "BlockDeviceMappings": [{
      "DeviceName": "/dev/xvda",          EBS root volume
      "Ebs": {                            (your OS lives here)
        "VolumeSize": "8",
        "VolumeType": "gp2"
      }
    }, {
      "DeviceName": "/dev/xvdb",
      "VirtualName": "ephemeral0"          The instance store
    }]                                     has a virtual name like
  }                                        ephemeral0 or ephemeral1.
}
```

The instance store will appear as /dev/xvdb.

> **Windows-based EC2 instances**
>
> The same `BlockDeviceMappings` applies to Windows-based EC2 instances. `Device-Name` isn't the same as the drive letter (C:/, D:/, and so on). To go from `DeviceName` to the drive letter, the volume must be mounted. The instance store volume from listing 8.1 will be mounted to Z:/. Read on to see how mounting works on Linux.

> **Cleaning up**
>
> Delete your manually started EC2 instance after you finish this section to clean up all used resources. Otherwise you'll likely be charged for the resources you use.

8.2.1   *Using an instance store*

To help you explore instance stores, we created the CloudFormation template located at https://s3.amazonaws.com/awsinaction/chapter8/instance_store.json.

> **WARNING** Starting a virtual server with instance type m3.medium will incur charges. See http://aws.amazon.com/ec2/pricing to find out the current hourly price.

Create a stack based on that template, copy the PublicName output, and connect via SSH. You can see the attached instance store volumes with the help of fdisk. Usually, instance stores are found at /dev/xvdb to /dev/xvde:

```
$ sudo fdisk -l
Disk /dev/xvda: 8589 MB [...]          ◁────┐ Root volume (your
Units = Sektoren of 1 * 512 = 512 bytes     │ OS lives here)
Sector size (logical/physical): 512 bytes / 512 bytes
I/O size (minimum/optimal): 512 bytes / 512 bytes
Disk label type: gpt


#        Start        End    Size  Type            Name
  1       4096   16777182      8G  Linux filesyste Linux
128       2048       4095      1M  BIOS boot parti BIOS Boot Partition

Disk /dev/xvdb: 4289 MB [...]          ◁──────── Instance store
Units = Sektoren of 1 * 512 = 512 bytes
Sector size (logical/physical): 512 bytes / 512 bytes
I/O size (minimum/optimal): 512 bytes / 512 bytes
```

To see the mounted volumes, use this command:

```
$ df -h
Filesystem   Size  Used Avail Use% Mounted on       ┐ Root volume (your
/dev/xvda1   7.8G  1.1G  6.6G  14% /          ◁──────┘ OS lives here)
devtmpfs     1.9G   60K  1.9G   1% /dev
tmpfs        1.9G     0  1.9G   0% /dev/shm
/dev/xvdb    3.9G  1.1G  2.7G  28% /media/ephemeral0  ◁─┐ The instance
                                                        │ store is mounted
                                                        │ automatically.
```

Your instance store is mounted automatically to /media/ephemeral0. If your EC2 instance has more than one instance store, ephemeral1, ephemeral2, and so on will be used. Now it's time to run some performance tests.

8.2.2 *Testing performance*

Let's take the same performance measurements to see the difference between the instance store and EBS volumes:

```
$ sudo dd if=/dev/zero of=/media/ephemeral0/tempfile bs=1M count=1024 \
conv=fdatasync,notrunc

1024+0 records in                                          ┐ 3 × write
1024+0 records out                                         │ performance
1073741824 bytes (1.1 GB) copied, 5.93311 s, 181 MB/s  ◁───┘ compared with EBS
```

```
$ echo 3 | sudo tee /proc/sys/vm/drop_caches
3

$ sudo dd if=/media/ephemeral0/tempfile of=/dev/null bs=1M count=1024
1024+0 records in
1024+0 records out
1073741824 bytes (1.1 GB) copied, 3.76702 s, 285 MB/s
```
⟵ **4 × read performance compared with EBS**

Keep in mind that performance can vary, depending on your actual workload. This example assumes a file size of 1 MB. If you're hosting websites, you'll most likely deal with lots of small files instead. But this performance measurement shows that the instance store is a normal hard disk and has performance characteristics like those of a normal hard disk.

> **Cleaning up**
>
> Delete your stack after you finish this section, to clean up all used resources. Otherwise you'll likely be charged for the resources you use.

8.2.3 *Backing up your data*

There is no built-in backup mechanism for instance store volumes. Based on what you learned in section 7.2, you can use a combination of cron and S3 to back up your data periodically:

```
$ aws s3 sync /path/to/data s3://$YourCompany-backup/serverdata
```

But if you need to back up data from an instance store, you should probably use more durable, block-level storage like EBS. An instance store is better used for ephemeral persistence requirements.

8.3 *Comparing block-level storage solutions*

Table 8.4 shows how S3, EBS, and instance stores differ. Use this table to decide what option is best for your use case. A rule of thumb: if your application supports S3, use S3; otherwise, choose EBS.

Table 8.4   S3 vs. block-level storage solutions in AWS

	S3	EBS	Instance store
Common use cases	Integrated into your application to store user uploads	Persistence for traditional databases or legacy applications that require block-level storage	Temporary persistence or high-performance storage for applications that handle replication internally to protect against data loss
Independent resource	Yes	Yes	No

Table 8.4   S3 vs. block-level storage solutions in AWS *(continued)*

	S3	EBS	Instance store
How it can be accessed	HTTPS API	EC2 instance / system calls	EC2 instance / system calls
Has a file system?	No	Yes	Yes
Protection against data loss	Very high	High	Low
Cost per GB stored	$$	$$$	$
Effort to maintain	None	Little	Medium

Next, you'll look at a real-world example using instance store and EBS volumes.

8.4   Hosting a shared file system backed by an instance store and EBS

There is an important problem that you can't solve with AWS block-level storage solutions: sharing block-level storage between multiple EC2 instances at the same time. You can solve this problem with the help of the Network File System (NFS) protocol.

> **Amazon Elastic File System is coming**
>
> AWS is working on a service called Amazon Elastic File System (EFS). EFS is a distributed file system service based on the Network File System version 4 (NFSv4) protocol. As soon as EFS is available, you should choose it if you need to share block-level storage between multiple servers. Find out if EFS is available in the meantime by visiting http://aws.amazon.com/efs.

Figure 8.4 shows how one EC2 instance acts as a NFS server and exports a share via NFS. Other EC2 instances (NFS clients) then mount the NFS share from the NFS server via a network connection. To enhance performance in terms of latency, an instance store is used on the NFS server. But you already learned that an instance store isn't very durable, so you must take care of that. An EBS volume is attached to the NFS server, and data is synchronized at a regular interval. The worst-case scenario would be if all data modified since the last sync was lost. In some scenarios (such as sharing PHP files between web servers), this data loss is acceptable because the files can be uploaded again.

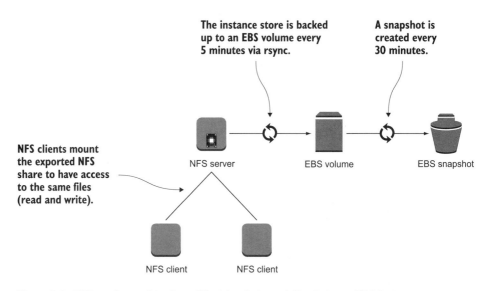

Figure 8.4   NFS can be used to share (block-level storage) files between EC2 instances.

NFS setup is a single point of failure

The NFS setup is most likely not what you want to run in mission-critical production environments. The NFS server is a single point of failure: if the EC2 instance fails, no NFS clients can access the shared files. Think twice about whether you want a shared file system. In most cases, S3 is a good alternative that can be used with a few changes to the application. If you really need a shared file system, consider Amazon EFS (when it's released) or set up GlusterFS.

You'll now create a CloudFormation template and Bash scripts to turn this system diagram into reality. Step by step you'll do the following:

1 Add security groups to create a secure NFS setup.
2 Add the NFS server EC2 instance and the EBS volume.
3 Create the installation and configuration script for the NFS server.
4 Add the NFS client EC2 instances.

Let's get started.

8.4.1 Security groups for NFS

Who talks to whom? That's the question determining how security groups must be designed. To make things easier (you won't use a bastion host here), SSH access should be allowed from the public internet (0.0.0.0/0) on all EC2 instances. The NFS server also must be reachable on the needed ports for NFS (TCP and UDP: 111, 2049), but only clients should have access to the NFS ports.

Listing 8.2   Security groups for NFS

Security group associated with NFS clients. This group contains no rules: it only marks traffic from clients.

```
"SecurityGroupClient": {
  "Type": "AWS::EC2::SecurityGroup",
  "Properties": {
    "GroupDescription": "My client security group",
    "VpcId": {"Ref": "VPC"}
  }
},
"SecurityGroupServer": {
  "Type": "AWS::EC2::SecurityGroup",
  "Properties": {
    "GroupDescription": "My server security group",
    "VpcId": {"Ref": "VPC"},
    "SecurityGroupIngress": [{
      "SourceSecurityGroupId": {"Ref": "SecurityGroupClient"},
      "IpProtocol": "tcp",
      "FromPort": 111,
      "ToPort": 111
    }, {
      "SourceSecurityGroupId": {"Ref": "SecurityGroupClient"},
      "IpProtocol": "udp",
      "FromPort": 111,
      "ToPort": 111
    }, {
      "SourceSecurityGroupId": {"Ref": "SecurityGroupClient"},
      "IpProtocol": "tcp",
      "FromPort": 2049,
      "ToPort": 2049
    }, {
      "SourceSecurityGroupId": {"Ref": "SecurityGroupClient"},
      "IpProtocol": "udp",
      "FromPort": 2049,
      "ToPort": 2049
    }]
  }
},
"SecurityGroupCommon": {
  "Type": "AWS::EC2::SecurityGroup",
  "Properties": {
    "GroupDescription": "My security group",
    "VpcId": {"Ref": "VPC"},
    "SecurityGroupIngress": [{
      "CidrIp": "0.0.0.0/0",
      "FromPort": 22,
      "IpProtocol": "tcp",
      "ToPort": 22
    }]
  }
}
```

Security group associated with NFS server

Allows inbound Portmapper port III (TCP) from NFS clients (SecurityGroupClient as the source)

Allows port III (UDP) as well

Allows inbound nfsd port 2049 (TCP and UDP) from NFS clients

Common security group associated with the NFS server and clients

Allows inbound SSH from the public internet

The interesting part is that `SecurityGroupClient` contains no rules. It's only needed to mark traffic from NFS clients. `SecurityGroupServer` uses `SecurityGroupClient` as a source to allow traffic only from NFS clients.

8.4.2   NFS server and volume

The instance type of the NFS server must provide an instance store. You'll use m3.medium in this example because it's the cheapest instance store available, but it offers only 4 GB. If you need a larger size, you must choose another instance type. The server has two security groups attached: `SecurityGroupCommon` to allow SSH and `SecurityGroupServer` to allow NFS-related ports. The server must also install and configure NFS on startup, so you'll use a bash script; you'll create this script in the next section. Using a bash script makes things more readable—the `UserData` format is a bit annoying over time. To prevent data loss, you'll create an EBS volume as a backup for the instance store.

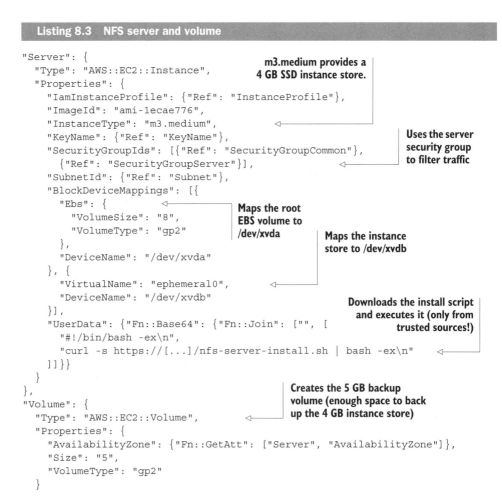

Listing 8.3   NFS server and volume

```
"Server": {
  "Type": "AWS::EC2::Instance",
  "Properties": {
    "IamInstanceProfile": {"Ref": "InstanceProfile"},
    "ImageId": "ami-1ecae776",
    "InstanceType": "m3.medium",              <—    m3.medium provides a
    "KeyName": {"Ref": "KeyName"},                  4 GB SSD instance store.
    "SecurityGroupIds": [{"Ref": "SecurityGroupCommon"},
      {"Ref": "SecurityGroupServer"}],        <—    Uses the server
    "SubnetId": {"Ref": "Subnet"},                  security group
    "BlockDeviceMappings": [{                       to filter traffic
      "Ebs": {                      <—    Maps the root
        "VolumeSize": "8",                EBS volume to
        "VolumeType": "gp2"               /dev/xvda      Maps the instance
      },                                                 store to /dev/xvdb
      "DeviceName": "/dev/xvda"
    }, {
      "VirtualName": "ephemeral0",    <—
      "DeviceName": "/dev/xvdb"               Downloads the install script
    }],                                       and executes it (only from
    "UserData": {"Fn::Base64": {"Fn::Join": ["", [      trusted sources!)
      "#!/bin/bash -ex\n",
      "curl -s https://[...]/nfs-server-install.sh | bash -ex\n"    <—
    ]]}}
  }
},
"Volume": {                         Creates the 5 GB backup
  "Type": "AWS::EC2::Volume",   <—  volume (enough space to back
  "Properties": {                   up the 4 GB instance store)
    "AvailabilityZone": {"Fn::GetAtt": ["Server", "AvailabilityZone"]},
    "Size": "5",
    "VolumeType": "gp2"
  }
```

```
  },
  "VolumeAttachment": {
    "Type": "AWS::EC2::VolumeAttachment",          ◁─────   Attaches the volume to
    "Properties": {                                           the server (to /dev/xvdf)
      "Device": "/dev/xvdf",
      "InstanceId": {"Ref": "Server"},
      "VolumeId": {"Ref": "Volume"}
    }
  }
}
```

You can now install and configure the NFS server with a bash script on startup.

8.4.3 *NFS server installation and configuration script*

To get NFS running, you need to install the relevant software packages with yum and configure and start them. To back up the instance store volumes at a regular interval, you also need to mount the EBS volume and run a cron job from time to time to copy the data to the EBS volume. Finally, you'll create an EBS snapshot from the EBS volume, as shown in the next listing.

Listing 8.4   NFS installation and configuration script

```
                    #!/bin/bash -ex                         Installs NFS packages

                    yum -y install nfs-utils nfs-utils-lib   ◁
 Starts          └─▷ service rpcbind start                                           Exports the
 rpcbind            service nfs start          ◁────── Starts the NFS daemon         instance store
 (an NFS       ┌──▷ chmod 777 /media/ephemeral0                                      volume via NFS
 dependency)       echo "/media/ephemeral0 *(rw,async)" >> /etc/exports   ◁────      to other NFS
               └─▷ exportfs -a                                                       clients
 Allows all
 users to read     while ! [ "$(fdisk -l | grep '/dev/xvdf' | wc -l)" -ge "1" ]; \  ◁────
 and write to      do sleep 10; done
 the instance                                                                      Waits until the EBS
 store volume                                                                      volume is available
                   if [[ "$(file -s /dev/xvdf)" != *"ext4"* ]]   ◁──────
 Reloads to          then
 apply export            mkfs -t ext4 /dev/xvdf                        Formats the EBS
 config changes    fi                                                  volume if not yet ext4
                                                                       (first server start)
 Mounts            mkdir /mnt/backup
 the EBS           echo "/dev/xvdf /mnt/backup ext4 defaults,nofail 0 2" >> /etc/fstab
 volume        └─▷ mount -a

                   INSTANCEID=$(curl -s http://169.254.169.254/latest/meta-data/instance-id)
                   VOLUMEID=$(aws --region us-east-1 ec2 describe-volumes \     ◁───────┐
                   --filters "Name=attachment.instance-id,Values=$INSTANCEID" \
                   --query "Volumes[0].VolumeId" --output text)
                                                                       Gets the EBS volume's ID
                   cat > /etc/cron.d/backup << EOF       ◁──────

                                        Copies all text in EOF to the
                                        cron job definition. /etc/dron.d/
                                        contains cron job definitions.
```

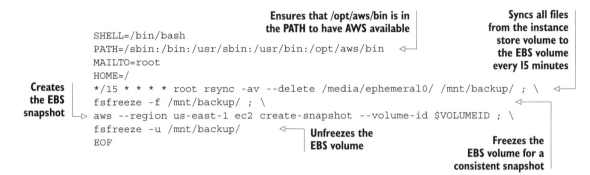

Ensures that /opt/aws/bin is in the PATH to have AWS available

Syncs all files from the instance store volume to the EBS volume every 15 minutes

Creates the EBS snapshot

Unfreezes the EBS volume

Freezes the EBS volume for a consistent snapshot

```
SHELL=/bin/bash
PATH=/sbin:/bin:/usr/sbin:/usr/bin:/opt/aws/bin
MAILTO=root
HOME=/
*/15 * * * * root rsync -av --delete /media/ephemeral0/ /mnt/backup/ ; \
fsfreeze -f /mnt/backup/ ; \
aws --region us-east-1 ec2 create-snapshot --volume-id $VOLUMEID ; \
fsfreeze -u /mnt/backup/
EOF
```

Because the script makes calls to the AWS API via the CLI, the EC2 instance needs permission to make those calls. This can be done with an IAM role, as shown in the next listing.

Listing 8.5 IAM role

```
"InstanceProfile": {
  "Type": "AWS::IAM::InstanceProfile",        Attaches the IAM
  "Properties": {                             profile to the
    "Path": "/",                              NFS server
    "Roles": [{"Ref": "Role"}]
  }
},
"Role": {
  "Type": "AWS::IAM::Role",        Defines the
  "Properties": {                  IAM role
    "AssumeRolePolicyDocument": {
      "Version": "2012-10-17",
      "Statement": [{
        "Effect": "Allow",
        "Principal": {
          "Service": ["ec2.amazonaws.com"]
        },
        "Action": ["sts:AssumeRole"]
      }]
    },
    "Path": "/",
    "Policies": [{
      "PolicyName": "ec2",
      "PolicyDocument": {
        "Version": "2012-10-17",
        "Statement": [{
          "Sid": "Stmt1425388787000",
          "Effect": "Allow",
          "Action": ["ec2:DescribeVolumes", "ec2:CreateSnapshot"],
          "Resource": ["*"]
        }]                                      Lets you describe
      }                                         volumes and
    }]                                          create snapshots
  }
}
```

> **rsync with lots of small files**
>
> If your use case requires many small files (more than 1 million), `rsync` will take a long time and consume many CPU cycles. You may want to consider DRBD to asynchronously sync the instance store to the EBS volume. The setup is slightly more complicated (at least, if you use Amazon Linux), but you get much better performance.

Only one thing is missing: clients. You'll add them next.

8.4.4 NFS clients

An NFS share can be mounted by multiple clients. For demonstration purposes, two clients will be enough: `Client1` and `Client2`. `Client2` is a copy of `Client1`.

Listing 8.6 NFC client

```
"Client1": {
  "Type": "AWS::EC2::Instance",
  "Properties": {
    "ImageId": "ami-1ecae776",
    "InstanceType": "t2.micro",
    "KeyName": {"Ref": "KeyName"},
    "SecurityGroupIds": [{"Ref": "SecurityGroupCommon"},        ←┐ Associates the
      {"Ref": "SecurityGroupClient"}],                            common and client
    "SubnetId": {"Ref": "Subnet"},                               security groups
    "UserData": {"Fn::Base64": {"Fn::Join": ["", [
      "#!/bin/bash -ex\n",
      "yum -y install nfs-utils nfs-utils-lib\n",              ←┐ NFS share
      "mkdir /mnt/nfs\n",                                        entry into
      "echo \"", {"Fn::GetAtt": ["Server", "PublicDnsName"]},    fstab
        ":/media/ephemeral0 /mnt/nfs nfs rw 0 0\" >> /etc/fstab\n",
      "mount -a\n"           ←┐ Mounts the
    ]]}}                        NFS share
  }
}
```

It's time to try sharing files via NFS.

8.4.5 Sharing files via NFS

To help you explore NFS, we've prepared a CloudFormation template located at https://s3.amazonaws.com/awsinaction/chapter8/nfs.json.

> **WARNING** Starting a virtual server with instance type m3.medium will incur charges. See http://aws.amazon.com/ec2/pricing/ if you want to find out the current hourly price.

Create a stack based on that template, copy the `Client1PublicName` output, and connect via SSH.

Place a file in /mnt/nfs/:

```
$ touch /mnt/nfs/test1
```

Now, connect to the second client via SSH by copying the `Client2PublicName` output from the stack. List all files in /mnt/nfs/:

```
$ ls /mnt/nfs/
test1
```

Voilà! You can share files between multiple EC2 instances.

Cleaning up

Delete your stack after you finish this section to clean up all used resources. Otherwise you'll be charged for the resources you use.

8.5   *Summary*

- Block-level storage can only be used in combination with an EC2 instance because the OS is needed to provide access to the block-level storage (including partitions, file systems, and read/write system calls).
- EBS volumes are connected to your EC2 instance via network. Depending on your instance type, this network connection can use more or less bandwidth.
- EBS snapshots are a powerful way to back up your EBS volumes to S3 because they use a block-level, incremental approach.
- An instance store is part of an EC2 instance, and it's fast and cheap. But all your data will be lost if the EC2 instance is stopped or terminated.
- You can use NFS to share files between EC2 instances.

Using a relational
database service: RDS

This chapter covers

- Launching and initializing relational databases with RDS
- Creating and restoring database snapshots
- Setting up a highly available database
- Tweaking database performance
- Monitoring a database

Relational databases are the de facto standard for storing and querying structured data, and many applications are built on top of a relational database system such as MySQL, Oracle Database, Microsoft SQL Server, or PostgreSQL. Typically, relational databases focus on data consistency and guarantee ACID database transactions (atomicity, consistency, isolation, and durability). Storing and querying structured data like the accounts and transactions in an accounting application is a typical task for a relational database.

225

If you want to use a relational database on AWS, you have two options:

- Use the managed relational database service *Amazon RDS*, which is offered by AWS.
- Operate a relational database yourself on top of virtual servers.

The Amazon Relational Database Service (Amazon RDS) offers ready-to-use relational databases. Under the hood, Amazon RDS operates a common relational database. As we write this book, MySQL, Oracle Database, Microsoft SQL Server, and PostgreSQL are supported. If your application supports one of these relational database systems, the migration to Amazon RDS is easy.

> **Amazon Aurora is coming**
>
> AWS is working on a database engine called Amazon Aurora. Aurora is MySQL compatible but offers better availability and performance at a lower cost. You can use Aurora to replace a MySQL setup. To find out if Aurora is available, visit https://aws.amazon.com/rds/aurora.

RDS is a managed service. A managed service is offered by a managed services provider—in the case of Amazon RDS, the managed service provider is AWS. The managed service provider is responsible for providing a defined set of services—in the case of Amazon RDS, for operating a relational database system. Table 9.1 compares using an RDS database and hosting a database on virtual servers yourself.

Table 9.1   Managed service RDS vs. a self-hosted database on virtual servers

	Amazon RDS	**Self-hosted on virtual servers**
Cost for AWS services	Higher because RDS costs more than virtual servers (EC2)	Lower because virtual servers (EC2) are cheaper than RDS
Total cost of ownership	Lower because operating costs are split among many customers	Much higher because you need your own manpower to manage your database
Quality	AWS professionals are responsible for the managed service.	You'll need to build a team of professionals and implement quality control yourself.
Flexibility	High, because you can choose a relational database system and most of the configuration parameters	Higher, because you can control every part of the relational database system you installed on virtual servers

You'd need considerable time and know-how to build a comparable relational database environment based on virtual servers, so we recommend using Amazon RDS for relational databases whenever possible to decrease operational costs and improve quality. That's why we won't cover hosting a relational database on virtual servers in this book. Instead, we'll introduce Amazon RDS in detail.

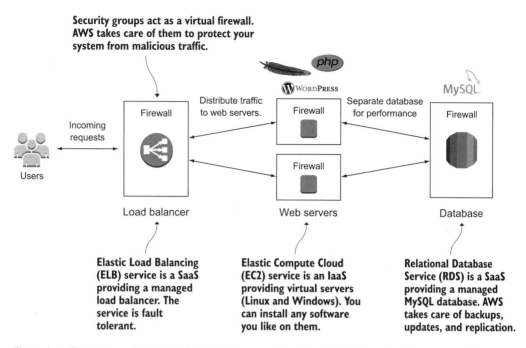

Figure 9.1 The company's blogging infrastructure consists of two load-balanced web servers running WordPress and a MySQL database server.

In this chapter, you'll launch a MySQL database with the help of Amazon RDS. Chapter 2 introduced a WordPress setup like the one shown in figure 9.1; you'll reuse this example in this chapter, focusing on the database part. After the MySQL database based on Amazon RDS is running, you'll learn how to import, back up, and restore data. More advanced topics like setting up a highly available database and improving the performance of the database will follow.

> **Examples are 100% covered by the Free Tier**
>
> The examples in this chapter are completely covered by the Free Tier. As long as you don't run the examples for longer than a few days, you won't pay anything. Keep in mind that this only applies if you created a fresh AWS account for this book and nothing else is going on in your AWS account. Try to complete the examples of the chapter within a few days; you'll clean up your account at the end of each example.

All the examples in this chapter use a MySQL database used by a WordPress application. You can easily transfer what you learn to other database engines such as Oracle Database, Microsoft SQL Server, and PostgreSQL, and to applications other than WordPress.

9.1   Starting a MySQL database

The popular blogging platform WordPress is built on top of a MySQL relational data-base. If you want to host a blog based on WordPress on your server, you'll need to run the PHP application—for example, with the help of an Apache web server—and you'll need to operate a MySQL database where WordPress stores the articles, comments, and authors. Amazon RDS offers a MySQL database as a managed service. You no longer need to install, configure, and operate a MySQL database yourself.

9.1.1   *Launching a WordPress platform with an Amazon RDS database*

Launching a database consists of two steps:

- Launching a database instance
- Connecting an application to the database endpoint

To set up a WordPress blogging platform with a MySQL database, you'll use the same CloudFormation template you used in chapter 2. You also used Amazon RDS there. The template can be found on GitHub and on S3. You can download a snapshot of the repository at https://github.com/AWSinAction/code/archive/master.zip. The file we talk about is located at chapter9/template.json. On S3, the same file is located at https://s3.amazonaws.com/awsinaction/chapter9/template.json.

Execute the following command to create a CloudFormation stack containing an RDS database instance with a MySQL engine and web servers serving the WordPress application:

```
$ aws cloudformation create-stack --stack-name wordpress --template-url \
https://s3.amazonaws.com/awsinaction/chapter9/template.json \
--parameters ParameterKey=KeyName,ParameterValue=mykey \
ParameterKey=AdminPassword,ParameterValue=test1234 \
ParameterKey=AdminEMail,ParameterValue=your@mail.com
```

It will take several minutes in the background until the CloudFormation stack is cre-ated, so you'll have enough time to learn the details of the RDS database instance while the template is launching. Listing 9.1 shows parts of the CloudFormation tem-plate used to create the wordpress stack.

Pitfall: media uploads and plugins

WordPress uses a MySQL database to store articles and users. But by default, Word-Press stores media uploads (such as images) and plugins in a folder called wp-content on the local file system. The server isn't stateless. You can't use multiple servers by default, because each request will be served by another server but media uploads and plugins are stored on only one of the servers.

The example in this chapter is incomplete because it doesn't handle this problem. If you're interested in a solution, see chapter 14, where plugins are installed automat-ically when you bootstrap virtual servers and media uploads are outsourced to an object store.

Table 9.2 shows the attributes needed when starting an RDS database with the help of CloudFormation or manually with the Management Console.

Table 9.2 Attributes needed to connect to an RDS database

Attribute	Description
AllocatedStorage	Storage size of your database in GB
DBInstanceClass	Size, also known as instance type, of the underlying virtual server
Engine	Database engine (MySQL, Oracle Database, Microsoft SQL Server, or PostgreSQL) you want to use
DBInstanceIdentifier	Identifier for the database instance
DBName	Identifier for the database
MasterUsername	Name for the master user
MasterUserPassword	Password for the master user

An RDS database can be deployed into a virtual private network (VPC). We recommend that you do so instead of deploying with a public reachable IP address to protect your data from the outside world. If you deploy your RDS instance into a VPC, you can use a private IP to communicate with the RDS instance. Thus you can't directly communicate with your database from the internet. If you want to deploy an RDS instance into your VPC, you need to specify the subnets for the database, as shown in the following listing.

Listing 9.1 Extract from the CloudFormation template setting up an RDS database

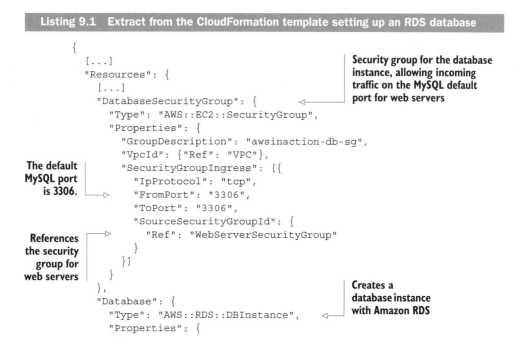

```
{
  [...]
  "Resources": {
    [...]
    "DatabaseSecurityGroup": {          ◁── Security group for the database
      "Type": "AWS::EC2::SecurityGroup",     instance, allowing incoming
      "Properties": {                        traffic on the MySQL default
        "GroupDescription": "awsinaction-db-sg",   port for web servers
        "VpcId": {"Ref": "VPC"},
        "SecurityGroupIngress": [{
          "IpProtocol": "tcp",
          "FromPort": "3306",           The default MySQL port is 3306.
          "ToPort": "3306",
          "SourceSecurityGroupId": {
            "Ref": "WebServerSecurityGroup"     References the security
          }                                     group for web servers
        }]
      }
    },
    "Database": {                       Creates a database instance
      "Type": "AWS::RDS::DBInstance",   ◁── with Amazon RDS
      "Properties": {
```

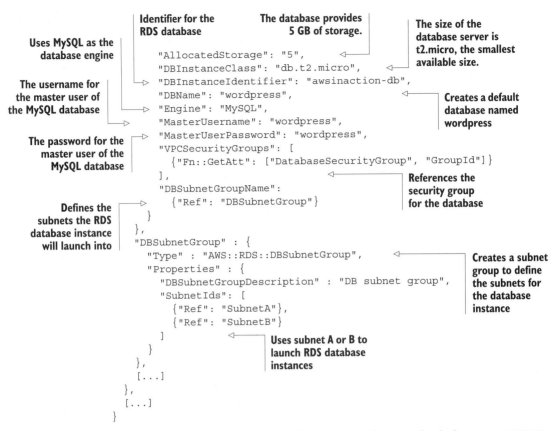

See if the CloudFormation stack named wordpress has reached the state CREATE
_COMPLETE with the following command:

```
$ aws cloudformation describe-stacks --stack-name wordpress
```

Search for *StackStatus* in the output, and check whether the status is CREATE_COMPLETE.
If not, you need to wait a few minutes longer (it can take up to 15 minutes to create the
stack) and re-run the command. If the status is CREATE_COMPLETE, you'll also find the
attribute OutputKey in the output section. The corresponding OutputValue contains
the URL for the WordPress blogging platform. The following listing shows the output in
detail. Open this URL in your browser; you'll find a running WordPress setup.

Listing 9.2 Checking the state of the CloudFormation stack

```
$ aws cloudformation describe-stacks --stack-name wordpress
{
  "Stacks": [{
    "StackId": "...",
    "Description": "AWS in Action: chapter 9",
    "Parameters": [{
      "ParameterValue": "mykey",
```

```
      "ParameterKey": "KeyName"
    }],
    "Tags": [],
    "Outputs": [{
      "Description": "Wordpress URL",          Open this URL in your
      "OutputKey": "URL",                      browser to open the
      "OutputValue": "http://[...].com/wordpress"  ◁─┘ WordPress application.
    }],
    "StackStatusReason": "",
    "CreationTime": "2015-05-16T06:30:40.515Z",
    "StackName": "wordpress",                  Wait for state
    "NotificationARNs": [],                     CREATE_COMPLETE for
    "StackStatus": "CREATE_COMPLETE",       ◁──  the CloudFormation stack.
    "DisableRollback": false
  }]
}
```

Launching and operating a relational database like MySQL is that simple. Of course, you can also use the Management Console to launch an RDS database instance instead of using a CloudFormation template. RDS is a managed service, and AWS handles most of the tasks necessary to operate your database in a secure and reliable way. You only need to do a few things:

- Monitor the available storage of your database and make sure you increase the allocated storage as needed.
- Monitor the performance of your database and make sure you increase I/O and computing performance as needed.

Both tasks can be handled with the help of CloudWatch monitoring, as you'll learn later in the chapter.

9.1.2 Exploring an RDS database instance with a MySQL engine

The CloudFormation stack created an RDS database instance with a MySQL engine. Each RDS database instance offers an endpoint for SQL requests. Applications can send their requests to this endpoint to query or store data. The endpoint and detailed information of an RDS database instance can be requested with a `describe` command:

```
$ aws rds describe-db-instances
```

The output of this request contains detailed information about the RDS database instance, as shown in listing 9.2. The most important attributes that are needed to connect to an RDS database are described in table 9.3.

Table 9.3   Attributes needed to connect to an RDS database

Attribute	Description
Endpoint	Host name and port of the database endpoint needed to connect your applications to the database. This interface receives SQL commands.
DBName	Name of the default database that's automatically created at launch.

Table 9.3   Attributes needed to connect to an RDS database *(continued)*

Attribute	Description
MasterUsername	Name of the master user for the database. The password isn't shown again; you have to remember it or look it up in the CloudFormation template. The master user can create additional database users. The handling depends on the underlying database.
Engine	Describes the relational database system offered by this RDS instance. This is MySQL in the example.

There are many other attributes. You'll learn more about most of them in this chapter. The following listing describes a MySQL relational database instance.

Listing 9.3   Describing a MySQL RDS database instance

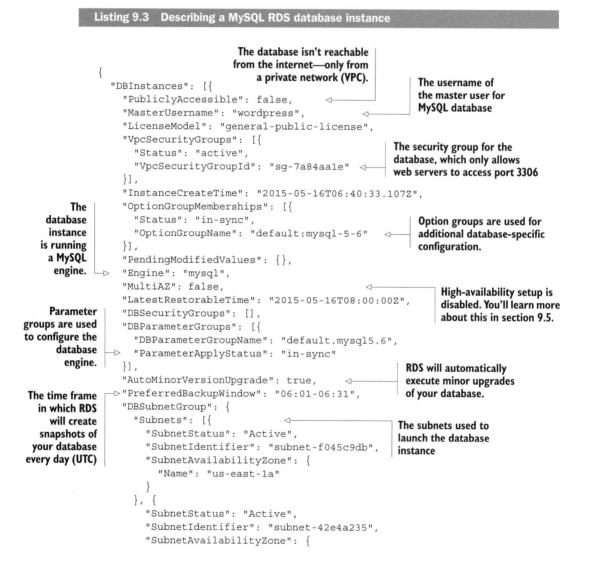

```
{
  "DBInstances": [{
    "PubliclyAccessible": false,            ◀── The database isn't reachable
                                                 from the internet—only from
                                                 a private network (VPC).
    "MasterUsername": "wordpress",          ◀── The username of
                                                 the master user for
                                                 MySQL database
    "LicenseModel": "general-public-license",
    "VpcSecurityGroups": [{
      "Status": "active",                       The security group for the
      "VpcSecurityGroupId": "sg-7a84aa1e"   ◀── database, which only allows
    }],                                         web servers to access port 3306
    "InstanceCreateTime": "2015-05-16T06:40:33.107Z",
    "OptionGroupMemberships": [{
      "Status": "in-sync",                      Option groups are used for
      "OptionGroupName": "default:mysql-5-6" ◀── additional database-specific
    }],                                         configuration.
    "PendingModifiedValues": {},
    "Engine": "mysql",                      ◀── The database instance is running a MySQL engine.
    "MultiAZ": false,                       ◀── High-availability setup is
    "LatestRestorableTime": "2015-05-16T08:00:00Z",  disabled. You'll learn more
    "DBSecurityGroups": [],                      about this in section 9.5.
    "DBParameterGroups": [{
      "DBParameterGroupName": "default.mysql5.6",   Parameter groups are used
      "ParameterApplyStatus": "in-sync"             to configure the database engine.
    }],
    "AutoMinorVersionUpgrade": true,        ◀── RDS will automatically
                                                execute minor upgrades
    "PreferredBackupWindow": "06:01-06:31",     of your database.
    "DBSubnetGroup": {
      "Subnets": [{                         ◀── The subnets used to
        "SubnetStatus": "Active",               launch the database
        "SubnetIdentifier": "subnet-f045c9db",  instance
        "SubnetAvailabilityZone": {
          "Name": "us-east-1a"
        }
      }, {
        "SubnetStatus": "Active",
        "SubnetIdentifier": "subnet-42e4a235",
        "SubnetAvailabilityZone": {
```

The time frame in which RDS will create snapshots of your database every day (UTC)

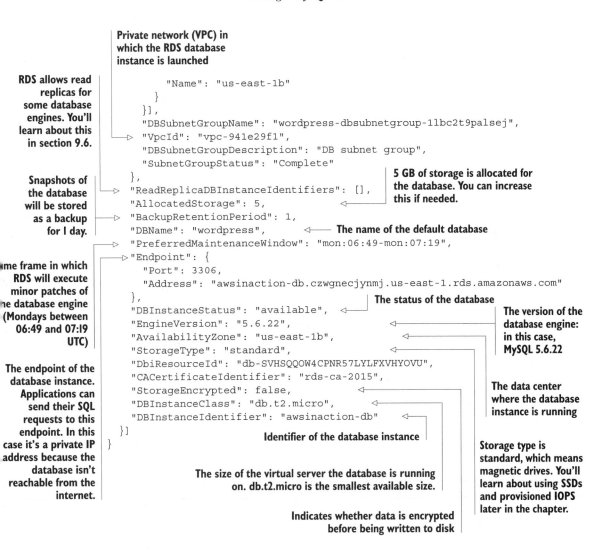

The RDS database is running, but what does it cost?

9.1.3 Pricing for Amazon RDS

A database on Amazon RDS is priced according to the size of the underlying virtual servers and the amount and type of allocated storage. Compared to a database running on a plain virtual server (EC2), you'll pay an extra charge of about 30%. In our opinion, the Amazon RDS service is worth the extra charge because you don't need to perform typical DBA tasks like installation, patching, upgrades, migration, backups, and recovery. Forester has analyzed that a DBA spends more than 50% of their time on these tasks.

Table 9.4 shows a pricing example for a medium-sized RDS database instance in the N. Virginia region without failover for high availability.

Table 9.4 Monthly cost for a medium-sized RDS instance

Description	Monthly price
Database instance db.m3.medium	$65.88 USD
50 GB of general purpose (SSD)	$5.75 USD
Additional storage for database snapshots (300 GB)	$28.50 USD
Total	$100.13 USD

You've launched an RDS database instance for use with a WordPress web application. You'll learn about importing data to the RDS database in the next section.

9.2   *Importing data into a database*

A database without data isn't useful. In many cases, you'll need to import data into a new database. If you move your on-premises environment to AWS, you'll need to transfer the database as well. This section will guide you through the process of importing a MySQL database dump to an RDS database with a MySQL engine. The process is similar for all other database engines (Oracle Database, Microsoft SQL Server, and PostgreSQL).

To import a database from your on-premises environment to Amazon RDS, follow these steps:

1 Export the on-premises database.
2 Start a virtual server in the same region and VPC as the RDS database.
3 Upload the database dump from export to the virtual server.
4 Run an import of the database dump to the RDS database on the virtual server.

We'll skip the first step of exporting a MySQL database. The following sidebar gives you some hints if you want to export an existing MySQL database.

Exporting a MySQL database

MySQL, and every other database system, offer a way to export and import databases. We recommend the command-line tools from MySQL for exporting and importing databases. You may need to install the MySQL client on your machine remove, as it includes these tools.

The following command exports all databases from localhost and dumps them into a file called dump.sql. Replace $UserName with the MySQL admin or master user, and enter the password when prompted:

```
$ mysqldump -u $UserName -p --all-databases > dump.sql
```

You can also specify only some databases for the export. To do so, replace $DatabaseName with the name of the database you want to export:

```
$ mysqldump -u $UserName -p $DatabaseName > dump.sql
```

> **(continued)**
>
> And of course you can export a database over a network connection. To connect to a database server to export a database, replace `$Host` with the host name or IP address of your database:
>
> ```
> $ mysqldump -u $UserName -p $DatabaseName --host $Host > dump.sql
> ```
>
> See the MySQL documentation if you need more information about the `mysqldump` tool.

Theoretically, you could import a database to RDS from any machine in your on-premises or local network. But the higher latency over the internet or VPN connection will slow down the import process dramatically. Because of this, we recommend adding a second step: upload the database dump to a virtual server running in the same region and VPC, and start to import the database to RDS from there.

To do so, we'll guide you through the following steps:

1 Get the public IP address of the virtual server running the WordPress application with a connection to the RDS database.
2 Connect to the virtual server via SSH.
3 Download the database dump from S3 to the virtual server.
4 Run an import of the database dump to the RDS database from the virtual server.

Fortunately, you already started two virtual servers that can connect to the MySQL database on RDS because they're serving the WordPress application. To find out the public IP address of one of these two virtual servers, run the following command on your local machine:

```
$ aws ec2 describe-instances --filters Name=tag-key,\
Values=aws:cloudformation:stack-name Name=tag-value,\
Values=wordpress --output text \
--query Reservations[0].Instances[0].PublicIpAddress
```

Open an SSH connection to the virtual server with the public IP address from the previous command. Use the SSH key mykey to authenticate, and replace `$PublicIpAddress` with the IP address of the virtual server running the WordPress application:

```
$ ssh -i $PathToKey/mykey.pem ec2-user@$PublicIpAddress
```

We prepared a MySQL database dump of a WordPress blog as an example. Download this database dump from S3 with the following command on the virtual server:

```
$ wget https://s3.amazonaws.com/awsinaction/chapter9/wordpress-import.sql
```

Now you're ready to import the MySQL database dump containing the data of a WordPress blog to the RDS database instance. You'll need the port and hostname, also called the endpoint, of the MySQL database on RDS to do so. Don't remember the endpoint? The following command will print it out for you. Run this on your local machine:

```
$ aws rds describe-db-instances --query DBInstances[0].Endpoint
```

Run the following command on the virtual server to import the data from the file wordpress-import.sql into the RDS database instance; replace $DBHostName with the RDS endpoint you printed to the terminal with the previous command. Type in the password wordpress when asked for a password:

```
$ mysql --host $DBHostName --user wordpress -p < wordpress-import.sql
```

Point your browser to the WordPress blog again, and you'll find many new posts and comments there. If you don't remember the URL, run the following command on your local machine to fetch it again:

```
$ aws cloudformation describe-stacks --stack-name wordpress \
--query Stacks[0].Outputs[0].OutputValue --output text
```

9.3   *Backing up and restoring your database*

Amazon RDS is a managed service, but you still need backups of your database in case something or someone harms your data and you need to restore from a snapshot in time, or you need to duplicate a database in the same or another region. RDS offers manual and automated *snapshots* for point-in-time recovery of RDS database instances.

In this section, you'll learn how to use RDS snapshots:

- Configuring the retention period and time frame for automated snapshots
- Creating snapshots manually
- Restoring snapshots by starting new database instances based on a snapshot
- Copying a snapshot to another region for disaster recovery or relocation

9.3.1   *Configuring automated snapshots*

The RDS database of the WordPress blogging platform you started in section 9.1 will automatically create snapshots of your database. Automated snapshots are created once a day during a specified time frame. If no time frame is specified, RDS picks a random 30-minute time frame during the night. Automated snapshots are deleted after one day by default; you can change this retention period to a value between 1 and 35.

Creating a snapshot requires a brief freeze of all disk activity. Requests to the database may be delayed or even fail because of a timeout, so we recommend that you choose a time frame for the automated snapshot that has the least impact on applications and users.

The following command changes the time frame for automated backups to 05:00–06:00 UTC and the retention period to three days. Use the terminal on your local machine to execute it:

```
$ aws cloudformation update-stack --stack-name wordpress --template-url \
https://s3.amazonaws.com/awsinaction/chapter9/template-snapshot.json \
--parameters ParameterKey=KeyName,UsePreviousValue=true \
ParameterKey=AdminPassword,UsePreviousValue=true \
ParameterKey=AdminEMail,UsePreviousValue=true
```

The RDS database will be modified based on a slightly modified CloudFormation template, as shown in the following listing.

Listing 9.4 Modifying an RDS database's snapshot time frame and retention time

```
[...]
"Database": {
  "Type": "AWS::RDS::DBInstance",
  "Properties": {
    "AllocatedStorage": "5",
    "DBInstanceClass": "db.t2.micro",
    "DBInstanceIdentifier": "awsinaction-db",
    "DBName": "wordpress",
    "Engine": "MySQL",
    "MasterUsername": "wordpress",
    "MasterUserPassword": "wordpress",
    "VPCSecurityGroups": [
      {"Fn::GetAtt": ["DatabaseSecurityGroup", "GroupId"]}
    ],
    "DBSubnetGroupName": {"Ref": "DBSubnetGroup"},
    "BackupRetentionPeriod": 3,
    "PreferredBackupWindow": "05:00-06:00"
  }
}
[...]
```

Keep snapshots for three days. → "BackupRetentionPeriod": 3,

Create snapshots automatically between 05:00 and 06:00 UTC.

If you want to disable automated snapshots, you need to change the retention period to 0. As usual, you can configure automated backups with the help of CloudFormation templates, the Management Console, or SDKs.

9.3.2 Creating snapshots manually

Manual snapshots can be triggered in addition to automated snapshots whenever needed. The following command creates a manual snapshot called wordpress-manual-snapshot:

```
$ aws rds create-db-snapshot --db-snapshot-identifier \
wordpress-manual-snapshot \
--db-instance-identifier awsinaction-db
```

It will take a few minutes for the snapshot to be created. You can check the current state of the snapshot with the following command:

```
$ aws rds describe-db-snapshots \
--db-snapshot-identifier wordpress-manual-snapshot
```

RDS doesn't delete manual snapshots automatically; you need to delete them yourself if you don't need them any longer. You'll learn how to do this at the end of the section.

Copying an automated snapshot as a manual snapshot

There's a difference between automated and manual snapshots. Automated snapshots are deleted automatically after the retention period is over, but manual snapshots aren't. If you want to keep an automated snapshot even after the retention period is over, you have to copy the automated snapshot to a new manual snapshot.

Get the snapshot identifier of an automated snapshot from the RDS database of the WordPress blogging platform you started in section 9.1 by running the following command at your local terminal:

```
$ aws rds describe-db-snapshots --snapshot-type automated \
--db-instance-identifier awsinaction-db \
--query DBSnapshots[0].DBSnapshotIdentifier \
--output text
```

The following command copies an automated snapshot to a manual snapshot named `wordpress-copy-snapshot`. Replace `$SnapshotId` with the output from the previous command:

```
$ aws rds copy-db-snapshot --source-db-snapshot-identifier \
$SnapshotId --target-db-snapshot-identifier \
wordpress-copy-snapshot
```

The copy of the automated snapshot is named `wordpress-copy-snapshot`. It won't be removed automatically.

9.3.3   Restoring a database

If you restore a database from an automated or a manual snapshot, a new database is created based on the snapshot. As figure 9.2 shows, you can't restore a snapshot to an existing database.

As figure 9.3 illustrates, a new database is created to restore a database snapshot.

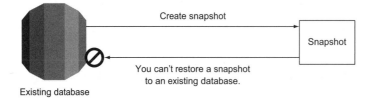

Existing database

Create snapshot

Snapshot

You can't restore a snapshot
to an existing database.

Figure 9.2   A snapshot can't be restored into an existing database.

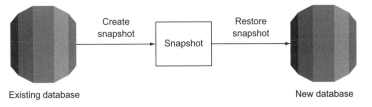

Existing database   New database

Figure 9.3 A new database is created to restore a snapshot.

Using a DNS CNAME to point to your database

Each RDS database instance gets a DNS name like awsinaction-db.czwgnecjynmj.us-east-1.rds.amazonaws.com. If you create a database instance from a snapshot, the new database instance will get a new name. If you hard-code the name into your application configuration, your application won't work because it doesn't use the new DNS name. To avoid this, you can create a DNS record like mydatabase.mycompany .com that points to the database's DNS name with a *CNAME*. If you need to restore your database, change the DNS record to point to the new name; your application will work again because the application uses mydatabase.mycompany.com to connect to the database. The DNS service in AWS is called Route 53.

To create a new database in the same VPC as the WordPress blogging platform you started in section 9.1, you need to find out the subnet group of the existing database. Execute the following command to do so:

```
$ aws cloudformation describe-stack-resource \
--stack-name wordpress --logical-resource-id DBSubnetGroup \
--query StackResourceDetail.PhysicalResourceId --output text
```

You're ready to create a new database based on the manual snapshot you created at the beginning of this section. Execute the following command after replacing $SubnetGroup with the output of the previous command:

```
$ aws rds restore-db-instance-from-db-snapshot \
--db-instance-identifier awsinaction-db-restore \
--db-snapshot-identifier wordpress-manual-snapshot \
--db-subnet-group-name $SubnetGroup
```

A new database named awsinaction-db-restore is created based on the manual snapshot. After the database is created, you can switch the WordPress application to the new endpoint.

   If you're using automated snapshots, you can also restore your database from a specified moment in time because RDS keeps the database's change logs. This allows you to jump back to any point in time from the backup retention period to the last five minutes.

Execute the following command after replacing $SubnetGroup with the output of the earlier describe-stack-resource command and replacing $Time with a UTC timestamp from five minutes ago (for example, 2015-05-23T12:55:00Z):

```
$ aws rds restore-db-instance-to-point-in-time \
--target-db-instance-identifier awsinaction-db-restore-time \
--source-db-instance-identifier awsinaction-db \
--restore-time $Time --db-subnet-group-name $SubnetGroup
```

A new database named awsinaction-db-restore-time is created based on the source database from five minutes ago. After the database is created, you can switch the WordPress application to the new endpoint.

9.3.4 Copying a database to another region

Copying a database to another region is easy with the help of snapshots. The main reasons for doing so are as follows:

- *Disaster recovery*—You can recover from an unlikely region-wide outage.
- *Relocating*—You can move your infrastructure to another region so you can serve your customers with lower latency.

You can easily copy a snapshot to another region. The following command copies the snapshot named wordpress-manual-snapshot from the region us-east-1 to the region eu-west-1. You need to replace $AccountId before you execute the command:

```
$ aws rds copy-db-snapshot --source-db-snapshot-identifier \
arn:aws:rds:us-east-1:$AccountId:snapshot:\
wordpress-manual-snapshot --target-db-snapshot-identifier \
wordpress-manual-snapshot --region eu-west-1
```

> **NOTE** Moving data from one region to another region may violate privacy laws or compliance rules, especially if the data crosses frontiers. Make sure you're allowed to copy the data to another region if you're working with real data.

If you can't remember your account ID, you can look it up with the help of the CLI:

```
$ aws iam get-user --query "User.Arn" --output text
arn:aws:iam::878533158213:user/mycli          ⟵——— Account ID has 12 digits (878533158213)
```

After the snapshot is copied to the region eu-west-1, you can restore a database from it as described in the previous section.

9.3.5 Calculating the cost of snapshots

Snapshots are billed based on the storage they use. You can store snapshots up to the size of your database instance for free. In the example setup for a WordPress blogging platform, you can store up to 5 GB of snapshots for free. On top of that, you pay per GB per month of used storage. As we're writing this book, the cost is $0.095 for each GB every month (region us-east-1).

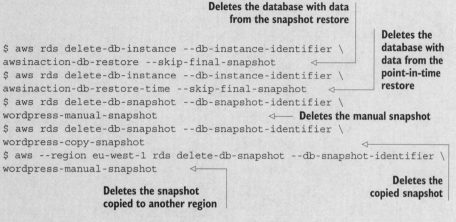

Cleaning up

It's time to clean up the snapshots and restore the databases. Execute the following commands step by step:

```
$ aws rds delete-db-instance --db-instance-identifier \
awsinaction-db-restore --skip-final-snapshot
$ aws rds delete-db-instance --db-instance-identifier \
awsinaction-db-restore-time --skip-final-snapshot
$ aws rds delete-db-snapshot --db-snapshot-identifier \
wordpress-manual-snapshot
$ aws rds delete-db-snapshot --db-snapshot-identifier \
wordpress-copy-snapshot
$ aws --region eu-west-1 rds delete-db-snapshot --db-snapshot-identifier \
wordpress-manual-snapshot
```

Deletes the database with data from the snapshot restore

Deletes the database with data from the point-in-time restore

◁— Deletes the manual snapshot

Deletes the copied snapshot

Deletes the snapshot copied to another region

Keep the rest of the setup, because you'll use it in the following sections.

9.4 Controlling access to a database

The shared-responsibility model applies to the RDS service, as well as to AWS services in general. AWS is responsible for security of the cloud in this case—for example, for the security of the underlying OS. You, the customer, need to specify the rules controlling access to the data and the RDS database.

Figure 9.4 shows the three layers that control access to an RDS database:

- Controlling access to the configuration of the RDS database
- Controlling network access to the RDS database
- Controlling data access with the help of the user and access management of the database itself

9.4.1 Controlling access to the configuration of an RDS database

Access to the RDS service is controlled with the help of the Identity and Access Management (IAM) service. The IAM service is responsible for controlling access to actions like creating, updating, and deleting an RDS database instance. IAM doesn't manage access inside the database; that's the job of the database engine (see section 9.4.3). An IAM policy defines the configuration and management actions a user or group is allowed to execute on the RDS service. Attaching the IAM policy to IAM users, groups, or roles controls which entity can use the policy to configure an RDS database.

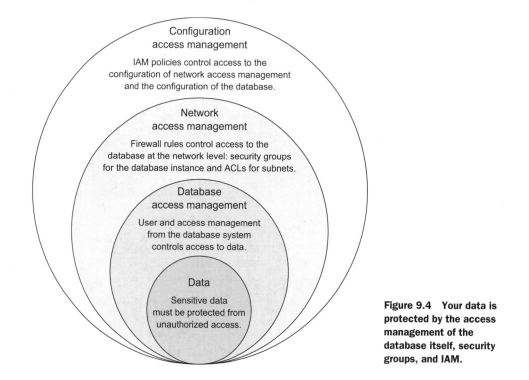

Figure 9.4 Your data is protected by the access management of the database itself, security groups, and IAM.

The following listing shows an IAM policy that allows access to all configuration and management actions of the RDS service. You could attach this policy to only certain IAM users and groups to limit access.

Listing 9.5 IAM policy allowing access to manage RDS

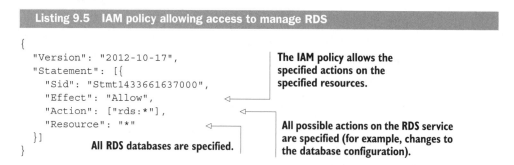

```
{
  "Version": "2012-10-17",
  "Statement": [{
    "Sid": "Stmt1433661637000",
    "Effect": "Allow",
    "Action": ["rds:*"],
    "Resource": "*"
  }]
}
```

The IAM policy allows the specified actions on the specified resources.

All possible actions on the RDS service are specified (for example, changes to the database configuration).

All RDS databases are specified.

Only people and machines that really need to make changes to RDS databases should be allowed to do so. See chapter 6 if you're interested in more details about the IAM service.

9.4.2 Controlling network access to an RDS database

An RDS database is linked to security groups. A security group consists of rules for a firewall controlling inbound and outbound database traffic. You already know about security groups in combination with virtual servers.

The next listing shows the configuration of the security group attached to the RDS database in the WordPress example. Inbound connections to port 3306, the default port for MySQL, are only allowed from virtual servers linked to the security group called `WebServerSecurityGroup`.

Listing 9.6 CloudFormation template extract: firewall rules for an RDS database

```
{
  [...]
  "Resources": {
    [...]
    "DatabaseSecurityGroup": {          ◁────┐  Security group for the
      "Type": "AWS::EC2::SecurityGroup",       database instance, allowing
      "Properties": {                          incoming traffic on the MySQL
        "GroupDescription": "awsinaction-db-sg",  default port for web servers
        "VpcId": {"Ref": "VPC"},
        "SecurityGroupIngress": [{
          "IpProtocol": "tcp",
          "FromPort": "3306",        ◁─── The default MySQL port is 3306.
          "ToPort": "3306",
          "SourceSecurityGroupId": {"Ref": "WebServerSecurityGroup"}   ◁──┐
        }]                                                                │
      }                                   References the security
    },                                    group for web servers │
    [...]
  },
  [...]
}
```

Only machines that really need to connect to the RDS database should be allowed to do so on the network level. See chapter 6 if you're interested in more details about firewall rules and security groups.

9.4.3 Controlling data access

A database engine implements access control. User management of the database engine has nothing to do with IAM users and access rights; it's only responsible for controlling access to the database. For example, you typically define a user for each application and grant rights to access and manipulate tables as needed.

Typical use cases are as follows:

- Limiting write access to a database to a few database users (for example, only for an application)

- Limiting access to specific tables to a few users (for example, to a department of the organization)
- Limiting access to tables to isolate different applications (for example, hosting multiple applications for different customers on the same database)

User and access management varies between database systems. We don't cover this topic in this book; refer to your database system's documentation for details.

9.5   *Relying on a highly available database*

A database is typically the most important part of a system. Applications won't work if they can't connect to the database, and the data stored in the database is mission-critical, so the database must be highly available and store data durably.

Amazon RDS lets you launch a highly available database. Compared to a default database consisting of a single database instance, a highly available RDS database consists of two database instances: a master and a standby database. You also pay for two instances if you run a highly available RDS database. All clients send requests to the master database. Data is replicated between the master and the standby database synchronously, as shown in figure 9.5.

If the master database becomes unavailable due to hardware or network failures, RDS starts the failover process. The standby database becomes the master database. As figure 9.6 shows, the DNS name is updated and clients begin to use the former standby database for their requests.

RDS detects the need for a failover automatically and executes it without human intervention. We highly recommend using high-availability deployment for all databases that handle production workloads.

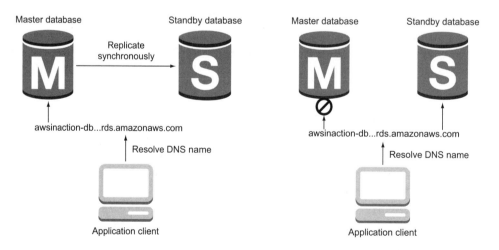

Figure 9.5   The master database is replicated to the standby database when running in high-availability mode.

Figure 9.6   The client fails over to the standby database if the master database fails, using DNS resolution.

9.5.1 *Enabling high-availability deployment for an RDS database*

Execute the following command at your local terminal to enable high-availability deployment for the RDS database of the WordPress blogging platform you started in section 9.1:

```
$ aws cloudformation update-stack --stack-name wordpress --template-url \
https://s3.amazonaws.com/awsinaction/chapter9/template-multiaz.json \
--parameters ParameterKey=KeyName,UsePreviousValue=true \
ParameterKey=AdminPassword,UsePreviousValue=true \
ParameterKey=AdminEMail,UsePreviousValue=true
```

> **WARNING** Starting a highly available RDS database will incur charges. See https://aws.amazon.com/rds/pricing/ if you want to find out the current hourly price.

The RDS database is updated based on a slightly modified CloudFormation template.

Listing 9.7 Modifying the RDS database by enabling high availability

```
[...]
"Database": {
  "Type": "AWS::RDS::DBInstance",
  "Properties": {
    "AllocatedStorage": "5",
    "DBInstanceClass": "db.t2.micro",
    "DBInstanceIdentifier": "awsinaction-db",
    "DBName": "wordpress",
    "Engine": "MySQL",
    "MasterUsername": "wordpress",
    "MasterUserPassword": "wordpress",
    "VPCSecurityGroups": [
      {"Fn::GetAtt": ["DatabaseSecurityGroup", "GroupId"]}
    ],
    "DBSubnetGroupName": {"Ref": "DBSubnetGroup"},
    "MultiAZ": true                          ⟵——————— Enables high-availability
  }                                                   deployment for the RDS
}                                                     database
[...]
```

It will take several minutes for the database to be deployed in high-availability mode. But there is nothing more you need to do—the database is now highly available.

> **What is Multi-AZ?**
>
> Each AWS region is split into multiple independent data centers, also called *availability zones*. We'll introduce the concept of availability zones in chapter 11. That's why we've skipped one aspect of high-availability deployment for RDS: the master and standby databases are launched into two different availability zones. AWS calls the high-availability deployment of RDS *Multi-AZ* deployment.

In addition to the fact that a high-availability deployment of an RDS database increases the reliability of your database, there's another important advantage. Reconfiguring or maintaining a single-mode database causes short downtimes. A high-availability deployment of an RDS database solves this problem because you can switch to the standby database during maintenance.

9.6   *Tweaking database performance*

An RDS database, or an SQL database in general, can only be scaled vertically. If the performance of your database becomes insufficient, you must increase the performance of the underlying hardware:

- Faster CPU
- More memory
- Faster I/O

In comparison, an object store like S3 or a NoSQL-database like DynamoDB can be scaled horizontally. You can increase performance by adding more nodes to the cluster.

9.6.1   *Increasing database resources*

When you start an RDS database, you choose an instance type. An instance type defines the computing power and memory of a virtual server (like when you start an EC2 instance). Choosing a bigger instance type increases computing power and memory for RDS databases.

You started an RDS database with instance type db.t2.micro, the smallest available instance type. You can change the instance type with the help of the CloudFormation template, the CLI, the Management Console, or AWS SDKs. The following listing shows how to change the CloudFormation template to increase the instance type from db.t2.micro with 1 virtual core and 615 MB memory to db.m3.large with 2 faster virtual cores and 7.5 GB memory. You'll do this only in theory—don't increase your running database.

Listing 9.8   Modifying the instance type to improve performance of an RDS database

```
{
  [...]
  "Resources": {
    [...]
    "Database": {
      "Type": "AWS::RDS::DBInstance",
      "Properties": {
        "AllocatedStorage": "5",
        "DBInstanceClass": "db.m3.large",        ◁─── Increases the size of the
        "DBInstanceIdentifier": "awsinaction-db",      underlying virtual server
        "DBName": "wordpress",                          for the database instance
        "Engine": "MySQL",                              from db.t2.micro to
        "MasterUsername": "wordpress",                  db.m3.large
```

```
        "MasterUserPassword": "wordpress",
        "VPCSecurityGroups": [
          {"Fn::GetAtt": ["DatabaseSecurityGroup", "GroupId"]}
        ],
        "DBSubnetGroupName": {"Ref": "DBSubnetGroup"}
      }
    },
    [...]
  },
  [...]
}
```

Because a database has to read and write data to a disk, I/O performance is important for the database's overall performance. RDS offers three different types of storage, as you already know from the block storage service EBS:

- General purpose (SSD)
- Provisioned IOPS (SSD)
- Magnetic

You should choose general purpose (SSD) or even provisioned IOPS (SSD) storage for production workloads. The options are exactly the same as for the block storage service EBS you can use for virtual servers. If you need to guarantee a high level of read or write throughput, you should use the provisioned IOPS (SSD) option. The general purpose (SSD) option offers moderate baseline performance with the ability to burst. The throughput for general purpose (SSD) depends on the initialized storage size. Magnetic storage is an option if you need to store data at a low cost or if you don't need to access it in a predictable, performant way. The next listing shows how to enable general purpose (SSD) storage with the help of a CloudFormation template.

Listing 9.9 Modifying the storage type to improve performance of an RDS database

```
{
  [...]
  "Resources": {
    [...]
    "Database": {
      "Type": "AWS::RDS::DBInstance",
      "Properties": {
        "AllocatedStorage": "5",
        "DBInstanceClass": "db.t2.micro",
        "DBInstanceIdentifier":  "awsinaction-db",
        "DBName": "wordpress",
        "Engine": "MySQL",
        "MasterUsername": "wordpress",
        "MasterUserPassword": "wordpress",
        "VPCSecurityGroups": [
          {"Fn::GetAtt": ["DatabaseSecurityGroup", "GroupId"]}
        ],
        "DBSubnetGroupName": {"Ref": "DBSubnetGroup"},
```

```
        "StorageType": "gp2"
      }
    },
    [...]
  },
  [...]
}
```

Uses general purpose (SSD) storage to increase I/O performance

9.6.2   *Using read replication to increase read performance*

SQL databases can also be scaled horizontally in special circumstances. A database suffering from many read requests can be scaled horizontally by adding additional database instances for read replication. As figure 9.7 shows, changes to the database are asynchronously replicated to an additional read-only database instance. The read requests can be distributed between the master database and its read-replication databases to increase read throughput.

Tweaking read performance with replication makes sense only if an application generates many read requests and few write requests. Fortunately, most applications read more than they write.

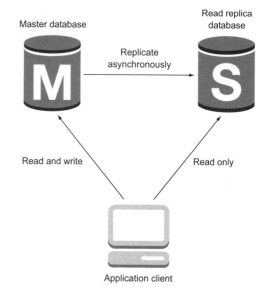

Figure 9.7   **Read requests are distributed between the master and read-replication databases for higher read performance.**

CREATING A READ-REPLICATION DATABASE

Amazon RDS supports read replication for MySQL and PostgreSQL databases. To use read replication, you need to enable automatic backups for your database, as shown in the last section of this chapter.

Execute the following command from your local machine to create a read-replication database for the database of the WordPress blogging platform you started in section 9.1:

```
$ aws rds create-db-instance-read-replica \
--db-instance-identifier awsinaction-db-read \
--source-db-instance-identifier awsinaction-db
```

RDS automatically triggers the following steps in the background:

1 Creating a snapshot from the source database, also called the master database
2 Launching a new database based on that snapshot
3 Activating replication between the master and read-replication databases
4 Creating an endpoint for SQL read requests to the read-replication database

After the read-replication database is successfully created, it's available to answer SQL read requests. The application using the SQL database must support the use of a read-replication database. WordPress, for example, doesn't support the use of a read replica by default, but you can use a plugin called HyperDB to do so; the configuration is a little tricky, so we'll skip this part. Creating or deleting a read replica doesn't affect the availability of the master database.

Using read replication to transfer data to another region

RDS supports read replication between regions for MySQL databases. You can replicate your data from the data centers in North Virginia to the data centers in Ireland, for example. There are three major use cases for this feature:

1 Backing up data to another region for the unlikely case of an outage of a complete region
2 Transferring data to another region to be able to answer read requests with lower latency
3 Migrating a database to another region

Creating read replication between two regions incurs an additional cost because you have to pay for the transferred data.

PROMOTING A READ REPLICA TO A STANDALONE DATABASE

If you create a read-replication database to migrate a database from one region to another, or if you have to perform heavy and load-intensive tasks on your database, such as adding an index, it's helpful to switch your workload from the master database to a read-replication database. The read replica must become the new master database. Promoting read-replication databases to become master databases is possible for MySQL and PostgreSQL databases with RDS.

The following command promotes the read-replication database you created in this section to a standalone master database. Note that the read-replication database will perform a restart and be unavailable for a few minutes:

```
$ aws rds promote-read-replica --db-instance-identifier awsinaction-db-read
```

The RDS database instance named awsinaction-db-read will accept write requests after the transformation from a read-replication database to a master database is successful.

Cleaning up

It's time to clean up to avoid unwanted expense. Execute the following command:

```
$ aws rds delete-db-instance --db-instance-identifier \
awsinaction-db-read --skip-final-snapshot
```

You've gained some experience with the AWS relational database service in this chapter. We'll end the chapter by having a closer look at the monitoring capabilities of RDS.

9.7   *Monitoring a database*

RDS is a managed service. Nevertheless, you need to monitor some metrics to make sure your database can respond to all requests from applications. RDS publishes several metrics to AWS CloudWatch, a monitoring service for the AWS cloud. You can watch these metrics through the Management Console, as shown in figure 9.8, and define alarms for when a metric reaches a threshold.

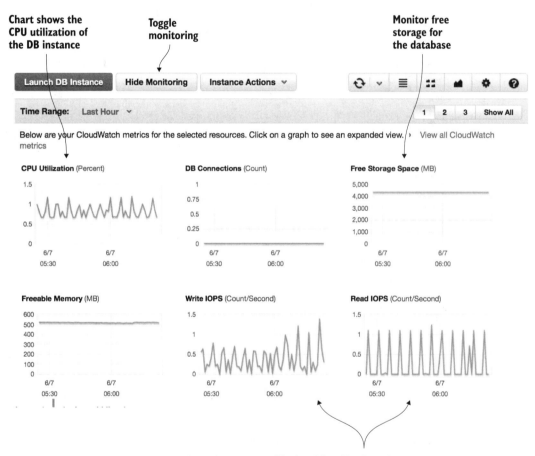

Figure 9.8   Metrics to monitor an RDS database from the Management Console

The following steps will guide you to the metrics of the RDS database you started for the WordPress blogging platform:

1 Open the Management Console at https://console.aws.amazon.com.
2 Select the CloudWatch service from the main navigation.
3 Choose RDS Metrics from the submenu at left.
4 Select a metric of your choice by selecting the check box in the table row.

There are up to 18 metrics per RDS database instance. Table 9.5 shows the most important ones; we recommend that you keep an eye on them by creating alarms.

Table 9.5   Important metrics for RDS databases from CloudWatch

Name	Description
FreeStorageSpace	Available storage in bytes. Make sure you don't run out of storage space.
CPUUtilization	The usage of the CPU as a percentage. High utilization can be an indicator of a bottleneck due to insufficient CPU performance.
FreeableMemory	Free memory in bytes. Running out of memory can cause performance problems.
DiskQueueDepth	Number of outstanding requests to the disk. A long queue indicates that the database has reached the storage's maximum I/O performance.

We recommend that you monitor these metrics in particular, to make sure your database isn't the cause of application performance problems.

> **Cleaning up**
> It's time to clean up, to avoid unwanted expense. Execute the following command to delete all resources corresponding to the WordPress blogging platform based on an RDS database:
>
> ```
> $ aws cloudformation delete-stack --stack-name wordpress
> ```

In this chapter, you've learned how to use the RDS service to manage relational databases for your applications. The next chapter will focus on a NoSQL database.

9.8   Summary

- RDS is a managed service providing relational databases.
- You can choose between MySQL, PostgreSQL, Microsoft SQL, and Oracle databases.
- The fastest way to import data into an RDS database is to copy it to a virtual server in the same region and pump it into the RDS database from there.

- You can control access to data with a combination of IAM policies and firewall rules, and on the database level.
- You can restore an RDS database to any time in the retention period (a maximum of 35 days).
- RDS databases can be highly available. You should launch RDS databases in Multi-AZ mode for production workloads.
- Read replication can improve the performance of read-intensive workloads on a SQL database.

Programming for the NoSQL database service: DynamoDB

This chapter covers

- The DynamoDB NoSQL database service
- Creating tables and secondary indexes
- Integrating DynamoDB into your service stack
- Designing a key-value optimized data model
- Tuning performance

Scaling a traditional, relational database is difficult because transactional guarantees (atomicity, consistency, isolation, and durability, also known as ACID) require communication among all nodes of the database. The more nodes you add, the slower your database becomes, because more nodes must coordinate transactions between each other. The way to tackle this has been to use databases that don't adhere to these guarantees. They're called NoSQL databases.

There are four types of NoSQL databases—document, graph, columnar, and key-value store—each with its own uses and applications. Amazon provides a NoSQL database service called DynamoDB. Unlike RDS, which effectively provides several common RDBMS engines like MySQL, Oracle Database, Microsoft SQL Server, and PostgreSQL, DynamoDB is a fully managed, proprietary, closed source key-value store. If you want to use a different type of NoSQL database—a document database like MongoDB, for example—you'll need to spin up an EC2 instance and install MongoDB directly on that. Use the instructions in chapters 3 and 4 to do so. DynamoDB is highly available and highly durable. You can scale from one item to billions and from one request per second to tens of thousands of requests per second.

This chapter looks in detail at how to use DynamoDB: both how to administer it like any other service and how to program your applications to use it. Administering DynamoDB is simple. You can create tables and secondary indexes, and there's only one option to tweak: its read and write capacity, which directly affects its cost and performance.

We'll look at the basics of DynamoDB and demonstrate them by walking through a simple to-do application called nodetodo, the Hello World of modern applications. Figure 10.1 shows the to-do application nodetodo in action.

Examples are 100% covered by the Free Tier

The examples in this chapter are totally covered by the Free Tier. As long as you don't run the examples longer than a few days, you won't pay anything for it. Keep in mind that this applies only if you created a fresh AWS account for this book and there are no other things going on in your AWS account. Try to complete the chapter within a few days, because you'll clean up your account at the end of the chapter.

```
●●●                         chapter10 — bash — 92×39
mwittig:chapter10 michael$ node index.js user-add michael michael@widdix.de +4971537507824
user added with uid michael
mwittig:chapter10 michael$ node index.js task-add michael "book flight to AWS re:Invent"
task added with tid 1433743784399
mwittig:chapter10 michael$ node index.js task-add michael "revise chapter 10"
task added with tid 1433743827724
mwittig:chapter10 michael$ node index.js task-ls michael
tasks [ { tid: '1433743784399',
    description: 'book flight to AWS re:Invent',
    created: '20150608',
    due: null,
    category: null,
    completed: null },
  { tid: '1433743827724',
    description: 'revise chapter 10',
    created: '20150608',
    due: null,
    category: null,
    completed: null } ]
mwittig:chapter10 michael$ node index.js task-done michael 1433743784399
task completed with tid 1433743784399
mwittig:chapter10 michael$ ▊
```

Figure 10.1 You can manage your tasks with the command-line to-do application nodetodo.

Before you get started with nodetodo, you need to know about DynamoDB 101.

10.1 Operating DynamoDB

DynamoDB doesn't require administration like a traditional relational database; instead, you have other tasks to take care of. Pricing depends mostly on your storage usage and performance requirements. This section also compares DynamoDB to RDS.

10.1.1 Administration

With DynamoDB, you don't need to worry about installation, updates, servers, storage, or backups:

- DynamoDB isn't software you can download. Instead, it's a NoSQL database as a service. Therefore, you really can't install DynamoDB like you install MySQL or MongoDB. This also means you don't have to update your database; the software is maintained by AWS.
- DynamoDB runs on a fleet of servers operated by AWS. They take care of the OS and all security-related questions. From a security perspective, it's your job to grant the right permissions in IAM to the users your of DynamoDB tables.
- DynamoDB replicates your data among multiple servers and across multiple data centers. There's no need for a backup from a durability point of view—the backup is already in the database.

Now you know some administrative tasks that are no longer necessary if you use DynamoDB. But you still have things to consider when using DynamoDB in production: creating tables (see section 10.4), creating secondary indexes (section 10.6), monitoring capacity usage, and provisioning read and write capacity (section 10.9).

10.1.2 Pricing

If you use DynamoDB, you pay the following monthly:

- $ 0.25 per used GB of storage (secondary indexes consume storage as well)
- $ 0.47 per provisioned write-capacity unit of throughput (throughput is explained in section 10.9)
- $ 0.09 per provisioned read-capacity unit of throughput

These prices are valid for the North Virginia (us-east-1) region. No additional traffic charges apply if you use AWS resources like EC2 servers to access DynamoDB in the same region

10.1.3 RDS comparison

Table 10.1 compares DynamoDB and RDS. Keep in mind that this is like comparing apples and oranges; the only thing DynamoDB and RDS have in common is that both are called databases.

Table 10.1   Differences between DynamoDB and RDS

Task	DynamoDB	RDS
Creating a table	Management Console, SDK, or CLI `aws dynamodb create-table`	SQL `CREATE TABLE` statement
Inserting, updating, or deleting data	SDK	SQL `INSERT`, `UPDATE`, or `DELETE` statement, respectively
Querying data	If you query the primary key: SDK. Querying non-key attributes isn't possible, but you can add a secondary index or scan the entire table.	SQL `SELECT` statement
Increasing storage	No action needed: DynamoDB grows with your items.	Provision more storage.
Increasing performance	Horizontal, by increasing capacity. DynamoDB will add more servers under the hood.	Vertical, by increasing instance size; or horizontal, by adding read replicas. There is an upper limit.
Installing the database on your machine	DynamoDB isn't available for download. You can only use it as a service.	Download MySQL, Oracle Database, Microsoft SQL Server, or PostgreSQL, and install it on your machine.
Hiring an expert	Search for special DynamoDB skills.	Search for general SQL skills or special skills, depending on the database engine.

10.2 DynamoDB for developers

DynamoDB is a key-value store that organizes your data in tables. Each table contains items (values) that are identified by keys. A table can also maintain secondary indexes for data look-up in addition to the primary key. In this section, you'll look at these basic building blocks of DynamoDB, ending with a brief comparison of NoSQL databases.

10.2.1 Tables, items, and attributes

A DynamoDB table has a name and organizes a collection of items. An *item* is a collection of attributes. An *attribute* is a name-value pair. The attribute value can be scalar (number, string, binary, boolean), multivalued (number set, string set, binary set), or a JSON document (object, array). Items in a table aren't required to have the same attributes; there is no enforced schema.

You can create a table with the Management Console, CloudFormation, SDKs, or the CLI. The following example shows how you create a table with the CLI (don't try to run this command now—you'll create a table later in the chapter):

**The attribute named
id is of type string.**

**Choose a name
for your table,
like app-entity.**

```
$ aws dynamodb create-table --table-name app-entity \
  --attribute-definitions AttributeName=id,AttributeType=S \
```

```
--key-schema AttributeName=id,KeyType=HASH \
--provisioned-throughput ReadCapacityUnits=5,WriteCapacityUnits=5
```

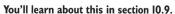

The primary key uses the id attribute.

You'll learn about this in section 10.9.

If you plan to run multiple applications that use DynamoDB, it's good practice to prefix your tables with the name of your application. You can also add tables via the Management Console. Keep in mind that you can't change the name of a table and the key schema. But you can add attribute definitions and change the provisioned throughput.

10.2.2 Primary keys

A primary key is unique within a table and identifies an item. You need the primary key to look up an item. The primary key is either a hash or a hash and a range. Hash keys

A hash key uses a single attribute of an item to create a hash index. If you want to look up an item based on its hash key, you need to know the exact hash key. A user table could use the user's email as a hash primary key. A user then can be retrieved if you know the hash key (email, in this case).

HASH AND RANGE KEYS

A hash and range key uses two attributes of an item to create a more powerful index. The first attribute is the hash part of the key, and the second part is the range. To look up an item, you need to know the exact hash part of the key, but you don't need to know the range part. The range part is sorted within the hash. This allows you to query the range part of the key from a certain starting point. A message table can use a hash and range as its primary key; the hash is the email of the user, and the range is a timestamp. You can now look up all messages of a user that are newer than a specific timestamp.

10.2.3 NoSQL comparison

Table 10.2 compares DynamoDB to several NoSQL databases. Keep in mind that all of these databases have pros and cons, and the table shows only a high-level comparison of how they can be used on top of AWS.

Table 10.2 Differences between DynamoDB and some NoSQL databases

Task	DynamoDB Key-value store	MongoDB Document store	Neo4j Graph store	Cassandra Columnar store	Riak KV Key-value store
Run the database on AWS in production.	One click: it's a managed service.	Cluster of EC2 instances, self-maintained.	Cluster of EC2 instances, self-maintained.	Cluster of EC2 instances, self-maintained.	Cluster of EC2 instances, self-maintained.
Increase available storage while running.	Not necessary. The database grows automatically.	Add more EC2 instances (replica set).	Not possible (the increasing size of EBS volumes requires downtime).	Add more EC2 instances.	Add more EC2 instances.

10.2.4 *DynamoDB Local*

Imagine a team of developers working on a new app using DynamoDB. During development, each developer needs an isolated database so as not to corrupt the other team members' data. They also want to write unit tests to make sure their app is working. You could create a unique set of DynamoDB tables with a CloudFormation stack per developer to separate them, or you could use a local DynamoDB. AWS provides a Java mockup of DynamoDB, which is available for download at http://mng.bz/27h5. Don't run it in production! It's only made for development purposes and provides the same functionality as DynamoDB, but it uses a different implementation: only the API is the same.

10.3   *Programming a to-do application*

To minimize the overhead of a programming language, you'll use Node.js/JavaScript to create a small to-do application that can be used via the terminal on your local machine. Let's call the application nodetodo. nodetodo will use DynamoDB as a database. With nodetodo, you can do the following:

- Create and delete users
- Create and delete tasks
- Mark tasks as done
- Get a list of all tasks with various filters

nodetodo supports multiple users and can track tasks with or without a due date. To help users deal with many tasks, a task can be assigned to a category. nodetodo is accessed via the terminal. Here's how you would use nodetodo via the terminal to add a user (don't try to run this command now—it's not yet implemented):

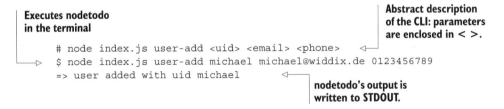

To add a new task, you would do the following (don't try to run this command now—it's not yet implemented):

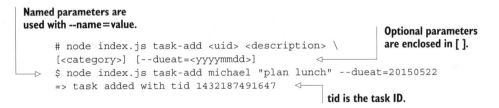

You would mark a task as finished as follows (don't try to run this command now—it's not yet implemented):

```
# node index.js task-done <uid> <tid>
$ node index.js task-done michael 1432187491647
=> task completed with tid 1432187491647
```

You should also be able to list tasks. Here's how you would use nodetodo to do that (don't try to run this command now—it's not yet implemented):

```
# node index.js task-ls <uid> [<category>] [--overdue|--due|...]
$ node index.js task-ls michael
=> tasks [...]
```

To implement an intuitive CLI, nodetodo uses docopt, a command-line interface description language, to describe the CLI interface. The supported commands are as follows:

- user-add—Adds a new user to nodetodo
- user-rm—Removes a user
- user-ls—Lists users
- user—Shows the details of a single user
- task-add—Adds a new task to nodetodo
- task-rm—Removes a task
- task-ls—Lists user tasks with various filters
- task-la—Lists tasks by category with various filters
- task-done—Marks a task as finished

In the rest of the chapter, you'll implement those commands. The following listing shows the full CLI description of all the commands, including parameters.

Listing 10.1 CLI description language docopt: using nodetodo (cli.txt)

```
nodetodo

Usage:
  nodetodo user-add <uid> <email> <phone>
  nodetodo user-rm <uid>
  nodetodo user-ls [--limit=<limit>] [--next=<id>]      <──┐  The named
                                                            │  parameters limit and
  nodetodo user <uid>                                       │  next are optional.
  nodetodo task-add <uid> <description> \
  [<category>] [--dueat=<yyyymmdd>]      <──┐  The category
  nodetodo task-rm <uid> <tid>               │  parameter is optional.
  nodetodo task-ls <uid> [<category>] \
  [--overdue|--due|--withoutdue|--futuredue]      <──┐
  nodetodo task-la <category> \                      │  Pipe indicates either/or.
  [--overdue|--due|--withoutdue|--futuredue]
  nodetodo task-done <uid> <tid>
  nodetodo -h | --help      <──┐  help prints information
                               │  about how to use nodetodo.
```

```
nodetodo --version              ←——— Version information

Options:
  -h --help        Show this screen.
  --version        Show version.
```

DynamoDB isn't comparable to a traditional relational database in which you create, read, update, or delete data with SQL. You'll access DynamoDB with an SDK to call the HTTP REST API. You must integrate DynamoDB into your application; you can't take an existing application that uses a SQL database and run it on DynamoDB. To use DynamoDB, you need to write code!

10.4   Creating tables

A table in DynamoDB organizes your data. You aren't required to define all the attributes that table items will have. DynamoDB doesn't need a static schema like a relational database, but you must define the attributes that are used as the primary key in your table. In other words, you must define the table's primary key. To do so, you'll use the AWS CLI. The `aws dynamodb create-table` command has four mandatory options:

- `table-name`—Name of the table (can't be changed).
- `attribute-definitions`—Name and type of attributes used as the primary key. A definition `AttributeName=attr1,AttributeType=S` can be repeated multiple times, separated by a space character. Valid types are `S` (String), `N` (Number), and `B` (Binary).
- `key-schema`—Name of attributes that are part of the primary key (can't be changed). Contains a single `AttributeName=attr1,KeyType=HASH` entry or two separated by spaces for the hash and range key. Valid types are `HASH` and `RANGE`.
- `provisioned-throughput`—Performance settings for this table defined as `ReadCapacityUnits=5,WriteCapacityUnits=5` (you'll learn about this in section 10.9).

You'll now create a table for the users of the nodetodo application and a table that will contain all the tasks.

10.4.1   Users with hash keys

Before you create a table for nodetodo users, you must think carefully about the table's name and primary key. We suggest that you prefix all your tables with the name of your application. In this case, the table name is `todo-user`. To choose a primary key, you have to think about the queries you'll make in the future and whether there is something unique about your data items. Users will have a unique ID, called `uid`, so it makes sense to choose the `uid` attribute as the primary key. You must also be able to look up users based on the `uid` to implement the `user` command. If you want a single attribute to be your primary key, you can always create a *hash index*: an unordered index based on the hash key. The following example shows a user table where uid is used as the primary hash key:

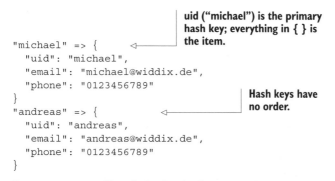

```
"michael" => {
  "uid": "michael",
  "email": "michael@widdix.de",
  "phone": "0123456789"
}
"andreas" => {
  "uid": "andreas",
  "email": "andreas@widdix.de",
  "phone": "0123456789"
}
```

uid ("michael") is the primary hash key; everything in { } is the item.

Hash keys have no order.

Because users will only be looked up based on the known uid, it's fine to use a hash key. Next you'll create the user table, structured like the previous example, with the help of the AWS CLI:

Items must at least have one attribute uid of type string.

Prefixing tables with the name of your application will prevent name clashes in the future.

```
$ aws dynamodb create-table --table-name todo-user \
--attribute-definitions AttributeName=uid,AttributeType=S \
--key-schema AttributeName=uid,KeyType=HASH \
--provisioned-throughput ReadCapacityUnits=5,WriteCapacityUnits=5
```

You'll learn about this in section 10.9.

The primary hash key uses the uid attribute.

Creating a table takes some time. Wait until the status changes to ACTIVE. You can check the status of a table as follows:

CLI command to check the table status

```
$ aws dynamodb describe-table --table-name todo-user
{
  "Table": {
    "AttributeDefinitions": [
      {
        "AttributeName": "uid",
        "AttributeType": "S"
      }
    ],
    "ProvisionedThroughput": {
      "NumberOfDecreasesToday": 0,
      "WriteCapacityUnits": 5,
      "ReadCapacityUnits": 5
    },
    "TableSizeBytes": 0,
    "TableName": "todo-user",
    "TableStatus": "ACTIVE",
    "KeySchema": [
```

Attributes defined for that table

Status of the table

Attributes used as the primary key

```
      {
        "KeyType": "HASH",
        "AttributeName": "uid"
      }
    ],
    "ItemCount": 0,
    "CreationDateTime": 1432146267.678
  }
}
```

10.4.2 *Tasks with hash and range keys*

Tasks always belong to a user, and all commands that are related to tasks include the user's ID. To implement the `task-ls` command, you need a way to query the tasks based on the user's ID. In addition to the hash key, you can use a hash and range key. Because all interactions with tasks require the user's ID, you can choose `uid` as the hash part and a task ID (`tid`), the timestamp of creation, as the range part of the key. Now you can make queries that include the user's ID and, if needed, the task's ID.

> **NOTE** This solution has one limitation: users can add only one task per timestamp. Our timestamp comes with millisecond resolution, so it should be fine. But you should take care to prevent strange things from happening when the user should be able to add two tasks at the same time.

A hash and range key uses two of your table attributes. For the hash part of the key, an unordered hash index is maintained; the range part is kept in a sorted range index. The combination of the hash and the range uniquely identifies the item. The following data set shows the combination of unsorted hash parts and sorted range parts:

```
                                      uid ("michael") is the hash portion
                                      and tid (I) is the range portion of
                                      the primary key.
["michael", 1] => {        ◁─────┘
  "uid": "michael",
  "tid": 1,
  "description": "prepare lunch"
}                                     The range is sorted
["michael", 2] => {        ◁─────┘   within a hash.
  "uid": "michael",
  "tid": 2,
  "description": "buy nice flowers for mum"
}
["michael", 3] => {
  "uid": "michael",
  "tid": 3,
  "description": "prepare talk for conference"
}
["andreas", 1] => {              ◁─────── There is no order in the hash.
  "uid": "andreas",
  "tid": 1,
  "description": "prepare customer presentation"
}
["andreas", 2] => {
```

```
    "uid": "andreas",
    "tid": 2,
    "description": "plan holidays"
}
```

nodetodo offers the ability to get all tasks for a user. If the tasks have only a primary hash key, this will be difficult, because you need to know the key to extract them from DynamoDB. Luckily, the hash and range key makes things easier, because you only need to know the hash portion of the key to extract the items. For the tasks, you'll use `uid` as the known hash portion. The range part is `tid`. The task ID is defined as the timestamp of task creation. You'll now create the task table, using two attributes to create a hash and range index:

At least two attributes are needed for a primary hash and range key.

```
$ aws dynamodb create-table --table-name todo-task \
--attribute-definitions AttributeName=uid,AttributeType=S \
 AttributeName=tid,AttributeType=N \
--key-schema AttributeName=uid,KeyType=HASH \
AttributeName=tid,KeyType=RANGE \
--provisioned-throughput ReadCapacityUnits=5,WriteCapacityUnits=5
```

The tid attribute is the range portion of the primary key.

Wait until the table status changes to `ACTIVE` when you run `aws dynamodb describe-table --table-name todo-task`. When both tables are ready, you'll add some data.

10.5 Adding data

You have two tables up and running. To use them, you need to add some data. You'll access DynamoDB via the Node.js SDK, so it's time to set up the SDK and some boilerplate code before you implement adding users and tasks.

> **Installing and getting started with Node.js**
>
> Node.js is a platform to execute JavaScript in an event-driven environment so you can easily build network applications. To install Node.js, visit https://nodejs.org and download the package that fits your OS.
>
> After Node.js is installed, you can verify if everything works by typing `node --version` into your terminal. Your terminal should respond with something similar to `v0.12.*`. Now you're ready to run JavaScript examples like nodetodo for AWS.

To get started with Node.js and docopt, you need some magic lines to load all the dependencies and do some configuration work. Listing 10.2 shows how this can be done.

> ### Where is the code located?
> As usual, you'll find the code in the book's code repository on GitHub: https://github.com/AWSinAction/code. nodetodo is located in /chapter10/.

Docopt is responsible for reading all the arguments passed to the process. It returns a JavaScript object, where the arguments are mapped to the described parameters in the CLI description.

Listing 10.2   nodetodo: using docopt in Node.js (index.js)

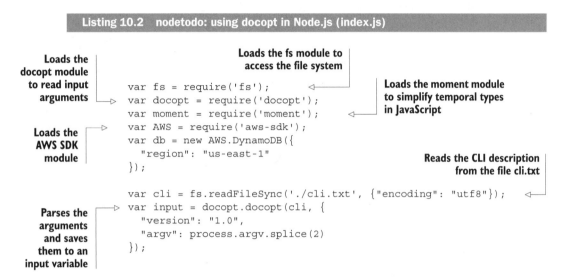

Loads the docopt module to read input arguments

Loads the fs module to access the file system

Loads the moment module to simplify temporal types in JavaScript

Loads the AWS SDK module

Reads the CLI description from the file cli.txt

Parses the arguments and saves them to an input variable

```
var fs = require('fs');
var docopt = require('docopt');
var moment = require('moment');
var AWS = require('aws-sdk');
var db = new AWS.DynamoDB({
  "region": "us-east-1"
});

var cli = fs.readFileSync('./cli.txt', {"encoding": "utf8"});
var input = docopt.docopt(cli, {
  "version": "1.0",
  "argv": process.argv.splice(2)
});
```

Next you'll implement the features of nodetodo. You can use the `putItem` SDK operation to add data to DynamoDB like this:

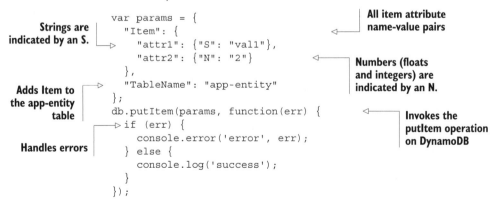

Strings are indicated by an S.

All item attribute name-value pairs

Numbers (floats and integers) are indicated by an N.

Adds Item to the app-entity table

Invokes the putItem operation on DynamoDB

Handles errors

```
var params = {
  "Item": {
    "attr1": {"S": "val1"},
    "attr2": {"N": "2"}
  },
  "TableName": "app-entity"
};
db.putItem(params, function(err) {
  if (err) {
    console.error('error', err);
  } else {
    console.log('success');
  }
});
```

The first step is to add data to nodetodo.

10.5.1 Adding a user

You can add a user to nodetodo by calling `nodetodo user-add <uid> <email> <phone>`. In Node.js, you do this using the code in the following listing.

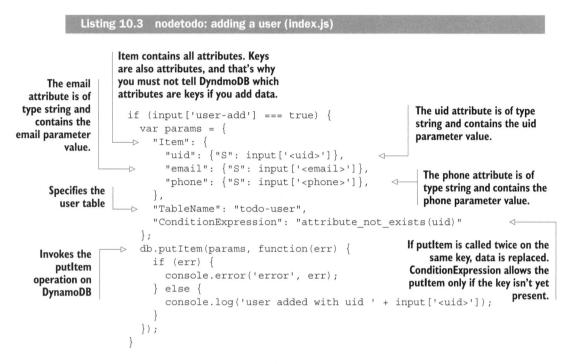

Listing 10.3   nodetodo: adding a user (index.js)

The email attribute is of type string and contains the email parameter value.

Item contains all attributes. Keys are also attributes, and that's why you must not tell DyndmoDB which attributes are keys if you add data.

Specifies the user table

Invokes the putItem operation on DynamoDB

The uid attribute is of type string and contains the uid parameter value.

The phone attribute is of type string and contains the phone parameter value.

If putItem is called twice on the same key, data is replaced. ConditionExpression allows the putItem only if the key isn't yet present.

```
if (input['user-add'] === true) {
  var params = {
    "Item": {
      "uid": {"S": input['<uid>']},
      "email": {"S": input['<email>']},
      "phone": {"S": input['<phone>']},
    },
    "TableName": "todo-user",
    "ConditionExpression": "attribute_not_exists(uid)"
  };
  db.putItem(params, function(err) {
    if (err) {
      console.error('error', err);
    } else {
      console.log('user added with uid ' + input['<uid>']);
    }
  });
}
```

When you make a call to the AWS API, you always do the following:

1 Create a JavaScript object (map) filled with the needed parameters (the `params` variable).
2 Invoke the function on the AWS SDK.
3 Check whether the response contains an error, or process the returned data.

Therefore you only need to change the content of `params` if you want to add a task instead of a user.

10.5.2 Adding a task

You can add a task to nodetodo by calling `nodetodo task-add <uid> <description> [<category>] [--dueat=<yyyymmdd>]`. In Node.js, you do this with the code shown in the following listing.

Listing 10.4   nodetodo: adding a task (index.js)

```
if (input['task-add'] === true) {
  var tid = Date.now();
  var params = {
```

Creates the task ID (tid) based on the current timestamp

The tid attribute is of type number and contains the tid value.

The created attribute is of type number (format 20150525).

Specifies the task table

If the optional named parameter dueat is set, add this value to the item.

If the optional named parameter category is set, add this value to the item.

Invokes the putItem operation on DynamoDB

```
"Item": {
  "uid": {"S": input['<uid>']},
  "tid": {"N": tid.toString()},
  "description": {"S": input['<description>']},
  "created": {"N": moment().format("YYYYMMDD")}
},
"TableName": "todo-task",
"ConditionExpression":
  "attribute_not_exists(uid) and attribute_not_exists(tid)"
};
if (input['--dueat'] !== null) {
  params.Item.due = {"N": input['--dueat']};
}
if (input['<category>'] !== null) {
  params.Item.category = {"S": input['<category>']};
}
db.putItem(params, function(err) {
  if (err) {
    console.error('error', err);
  } else {
    console.log('task added with tid ' + tid);
  }
});
}
```

Now you can add users and tasks to nodetodo. Wouldn't it be nice if you could retrieve all this data?

10.6   *Retrieving data*

DynamoDB is a key-value store. The key is usually the only way to retrieve data from such a store. When designing a data model for DynamoDB, you must be aware of that limitation when you create tables (you did so in section 10.4). If you can use only one key to look up data, you'll soon or later experience difficulties. Luckily, DynamoDB provides two other ways to look up items: a secondary index key lookup and the scan operation. You'll start by retrieving data with its primary key and continue with more sophisticated methods of data retrieval.

DynamoDB Streams

DynamoDB lets you retrieve changes to a table as soon as they're made. A *stream* provides all write (create, update, delete) operations to your table items. The order is consistent within a hash key:

- If your application polls the database for changes, DynamoDB Streams solves the problem in a more elegant way.
- If you want to populate a cache with the changes made to a table, DynamoDB Streams can help.
- If you want to replicate a DynamoDB table to another region, DynamoBD Streams can do it.

10.6.1 Getting by key

The simplest form of data retrieval is looking up a single item by its primary key. The getItem SDK operation to get a single item from DynamoDB can be used like this:

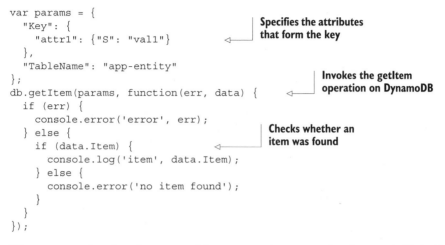

```
var params = {
  "Key": {
    "attr1": {"S": "val1"}                    Specifies the attributes
  },                                          that form the key
  "TableName": "app-entity"
};                                                  Invokes the getItem
db.getItem(params, function(err, data) {            operation on DynamoDB
  if (err) {
    console.error('error', err);
  } else {                                    Checks whether an
    if (data.Item) {                          item was found
      console.log('item', data.Item);
    } else {
      console.error('no item found');
    }
  }
});
```

The command nodetodo user <uid> must retrieve a user by the user's ID (uid). Translated to the Node.js AWS SDK, this looks like the following listing.

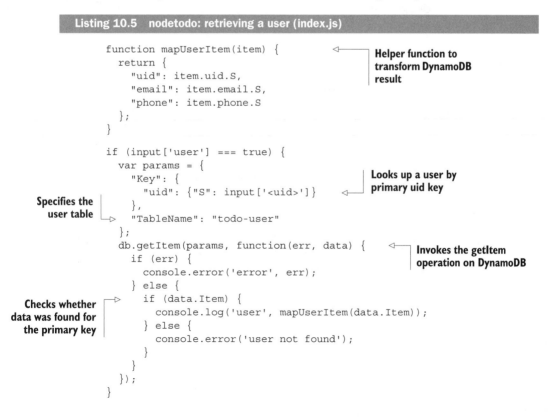

Listing 10.5   nodetodo: retrieving a user (index.js)

```
function mapUserItem(item) {                 Helper function to
  return {                                   transform DynamoDB
    "uid": item.uid.S,                       result
    "email": item.email.S,
    "phone": item.phone.S
  };
}

if (input['user'] === true) {
  var params = {
    "Key": {                                 Looks up a user by
      "uid": {"S": input['<uid>']}           primary uid key
    },
    "TableName": "todo-user"
  };                          Specifies the
                              user table
  db.getItem(params, function(err, data) {      Invokes the getItem
    if (err) {                                  operation on DynamoDB
      console.error('error', err);
    } else {
      if (data.Item) {
        console.log('user', mapUserItem(data.Item));
      } else {
        console.error('user not found');
      }
    }
  });
}
```

Specifies the user table

Checks whether data was found for the primary key

You can also use the `getItem` operation to retrieve data by primary hash and range key. The only change is that that `Key` has two entries instead of one. `getItem` returns one item or no items; if you want to get multiple items, you need to query DynamoDB.

10.6.2 Querying by key and filter

If you want to retrieve not a single item but a collection of items, you must query DynamoDB. Retrieving multiple items by primary key only works if your table has a hash and range key. Otherwise, the hash will only identify a single item. The `query` SDK operation to get a collection of items from DynamoDB can be used like this:

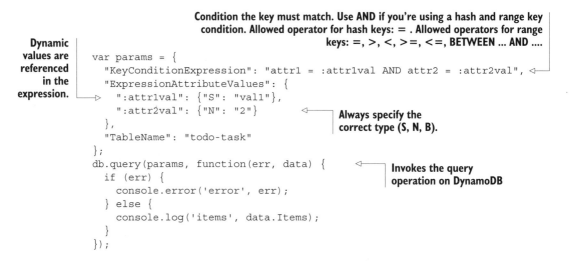

```
var params = {
  "KeyConditionExpression": "attr1 = :attr1val AND attr2 = :attr2val",
  "ExpressionAttributeValues": {
    ":attr1val": {"S": "val1"},
    ":attr2val": {"N": "2"}
  },
  "TableName": "todo-task"
};
db.query(params, function(err, data) {
  if (err) {
    console.error('error', err);
  } else {
    console.log('items', data.Items);
  }
});
```

Condition the key must match. Use AND if you're using a hash and range key condition. Allowed operator for hash keys: = . Allowed operators for range keys: =, >, <, >=, <=, BETWEEN ... AND ....

Dynamic values are referenced in the expression.

Always specify the correct type (S, N, B).

Invokes the query operation on DynamoDB

The `query` operations also lets you specify an optional `FilterExpression`. The syntax of `FilterExpression` works like `KeyConditionExpression`, but no index is used for filters. Filters are applied to all matches that `KeyConditionExpression` returns.

To list all tasks for a certain user, you must query DynamoDB. The primary key of a task is the combination of the `uid` hash part and the `tid` range part. To get all tasks for a user, `KeyConditionExpression` only requires the equality of the hash part of the primary key. The implementation of `nodetodo task-ls <uid> [<category>] [--overdue |--due|--withoutdue|--futuredue]` is shown next.

> **Listing 10.6   nodetodo: retrieving tasks (index.js)**

```
function getValue(attribute, type) {
  if (attribute === undefined) {
    return null;
  }
  return attribute[type];
}

function mapTaskItem(item) {
  return {
    "tid": item.tid.N,
```

Helper function to access optional attributes

Helper function to transform the DynamoDB result

```
      "description": item.description.S,
      "created": item.created.N,
      "due": getValue(item.due, 'N'),
      "category": getValue(item.category, 'S'),
      "completed": getValue(item.completed, 'N')
  };
}

if (input['task-ls'] === true) {
  var now = moment().format("YYYYMMDD");
  var params = {
    "KeyConditionExpression": "uid = :uid",
    "ExpressionAttributeValues": {
      ":uid": {"S": input['<uid>']}
    },
    "TableName": "todo-task"
  };
  if (input['--overdue'] === true) {
    params.FilterExpression = "due < :yyyymmdd";
    params.ExpressionAttributeValues[':yyyymmdd'] = {"N": now};
  } else if (input['--due'] === true) {
    params.FilterExpression = "due = :yyyymmdd";
    params.ExpressionAttributeValues[':yyyymmdd'] = {"N": now};
  } else if (input['--withoutdue'] === true) {
    params.FilterExpression = "attribute_not_exists(due)";
  } else if (input['--futuredue'] === true) {
    params.FilterExpression = "due > :yyyymmdd";
    params.ExpressionAttributeValues[':yyyymmdd'] = {"N": now};
  }
  if (input['<category>'] !== null) {
    if (params.FilterExpression === undefined) {
      params.FilterExpression = '';
    } else {
      params.FilterExpression += ' AND ';
    }
    params.FilterExpression += 'category = :category';
    params.ExpressionAttributeValues[':category'] = {"S": input['<category>']};
  }
  db.query(params, function(err, data) {
    if (err) {
      console.error('error', err);
    } else {
      console.log('tasks', data.Items.map(mapTaskItem));
    }
  });
}
```

Query attributes must be passed this way.

Primary key query. The task table uses a primary hash and range key. Only the hash is defined in the query, so all ranges are returned.

Filtering uses no index; it's applied over all elements returned from the primary key query.

Filter attributes must be passed this way.

Multiple filters can be combined with logical operators.

Attribute_not_exists(due) is true when the attribute is missing (opposite of attribute_exists).

Invokes the query operation on DynamoDB

Two problems arise with the query approach:

- Depending on the result size from the primary key query, filtering may be slow. Filters work without an index: every item must be inspected. Imagine you have stock prices in DynamoDB, with a primary hash and range key: the hash is AAPL, and the range is a timestamp. You can make a query to retrieve all stock prices of Apple (AAPL) between two timestamps (20100101 and 20150101). But if you only want to return prices on Mondays, you need to filter over all prices to return only 20% of them. That's wasting a lot of resources!

- You can only query the primary key. Returning a list of all tasks that belong to a certain category for all users isn't possible, because you can't query the `category` attribute.

You can solve those problems with secondary indexes. Let's look at how they work.

10.6.3   *Using secondary indexes for more flexible queries*

A *secondary index* is a projection of your original table that's automatically maintained by DynamoDB. You can query a secondary index like you query the index containing all the primary keys of a table. You can imagine a global secondary index as a read-only DynamoDB table that's automatically updated by DynamoDB: whenever you change the parent table, all indexes are asynchronously (eventually consistent!) updated as well. Figure 10.2 shows how a secondary index works.

A secondary index comes at a price: the index requires storage (the same cost as for the original table). You must provision additional write-capacity units for the index as well because a write to your table will cause a write to the secondary index.

A huge benefit of DynamoDB is that you can provision capacity based on your workload. If one of your table indexes gets tons of read traffic, you can increase the read capacity of that index. You can fine-tune your database performance by provisioning sufficient capacity for your tables and indexes. You'll learn more about that in section 10.9.

Back to nodetodo. To implement the retrieval of tasks by category, you'll add a secondary index to the `todo-task` table. This will allow you to make queries by category. A hash and range key is used: the hash is the `category` attribute, and the range is the

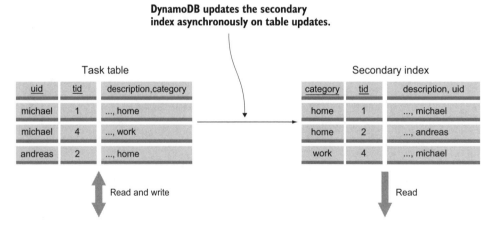

Figure 10.2   A secondary index contains a copy (projection) of your table's data to provide fast lookup on another key.

tid attribute. The index also needs a name: category-index. You can find the following CLI command in the README.md file in nodetodo's code folder:

Adds a category attribute because the attribute will be used in the index.

You can add a global secondary index after the table is created.

```
$ aws dynamodb update-table --table-name todo-task \
--attribute-definitions AttributeName=uid,AttributeType=S \
AttributeName=tid,AttributeType=N \
AttributeName=category,AttributeType=S \
--global-secondary-index-updates '[{\
"Create": {\
"IndexName": "category-index", \
"KeySchema": [{"AttributeName": "category", "KeyType": "HASH"}, \
{"AttributeName": "tid", "KeyType": "RANGE"}], \
"Projection": {"ProjectionType": "ALL"}, \
"ProvisionedThroughput": {"ReadCapacityUnits": 5, \
"WriteCapacityUnits": 5}\
}}]'
```

Creates a new secondary index

The category attribute is the hash portion of the key, and the tid attribute is the range portion.

All attributes are projected into the index.

A global secondary index takes some time to be created. You can use the CLI to find out if the index is active:

```
$ aws dynamodb describe-table --table-name=todo-task \
--query "Table.GlobalSecondaryIndexes"
```

The following listing shows how the implementation of nodetodo task-la <category> [--overdue|...] uses the query operation.

Listing 10.7 nodetodo: retrieving tasks from a category index (index.js)

```
if (input['task-la'] === true) {
  var now = moment().format("YYYYMMDD");
  var params = {
    "KeyConditionExpression": "category = :category",
    "ExpressionAttributeValues": {
      ":category": {"S": input['<category>']}
    },
    "TableName": "todo-task",
    "IndexName": "category-index"
  };
  if (input['--overdue'] === true) {
    params.FilterExpression = "due < :yyyymmdd";
    params.ExpressionAttributeValues[':yyyymmdd'] = {"N": now};
  }
  [...]
  db.query(params, function(err, data) {
    if (err) {
      console.error('error', err);
    } else {
      console.log('tasks', data.Items.map(mapTaskItem));
    }
  });
}
```

A query against an index works the same as a query against the primary key ...

... but you must specify the index you want to use.

Filtering works the same as with primary keys.

But there are still situations where a query doesn't work: you can't retrieve all users. Let's look at what a table scan can do for you.

10.6.4 Scanning and filtering all of your table's data

Sometime you can't work with keys; instead, you need to go through all the items in the table. That's not efficient, but in some situations, it's okay. DynamoDB provides the scan operation to scan all items in a table:

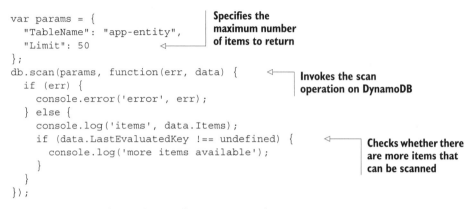

```
var params = {
  "TableName": "app-entity",
  "Limit": 50
};
db.scan(params, function(err, data) {
  if (err) {
    console.error('error', err);
  } else {
    console.log('items', data.Items);
    if (data.LastEvaluatedKey !== undefined) {
      console.log('more items available');
    }
  }
});
```

Specifies the maximum number of items to return

Invokes the scan operation on DynamoDB

Checks whether there are more items that can be scanned

The next listing shows the implementation of `nodetodo user-ls [--limit=<limit>] [--next=<id>]`. A paging mechanism is used to prevent too many items from being returned.

Listing 10.8 nodetodo: retrieving all users with paging (index.js)

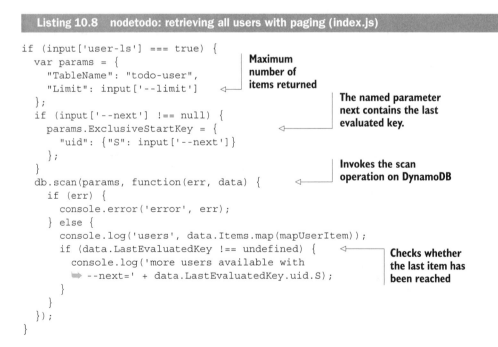

```
if (input['user-ls'] === true) {
  var params = {
    "TableName": "todo-user",
    "Limit": input['--limit']
  };
  if (input['--next'] !== null) {
    params.ExclusiveStartKey = {
      "uid": {"S": input['--next']}
    };
  }
  db.scan(params, function(err, data) {
    if (err) {
      console.error('error', err);
    } else {
      console.log('users', data.Items.map(mapUserItem));
      if (data.LastEvaluatedKey !== undefined) {
        console.log('more users available with
          ➥ --next=' + data.LastEvaluatedKey.uid.S);
      }
    }
  });
}
```

Maximum number of items returned

The named parameter next contains the last evaluated key.

Invokes the scan operation on DynamoDB

Checks whether the last item has been reached

The scan operation reads all items in the table. This example didn't filter any data, but you can use FilterExpression as well. Note that you shouldn't use the scan operation too often—it's flexible but not efficient.

10.6.5 *Eventually consistent data retrieval*

DynamoDB doesn't support transactions the same way a traditional database does. You can't modify (create, update, delete) multiple documents in a single transaction—the atomic unit in DynamoDB is a single item.

In addition, DynamoDB is eventually consistent. That means it's possible that if you create an item (version 1), update that item to version 2, and then get that item, you may see the old version 1; if you wait and get the item again, you'll see version 2. Figure 10.3 shows this process. The reason for this behavior is that the item is persisted on multiple servers in the background. Depending on which server answers your request, the server may not have the latest version of the item.

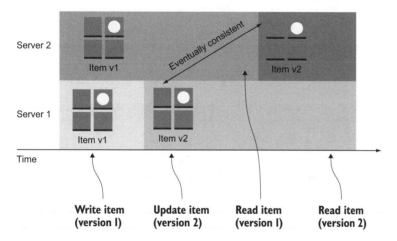

Figure 10.3 Eventually consistent reads can return old values after a write operation until the change is propagated to all servers.

You can prevent eventually consistent reads by adding "ConsistentRead": true to the DynamoDB request to get *strongly consistent reads*. Strongly consistent reads are supported by getItem, query, and scan operation. But a strongly consistent read takes longer and consumes more read capacity than an eventually consistent read. Reads from a global secondary index are always eventually consistent because the index itself is eventually consistent.

10.7 *Removing data*

Like the getItem operation, the deleteItem operation requires that you specify the primary key you want to delete. Depending on whether your table uses a hash or a hash and range key, you must specify one or two attributes.

You can remove a user with nodetodo by calling `nodetodo user-rm <uid>`. In Node.js, this is as shown in the following listing.

Listing 10.9   nodetodo: removing a user (index.js)

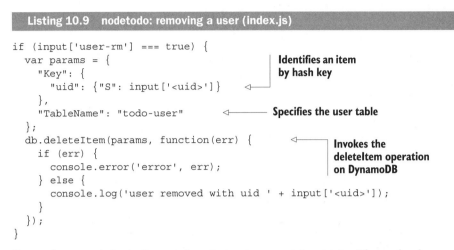

```
if (input['user-rm'] === true) {
  var params = {
    "Key": {                              Identifies an item
      "uid": {"S": input['<uid>']}        by hash key
    },
    "TableName": "todo-user"        Specifies the user table
  };
  db.deleteItem(params, function(err) {        Invokes the
    if (err) {                                 deleteItem operation
      console.error('error', err);             on DynamoDB
    } else {
      console.log('user removed with uid ' + input['<uid>']);
    }
  });
}
```

Removing a task is similar: `nodetodo task-rm <uid> <tid>`. The only change is that the item is identified by a hash and range key and the table name, as shown in the next listing.

Listing 10.10   nodetodo: removing a task (index.js)

```
if (input['task-rm'] === true) {
  var params = {
    "Key": {                                   Identifies an item by
      "uid": {"S": input['<uid>']},            hash and range key
      "tid": {"N": input['<tid>']}
    },
    "TableName": "todo-task"        Specifies the task table
  };
  db.deleteItem(params, function(err) {
    if (err) {
      console.error('error', err);
    } else {
      console.log('task removed with tid ' + input['<tid>']);
    }
  });
}
```

You're now able to create, read, and delete items in DynamoDB. The only operation missing is updating.

10.8   Modifying data

You can update an item with the `updateItem` operation. You must identify the item you want to update by its key; you can also provide an `UpdateExpression` to specify the updates you want to perform. You can use one or a combination of the following update actions:

- Use SET to override or create a new attribute. Examples: SET attr1 = :attr1val, SET attr1 = attr2 + :attr2val, SET attr1 = :attr1val, attr2 = :attr2val.
- Use REMOVE to remove an attribute. Examples: REMOVE attr1, REMOVE attr1, attr2.

In nodetodo, you can mark a task as done by calling nodetodo task-done <uid> <tid>. To implement this feature, you need to update the task item, as shown in Node.js in the following listing.

Listing 10.11   nodetodo: updating a task as done (index.js)

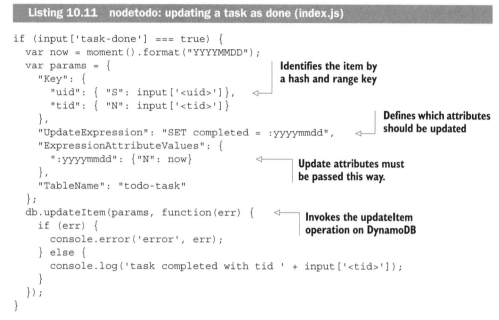

```
if (input['task-done'] === true) {
  var now = moment().format("YYYYMMDD");
  var params = {
    "Key": {                                      Identifies the item by
      "uid": { "S": input['<uid>']},              a hash and range key
      "tid": { "N": input['<tid>']}
    },                                                   Defines which attributes
    "UpdateExpression": "SET completed = :yyyymmdd",      should be updated
    "ExpressionAttributeValues": {
      ":yyyymmdd": {"N": now}                    Update attributes must
    },                                           be passed this way.
    "TableName": "todo-task"
  };
  db.updateItem(params, function(err) {       Invokes the updateItem
    if (err) {                                operation on DynamoDB
      console.error('error', err);
    } else {
      console.log('task completed with tid ' + input['<tid>']);
    }
  });
}
```

That's it! You've implemented all of nodetodo's features.

10.9   Scaling capacity

When you create a DynamoDB table or a global secondary index, you must provision throughput. Throughput is divided into read and write capacity. DynamoDB uses ReadCapacityUnits and WriteCapacityUnits to specify the throughput of a table or global secondary index. But how is a capacity unit defined? Let's start by doing some experimentation with the command-line interface:

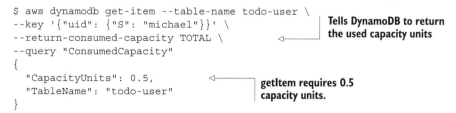

```
$ aws dynamodb get-item --table-name todo-user \
--key '{"uid": {"S": "michael"}}' \            Tells DynamoDB to return
--return-consumed-capacity TOTAL \             the used capacity units
--query "ConsumedCapacity"
{
  "CapacityUnits": 0.5,                getItem requires 0.5
  "TableName": "todo-user"             capacity units.
}
```

```
$ aws dynamodb get-item --table-name todo-user \
--key '{"uid": {"S": "michael"}}' \
--consistent-read --return-consumed-capacity TOTAL \      ⟵    A consistent read ...
--query "ConsumedCapacity"
{
    "CapacityUnits": 1.0,              ⟵ ─────────── ... needs twice as
    "TableName": "todo-user"                         many capacity units.
}
```

More abstract rules for throughput consumption are as follows:

- An eventually consistent read takes half the capacity compared to a strongly consistent read.
- A strongly consistent `getItem` requires one read capacity unit if the item isn't larger than 4 KB. If the item is larger than 4 KB, you need additional read capacity units. You can calculate the required read capacity units using `roundUP(itemSize / 4)`.
- A strongly consistent `query` requires one read capacity unit per 4 KB of item size. This means if your query returns 10 items, and each item is 2 KB, the item size is 20 KB and you need 5 read units. This is in contrast to 10 `getItem` operations, for which you would need 10 read capacity units.
- A write operation needs one write capacity unit per 1 KB of item size. If your item is larger than 1 KB, you can calculate the required write capacity units using `roundUP(itemSize)`.

If capacity units aren't your favorite unit, you can use the AWS Simple Monthly Calculator at http://aws.amazon.com/calculator to calculate your capacity needs by providing details of your read and write workload.

The provision throughput of a table or a global secondary index is defined in seconds. If you provision five read capacity units per second with `ReadCapacityUnits=5`, you can make five strongly consistent `getItem` requests for that table if the item size isn't larger than 4 KB per second. If you make more requests than are provisioned, DynamoDB will first throttle your request. If you make many more requests than are provisioned, DynamoDB will reject your requests.

It's important to monitor how many read and write capacity units you require. Fortunately, DynamoDB sends some useful metrics to CloudWatch every minute. To see the metrics, open the AWS Management Console, navigate to the DynamoDB service, and select one of the tables. Figure 10.4 shows the CloudFormation metrics for the `todo-user` table.

You can modify the provisioned throughput whenever you like, but you can only decrease the throughput capacity of a single table four times a day.

Cleaning up

Don't forget to delete your DynamoDB tables after you finish this section. Use the Management Console to do so.

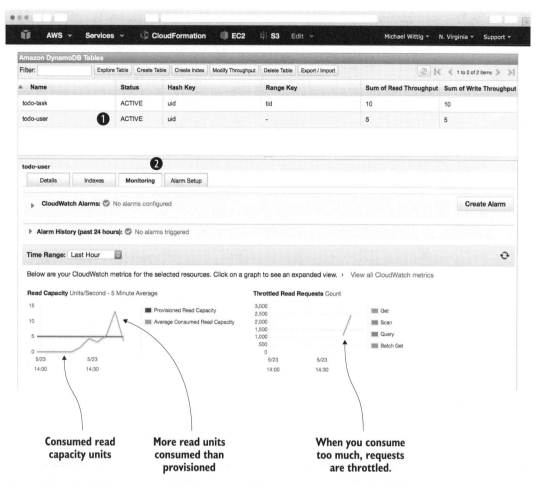

Figure 10.4 Monitoring provisioned and consumed capacity units of the DynamoDB table

10.10 Summary

- DynamoDB is a NoSQL database service that removes all the operational burdens from you, scales well, and can be used in many ways as the storage back end of your applications.
- Looking up data in DynamoDB is based on keys. A hash key can only be looked up if you know the key. But DynamoDB also supports hash and range keys, which combine the power of a hash key with another key that is sorted.
- You can retrieve a single item by its key with the getItem operation.
- Strongly consistent reads (getItem, query, and scan) can be enforced if needed. Reads from a global secondary index are always eventually consistent.

- DynamoDB doesn't support SQL. Instead, you must use the SDK to communicate with DynamoDB from your application. This also implies that you can't use an existing application to run with DynamoDB without touching the code.
- DynamoDB uses expressions to make more complex interactions with the database possible, such as when you update an item.
- Monitoring consumed read and write capacity is important if you want to provision enough capacity for your tables and indices.
- DynamoDB is charged for per gigabyte of storage and per provisioned read or write capacity.
- You can use the `query` operation to query primary keys or secondary indexes.
- The `scan` operation is flexible but not efficient and shouldn't be used too often.

Part 4

Architecting on AWS

Werner Vogels, CTO of Amazon.com, is quoted as saying, "Everything fails all the time." This is an important concept behind AWS. Instead of trying to reach the unreachable goal of being an unbreakable system, AWS is built for failure. Hard drives fail, so S3 stores data on multiple hard drives to prevent loss of data. Computing hardware fails, so virtual servers can be automatically restarted on another machine if necessary. Data centers fail, so there are multiple data centers per region that can be used in parallel or on demand.

In this part of the book, you'll learn how to prevent an outage of your applications running on AWS by using the right tools and architecture. The following table lists the most important services and their approach to handling failure:

	Description	Examples
Fault tolerant	Services can recover from failure automatically without any downtime.	S3 (object storage), DynamoDB (NoSQL database), Route 53 (DNS)
Highly available	Services can recover from some failures automatically with a brief downtime.	RDS (relational database), EBS (network attached storage)
Manual failure handling	Services don't recover from failure by default but offer tools to build a highly available infrastructure on top of them.	EC2 (virtual server)

Designing for failure is a fundamental principle of AWS; another is using the elasticity of the cloud. You'll also learn how to increase the number of virtual servers based on the current workload and architect reliable systems on AWS.

Chapter 11 lays the foundation for becoming independent of the risk of losing a single server or a complete data center. You'll learn how to recover a single EC2 instance in the same data center or in another data center. Chapter 12 discusses decoupling your system to increase reliability: using synchronous decoupling with the help of load balancers, and using asynchronous decoupling via Amazon SQS, a distributed queuing service, to build a fault-tolerant system. Chapter 13 covers designing a fault-tolerant web application based on EC2 instances (which aren't fault-tolerant by default). Chapter 14 is all about elasticity and auto-scaling; you'll learn to scale capacity based on a schedule or on the current system load.

11

Achieving high availability: availability zones, auto-scaling, and CloudWatch

This chapter covers

- Using a CloudWatch alarm to recover a failed virtual server
- Understanding availability zones in an AWS region
- Using auto-scaling to guarantee running virtual servers
- Analyzing disaster-recovery requirements

In this chapter, we'll teach you how to build a high-availability architecture based on EC2 instances. A virtual server isn't highly available by default. The following scenarios cause an outage of your virtual server:

- The virtual server fails because of a software issue (the OS of the virtual server).

- A software issue occurs on the host server, causing the virtual server to crash (the OS of the host server or virtualization layer).
- The computing, storage, or networking hardware of the physical host fails.
- Necessary parts of the data center that the virtual server depends on fail: network connectivity, the power supply, or the cooling system.

For example, if the computing hardware of a physical host server fails, all EC2 instances running on this host server will fail. If you're running an application on an affected virtual server, this application will fail and cause downtime until somebody—probably you—intervenes by starting a new virtual server running on another physical host server. To avoid this, you should aim for a highly available virtual server that can recover from failure automatically without human intervention.

Examples are 100% covered by the Free Tier

The examples in this chapter are completely covered by the Free Tier. As long as you don't run the examples for longer than a few days, you won't pay anything. Keep in mind that this only applies if you created a fresh AWS account for this book and nothing else is going on in your AWS account. Try to complete the examples of the chapter within a few days; you'll clean up your account at the end of each example.

High availability describes a system that's operating with almost no downtime. Even if a failure occurs, the system can provide its services at a high probability. Although a short interruption might be necessary to recover from a failure, there's no need for human interaction. The Harvard Research Group (HRG) defines high availability with the classification AEC-2, which requires an uptime of 99.99 % over a year.

High availability vs. fault tolerance

A highly available system can recover from a failure automatically with a short downtime. A fault-tolerant system, in contrast, requires the system to provide its services without interruption in case of a component failure. We'll show you how to build a fault-tolerant system in chapter 13.

AWS offers tools for building highly available systems based on EC2 instances:

- Monitoring the health of virtual servers with CloudWatch and triggering recovery automatically if needed
- Building a highly available infrastructure by using multiple isolated data centers, called *availability zones*, within a region
- Using auto-scaling to have a guaranteed number of virtual servers running and replace failed instances automatically

11.1 Recovering from server failure with CloudWatch

The status of every virtual server is checked by the EC2 service automatically. Checks are performed every minute and are available as CloudWatch metrics. *AWS CloudWatch* is a service offering metrics, logs, and alarms for AWS resources. You used CloudWatch to gain insights into the current load of a relational database instance in chapter 9. Figure 11.1 shows how to manually set up a CloudWatch alarm based on the system check of an EC2 instance from the details page of an EC2 instance.

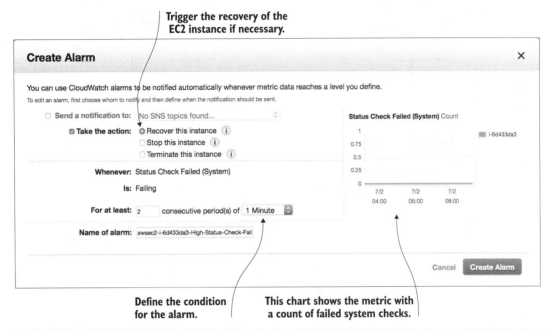

Figure 11.1   Creating a CloudWatch alarm based on a system-check metric, to trigger a recovery of the EC2 instance in case of a failure

A *system status check* detects a loss of network connectivity or power and software or hardware issues on the physical host. AWS needs to be involved to repair failures detected by the system status check. One possible strategy to resolve such failures is to recover by moving the virtual machine to another physical host.

Figure 11.2 shows the process in the case of an outage affecting a virtual server:

1 The physical server's hardware fails and causes the virtual server to fail as well.
2 The EC2 service detects the outage and reports the failure to CloudWatch metrics.
3 Recovery of the virtual server is triggered by the CloudWatch alarm.
4 The virtual server is launched on another physical host.
5 The EBS volume and Elastic IP stay the same and are linked to the new virtual server.

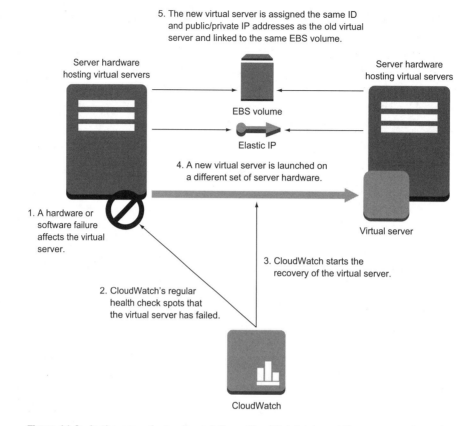

Figure 11.2   In the case of a hardware failure, CloudWatch triggers the recovery of the virtual server.

After the recovery, a new virtual server is running with the same ID and private IP address. Data on EBS volumes, the network-attached storage, is restored as well. No data is lost because the EBS volume stays the same. Virtual servers with local disks (instance storage) aren't supported for the CloudWatch alarm-based recovery process. If the old virtual server was connected to an Elastic IP address, the new server is connected to the same public IP address.

Requirements for recovering EC2 instances

A virtual server must fulfill the following requirements if you want to use the recovery feature:

- It must be running in a virtual private cloud (VPC) network.
- The instance family must be c3 (compute optimized), c4 (compute optimized), m3 (general), r3 (memory optimized), or t2 (burstable performance). Earlier instance families aren't supported (such as t1).
- The EC2 instance must use EBS volumes exclusively because data on instance storage would be lost after a recovery of the instance.

11.1.1 Creating a CloudWatch alarm

A CloudWatch alarm consists of the following:

- A metric that monitors data (health check, CPU usage, and so on)
- A rule defining a threshold based on a statistical function over a period of time
- Actions to trigger if the state of the alarm changes (such as triggering a recovery of an EC2 instance if the state changes to ALARM)

The following states are available for an alarm:

- OK—Everything is fine; the threshold hasn't been reached.
- INSUFFICIENT_DATA—There isn't enough data to evaluate the alarm.
- ALARM—Something is broken: the threshold has been overstepped.

To monitor the health of a virtual server and recover it in case of a failure of the underlying host system, you can use a CloudWatch alarm like the one shown in listing 11.1. This listing is an excerpt from a CloudFormation template.

Listing 11.1 creates a CloudWatch alarm based on a metric called StatusCheckFailed_System (linked by attribute MetricName). This metric contains the results of the system status checks for a virtual server performed by the EC2 service every minute. If the check fails, a measurement point with value of 1 is added to the metric StatusCheckFailed_System. Because the EC2 service publishes this metric, the Namespace is called AWS/EC2 and the Dimension of the metric is the ID of a virtual server.

The CloudWatch alarm checks the metric every 60 seconds as defined by the Period attribute. As defined in EvaluationPeriods, the alarm will check the last five periods, which means the last five minutes in this case. The check runs a statistical function specified in Statistic on the periods. The result of the statistical function, a minimum function in this case, is compared with ComparisonOperator against Threshold. If the result is negative, the alarm actions defined in AlarmActions are executed—in the following listing, the recovery of the virtual server—a built-in action for EC2 instances.

Listing 11.1 Creating a CloudWatch alarm to monitor the health of an EC2 instance

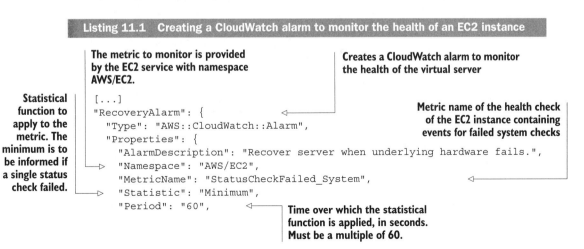

The metric to monitor is provided by the EC2 service with namespace AWS/EC2.

Creates a CloudWatch alarm to monitor the health of the virtual server

Statistical function to apply to the metric. The minimum is to be informed if a single status check failed.

Metric name of the health check of the EC2 instance containing events for failed system checks

```
[...]
"RecoveryAlarm": {
  "Type": "AWS::CloudWatch::Alarm",
  "Properties": {
    "AlarmDescription": "Recover server when underlying hardware fails.",
    "Namespace": "AWS/EC2",
    "MetricName": "StatusCheckFailed_System",
    "Statistic": "Minimum",
    "Period": "60",
```

Time over which the statistical function is applied, in seconds. Must be a multiple of 60.

Operator for comparing
the output of the statistical
function with the threshold

Number of periods over which data is
compared to the threshold

```
      "EvaluationPeriods": "5",
      "ComparisonOperator": "GreaterThanThreshold",
      "Threshold": "0",
      "AlarmActions": [{
        "Fn::Join": ["", ["arn:aws:automate:", {"Ref": "AWS::Region" },
        ":ec2:recover" ]]
      }],
      "Dimensions": [{"Name": "InstanceId", "Value": {"Ref": "Server"}}]
    }
  }
  [...]
```

Threshold
triggering
an alarm

Action to perform in case of
an alarm. Uses the predefined
recovery action for EC2 instances.

The virtual server is a
dimension of the metric.

In summary, the status of the virtual server is checked every minute by AWS. The result of these checks is written to the StatusCheckFailed_System metric. The alarm checks this metric. If there are five consecutive failed checks, the alarm trips.

11.1.2 *Monitoring and recovering a virtual server based on a CloudWatch alarm*

Suppose that your team is developing software in an agile development process. To accelerate the process, your team decides to automate the testing, build, and deployment of the software. You've been asked to set up a continuous integration server (CI server). You've chosen to use Jenkins, an open source application written in Java and running in a servlet container such as Apache Tomcat. Because you're using infrastructure as code, you're planning to deploy changes to your infrastructure with Jenkins as well.[1]

A Jenkins server is a typical use case for a high-availability setup. It's an important part of your infrastructure because your colleagues won't be able to test and deploy new software if the application suffers from downtime. But a short downtime in the case of a failure with automatic recovery won't break your business, so you don't need a fault-tolerant system.

In this example, you'll do the following:

1 Create a virtual network in the cloud (VPC).
2 Launch a virtual server in the VPC, and automatically install Jenkins during bootstrap.
3 Create a CloudWatch alarm to monitor the health of the virtual server.

We'll guide you through these steps with the help of a CloudFormation template.

You can find the CloudFormation template for this example on Github and on S3. You can download a snapshot of the repository at https://github.com/AWSinAction/code/archive/master.zip. The file we talk about is located at chapter11/recovery.json. On S3, the same file is located at https://s3.amazonaws.com/awsinaction/chapter11/recovery.json.

---

[1] Learn more about Jenkins by using its documentation at https://wiki.jenkins-ci.org/display/JENKINS/Use+Jenkins.

The following command starts a CloudFormation template containing an EC2 instance with a CloudWatch alarm triggering a recovery if the virtual server fails. Replace $Password with a password consisting of 8–40 characters and digits. A Jenkins server is automatically installed while starting the virtual server:

```
$ aws cloudformation create-stack --stack-name jenkins-recovery \
--template-url https://s3.amazonaws.com/\
awsinaction/chapter11/recovery.json \
--parameters ParameterKey=JenkinsAdminPassword,ParameterValue=$Password
```

The CloudFormation template contains the definition of a private network and security configuration. But the most important parts of the template are these:

- Virtual server with user data containing a bash script to install a Jenkins server during bootstrapping
- Public IP address assigned to the virtual server so you can access the new server after a recovery under the same public IP address as before
- CloudWatch alarm based on the system-status metric published by the EC2 service

The following listing shows the important parts of the template.

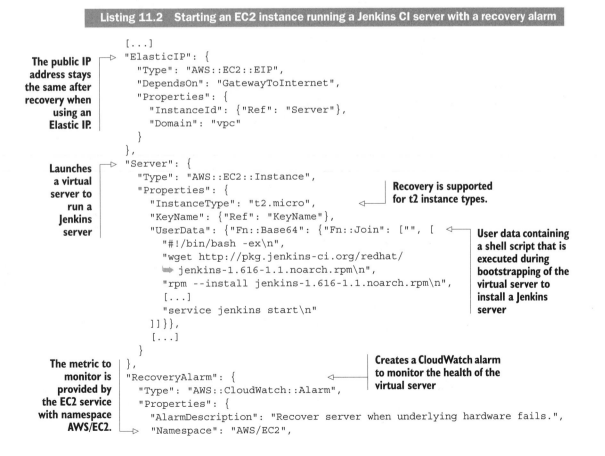

Listing 11.2 Starting an EC2 instance running a Jenkins CI server with a recovery alarm

The public IP address stays the same after recovery when using an Elastic IP.

```
[...]
"ElasticIP": {
  "Type": "AWS::EC2::EIP",
  "DependsOn": "GatewayToInternet",
  "Properties": {
    "InstanceId": {"Ref": "Server"},
    "Domain": "vpc"
  }
},
```

Launches a virtual server to run a Jenkins server

```
"Server": {
  "Type": "AWS::EC2::Instance",
  "Properties": {
    "InstanceType": "t2.micro",
    "KeyName": {"Ref": "KeyName"},
    "UserData": {"Fn::Base64": {"Fn::Join": ["", [
      "#!/bin/bash -ex\n",
      "wget http://pkg.jenkins-ci.org/redhat/
➥ jenkins-1.616-1.1.noarch.rpm\n",
      "rpm --install jenkins-1.616-1.1.noarch.rpm\n",
      [...]
      "service jenkins start\n"
    ]]}},
    [...]
  }
},
```

Recovery is supported for t2 instance types.

User data containing a shell script that is executed during bootstrapping of the virtual server to install a Jenkins server

The metric to monitor is provided by the EC2 service with namespace AWS/EC2.

```
"RecoveryAlarm": {
  "Type": "AWS::CloudWatch::Alarm",
  "Properties": {
    "AlarmDescription": "Recover server when underlying hardware fails.",
    "Namespace": "AWS/EC2",
```

Creates a CloudWatch alarm to monitor the health of the virtual server

Time over which the statistical function is applied, in seconds. Must be a multiple of 60.

Statistical function to apply to the metric. The minimum is to be informed if a single status check failed.

Metric name of the health check of the EC2 instance containing events for failed system checks

Operator for comparing the output of the statistical function with the threshold

The virtual server is a dimension of the metric.

```
    "MetricName": "StatusCheckFailed_System",
    "Statistic": "Minimum",
    "Period": "60",
    "EvaluationPeriods": "5",
    "ComparisonOperator": "GreaterThanThreshold",
    "Threshold": "0",
    "AlarmActions": [{
      "Fn::Join": ["", ["arn:aws:automate:", {"Ref": "AWS::Region" },
      ":ec2:recover" ]]
    }],
    "Dimensions": [{"Name": "InstanceId", "Value": {"Ref": "Server"}}]
  }
}
[...]
```

Number of periods over which data is compared to the threshold

Threshold triggering an alarm

Action to perform in case of an alarm. Uses the predefined recovery action for EC2 instances.

It will take a few minutes for the CloudFormation stack to be created and Jenkins to be installed on the virtual server. Run the following command to get the output of the stack. If the output is empty, retry after a few more minutes:

```
$ aws cloudformation describe-stacks --stack-name jenkins-recovery \
--query Stacks[0].Outputs
```

If the query returns output as shown here, containing a URL, a user, and a password, the stack has been created and the Jenkins server is ready to use. Open the URL in your browser, and log in to the Jenkins server with user admin and the password you've chosen:

```
[
  {
    "Description": "URL to access web interface of Jenkins server.",
    "OutputKey": "JenkinsURL",
    "OutputValue": "http://54.152.240.91:8080"
  },
  {
    "Description": "Administrator user for Jenkins.",
    "OutputKey": "User",
    "OutputValue": "admin"
  },
  {
    "Description": "Password for Jenkins administrator user.",
    "OutputKey": "Password",
    "OutputValue": "********"
  }
]
```

Open this URL in your browser to access the web interface of the Jenkins server.

Use this user to log in to the Jenkins server.

Use this password to log in to the Jenkins server.

You're now ready to create your first job on the Jenkins server. To do so, you have to log in with the username and password from the previous output. Figure 11.3 shows the Jenkins server's login form.

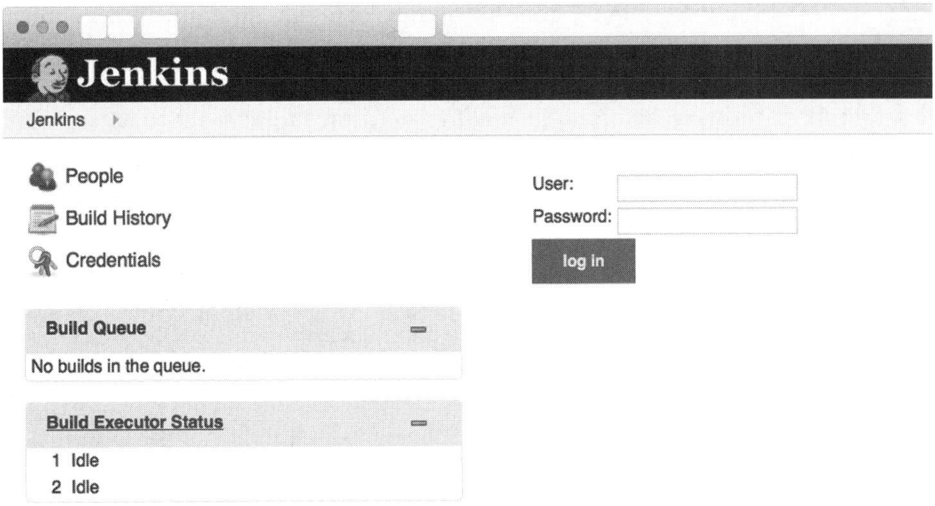

Figure 11.3   Web interface of the Jenkins server

The Jenkins server runs on a virtual server with automated recovery. If the virtual server fails because of issues with the host system, it will be recovered with all data and the same public IP address. The URL doesn't change because you use an Elastic IP for the virtual server. All data is restored because the new virtual server uses the same EBS volume as the previous virtual server.

Unfortunately, you can't test the recovery process. The CloudWatch alarm monitors the health of the host system, which can only be controlled by AWS.

Cleaning up

Now that you've finished this example, it's time to clean up to avoid unwanted costs. Execute the following command to delete all resources corresponding to the Jenkins setup:

```
$ aws cloudformation delete-stack --stack-name jenkins-recovery
$ aws cloudformation describe-stacks --stack-name jenkins-recovery    ⟵
```

> **Rerun this command until the status changes to DELETE_COMPLETE or an errors occurs stating that the stack does not exist.**

11.2   Recovering from a data center outage

Recovering a virtual server after a failure of the underlying software and hardware is possible with system status checks and CloudWatch, as described in the previous section. But what happens if the entire data center fails because of a power outage, a fire, or some other issue? The recovery of a virtual server as described in section 11.1 will fail because it tries to launch an EC2 instance in the same data center.

AWS is built for failure, even in the rare case that an entire data center fails. The AWS regions consist of multiple data centers called *availability zones.* Combined with the ability to define the number and type of virtual servers AWS should always keep running, with the help of auto-scaling, you can start virtual servers that can recover from a data center outage with a short downtime. There are two pitfalls when building a highly available setup over multiple availability zones:

- Data stored on network-attached storage (EBS) won't be available after a failover to another data center by default.
- You can't start a new virtual server into another data center with the same private IP address. In addition, you can't keep the same public IP address automatically after a recovery, as was the case in the previous section with a CloudWatch alarm triggering a recovery.

In this section, you'll improve the Jenkins setup from the previous section, add the ability to recover from an outage of an entire data center, and work around the pitfalls afterward.

11.2.1 *Availability zones: multiple data centers per region*

As you've learned, AWS operates multiple locations worldwide, called *regions.* You've used region US East (N. Virginia), also called us-east-1, if you've followed the examples so far. In total, there are nine public available regions in the US, South America, Europe, and Asia Pacific.

Each region consists of multiple *availability zones.* You can think of an availability zone as an isolated data center and a region as an area where multiple isolated data centers are located at a sufficient distance. The availability zones are connected through low-latency links, so requests between different availability zones aren't as expensive as requests across the internet in terms of latency. The number of availability zones depends on the region. Region US East (N. Virginia) consists of four availability zones, and region EU (Frankfurt) offers two availability zones at the moment. Figure 11.4 illustrates the concept of availability zones within a region.

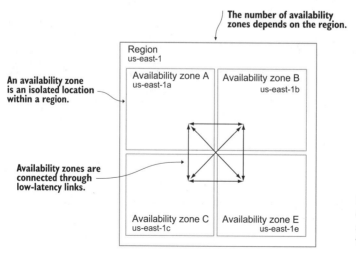

Figure 11.4   A region consists of multiple availability zones connected through low-latency links.

Some AWS services are highly available or even fault-tolerant by default. For some services, you have to use the available tools to build a highly available architecture yourself. The same is true for using multiple availability zones or even multiple regions to build a highly available architecture, as figure 11.5 shows:

- There are services operating globally over multiple regions: Route 53 (DNS) and CloudFront (CDN).
- Some services are using multiple availability zones within a region so they can recover from a data center outage: S3 (object store) and DynamoDB (NoSQL database).
- The relational database service (RDS) offers the ability to deploy a master-standby setup, called Multi-AZ deployment, so you can failover into another availability zone if necessary.
- A virtual server runs in a single availability zone. But AWS offers tools to build an architecture based on EC2 instances that can failover into another availability zone.

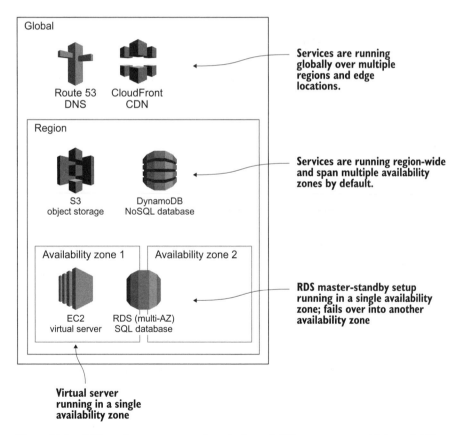

Figure 11.5 AWS services can operate in a single availability zone, over multiple availability zones within a region, or even globally.

The identifier of an availability zone consists of the identifier of the region (such as us-east-1) and a character (a, b, c, d, or e). us-east-1a is the identifier of an availability zone in region us-east-1. To distribute resources across the different availability zones, the identifier of an availability zone is generated randomly for each AWS account. This means us-east-1a points to another physical data center in your AWS account, as it does in our AWS account.

You can use the following commands to discover all regions available for your AWS account:

```
$ aws ec2 describe-regions
{
  "Regions": [
    {
    "Endpoint": "ec2.eu-central-1.amazonaws.com",
    "RegionName": "eu-central-1"
    },
    {
      "Endpoint": "ec2.sa-east-1.amazonaws.com",
      "RegionName": "sa-east-1"
    },
    {
      "Endpoint": "ec2.ap-northeast-1.amazonaws.com",
      "RegionName": "ap-northeast-1"
    },
    {
      "Endpoint": "ec2.eu-west-1.amazonaws.com",
      "RegionName": "eu-west-1"
    },
    {
      "Endpoint": "ec2.us-east-1.amazonaws.com",
      "RegionName": "us-east-1"
    },
    {
      "Endpoint": "ec2.us-west-1.amazonaws.com",
      "RegionName": "us-west-1"
    },
    {
      "Endpoint": "ec2.us-west-2.amazonaws.com",
      "RegionName": "us-west-2"
    },
    {
      "Endpoint": "ec2.ap-southeast-2.amazonaws.com",
      "RegionName": "ap-southeast-2"
    },
    {
      "Endpoint": "ec2.ap-southeast-1.amazonaws.com",
      "RegionName": "ap-southeast-1"
    }
  ]
}
```

To list all availability zones for a region, execute the following command and replace `$Region` with a `RegionName` from the previous command:

```
$ aws ec2 describe-availability-zones --region $Region
{
  "AvailabilityZones": [
    {
      "State": "available",
      "RegionName": "us-east-1",
      "Messages": [],
      "ZoneName": "us-east-1a"
    },
    {
      "State": "available",
      "RegionName": "us-east-1",
      "Messages": [],
      "ZoneName": "us-east-1b"
    },
    {
      "State": "available",
      "RegionName": "us-east-1",
      "Messages": [],
      "ZoneName": "us-east-1c"
    },
    {
      "State": "available",
      "RegionName": "us-east-1",
      "Messages": [],
      "ZoneName": "us-east-1e"
    }
  ]
}
```

Before you start to create a high-availability architecture based on EC2 instances with failover to multiple availability zones, there's one more lesson to learn. If you define a private network in AWS with the help of the virtual private cloud (VPC) service, you need to know the following:

- A VPC is always bound to a region.
- A subnet within a VPC is linked to an availability zone.
- A virtual server is launched into a single subnet.

Figure 11.6 illustrates these dependencies.

Next, you'll learn how to launch a virtual server that will automatically restart in another availability zone if a failure occurs.

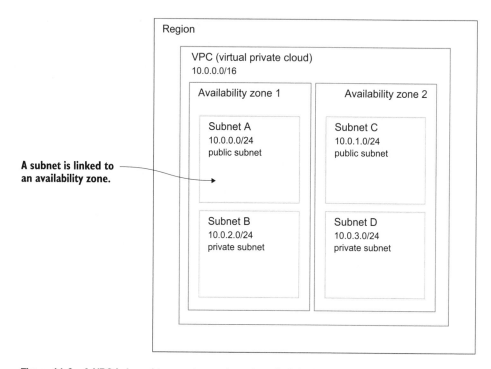

Figure 11.6 A VPC is bound to a region, and a subnet is linked to an availability zone.

11.2.2 *Using auto-scaling to ensure that a virtual server is always running*

Auto-scaling is part of the EC2 service and helps you to ensure that a specified number of virtual servers is running. You can use auto-scaling to launch a virtual server and make sure a new virtual server is started if the original virtual server fails. With auto-scaling, you can start EC2 instances in multiple subnets. In case of an outage of an entire availability zone, a new virtual server can be launched into another subnet in another availability zone.

To configure auto-scaling, you need to create two parts of the configuration:

- A *launch configuration* contains all information needed to launch a virtual server: instance type (size of virtual server) and image (AMI) to start from.
- An *auto-scaling group* tells the EC2 service how many virtual servers should be started with a specific launch configuration, how to monitor the instances, and in which subnets virtual servers should be started.

Figure 11.7 illustrates this process.

Listing 11.3 shows how to use auto-scaling to make sure a single EC2 instance is always running. The parameters are explained in table 11.1.

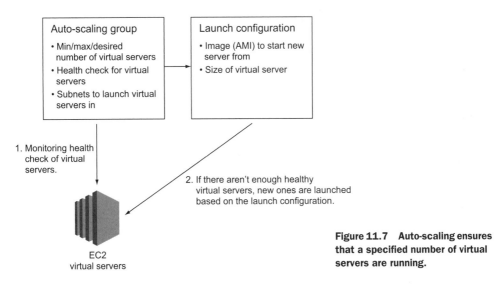

Figure 11.7 Auto-scaling ensures that a specified number of virtual servers are running.

Table 11.1 Required parameters for the launch configuration and auto-scaling group

Context	Property	Description	Values
LaunchConfiguration	ImageId	The ID of the AMI the virtual server should be started from.	Any AMI ID accessible from your account.
LaunchConfiguration	InstanceType	The size of the virtual server.	All available instance sizes, such as t2.micro, m3.medium, and c3.large.
AutoScalingGroup	DesiredCapacity	The number of virtual servers desired at the moment.	Any positive number. Use 1 if you want a single virtual server to be started based on the launch configuration.
AutoScalingGroup	MinSize	The minimum number of virtual servers this auto-scaling group ensures are running at the same time.	Any positive number. Use 1 if you want a single virtual server to be started based on the launch configuration.
AutoScalingGroup	MaxSize	The maximum number of virtual servers this auto-scaling group allows to run at the same time.	Any positive number. Use 1 if you want a single virtual server to be started based on the launch configuration.
AutoScalingGroup	VPCZoneIdentifier	The subnet IDs you want to start virtual servers in.	Any subnet ID from a VPC from your account. Subnets must belong to the same VPC.
AutoScalingGroup	HealthCheckType	The health check used to identify failed virtual servers. If the health check fails, the auto-scaling group replaces the virtual server with a new one.	EC2 to use the status checks of the virtual server, or ELB to use the health check of the load balancer (see chapter 13).

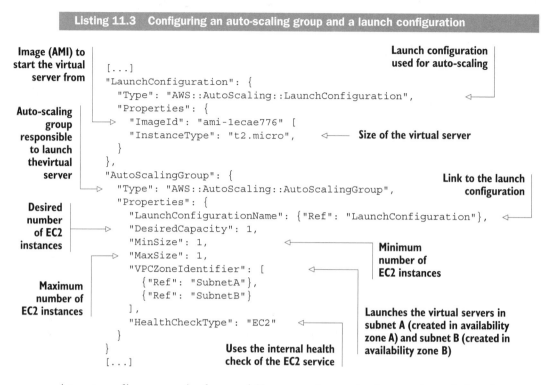

Listing 11.3   Configuring an auto-scaling group and a launch configuration

An auto-scaling group is also used if you need to scale the number of virtual servers based on usage of your system. You'll learn how to scale the number of servers based on current load in chapter 14. In this chapter, you only need to make sure a single virtual server is always running. Because you need a single virtual server, set the following parameters for auto-scaling to 1:

- DesiredCapacity
- MinSize
- MaxSize

The next section will reuse the Jenkins example from the beginning of the chapter to show you how high availability can be achieved with auto-scaling in practice.

11.2.3   *Recovering a failed virtual server to another availability zone with the help of auto-scaling*

In the first part of the chapter, you used a CloudWatch alarm to trigger the recovery of a virtual server, running a Jenkins CI server, in case of a failure. This mechanism launches an identical copy of the original virtual server if necessary. Doing so is only possible in the same availability zone because the private IP address and the EBS volume of a virtual server are bound to a single subnet and a single availability zone. But suppose your team isn't happy about the fact that they won't be able to use the Jenkins server to test, build, and deploy new software in case of a data center outage in a AWS region. You begin looking for a tool that will let you recover in another availability zone.

A failover into another availability zone for a virtual server running Jenkins is possible with the help of auto-scaling. You can find the CloudFormation template for this example on Github and on S3. You can download a snapshot of the repository at https://github.com/AWSinAction/code/archive/master.zip. The file we talked about is located at chapter11/multiaz.json. On S3, the same file is located at https://s3.amazonaws.com/awsinaction/chapter11/multiaz.json.

Execute the following command to create a virtual server that can recover in another availability zone if necessary with the help of auto-scaling. Replace $Password with a password consisting of 8–40 characters and digits. The command uses the CloudFormation template shown in listing 11.3 to set up the environment:

```
$ aws cloudformation create-stack --stack-name jenkins-multiaz \
--template-url https://s3.amazonaws.com/\
awsinaction/chapter11/multiaz.json \
--parameters ParameterKey=JenkinsAdminPassword,ParameterValue=$Password
```

You'll find both a launch configuration and an auto-scaling group in the CloudFormation template shown in listing 11.4. The most important parameters for the launch configuration were already used when starting a single virtual server with the CloudWatch recovery alarm in the previous section:

- `ImageId`—ID of the image (AMI) for virtual server
- `InstanceType`—Size of the virtual server
- `KeyName`—Name of the SSH key pair
- `SecurityGroupIds`—Link to the security groups
- `UserData`—Script executed during bootstrap to install the Jenkins CI server

There's one important difference between the definition of a single EC2 instance and the launch configuration: the subnet for the virtual server isn't defined in the launch configuration but in the auto-scaling group, as shown in the next listing.

Listing 11.4 Jenkins CI server with auto-scaling in two availability zones

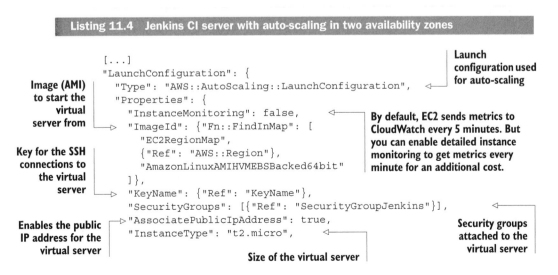

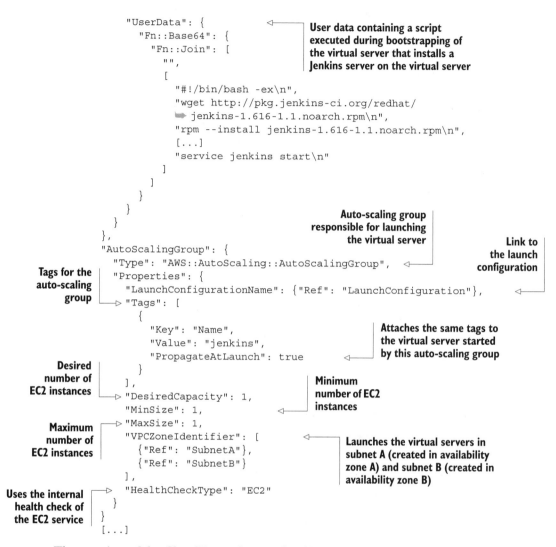

```
"UserData": {                          ◁────  User data containing a script
  "Fn::Base64": {                              executed during bootstrapping of
    "Fn::Join": [                              the virtual server that installs a
      "",                                      Jenkins server on the virtual server
      [
        "#!/bin/bash -ex\n",
        "wget http://pkg.jenkins-ci.org/redhat/
        ➥ jenkins-1.616-1.1.noarch.rpm\n",
        "rpm --install jenkins-1.616-1.1.noarch.rpm\n",
        [...]
        "service jenkins start\n"
      ]
    ]
  }
}
},                                                Auto-scaling group
"AutoScalingGroup": {                         responsible for launching
  "Type": "AWS::AutoScaling::AutoScalingGroup",  the virtual server          Link to
  "Properties": {                            ◁─────────────────           the launch
    "LaunchConfigurationName": {"Ref": "LaunchConfiguration"},          configuration
    "Tags": [                                                      ◁─────
      {
        "Key": "Name",                          Attaches the same tags to
        "Value": "jenkins",                     the virtual server started
        "PropagateAtLaunch": true     ◁─────   by this auto-scaling group
      }
    ],                                    Minimum
    "DesiredCapacity": 1,                 number of EC2
    "MinSize": 1,                    ◁──  instances
    "MaxSize": 1,
    "VPCZoneIdentifier": [           ◁────
      {"Ref": "SubnetA"},                     Launches the virtual servers in
      {"Ref": "SubnetB"}                      subnet A (created in availability
    ],                                        zone A) and subnet B (created in
    "HealthCheckType": "EC2"                  availability zone B)
  }
}
[...]
```

- Tags for the auto-scaling group → "Tags": [
- Desired number of EC2 instances → "DesiredCapacity": 1,
- Maximum number of EC2 instances → "MaxSize": 1,
- Uses the internal health check of the EC2 service → "HealthCheckType": "EC2"

The creation of the CloudFormation stack will take a few minutes—time to grab some coffee or tea and take a short break. Execute the following command to grab the public IP address of the virtual server. If no IP address appears, the virtual server isn't started yet. Wait another minute, and try again:

```
$ aws ec2 describe-instances --filters "Name=tag:Name,\
Values=jenkins-multiaz" "Name=instance-state-code,Values=16" \
--query "Reservations[0].Instances[0].\
[InstanceId, PublicIpAddress, PrivateIpAddress, SubnetId]"
[
  "i-e8c2063b",
  "52.4.11.10",
  "10.0.1.56",
  "subnet-36257a41"
]
```

- Instance ID of the virtual server → "i-e8c2063b",
- Public IP address of the virtual server → "52.4.11.10"
- Private IP address of the virtual server → "10.0.1.56",
- Subnet ID of the virtual server → "subnet-36257a41"

Open http://$PublicIP:8080 in your browser, and replace $PublicIP with the public IP address from the output of the previous describe command. The web interface from the Jenkins server appears.

Execute the following command to terminate the virtual server and test the recovery process with auto-scaling. Replace $InstanceId with the instance ID from the output of the previous describe command:

```
$ aws ec2 terminate-instances --instance-ids $InstanceId
```

After a few minutes, the auto-scaling group detects that the virtual server was terminated and starts a new virtual server. Rerun the describe-instances command until the output contains a new running virtual server:

```
$ aws ec2 describe-instances --filters "Name=tag:Name,\
Values=jenkins-multiaz" "Name=instance-state-code,Values=16" \
--query "Reservations[0].Instances[0].\
[InstanceId, PublicIpAddress, PrivateIpAddress, SubnetId]"
[
  "i-5e4f68f7",
  "54.88.118.96",
  "10.0.0.36",
  "subnet-aa29b281"
]
```

The instance ID, the public IP address, the private IP address, and probably even the subnet ID have changed for the new instance. Open http://$PublicIP:8080 in your browser, and replace $PublicIP with the public IP address from the output of the previous describe command. The web interface from the Jenkins server appears.

You've built a highly available architecture consisting of an EC2 server with the help of auto-scaling. There are two issues with the current setup:

- The Jenkins server stores data on disk. When a new virtual server is started to recover from a failure, this data is lost because a new disk is created.
- The public and private IP addresses of the Jenkins server change after a new virtual server is started for recovery. The Jenkins server is no longer available under the same endpoint.

You'll learn how to solve these problems in the next part of the chapter.

11.2.4 *Pitfall: network-attached storage recovery*

The EBS service offers network-attached storage for virtual servers. EC2 instances are linked to a subnet, which is linked to an availability zone. EBS volumes are also located in a single availability zone. If your virtual server is started in another availability zone because of an outage, the data stored on the EBS volume is no longer available. Figure 11.8 illustrates the problem.

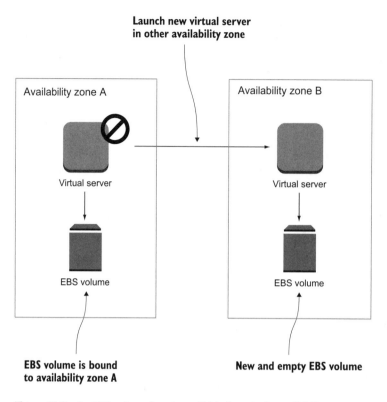

Figure 11.8   An EBS volume is only available in a single availability zone.

There are multiple solutions to this problem:

- Outsource the state of your virtual server to a managed service that uses multiple availability zones by default: relational database service (RDS), DynamoDB (NoSQL database), or S3 (object store).
- Create snapshots of your EBS volumes, and use these snapshots if a virtual server needs to recover in another availability zone. EBS snapshots are stored on S3 to be available in multiple availability zones.
- Use a distributed third-party storage solution to store your data in multiple availability zones: GlusterFS, DRBD, MongoDB, and so on.

The Jenkins server stores data directly on disk. To outsource the state of the virtual server, you can't use RDS, DynamoDB, or S3; you need a block-level storage solution instead. As you learned, an EBS volume is only available in a single availability zone, so this isn't the best fit for the problem. Using a distributed third-party storage solution would be possible but introduces a lot of complexity that's out of the scope of this book. You'll learn how to use EBS snapshots to recover a virtual server in another availability zone without losing the complete state stored on the EBS volume. Instead, you'll lose all data since the last snapshot.

You can specify a custom image (AMI) for a virtual server started by auto-scaling with the help of the launch configuration, as shown in listing 11.5. An AMI is similar to an EBS snapshot; it contains additional information regarding the virtualization of the OS. You can also launch a new virtual server based on a AMI. But it's not possible to use an EBS snapshot to create a root volume. You can create an image (AMI) of every running virtual server. In comparison to the EBS volume itself, an EBS snapshot or AMI is stored in multiple availability zones within a region, so you can use it to recover in another availability zone.

Listing 11.5 Updating the image a new virtual server starts from in case of recovery

```
[...]
"LaunchConfiguration": {
  "Type": "AWS::AutoScaling::LaunchConfiguration",
  "Properties": {
    "InstanceMonitoring": false,
    "ImageId": {"Ref": "AMISnapshot"},          <──  Auto-scaling starts new
    "KeyName": {"Ref": "KeyName"},                    virtual servers based
    "SecurityGroups": [{"Ref": "SecurityGroupJenkins"}],   on the specified AMI.
    "AssociatePublicIpAddress": true,
    "InstanceType": "t2.micro",
    "UserData": {
      "Fn::Base64": {
        "Fn::Join": [
          "",
          [
            "#!/bin/bash -ex\n",
            "wget http://pkg.jenkins-ci.org/redhat/
➥ jenkins-1.616-1.1.noarch.rpm\n",
            "rpm --install jenkins-1.616-1.1.noarch.rpm\n",
            [...]
            "service jenkins start\n"
          ]
        ]
      }
    }
  }
}
[...]
```

We'll guide you through the following steps:

1 Add a job for Jenkins CI server.
2 Create an AMI with a snapshot of the current state of the virtual server.
3 Update the launch configuration.
4 Test the recovery.

Execute the following command to get the instance ID and public IP address of the running virtual server:

```
$ aws ec2 describe-instances --filters "Name=tag:Name,\
Values=jenkins-multiaz" "Name=instance-state-code,Values=16" \
--query "Reservations[0].Instances[0].[InstanceId, PublicIpAddress]"
[
  "i-5e4f68f7",
  "54.88.118.96"
]
```

Now, create a new Jenkins job by following these steps:

1   Open http://$PublicIP:8080/newJob in your browser, and replace $PublicIP with the public IP address from the output of the previous describe command.

2   Log in with user admin and the password you chose when starting the Cloud-Formation template.

3   Type in AWS in Action as the name for the new job.

4   Select Freestyle Project as the job type, and click OK to save the job.

You've made some changes to the state of the virtual server stored on the EBS root volume.

To make sure this new job doesn't get lost if a new virtual server is started by the auto-scaling group in case of a failure, you need to create an AMI as a snapshot of the current state. Execute the following command to do so, replacing $InstanceId with the instance ID from the previous describe command:

```
$ aws ec2 create-image --instance-id $InstanceId --name jenkins-multiaz
{
  "ImageId": "ami-0dba4266"          ◁─────────   ID of new AMI used to update
}                                                 the launch configuration with
                                                  the help of the CloudFormation
```

Wait until the AMI is available. Execute the following command to check the current status, replacing $ImageId with the ImageId printed from the create-image command:

```
$ aws ec2 describe-images --image-id $ImageId --query "Images[].State"
```

You need to update the launch configuration with the CloudFormation template shown in listing 11.5. Execute the following command to do so, replacing $ImageId with the ImageId:

```
$ aws cloudformation update-stack --stack-name jenkins-multiaz \
--template-url https://s3.amazonaws.com/awsinaction/\
chapter11/multiaz-ebs.json --parameters \
ParameterKey=JenkinsAdminPassword,UsePreviousValue=true \
ParameterKey=AMISnapshot,ParameterValue=$ImageId
```

Wait a few minutes until CloudFormation has changed the launch configuration. Check the status by running aws cloudformation describe-stacks --stack-name jenkins-multiaz and wait until status changes to UPDATE_COMPLETE. It's now time to simulate an outage of the virtual server. Execute the following command to terminate the virtual server, replacing $InstanceId with the output from the describe command:

```
$ aws ec2 terminate-instances --instance-ids $InstanceId
```

It will take up to five minutes for the auto-scaling group to detect the missing virtual server and start a new virtual server. Run the following command to get information about the new virtual server. If the output is empty, retry the command after a few minutes:

```
$ aws ec2 describe-instances --filters "Name=tag:Name,\
Values=jenkins-multiaz" "Name=instance-state-code,Values=16" \
--query "Reservations[0].Instances[0].[InstanceId, PublicIpAddress]"
```

Open http://$PublicIP:8080 in your browser, and replace $PublicIP with the public IP address from the output of the previous describe command. You should find a job named AWS in Action available in the Jenkins web interface.

> **Cleaning up**
>
> It's time to clean up to avoid unwanted costs. Execute the following command to prepare for the deletion of unused resources:
>
> ```
> $ aws ec2 describe-images --owners self \
> --query Images[0].[ImageId,BlockDeviceMappings[0]\
> .Ebs.SnapshotId]
> ```
>
> The output contains the ID of the image (AMI) and the ID of the corresponding snapshot. Execute the following commands to delete all resources corresponding to the Jenkins setup, replacing $ImageId with the image ID and $SnapshotId with the snapshot ID from the previous output:
>
> ```
> $ aws cloudformation delete-stack --stack-name jenkins-multiaz
> $ aws cloudformation describe-stacks --stack-name jenkins-multiaz   <──┐
> $ aws ec2 deregister-image --image-id $ImageId
> $ aws ec2 delete-snapshot --snapshot-id $SnapshotId
> ```
>
> **Rerun this command until the status changes to DELETE_COMPLETE or an error occurs stating that the stack doesn't exist.**

11.2.5 Pitfall: network interface recovery

Recovering a virtual server with the help of a CloudWatch alarm in the same availability zone, as described at the beginning of this chapter, is easy because the private IP address and the public IP address stay the same automatically. You can use these IP addresses as an endpoint to access the server even after a failover.

You can't do this when using auto-scaling to recover from a server or data center outage. If a virtual server has to be started in another availability zone to recover from a data center outage, it must be started in another subnet. It's not possible to use the same private IP address for the new virtual server, as figure 11.9 shows.

By default, you also can't use an Elastic IP as a public IP address for a virtual server launched by auto-scaling. But the requirement for a static endpoint to receive requests is common. For the use case of a Jenkins server, developers want to bookmark

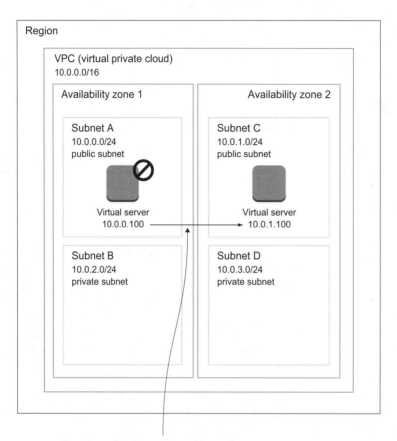

The private IP address has to change because
the virtual server is recovered in another subnet.

Figure 11.9   The virtual server starts in another subnet in case of a failover and
changes the private IP address.

an IP address or a hostname to reach the web interface. There are different possibilities to provide a static endpoint when using auto-scaling to build high availability for a single virtual server:

- Allocate an Elastic IP, and associate this public IP address during the bootstrap of the virtual server.
- Create or update a DNS entry linking to the current public or private IP address of the virtual server.
- Use an Elastic Load Balancer (ELB) as a static endpoint that forwards requests to the current virtual server.

To use the second solution, you need to link a domain with the Route 53 (DNS) service; we've chosen to skip this solution because you need a registered domain to implement it. The ELB solution is covered in chapter 12, so we'll skip it in this chapter as well. We'll focus on the first solution: allocating an Elastic IP and associating this public IP address during the bootstrap of the virtual server started by auto-scaling.

Execute the following command to create the Jenkins setup based on auto-scaling again, using an Elastic IP address as static endpoint:

```
$ aws cloudformation create-stack --stack-name jenkins-elasticip \
--template-url https://s3.amazonaws.com/\
awsinaction/chapter11/multiaz-elasticip.json \
--parameters ParameterKey=JenkinsAdminPassword,ParameterValue=$Password \
--capabilities CAPABILITY_IAM
```

The command creates a stack based on the template shown in listing 11.6. The differences from the original template spinning up a Jenkins server with auto-scaling are as follows:

- Allocating an Elastic IP
- Adding the association of an Elastic IP to the script in the user data
- Creating an IAM role and policy to allow the EC2 instance to associate an Elastic IP

> **Listing 11.6   Using an Elastic IP as a static endpoint**

```
[...]
"IamRole": {                    ◁————————   Creates an IAM
  "Type": "AWS::IAM::Role",                 role used by the
  "Properties": {                           EC2 instance
    "AssumeRolePolicyDocument": {
      "Version": "2012-10-17",
      "Statement": [
        {
          "Effect": "Allow",
          "Principal": {"Service": ["ec2.amazonaws.com"]
        },
          "Action": ["sts:AssumeRole"]
        }
      ]
    },
    "Path": "/",
    "Policies": [
      {
        "PolicyName": "root",
        "PolicyDocument": {
          "Version": "2012-10-17",
          "Statement": [                     Associating an Elastic IP is
            {                                 allowed for EC2 instances
              "Action": ["ec2:AssociateAddress"],  ◁┘ using this IAM role.
              "Resource": ["*"],
              "Effect": "Allow"
            }
          ]
        }
      }
    ]
  }
```

```
    },
    "IamInstanceProfile": {
      "Type": "AWS::IAM::InstanceProfile",
      "Properties": {
        "Path": "/",
        "Roles": [{"Ref": "IamRole"}]
      }
    },
    "ElasticIP": {                          ⟵
      "Type": "AWS::EC2::EIP",
      "Properties": {
        "Domain": "vpc"                     ⟵
      }
    },
    "LaunchConfiguration": {
      "Type": "AWS::AutoScaling::LaunchConfiguration",
      "DependsOn": "ElasticIP",                          ⟵
      "Properties": {
        "InstanceMonitoring": false,
        "IamInstanceProfile": {"Ref": "IamInstanceProfile"},
        "ImageId": {"Fn::FindInMap": [
          "EC2RegionMap",
          {"Ref": "AWS::Region"},                        ⟵
          "AmazonLinuxAMIHVMEBSBacked64bit"
        ]},
        "KeyName": {"Ref": "KeyName"},
        "SecurityGroups": [{"Ref": "SecurityGroupJenkins"}],
        "AssociatePublicIpAddress": true,
        "InstanceType": "t2.micro",
        "UserData": {
          "Fn::Base64": {
            "Fn::Join": [
              "",
              [
                "#!/bin/bash -ex\n",
                "aws configure set default.region ", {"Ref": "AWS::Region"},",",  ⟵
                "aws ec2 associate-address --instance-id ",
                "$INSTANCE_ID --allocation-id ",
                {"Fn::GetAtt": ["ElasticIP", "AllocationId"]},
                "\n",
                "wget http://pkg.jenkins-ci.org/redhat/
                ➡ jenkins-1.616-1.1.noarch.rpm\n",
                "rpm --install jenkins-1.616-1.1.noarch.rpm\n",
                [...]
                "service jenkins start\n"
              ]
            ]
          }
        }
      }
    }
    [...]
```

Allocates an Elastic IP for the virtual server running Jenkins

Creates an Elastic IP for VPC

Waits for the Elastic IP to be available

Sets the default region for AWS CLI to the region the virtual server is running in.

Gets the instance ID from the instance metadata

Associates the Elastic IP with the virtual server

If the following query returns output containing a URL, a user, and a password, the stack is created and the Jenkins server is ready to use. Open the URL in your browser, and log in to the Jenkins server with user admin and the password you've chosen. If the output is empty, try again in a few minutes:

```
$ aws cloudformation describe-stacks --stack-name jenkins-elasticip \
--query Stacks[0].Outputs
```

You can now test whether the recovery of the virtual server works as expected. To do so, you'll need to know the instance ID of the running virtual server. Run the following command to get this information:

```
$ aws ec2 describe-instances --filters "Name=tag:Name,\
Values=jenkins-elasticip" "Name=instance-state-code,Values=16" \
--query "Reservations[0].Instances[0].InstanceId" --output text
```

Execute the following command to terminate the virtual server and test the recovery process triggered by auto-scaling. Replace $InstanceId with the instance from the output of the previous command:

```
$ aws ec2 terminate-instances --instance-ids $InstanceId
```

Wait a few minutes for the recovery of your virtual server. Because you're using an Elastic IP assigned to the new virtual server on bootstrapping, you can open the same URL in your browser as you did before the termination of the old instance.

Cleaning up

It's time to clean up to avoid unwanted costs. Execute the following command to delete all resources corresponding to the Jenkins setup:

```
$ aws cloudformation delete-stack --stack-name jenkins-elasticip
$ aws cloudformation describe-stacks --stack-name jenkins-elasticip
```

> **Rerun this command until the status changes to DELETE_COMPLETE or an errors occurs stating that the stack does not exist.**

Now the public IP address of your virtual server running Jenkins won't change even if the running virtual server needs to be replaced by another virtual server in another availability zone.

11.3 *Analyzing disaster-recovery requirements*

Before you begin implementing highly available or even fault-tolerant architectures on AWS, you should start by analyzing your disaster-recovery requirements. Disaster recovery is easier and cheaper in the cloud than in a traditional data center, but it increases the complexity and therefore the initial and operating costs of your system. The recovery time objective (RTO) and recovery point objective (RPO) are standard for defining the importance of disaster recovery for a system from the business point of view.

The *recovery time objective (RTO)* is the time it takes for a system to recover from a failure; it's the length of time until the system service level is reached after an outage. In the example with a Jenkins server, the RTO would be the time until a new virtual server is started and Jenkins is installed and running after an outage of a virtual server or an entire data center.

The *recovery point objective (RPO)* is the acceptable data-loss time caused by a failure. The amount of data loss is measured in time. If an outage happens at 10:00 AM and the system recovers with a data snapshot from 09:00 AM, the time span of the data loss is one hour. In the example with a Jenkins server using auto-scaling, the RPO would be the maximum time span between two EBS snapshots. Configuration and results from Jenkins jobs that changed after the last EBS snapshot would be lost in case of a recovery in another data center. Figure 11.10 illustrates the definitions of RTO and RPO.

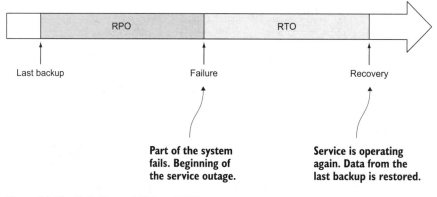

Figure 11.10   Definitions of RTO and RPO

11.3.1   RTO and RPO comparison for a single virtual server

You've learned about two possible solutions to make a single server highly available. Table 11.2 compares the solutions.

Table 11.2   Comparison of high availability for a single virtual server

	RTO	RPO	Availability
Virtual server with recovery triggered by a Cloud-Watch alarm	About 10 minutes	No data loss.	Recovers from a failure of a virtual server but not from an outage of an entire availability zone
Virtual server with auto-scaling for recovery	About 10 minutes	All data since the last snapshot is lost. Practicable time span for snapshots is between 30 minutes and 24 hours.	Recovers from a failure of a virtual server and from an outage of an entire availability zone

If you want to be able to recover from an outage of an availability zone and need to decrease the RPO, you should try to achieve a stateless server. Using storage services like RDS, S3, and DynamoDB can help you to do so. See part 3 of the book if you need help with using these services.

11.4 Summary

- A virtual server fails if the underlying hardware or software fails.
- You can recover a failed virtual server with the help of a CloudWatch alarm.
- An AWS region consists of multiple isolated data centers called availability zones.
- Recovering from a data center outage is possible when using multiple availability zones.
- Some AWS services use multiple availability zones by default, but virtual servers run in a single availability zone.
- You can use auto-scaling to guarantee that a single virtual server is always running even if an availability zone fails.
- Recovering data in another availability zone is tricky when stored on EBS volumes instead of managed storage services like RDS, S3, and DynamoDB.

Decoupling
your infrastructure:
ELB and SQS

This chapter covers

- The reasons for decoupling a system
- Synchronous decoupling with load balancers
- Asynchronous decoupling with message queues

Imagine that you want some advice on using AWS from us, and therefore we plan to meet in a café. To make this meeting successful, we must

- Be available at the same time
- Be at the same place
- Find each other at the café

The problem with our meeting is that it's tightly coupled to a location. We can solve that issue by decoupling our meeting from the location, so we change plans and schedule a Google Hangout session. Now we must

- Be available at the same time
- Find each other in Google Hangout

Google Hangout (this also works with all other video/voice chats) does synchronous decoupling. It removes the need to be at the same place while still requiring us to meet at the same time.

We can even decouple from time by using an e-mail conversation. Now we must

- Find each other via email

Email does asynchronous decoupling. You can send an email when the recipient is asleep, and they'll respond when they're awake.

Examples are 100% covered by the Free Tier

The examples in this chapter are totally covered by the Free Tier. As long as you don't run the examples longer than a few days, you won't pay anything for it. Keep in mind that this applies only if you created a fresh AWS account for this book and there are no other things going on in your AWS account. Try to complete the chapter within a few days, because you'll clean up your account at the end of the chapter.

NOTE To fully understand this chapter, you'll need to have read and understood the concept of auto-scaling covered in chapter 11.

A meeting isn't the only thing that can be decoupled. In software systems, you can find a lot of tightly coupled components:

- A public IP address is like the location of our meeting. To make a request to a web server, you must know its public IP address, and the server must be connected to that address. If you want to change the public IP address, both parties are involved in making the appropriate changes.
- If you want to make a request to a web server, the web server must be online at the same time. Otherwise your request will fail. There are many reasons a web server can be offline: someone is installing updates, a hardware failure, and so on.

AWS offers a solution for both of these problems. The *Elastic Load Balancing (ELB)* service provides a load balancer that sits between your web servers and the public internet to decouple your servers synchronously. For asynchronous decoupling, AWS offers a *Simple Queue Service (SQS)* that provides a message queue infrastructure. You'll learn about both services in this chapter. Let's start with ELB.

12.1 *Synchronous decoupling with load balancers*

Exposing a single web server to the outside world introduces a dependency: the public IP address of the EC2 instance. From this point on, you can't change the public IP address again because it's used by many clients sending requests to your server. You're faced with the following issues:

- Changing the public IP address is no longer possible because many clients rely on it.
- If you add an additional server (and IP address) to handle increasing load, it's ignored by all current clients: they're still sending all requests to the public IP address of the first server.

You can solve these issues with a DNS name pointing to your server. But DNS isn't fully under your control. DNS servers cache entries, and sometimes they don't respect your time to live (TTL) settings. A better solution is to use a load balancer.

A load balancer can help to decouple a system where the requester awaits an immediate response. Instead of exposing your web servers to the outside world, you only expose the load balancer to the outside world. The load balancer then redirects requests to the web servers behind it. Figure 12.1 shows how this works.

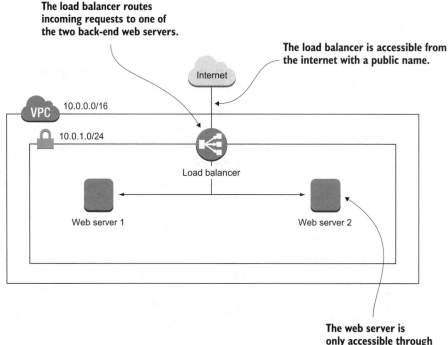

Figure 12.1 A load balancer synchronously decouples your server.

AWS offers load balancers through the ELB service. The AWS load balancer is fault-tolerant and scalable. For each ELB, you pay $ 0.025 per hour and $ 0.008 per GB of processed traffic. The prices are valid for the North Virginia (us-east-1) region.

> **NOTE** The ELB service doesn't have an independent Management Console. It's integrated into the EC2 service.

A load balancer can be used with more than web servers—you can use load balancers in front of any systems that deal with request/response kind of communication.

12.1.1 Setting up a load balancer with virtual servers

AWS shines when it comes to integrating services together. In chapter 11, you learned about auto-scaling groups. You'll now put a Elastic Load Balancer (ELB) in front of an auto-scaling group to decouple traffic to web servers. The auto-scaling group will make sure you always have two servers running. Servers that are started in the auto-scaling group will automatically register with the ELB. Figure 12.2 shows how the setup will look. The interesting part is that the web servers are no longer accessible directly from the public internet. Only the load balancer is accessible and redirects request to the back-end servers behind it; this is done with security groups, which you learned about in chapter 6.

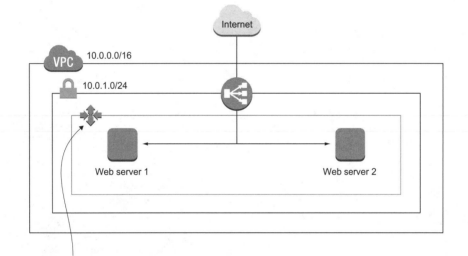

The auto-scaling group observes two web servers. If a new server is started, the auto-scaling group registers it with the ELB.

Figure 12.2 Auto-scaling groups work closely with ELB: they register a new server with the load balancer.

An ELB is described by the following:

- The subnets it's attached to. There can be more than one.
- A mapping of the load balancer port to the port on the servers behind the ELB.
- The security groups that are assigned to the ELB. You can restrict traffic to the ELB in the same ways you can with EC2 instances.
- Whether the load balancer should be accessible from the public internet.

The connection between the ELB and the auto-scaling group is made in the auto-scaling group description by specifying LoadBalancerNames.

The next listing shows a CloudFormation template snippet to create an ELB and connect it with an auto-scaling group. The listing implements the example shown in figure 12.2.

Listing 12.1   Creating a load balancer and connecting it with an auto-scaling group

```
[...]
"LoadBalancerSecurityGroup": {
  "Type": "AWS::EC2::SecurityGroup",
  "Properties": {
    "GroupDescription": "elb-sg",
    "VpcId": {"Ref": "VPC"},
    "SecurityGroupIngress": [{          ◁──── The load balancer only
      "CidrIp": "0.0.0.0/0",                  accepts traffic on port 80.
      "FromPort": 80,
      "ToPort": 80,
      "IpProtocol": "tcp"
    }]
  }
},
"LoadBalancer": {
  "Type": "AWS::ElasticLoadBalancing::LoadBalancer",
  "Properties": {                              Attaches the ELB
    "Subnets": [{"Ref": "Subnet"}],     ◁──── to the subnet
    "LoadBalancerName": "elb",
    "Listeners": [{          ◁────          Maps the load-balancer
      "InstancePort": "80",                port to a port on the
      "InstanceProtocol": "HTTP",          servers behind it.
      "LoadBalancerPort": "80",
      "Protocol": "HTTP"
    }],
    "SecurityGroups": [{"Ref": "LoadBalancerSecurityGroup"}],
    "Scheme": "internet-facing"     ◁────
  }                                        The ELB is publicly
},                                         accessible (use internal
"LaunchConfiguration": {                   instead of internet-facing
  "Type": "AWS::AutoScaling::LaunchConfiguration",   to define a load balancer
  "Properties": {                          reachable from private
    [...]                                  network only).
  }
},
```

Assigns a security group.

```
"AutoScalingGroup": {
  "Type": "AWS::AutoScaling::AutoScalingGroup",
  "Properties": {
    "LoadBalancerNames": [{"Ref": "LoadBalancer"}],
    "LaunchConfigurationName": {"Ref": "LaunchConfiguration"},
    "MinSize": "2",
    "MaxSize": "2",
    "DesiredCapacity": "2",
    "VPCZoneIdentifier": [{"Ref": "Subnet"}]
  }
}
```

Connects the auto-scaling group with the ELB. (points to `"LoadBalancerNames"`)

Belongs to MinSize, MaxSize and DesiredCapacity. (points to `"DesiredCapacity": "2"`)

To help you explore ELBs, we created a CloudFormation template, located at https:// s3.amazonaws.com/awsinaction/chapter12/loadbalancer.json. Create a stack based on that template, and then visit the URL output of your stack with your browser. Every time you reload the page, you should see one of the private IP addresses of a back-end web server.

> **Cleaning up**
> Delete the stack you created.

12.1.2 Pitfall: connecting a server too early

The auto-scaling group is responsible for connecting a newly launched EC2 instance with the load balancer. But how does the auto-scaling group knows when the EC2 instance is installed and ready to accept traffic? Unfortunately, the auto-scaling group doesn't know whether the server is ready; it will register the EC2 instance with the load balancer as soon as the instance is launched. If traffic is sent to a server that's launched but not installed, the request will fail and your users will be unhappy.

But the ELB can send periodic health checks to each server that's connected to find out whether the server can serve requests. In the web server example, you want to check whether you get a status code 200 response for a particular resource, such as /index.html. The following listing shows how this can be done with CloudFormation.

Listing 12.2 ELB health checks to determine whether a server can answer requests

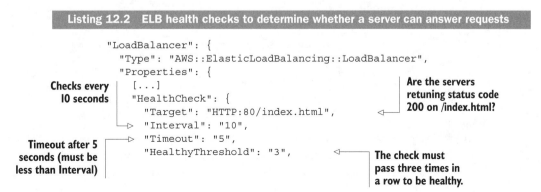

```
"LoadBalancer": {
  "Type": "AWS::ElasticLoadBalancing::LoadBalancer",
  "Properties": {
    [...]
    "HealthCheck": {
      "Target": "HTTP:80/index.html",
      "Interval": "10",
      "Timeout": "5",
      "HealthyThreshold": "3",
```

Checks every 10 seconds (points to `"Interval": "10"`)

Timeout after 5 seconds (must be less than Interval) (points to `"Timeout": "5"`)

Are the servers retuning status code 200 on /index.html? (points to `"Target": "HTTP:80/index.html"`)

The check must pass three times in a row to be healthy. (points to `"HealthyThreshold": "3"`)

```
                          "UnhealthyThreshold": "2"
The check must       }
fail two times     }
in a row to be
unhealthy.      }
```

Instead of /index.html, you can also request a dynamic page like /healthy.php that does some additional checks to decide whether the web server is ready to handle requests. The contract is that you must return an HTTP status code 200 when the server is ready. That's it.

> **Aggressive health checks can cause downtime**
>
> If a server is too busy to answer a health check, the ELB will stop sending traffic to that server. If the situation is caused by a general load increase on your system, the ELB's response will make the situation worse! We've seen applications experience downtime due to overly aggressive health checks. You need proper load testing to understand what's going on. An appropriate solution is application-specific and can't be generalized.

By default, an auto-scaling group determines if an EC2 instance is healthy based on the heath check that EC2 performs every minute. You can configure an auto-scaling group to use the health check of the load balancer instead. The auto-scaling group will now terminate servers not only if the hardware fails, but also if the application fails. Set `"HealthCheckType": "ELB"` in the auto-scaling group description. Sometimes this setting makes sense because restarting can solve issues like memory, thread pool, or disk overflow, but it can also cause unwanted restarts of EC2 instances in the case of a broken application.

12.1.3 More use cases

So far, you've seen the most common use case for ELB: load-balancing incoming web requests to some web servers over HTTP. As mentioned earlier, ELB can do far more than that. In this section, we'll look at four more typical use cases:

1. ELB can balance TCP traffic. You can place almost any application behind a load balancer.
2. ELB can turn SSL-encrypted traffic into plain traffic if you add your SSL certificate to AWS.
3. ELB can log each request. Logs are stored on S3.
4. ELB can distribute your requests evenly across multiple availability zones.

HANDLING TCP TRAFFIC

Until now, you've only used ELB to handle HTTP traffic. You can also configure ELB to redirect plain TCP traffic, to decouple databases or legacy applications with proprietary interfaces. Compared to an ELB configuration that handles HTTP traffic, you must change `Listeners` and `HealthCheck` to handle TCP traffic with ELB. The health check doesn't check for a specific response as it did when dealing with HTTP; health checks for TCP traffic are healthy when the ELB can open a socket. The following listing shows how you can redirect TCP traffic to MySQL back ends.

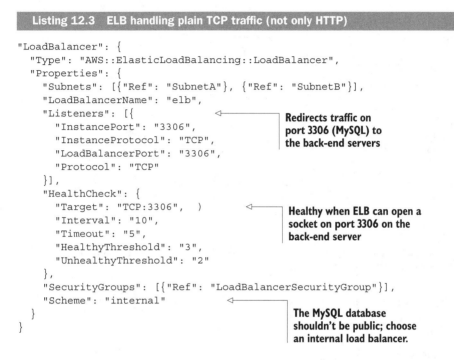

Listing 12.3 ELB handling plain TCP traffic (not only HTTP)

```
"LoadBalancer": {
  "Type": "AWS::ElasticLoadBalancing::LoadBalancer",
  "Properties": {
    "Subnets": [{"Ref": "SubnetA"}, {"Ref": "SubnetB"}],
    "LoadBalancerName": "elb",
    "Listeners": [{                          Redirects traffic on
      "InstancePort": "3306",                port 3306 (MySQL) to
      "InstanceProtocol": "TCP",             the back-end servers
      "LoadBalancerPort": "3306",
      "Protocol": "TCP"
    }],
    "HealthCheck": {
      "Target": "TCP:3306",   )             Healthy when ELB can open a
      "Interval": "10",                     socket on port 3306 on the
      "Timeout": "5",                       back-end server
      "HealthyThreshold": "3",
      "UnhealthyThreshold": "2"
    },
    "SecurityGroups": [{"Ref": "LoadBalancerSecurityGroup"}],
    "Scheme": "internal"
  }                                         The MySQL database
}                                           shouldn't be public; choose
                                            an internal load balancer.
```

You can also configure port 80 to be handled as TCP traffic, but you'll lose the ability to do health checks based on the status code that's returned by your web server.

TERMINATING SSL

An ELB can be used to terminate SSL without the need to do the configuration on your own. Terminating SSL means the ELB offers an SSL-encrypted endpoint that forwards requests unencrypted to your back-end servers. Figure 12.3 shows how this works.

You can use predefined security policies from AWS to get a secure SSL configuration that takes care of SSL vulnerabilities in the wild. You can accept requests on port 443 (HTTPS); the ELB terminates SSL and forwards the request to port 80 on a web server. That's an easy solution to offer SSL-encrypted communication. SSL termination doesn't just work for HTTP requests; it also works for TCP traffic (such as POP3, SMTP, FTP).

> **NOTE** The following example only works if you already own an SSL certificate. If you don't, you need to buy an SSL certificate or skip the example. AWS doesn't offer SSL certificates at the moment. You could use a self-signed certificate for testing purposes.

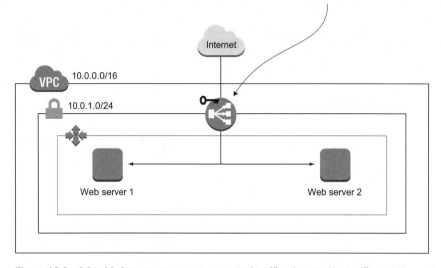

SSL-encrypted traffic on port 443 reaches the ELB.
Internally, the traffic is decrypted with the private
key. The ELB forwards decrypted (plain HTTP)
traffic to back-end servers on port 80.

**Figure 12.3   A load balancer can accept encrypted traffic, decrypt the traffic, and forward
unencrypted traffic to the back end.**

Before you can activate SSL encryption, you must upload your SSL certificate to IAM
with the help of the CLI:

```
$ aws iam upload-server-certificate \
--server-certificate-name my-ssl-cert \
--certificate-body file://my-certificate.pem \
--private-key file://my-private-key.pem \
--certificate-chain file://my-certificate-chain.pem
```

Now you can use your SSL certificate by referencing `my-ssl-cert`. The following listing shows how encrypted HTTP communication can be configured with the help of
the ELB.

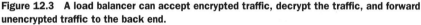

Listing 12.4   Terminating SSL with ELB to offer encrypted communication

```
"LoadBalancer": {
  "Type": "AWS::ElasticLoadBalancing::LoadBalancer",
  "Properties": {
    "Subnets": [{"Ref": "SubnetA"}, {"Ref": "SubnetB"}],
    "LoadBalancerName": "elb",
    "Policies": [{
      "PolicyName": "ELBSecurityPolicyName",
      "PolicyType": "SSLNegotiationPolicyType",
      "Attributes": [{
        "Name": "Reference-Security-Policy",
        "Value": "ELBSecurityPolicy-2015-05"
```

Configures
SSL

Uses a predefined
security policy as
a configuration

```
      }]
    }],
    "Listeners": [{
      "InstancePort": "80",          ◁────┐
      "InstanceProtocol": "HTTP",
      "LoadBalancerPort": "443",     ◁──┐
      "Protocol": "HTTPS",
      "SSLCertificateId": "my-ssl-cert",  ◁──┐
      "PolicyNames": ["ELBSecurityPolicyName"]
    }],
    "HealthCheck": {
      [...]
    },
    "SecurityGroups": [{"Ref": "LoadBalancerSecurityGroup"}],
    "Scheme": "internet-facing"
  }
}
```

The back-end servers listen on port 80 (HTTP).

The ELB accepts requests on port 443 (HTTPS).

References the previously uploaded SSL certificate

Terminating SSL with the help of the ELB eliminates many administrative tasks that are critical to providing secure communication. We encourage you to offer HTTPS with the help of an ELB to protect your customers from all kinds of attacks while they're communicating with your servers.

> **WARNING** It's likely that the security policy `ELBSecurityPolicy-2015-05` is no longer the most up-to-date. The security policy defines what versions of SSL are supported, what ciphers are supported, and other security-related options. If you aren't using the latest security policy version, your SSL setup is probably vulnerable. Visit http://mng.bz/916U to get the latest version.

We recommend that you offer only SSL-encrypted communication to your users. In addition to protecting sensitive data, it also has a positive impact on Google rankings.

LOGGING

ELB can integrate with S3 to provide access logs. Access logs contain all the requests processed by the ELB. You may be familiar with access logs from web servers like Apache web server; you can use access logs to debug problems with your back end and analyze how many requests have been made to your system.

To activate access logging, the ELB must know to which S3 bucket logs should be written. You can also specify how often the access logs should be written to S3. You need to set up an S3 bucket policy to allow the ELB to write to the bucket, as shown in the following listing.

Listing 12.5 policy.json

```
{
  "Id": "Policy1429136655940",
  "Version": "2012-10-17",
  "Statement": [{
    "Sid": "Stmt1429136633762",
```

```
    "Action": ["s3:PutObject"],
    "Effect": "Allow",
    "Resource": "arn:aws:s3:::elb-logging-bucket-$YourName/*",
    "Principal": {
      "AWS": [
        "127311923021", "027434742980", "797873946194",
        "156460612806", "054676820928", "582318560864",
        "114774131450", "783225319266", "507241528517"
      ]
    }
  }]
}
```

To create the S3 bucket with the policy, use the CLI—but don't forget to replace
$YourName with your name or nickname to prevent name clashes with other readers.
This also applies to the policy.json file. To save some time, you can download the policy from https://s3.amazonaws.com/awsinaction/chapter12/policy.json:

```
$ aws s3 mb s3://elb-logging-bucket-$YourName
$ aws s3api put-bucket-policy --bucket elb-logging-bucket-$YourName \
--policy file://policy.json
```

You can activate access logging with the following CloudFormation description.

Listing 12.6   Activating access logs written by ELB

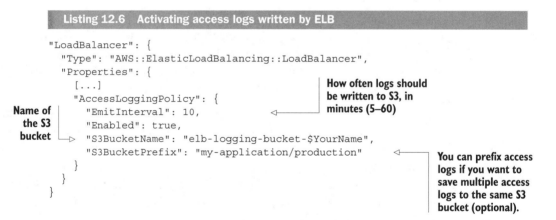

The ELB will now write access-log files to the specified S3 bucket from time to time.
The access log is similar to the one created by the Apache web server, but you can't
change the format of the information it contains. The following snippet shows a single
line of an access log:

```
2015-06-23T06:40:08.771608Z elb 92.42.224.116:17006 172.31.38.190:80
0.000063 0.000815 0.000024 200 200 0 90
"GET http://elb-....us-east-1.elb.amazonaws.com:80/ HTTP/1.1"
"Mozilla/5.0 (Macintosh; ...) Gecko/20100101 Firefox/38.0" - -
```

Here are examples of the pieces of information an access log always contains:

- Time stamp: 2015-06-23T06:40:08.771608Z
- Name of the ELB: elb

- Client IP address and port: `92.42.224.116:17006`
- Back-end IP address and port: `172.31.38.190:80`
- Number of seconds the request was processed in the load balancer: `0.000063`
- Number of seconds the request was processed in the back end: `0.000815`
- Number of seconds the response was processed in the load balancer: `0.000024`
- HTTP status code returned by the load balancer: `200`
- HTTP status code returned by back end: `200`
- Number of bytes received: `0`
- Number of bytes sent: `90`
- Request: `"GET http://elb-....us-east-1.elb.amazonaws.com:80/ HTTP/1.1"`
- User agent: `"Mozilla/5.0 (Macintosh; ...) Gecko/20100101 Firefox/38.0"`

Cleaning up

Remove the S3 bucket you created in the logging example:

```
$ aws s3 rb --force s3://elb-logging-bucket-$YourName
```

CROSS-ZONE LOAD BALANCING

The ELB is a fault-tolerant service. If you create an ELB, you receive a public name like `elb-1079556024.us-east-1.elb.amazonaws.com` as the endpoint. It's interesting to see what's behind that name. You can use the command-line application `dig` (or `nslookup` on Windows) to ask a DNS server about a particular name:

```
$ dig elb-1079556024.us-east-1.elb.amazonaws.com
[...]
;; ANSWER SECTION:
elb-1079556024.us-east-1.elb.amazonaws.com. 42 IN A 52.0.40.9
elb-1079556024.us-east-1.elb.amazonaws.com. 42 IN A 52.1.152.202
[...]
```

The name `elb-1079556024.us-east-1.elb.amazonaws.com` resolves to two IP addresses: 52.0.40.9 and 52.1.152.202. When you create a load balancer, AWS starts two instances in the background and uses DNS to distributed between the two. To make the servers fault-tolerant, AWS spawns the load-balancer instances in different availability zones. By default, each load-balancer instance of the ELB sends traffic only to EC2 instances in the same availability zone. If you want to distribute requests across availability zones, you can enable *cross-zone load balancing*. Figure 12.4 shows a scenario in which cross-zone load balancing is important.

The following CloudFormation snippet shows how this can be activated:

```
"LoadBalancer": {
  "Type": "AWS::ElasticLoadBalancing::LoadBalancer",
  "Properties": {
    [...]
    "CrossZone": true
  }
}
```

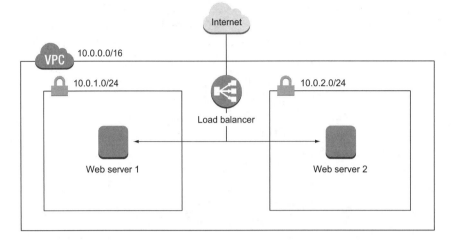

Figure 12.4   Enabling cross-zone load balancing to distribute traffic between availability zones

We recommend that you enable cross-zone load balancing, which is disabled by default, to ensure that requests are routed evenly across all back-end servers.

In the next section, you'll learn more about asynchronous decoupling.

12.2   *Asynchronous decoupling with message queues*

Synchronous decoupling with ELB is easy; you don't need to change your code to do it. But for asynchronous decoupling, you have to adapt your code to work with a message queue.

A message queue has a head and a tail. You can add new messages to the tail while reading messages from the head. This allows you to decouple the production and consumption of messages. The producers and consumers don't know each other; they both only know about the message queue. Figure 12.5 illustrates this principle.

You can put new messages onto the queue while no one is reading messages, and the message queue acts as a buffer. To prevent message queues from growing infinitely large, messages are only saved for a certain amount of time. If you consume a message from a message queue, you must acknowledge the successful processing of the message to permanently delete it from the queue.

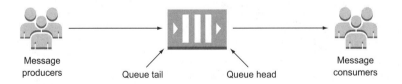

Figure 12.5   Producers send messages to a message queue, and consumers read messages.

The Simple Queue Service (SQS) is a fully managed AWS service. SQS offers message queues that guarantee the delivery of messages at least once:

- Under rare circumstances, a single message will be available for consumption twice. This may sound strange if you compare it to other message queues, but you'll see how to deal with this problem later in the chapter.
- SQS doesn't guarantee the order of messages, so you may read messages in a different order than they were produced.

This limitation of SQS is also beneficial:

- You can put as many messages into SQS as you like.
- The message queue scales with the number of messages you produce and consume.

The pricing model is also simple: you pay $0.00000050 per request to SQS or $0.5 per million requests. Producing a message is one request, and consuming is another request (if your payload is larger than 64 KB, every 64 KB chunk counts as one request).

12.2.1 *Turning a synchronous process into an asynchronous one*

A typical synchronous process looks like this: a user makes a request to your server, something happens on the server, and a result is returned to the user. To make things more concrete, we'll talk about the process of creating a preview image of an URL in the following example:

1. The user submits a URL.
2. The server downloads the content at the URL and converts it into a PNG image.
3. The server returns the PNG to the user.

With one small trick, this process can be made asynchronous:

1. The user submits a URL.
2. The server puts a message onto a queue that contains a random ID and the URL.
3. The server returns a link to the user where the PNG image will be found in the future. The link contains the random ID (http://$Bucket.s3-website-us-east-1 .amazonaws.com/$RandomId.png).
4. In the background, a worker consumes the message from the queue, downloads the content, converts the content into a PNG, and uploads the image to S3.
5. At some point in time, the user tries to download the PNG at the known location.

If you want to make a process asynchronous, you must manage the way the process initiator tracks the status of the process. One way of doing that is to return an ID to the initiator that can be used to look up the process. During the process, the ID is passed from step to step.

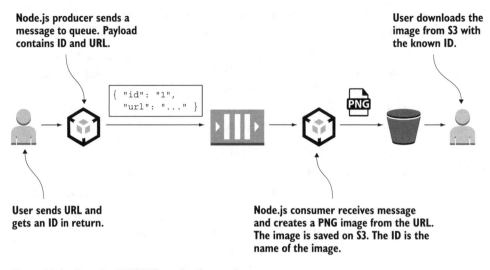

Figure 12.6   How the URL2PNG application works

12.2.2   *Architecture of the URL2PNG application*

You'll now create a simple but decoupled piece of software named URL2PNG that converts the URL of a web page into a PNG. Again, you'll use Node.js to do the programming part, and you'll use SQS. Figure 12.6 shows how the URL2PNG application works.

To complete the example, you need to create an S3 bucket with web hosting enabled. Execute the following commands, replacing $YourName with your name or nickname to prevent name clashes with other readers:

```
$ aws s3 mb s3://url2png-$YourName
$ aws s3 website s3://url2png-$YourName --index-document index.html \
--error-document error.html
```

Web hosting is needed so users can later download the images from S3. Now it's time to create the message queue.

12.2.3   *Setting up a message queue*

Creating an SQS queue is simple—you only need to specify the name of the queue:

```
$ aws sqs create-queue --queue-name url2png
{
    "QueueUrl": "https://queue.amazonaws.com/878533158213/url2png"
}
```

The returned QueueUrl is needed later in the example, so be sure to save it.

12.2.4   *Producing messages programmatically*

You now have an SQS queue to send messages to. To produce a message, you need to specify the queue and a payload. You'll again use Node.js in combination with the AWS SDK to connect your program with AWS.

> ### Installing and getting started with Node.js
> To install Node.js, visit https://nodejs.org and download the package that fits your OS.

Here's how the message is produced with the help of the AWS SDK for Node.js; it will later be consumed by the URL2PNG worker. The Node.js script can then be used like this (don't try to run this command now—you need to install and configure URL2PNG first):

```
$ node index.js "http://aws.amazon.com"
PNG will be available soon at
http://url2png-$YourName.s3-website-us-east-1.amazonaws.com/XYZ.png
```

As usual, you'll find the code in the book's code repository on GitHub https://github.com/AWSinAction/code. The URL2PNG example is located at /chapter12/url2png/. The following listing shows the implementation of index.js.

Listing 12.7 index.js: sending a message to the queue

```
var AWS = require('aws-sdk');
var uuid = require('node-uuid');
var sqs = new AWS.SQS({          ◁──── Creates an SQS endpoint
  "region": "us-east-1"
});

if (process.argv.length !== 3) {         Checks whether a
  console.log('URL missing');       ◁──┘ URL was provided
  process.exit(1);
}
                                   Creates a
var id = uuid.v4();           ◁──┘ random ID
var body = {              ◁────┐
  "id": id,                    │ The payload contains
  "url": process.argv[2]       │ the random ID and
};                             │ the URL.
                    ┌──────────┘
var params = {      │
  "MessageBody": JSON.stringify(body),    Queue to which the message
  "QueueUrl": "$QueueUrl"        ◁───┤    is sent (was returned when
};                                      creating the queue)

sqs.sendMessage(params, function(err) {   ◁──┐
  if (err) {                                  Invokes the sendMessage
    console.log('error', err);                operation on SQS
  } else {
    console.log('PNG will be available soon at http://url2png-$YourName.s3-
    ➥ website-us-east-1.amazonaws.com/' + id + '.png');
  }
});
```

Converts the payload into a JSON string

Before you can run the script, you need to install the Node.js modules. Run npm install in your terminal to install the dependencies. You'll find a config.json file that needs to be modified. Make sure to change QueueUrl to the queue you created at the beginning of this example and change Bucket to url2png-$YourName.

Now you can run the script with node index.js "http://aws.amazon.com". The program should response with something like "PNG will be available soon at http://url2png-$YourName.s3-website-us-east-1.amazonaws.com/XYZ.png". To verify that the message is ready for consumption, you can ask the queue how many messages are inside:

```
$ aws sqs get-queue-attributes \
--queue-url $QueueUrl \
--attribute-names ApproximateNumberOfMessages
{
  "Attributes": {
    "ApproximateNumberOfMessages": "1"
  }
}
```

Next, it's time to work on the worker that consumes the message and does all the work of generating a PNG.

12.2.5 *Consuming messages programmatically*

Processing a message with SQS takes three steps:

1 Receive a message.
2 Process the message.
3 Acknowledge successful message processing.

You'll now implement each of these steps to change a URL into a PNG.

To receive a message from an SQS queue, you must specify the following:

- The queue
- The maximum number of messages you want to receive. To get higher throughput, you can get batches of messages.
- The number of seconds you want to take this message from the queue to process it. Within that time, you must delete the message from the queue, or it will be received again.
- The maximum number of seconds you want to wait to receive messages. Receiving messages from SQS is done by polling the API. But the API allows long-polling for a maximum of 10 seconds.

The next listing shows how this is done with the SDK.

Listing 12.8   worker.js: receiving a message from the queue

```
var fs = require('fs');
var AWS = require('aws-sdk');
var webshot = require('webshot');
```

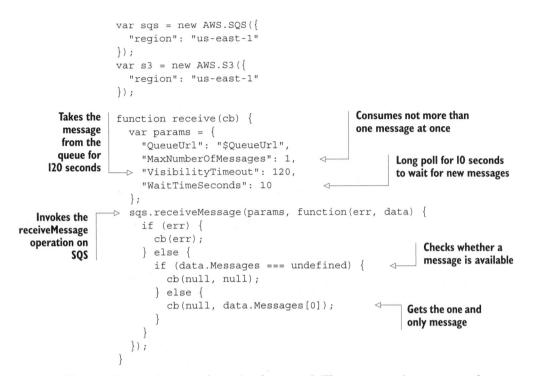

```
var sqs = new AWS.SQS({
  "region": "us-east-1"
});
var s3 = new AWS.S3({
  "region": "us-east-1"
});
```

Takes the message from the queue for 120 seconds

Consumes not more than one message at once

```
function receive(cb) {
  var params = {
    "QueueUrl": "$QueueUrl",
    "MaxNumberOfMessages": 1,
    "VisibilityTimeout": 120,
    "WaitTimeSeconds": 10
  };
```

Long poll for 10 seconds to wait for new messages

Invokes the receiveMessage operation on SQS

```
  sqs.receiveMessage(params, function(err, data) {
    if (err) {
      cb(err);
    } else {
      if (data.Messages === undefined) {
        cb(null, null);
      } else {
        cb(null, data.Messages[0]);
      }
    }
  });
}
```

Checks whether a message is available

Gets the one and only message

The receive step has now been implemented. The next step is to process the message. Thanks to a Node.js module called webshot, it's easy to create a screenshot of a website.

Listing 12.9 worker.js: processing a message (take screenshot and upload to S3)

Creates the screenshot with the webshot module

```
function process(message, cb) {
  var body = JSON.parse(message.Body);
  var file = body.id + '.png';
  webshot(body.url, file, function(err) {
    if (err) {
      cb(err);
    } else {
      fs.readFile(file, function(err, buf) {
        if (err) {
          cb(err);
        } else {
          var params = {
            "Bucket": "url2png-$YourName",
            "Key": file,
            "ACL": "public-read",
            "ContentType": "image/png",
            "Body": buf
          };
          s3.putObject(params, function(err) {
            if (err) {
              cb(err);
```

The message body is a JSON string. You convert it back into a JavaScript object.

Opens the screenshot that was saved to local disk by the webshot module

Allows everyone to read the screenshot on S3

Uploads the screenshot to S3

```
        } else {
          fs.unlink(file, cb);
        }
      });
    }
  });
}
```

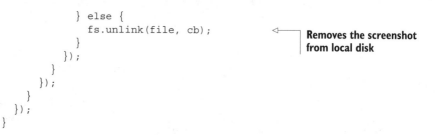
Removes the screenshot from local disk

The only step that's missing is to acknowledge that the message was successfully consumed. If you receive a message from SQS, you get a `ReceiptHandle`, which is a unique ID that you need to specify when you delete a message from a queue.

Listing 12.10   worker.js: acknowledging a message (deletes the message from the queue)

```
function acknowledge(message, cb) {
  var params = {
    "QueueUrl": "$QueueUrl",
    "ReceiptHandle": message.ReceiptHandle
  };
  sqs.deleteMessage(params, cb);
}
```

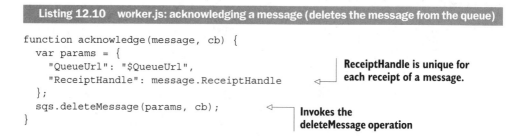
ReceiptHandle is unique for each receipt of a message.

Invokes the deleteMessage operation

You have all the parts; now it's time to connect them.

Listing 12.11   worker.js: connecting the parts

```
function run() {
  receive(function(err, message) {
    if (err) {
      throw err;
    } else {
      if (message === null) {
        console.log('nothing to do');
        setTimeout(run, 1000);
      } else {
        console.log('process');
        process(message, function(err) {
          if (err) {
            throw err;
          } else {
            acknowledge(message, function(err) {
              if (err) {
                throw err;
              } else {
                console.log('done');
                setTimeout(run, 1000);
              }
            });
          }
        });
      }
    }
  });
```

Receives a message

Checks whether a message is available

Calls the run method again in one second

Processes the message

Acknowledges the message

Calls the run method again in one second

```
      }
    }
  });
}

run();
```

Calls the run
method to start

Now you can start the worker to process the message that is already in the queue. Run the script with `node worker.js`. You should see some output that says the worker is in the process step and that then switches to Done. After a few seconds, the screenshot should be uploaded to S3. Your first asynchronous application is complete.

You've created an application that is asynchronously decoupled. If the URL2PNG service becomes popular and millions of users start using it, the queue will become longer and longer because your worker can't produce that many PNGs from URLs. The cool thing is that you can add as many workers as you like to consume those messages. Instead of only 1 worker, you can start 10 or 100. The other advantage is that if a worker dies for some reason, the message that was in flight will become available for consumption after two minutes and will be picked up by another worker. That's fault-tolerant! If you design your system asynchronously decoupled, it's easy to scale and a good foundation to be fault-tolerant. The next chapter will concentrate on this topic.

Cleaning up

Delete the message queue as follows:

```
$ aws sqs delete-queue --queue-url $QueueUrl
```

And don't forget to clean up and delete the S3 bucket used in the example. Issue the following command, replacing $YourName with your name:

```
$ aws s3 rb --force s3://url2png-$YourName
```

12.2.6 *Limitations of messaging with SQS*

Earlier in the chapter, we mentioned a few limitations of SQS. This section covers them in more detail.

SQS DOESN'T GUARANTEE THAT A MESSAGE IS DELIVERED ONLY ONCE

If a received message isn't deleted within `VisibilityTimeout`, the message will be received again. This problem can be solved by making the receive idempotent. *Idempotent* means that no matter how often the message is consumed, the result stays the same. In the URL2PNG example, this is true by design: if you process the message multiple times, the same image is uploaded to S3 multiple times. If the image is already available on S3, it's replaced. Idempotence solves many problems in distributed systems that guarantee at least single delivery of messages.

Not everything can be made idempotent. Sending an e-mail is a good example: if you process a message multiple times and it sends an email each time, you'll annoy the addressee. As a workaround, you can use a database to track whether you already sent the email.

In many cases, at least once is a good trade-off. Check your requirements before using SQS if this trade-off fits your needs.

SQS DOESN'T GUARANTEE THE MESSAGE ORDER

Messages may be consumed in a different order than the order in which you produced them. If you need a strict order, you should search for something else. SQS is a fault-tolerant and scalable message queue. If you need a stable message order, you'll have difficulty finding a solution that scales like SQS. Our advice is to change the design of your system so you no longer need the stable order or produce the order at the client side.

SQS DOESN'T REPLACE A MESSAGE BROKER

SQS isn't a message broker like ActiveMQ—SQS is only a message queue. Don't expect features like those offered by message brokers. Considering SQS versus ActiveMQ is like comparing DynamoDB to MySQL.

12.3 Summary

- Decoupling makes things easier because it reduces dependencies.
- Synchronous decoupling requires two sides to be available at the same time, but the sides don't know each other.
- With asynchronous decoupling, you can communicate without both sides being available.
- Most applications can be synchronously decoupled without touching the code, using the load balancer offered by the Elastic Load Balancing service.
- A load balancer can make periodic health checks to your application to determine whether the back end is ready to serve traffic.
- Asynchronous decoupling is only possible with asynchronous processes. But you can modify a synchronous process to be an asynchronous one most of the time.
- Asynchronous decoupling with SQS requires programming against SQS with one of the SDKs.

13

Designing
for fault-tolerance

This chapter covers

- What fault-tolerance is and why you need it
- Using redundancy to remove single point of failures
- Retrying on failure
- Using idempotent operations to achieve retry on failure
- AWS service guarantees

Failure is inevitable for hard disks, networks, power, and so on. Fault-tolerance deals with that problem. A fault-tolerant system is built for failure. If a failure occurs, the system isn't interrupted, and it continues to handle requests. If your system has a single point of failure, it's not fault-tolerant. You can achieve fault-tolerance by introducing redundancy into your system and by decoupling the parts of your system in such a way that one side doesn't rely on the uptime of the other.

The most convenient way to make your system fault-tolerant is to compose the system of fault-tolerant blocks. If all blocks are fault-tolerant, the system is fault-tolerant as well. Many AWS services are fault-tolerant by default. If possible, use them. Otherwise you'll need to deal with the consequences.

Unfortunately, one important service isn't fault-tolerant by default: EC2 instances. A virtual server isn't fault-tolerant. This means a system that uses EC2 isn't fault-tolerant by default. But AWS provides the building blocks to deal with that issue. The solution consists of auto-scaling groups, Elastic Load Balancing (ELB), and SQS.

It's important to differentiate among services that guarantee the following:

- *Nothing (single point of failure)*—No requests are served in case of failure.
- *High availability*—In case of failure, it takes some time until requests are served as before.
- *Fault-tolerance*—In case of failure, requests are served as before without any availability issues.

Following are the guarantees of the AWS services covered in this book in detail. *Single point of failure* (SPOF) means this service will fail if, for example, a hardware failure occurs:

- *Amazon Elastic Compute Cloud (EC2) instance*—A single EC2 instance can fail for many reasons: hardware failure, network problems, availability-zone problems, and so on. Use auto-scaling groups to have a fleet of EC2 instances serve requests in a redundant way to achieve high availability or fault-tolerance.
- *Amazon Relational Database Service (RDS) single instance*—A single RDS instance can fail for many reasons: hardware failure, network problems, availability zone problems, and so on. Use Multi-AZ mode to achieve high availability.

Highly available (HA) means that when a failure occurs the service won't be available for a short time but will come back automatically:

- *Elastic Network Interface (ENI)*—A network interface is bound to an AZ (availability zone), so if this AZ goes down, your network interface is down.
- *Amazon Virtual Private Cloud (VPC) subnet*—A VPC subnet is bound to an AZ, so if this AZ goes down, your subnet is down. Use multiple subnets in different AZs to remove the dependency on a single AZ.
- *Amazon Elastic Block Store (EBS) volume*—An EBS volume is bound to an AZ, so if this AZ goes down, your volume is unavailable (your data won't be lost). You can create EBS snapshots from time to time so you can recreate an EBS volume in another AZ.
- *Amazon Relational Database Service (RDS) Multi-AZ instance*—When running in Multi-AZ mode, a short downtime (one minute) is expected if an issue occurs with the master instance while changing DNS records to switch to the standby instance.

Fault-tolerant means that if a failure occurs, you won't notice it:

- Elastic Load Balancing (ELB), deployed to at least two AZs
- Amazon EC2 Security Group
- Amazon Virtual Private Cloud (VPC) with an ACL and a route table
- Elastic IP Address (EIP)
- Amazon Simple Storage Service (S3)

- Amazon Elastic Block Store (EBS) snapshot
- Amazon DynamoDB
- Amazon CloudWatch
- Auto-scaling group
- Amazon Simple Queue Service (SQS)
- AWS Elastic Beanstalk
- AWS OpsWorks
- AWS CloudFormation
- AWS Identity and Access Management (IAM, not bound to a single region; if you create an IAM user, that user is available in all regions)

Why should you care about fault-tolerance? Because in the end, a fault-tolerant system provides the highest quality to your end users. No matter what happens in your system, the user is never affected and can continue to consume content, buy stuff, or have conversations with friends. A few years ago it was expensive to achieve fault-tolerance, but in AWS, providing fault-tolerant systems is an affordable standard.

> **Chapter requirements**
> To fully understand this chapter, you need to have read and understood the following concepts:
>
> - EC2 (chapter 3)
> - Auto-scaling (chapter 11)
> - Elastic Load Balancing (chapter 12)
> - SQS (chapter 12)
>
> The example makes intensive use of the following:
>
> - Elastic Beanstalk (chapter 5)
> - DynamoDB (chapter 10)
> - Express, a Node.js web application framework

In this chapter, you'll learn everything you need to design a fault-tolerant web application based on EC2 instances (which aren't fault-tolerant by default).

13.1 Using redundant EC2 instances to increase availability

Unfortunately, EC2 instances aren't fault-tolerant. Under your virtual server is a host system. These are a few reasons your virtual server might suffer from a crash caused by the host system:

- If the host hardware fails, it can no longer host the virtual server on top of it.
- If the network connection to/from the host is interrupted, the virtual server loses the ability to communicate via network as well.
- If the host system is disconnected from a power supply, the virtual server also goes down.

But the software running on top of the virtual server may also cause a crash:

- If your software has a memory leak, you'll run out of memory. It may take a day, a month, a year, or more, but eventually it will happen.
- If your software writes to disk and never deletes its data, you'll run out of disk space sooner or later.
- Your application may not handle edge cases properly and instead just crashes.

Regardless of whether the host system or your software is the cause of a crash, a single EC2 instance is a single point of failure. If you rely on a single EC2 instance, your system will blow up—the only question is when.

13.1.1 Redundancy can remove a single point of failure

Imagine a production line that makes fluffy cloud pies. Producing a fluffy cloud pie requires several production steps (simplified!):

1. Produce a pie crust.
2. Cool the pie crust.
3. Put the fluffy cloud mass on top of the pie crust.
4. Cool the fluffy cloud pie.
5. Package the fluffy cloud pie.

The current setup is a single production line. The big problem with this setup is that whenever one of the steps crashes, the entire production line must be stopped. Figure 13.1 illustrates the problem when the second step (cooling the pie crust) crashes. The following steps no longer work, either, because they don't receive cool pie crusts.

Why not have multiple production lines? Instead of one line, suppose we have three. If one of the lines fails, the other two can still produce fluffy cloud pies for all the hungry customers in the world. Figure 13.2 shows the improvements; the only downside is that we need three times as many machines.

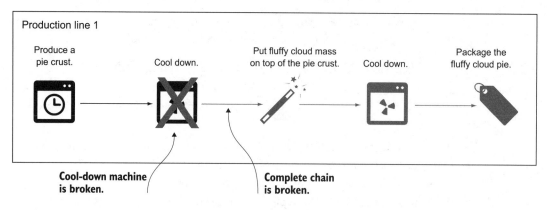

Figure 13.1 A single point of failure affects not only itself, but the entire system.

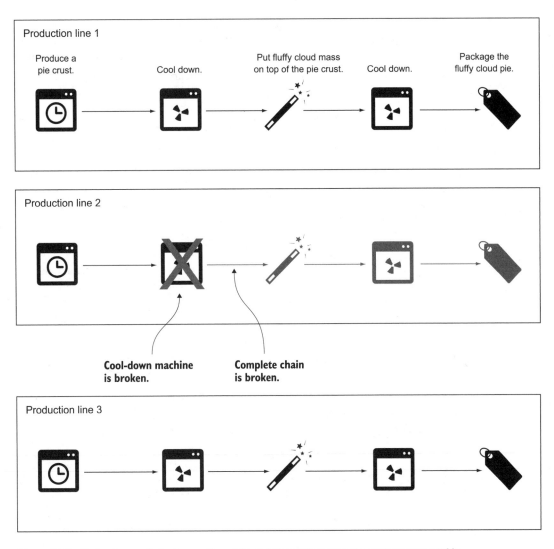

Figure 13.2   Redundancy eliminates single points of failure and makes the system more stable.

The example can be transferred to EC2 instances as well. Instead of having only one EC2 instance, you can have three of them running your software. If one of those instances crashes, the other two are still able to serve incoming requests. You can also minimize the cost impact of one versus three instances: instead of one large EC2 instance, you can choose three small ones. The problem that arises with a dynamic server pool is, how can you communicate with the instances? The answer is *decoupling*: put a load balancer between your EC2 instances and the requestor or a message queue. Read on to learn how this works.

13.1.2 *Redundancy requires decoupling*

Figure 13.3 shows how EC2 instances can be made fault-tolerant by using redundancy and synchronous decoupling. If one of the EC2 instances crashes, ELB stops to route requests to the crashed instances. The auto-scaling group replaces the crashed EC2 instance within minutes, and ELB begins to route requests to the new instance.

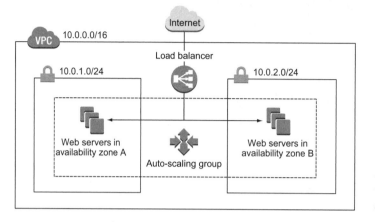

Figure 13.3   Fault-tolerant EC2 servers with an auto-scaling group and ELB

Take a second look at figure 13.3 and see what parts are redundant:

- *Availability zones*—Two are used. If one AZ goes down, we still have EC2 instances running in the other AZ.
- *Subnets*—A subnet is tightly coupled to an AZ. Therefore we need one subnet in each AZ, and subnets are also redundant.
- *EC2 instances*—We have multi-redundancy for EC2 instances. We have multiple instances in a single subnet (AZ), and we have instances in two subnets (AZs).

Figure 13.4 shows a fault-tolerant system built with EC2 that uses the power of redundancy and asynchronous decoupling to process messages from an SQS queue.

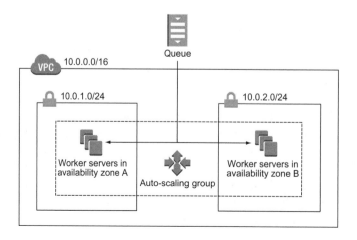

Figure 13.4   Fault-tolerant EC2 servers with an auto-scaling group and SQS

In both figures, the load balancer/SQS queue appears only once. This doesn't mean ELB or SQS is a single point of failure; on the contrary, ELB and SQS are fault-tolerant by default.

13.2 Considerations for making your code fault-tolerant

If you want fault-tolerance, you must achieve it within your code. You can design fault-tolerance into your code by following two suggestions presented in this section.

13.2.1 Let it crash, but also retry

The Erlang programming language is famous for the concept of "let it crash." That simply means whenever the program doesn't know what to do, it crashes, and someone needs to deal with the crash. Most often people overlook the fact that Erlang is also famous for retrying. Letting it crash without retrying isn't useful—if you can't recover from a crashed situation, your system will be down, which is the opposite of what you want.

You can apply the "let it crash" concept (some people call it "fail-fast") to synchronous and asynchronous decoupled scenarios. In a synchronous decoupled scenario, the sender of a request must implement the retry logic. If no response is returned within a certain amount of time, or an error is returned, the sender retries by sending the same request again. In an asynchronous decoupled scenario, things are easier. If a message is consumed but not acknowledged within a certain amount of time, it goes back to the queue. The next consumer then grabs the message and processes it again. Retrying is built into asynchronous systems by default.

"Let it crash" isn't useful in all situations. If the program wants to respond to tell the sender that the request contained invalid content, this isn't a reason for letting the server crash: the result will stay the same no matter how often you retry. But if the server can't reach the database, it makes a lot of sense to retry. Within a few seconds the database may be available again and able to successfully process the retried request.

Retrying isn't that easy. Imagine that you want to retry the creation of a blog post. With every retry, a new entry in the database is created, containing the same data as before. You end up with many duplicates in the database. Preventing this involves a powerful concept that's introduced next: idempotent retry.

13.2.2 Idempotent retry makes fault-tolerance possible

How can you prevent a blog post from being added to the database multiple times because of a retry? A naïve approach would be to use the title as primary key. If the primary key is already used, you can assume that the post is already in the database and skip the step of inserting it into the database. Now the insertion of blog posts is *idempotent*, which means no matter how often a certain action is applied, the outcome must be the same. In the current example, the outcome is a database entry.

Let's try it with a more complicated example. Inserting a blog post is more complicated in reality, and the process looks something like this:

1 Create a blog post entry in the database.
2 Invalidate the cache because data has changed.
3 Post the link to the blog's Twitter feed.

Let's take a close look at each step.

1. CREATING A BLOG POST ENTRY IN THE DATABASE

We covered this step earlier by using the title as
a primary key. But this time, let's use a univer-
sally unique identifier (UUID) instead of the
title as the primary key. A UUID like `550e8400-`
`e29b-11d4-a716-446655440000` is a random ID
that's generated by the client. Because of the
nature of a UUID, it's unlikely that two equal
UUIDs will be generated. If the client wants to
create a blog post, it must send a request to the
ELB containing the UUID, title, and text. The
ELB routes the request to one of the back-end
servers. The back-end server checks whether
the primary key already exists. If not, a new
record is added to the database. If it exists, the
insertion continues. Figure 13.5 shows the flow.

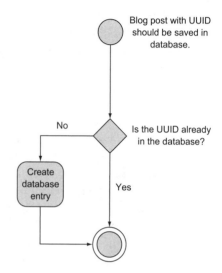

Figure 13.5   Idempotent database insert:
creating a blog post entry in the database
only if it doesn't already exist

Creating a blog post is a good example of an
idempotent operation that's guaranteed by
code. You can also use your database to handle
this problem. Just send an insert to your database. Three things can happen:

- Your database inserts the data. The step is successfully completed.
- Your database responds with an error that the primary key is already in use. The
  step is successfully completed.
- Your database responds with a different error. The step crashes.

Think twice about the best way of implementing idempotence!

2. INVALIDATING THE CACHE

This step sends an invalidation message to a caching layer. You don't need to worry
about idempotency too much here: it doesn't hurt if the cache is invalidated more
often than needed. If the cache is invalidated, then the next time a request hits the
cache, the cache won't contain data, and the original source (in this case, the database) will be queried for the result. The result is then put in the cache for subsequent
requests. If you invalidate the cache multiple times because of a retry, the worst thing
that can happen is that you may need to make a few more calls to your database.
That's easy.

3. POSTING TO THE BLOG'S TWITTER FEED

To make this step idempotent, you need to use some tricks because you interact with a third party that doesn't support idempotent operations. Unfortunately, no solution will guarantee that you post exactly one status update to Twitter. You can guarantee the creation is at least one (one or more than one) status update, or at most one (one or none) status update. An easy approach could be to ask the Twitter API for the latest status updates; if one of them matches the status update that you want to post, you skip the step because it's already done.

But Twitter is an eventually consistent system: there's no guarantee that you'll see a status update immediately after you post it. You can end up having your status update posted multiple times. Another approach would be to save in a database whether you already posted the blog post status update. But imagine saving to the database that you posted to Twitter and then making the request to the Twitter API—but at that moment, the system crashes. Your database will say that the Twitter status update was posted, but in reality it wasn't. You need to make a choice: tolerate a missing status update, or tolerate multiple status updates. Hint: it's a business decision. Figure 13.6 shows the flow of both solutions.

Now it's time for a practical example! You'll design, implement, and deploy a distributed, fault-tolerant web application on AWS. This example will demonstrate how distributed systems work and will combine most of the knowledge in this book.

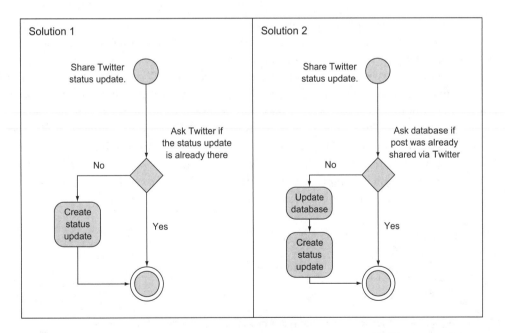

Figure 13.6 Idempotent Twitter status update: only share a status update if it hasn't already been done.

13.3   *Architecting a fault-tolerant web application: Imagery*

Before you begin the architecture and design of the fault-tolerant Imagery application, we'll talk briefly about what the application should do in the end. A user should be able to upload an image. This image is then transformed with a sepia filter so that it looks old. The user can then view the sepia image. Figure 13.7 shows the process.

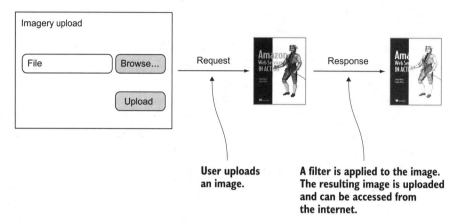

User uploads
an image.

A filter is applied to the image.
The resulting image is uploaded
and can be accessed from
the internet.

Figure 13.7   The user uploads an image to Imagery, where a filter is applied.

The problem with the process shown in figure 13.7 is that it's synchronous. If the server dies during request and response, the user's image won't be processed. Another problem arises when many users want to use the Imagery app: the system becomes busy and may slow down or stop working. Therefore the process should be turned into an asynchronous one. Chapter 12 introduced the idea of asynchronous decoupling by using a SQS message queue, as shown in figure 13.8.

When designing an asynchronous process, it's important to keep track of the process. You need some kind of identifier for it. When a user wants to upload an image, the user creates a process first. This process creation returns a unique ID. With that ID, the user is able to upload an image. If the image upload is finished, the server begins to process the image in the background. The user can look up the process at any time

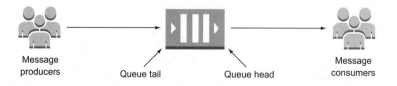

Message
producers

Queue tail   Queue head

Message
consumers

Figure 13.8   Producers send messages to a message queue, and consumers read messages.

with the process ID. While the image is being processed, the user can't see the sepia image. But as soon as the image is processed, the lookup process returns the sepia image. Figure 13.9 shows the asynchronous process.

Now that you have an asynchronous process, it's time to map that process to AWS services. Keep in mind that most services on AWS are fault-tolerant by default, so it makes sense to pick them whenever possible. Figure 13.10 shows one way of doing it.

To make things as easy as possible, all the actions will be accessible via a REST API, which will be provided by EC2 instances. In the end, EC2 instances will provide the process and make calls to all the AWS services shown in figure 13.10.

You'll use many AWS services to implement the Imagery application. Most of them are fault-tolerant by default, but EC2 isn't. You'll deal with that problem using an idempotent image-state machine, as introduced in the next section.

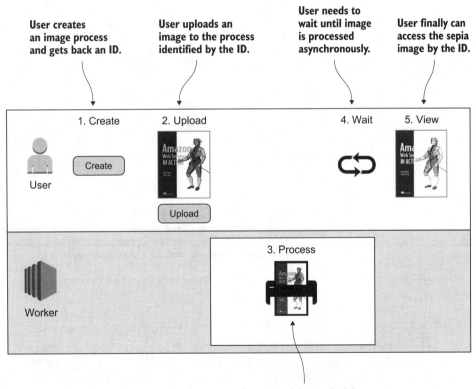

Figure 13.9   The user asynchronously uploads an image to Imagery, where a filter is applied.

User creates a process with a unique ID. Process is stored in DynamoDB.

With the process ID, the user uploads an image to S3. The S3 key is persisted to DynamoDB together with the new process state "uploaded". A SQS message is produced to trigger processing.

DynamoDB contains the current state of the process. Wait until state switches to "processed".

S3 contains the sepia image. DynamoDB knows the S3 key.

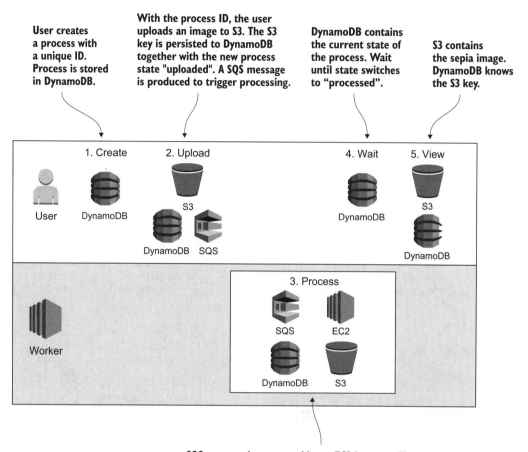

SQS message is consumed by an EC2 instance. The raw message is downloaded from S3 and processed, and the sepia image is uploaded to S3. The process in DynamoDB is updated with the new state "processed" and the S3 key of the sepia image.

Figure 13.10   Combining AWS services to implement the asynchronous Imagery process

Example is 100% covered by the Free Tier

The examples in this chapter are totally covered by the Free Tier. As long as you don't run the examples longer than a few days, you won't pay anything for it. Keep in mind that this applies only if you created a fresh AWS account for this book and there are no other things going on in your AWS account. Try to complete the chapter within a few days, because you'll clean up your account at the end of the chapter.

> ## AWS Lambda and Amazon API Gateway are coming
>
> AWS is working on a service called Lambda. With Lambda, you can upload a code function to AWS and then execute that function on AWS. You no longer need to provide your own EC2 instances; you only have to worry about the code. AWS Lambda is made for short-running processes (up to 60 seconds), so you can't create a web server with Lambda. But AWS will offer many integration hooks: for example, each time an object is added to S3, AWS can trigger a Lambda function; or a Lambda function is triggered when a new message arrives on SQS. Unfortunately, AWS Lambda isn't available in all regions at the time of writing, so we decided not to include this service.
>
> Amazon API Gateway gives you the ability to run a REST API without having to run any EC2 instances. You can specify that whenever a `GET /some/resource` request is received, it will trigger a Lambda function. The combination of Lambda and Amazon API Gateway lets you build powerful services without a single EC2 instance that you must maintain. Unfortunately, Amazon API Gateway isn't available in all regions at the time of writing.

13.3.1 *The idempotent image-state machine*

An idempotent image-state machine sounds complicated. We'll take some time to explain it because it's the heart of the Imagery application. Let's look at what a *state machine* is and what *idempotent* means in this context.

THE FINITE STATE MACHINE

A state machine has at least one start state and one end state (we're talking about finite state machines). Between the start and the end state, the state machine can have many other states. The machine also defines transitions between states. For example, a state machine with three states could look like this:

```
(A) -> (B) -> (C).
```

This means

- State A is the start state.
- There is a transition possible from state A to B.
- There is a transition possible from state B to C.
- State C is the end state.

But there's no transition possible between (A) -> (C) or (B) -> (A). The Imagery state machine could look like this:

```
(Created) -> (Uploaded) -> (Processed)
```

Once a new process (state machine) is created, the only transition possible is to `Uploaded`. To make this transition happen, you need the S3 key of the uploaded raw image. The transition between `Created -> Uploaded` can be defined by the function `uploaded(s3Key)`. Basically, the same is true for the transition `Uploaded -> Processed`. This transition can be done with the S3 key of the sepia image: `processed(s3Key)`.

Don't be confused because the upload and the image filter processing don't appear in the state machine. These are the basic actions that happen, but we're only interested in the results; we don't track the progress of the actions. The process isn't aware that 10% of the data has been uploaded or that 30% of the image processing is done. It only cares whether the actions are 100% done. You can probably imagine a bunch of other states that could be implemented but that we're skipping for the purpose of simplicity in this example; `Resized` and `Shared` are just two examples.

IDEMPOTENT STATE TRANSITIONS

An idempotent state transition must have the same result no matter how often the transition takes place. If you know that your state transitions are idempotent, you can do a simple trick: in case of a failure during transitioning, you retry the entire state transition.

Let's look at the two state transitions you need to implement. The first transition `Created -> Uploaded` can be implemented like this (pseudo code):

```
uploaded(s3Key) {
  process = DynamoDB.getItem(processId)
  if (process.state !== "Created") {
    throw new Error("transition not allowed")
  }
  DynamoDB.updateItem(processId, {"state": "Uploaded", "rawS3Key": s3Key})
  SQS.sendMessage({"processId": processId, "action": "process"});
}
```

The problem with this implementation is that it's not idempotent. Imagine that `SQS.sendMessage` fails. The state transition will fail, so you retry. But the second call to `uploaded(s3Key)` will throw a "transition not allowed" error because `DynamoDB.updateItem` was successful during the first call.

To fix that, you need to change the `if` statement to make the function idempotent:

```
uploaded(s3Key) {
  process = DynamoDB.getItem(processId)
  if (process.state !== "Created" && process.state !== "Uploaded") {
    throw new Error("transition not allowed")
  }
  DynamoDB.updateItem(processId, {"state": "Uploaded", "rawS3Key": s3Key})
  SQS.sendMessage({"processId": processId, "action": "process"});
}
```

If you retry now, you'll make multiple updates to DynamoDB, which doesn't hurt. And you may send multiple SQS messages, which also doesn't hurt, because the SQS message consumer must be idempotent as well. The same applies to the transition `Uploaded -> Processed`.

Next, you'll begin to implement the Imagery server.

13.3.2 Implementing a fault-tolerant web service

We'll split the Imagery application into two parts: a server and a worker. The server is responsible for providing the REST API to the user, and the worker handles consuming SQS messages and processing images.

> **Where is the code located?**
>
> As usual, you'll find the code in the book's code repository on GitHub: https://github.com/AWSinAction/code. Imagery is located in /chapter13/.

The server will support the following routes:

- POST /image—A new image process is created when executing this route.
- GET /image/:id—This route returns the state of the process specified with the path parameter :id.
- POST /image/:id/upload—This route offers a file upload for the process specified with the path parameter :id.

To implement the server, you'll again use Node.js and the Express web application framework. You'll only use Express framework a little, so you won't be bothered by it.

SETTING UP THE SERVER PROJECT

As always, you need some boilerplate code to load dependencies, initial AWS endpoints, and things like that, as shown in the next listing.

Listing 13.1   Initializing the Imagery server (server/server.js)

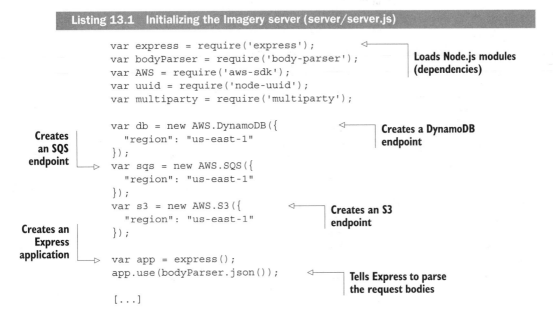

```
var express = require('express');           ◁──┐ Loads Node.js modules
var bodyParser = require('body-parser');        │ (dependencies)
var AWS = require('aws-sdk');                    │
var uuid = require('node-uuid');                 │
var multiparty = require('multiparty');          │

var db = new AWS.DynamoDB({                  ◁──┐ Creates a DynamoDB
  "region": "us-east-1"                          │ endpoint
});                                              │
var sqs = new AWS.SQS({
  "region": "us-east-1"
});
var s3 = new AWS.S3({                        ◁──┐ Creates an S3
  "region": "us-east-1"                          │ endpoint
});                                              │

var app = express();
app.use(bodyParser.json());                  ◁──┐ Tells Express to parse
                                                 │ the request bodies
[...]
```

Creates an SQS endpoint

Creates an Express application

```
app.listen(process.env.PORT || 8080, function() {
  console.log("Server started. Open http://localhost:"
  + (process.env.PORT || 8080) + " with browser.");
});
```

**Starts Express on the port defined by the
environment variable PORT, or defaults to 8080**

Don't worry too much about the boilerplate code; the interesting parts will follow.

CREATING A NEW IMAGERY PROCESS

To provide a REST API to create image processes, a fleet of EC2 instances will run
Node.js code behind a load balancer. The image processes will be stored in DynamoDB. Figure 13.11 shows the flow of a request to create a new image process.

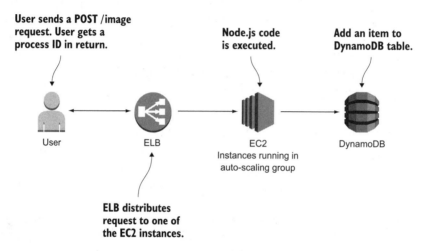

Figure 13.11   Creating a new image process in Imagery

You'll now add a route to the Express application to handle POST /image requests, as
shown in the next listing.

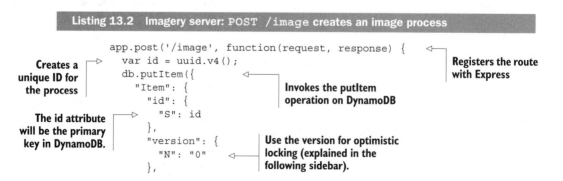

Listing 13.2   Imagery server: POST /image creates an image process

The process is now in the created state: this attribute will change when state transitions happen.

The DynamoDB table will be created later in the chapter.

Prevents the item from being replaced if it already exists.

Responds with the process ID

```
    "state": {
        "S": "created"
    }
},
    "TableName": "imagery-image",
    "ConditionExpression": "attribute_not_exists(id)"
}, function(err, data) {
    throw err;
} else {
    response.json({"id": id, "state": "created"});
}
});
});
```

A new process can now be created.

> ## Optimistic locking
>
> To prevent multiple updates to a DynamoDB item, you can use a trick called *optimistic locking*. When you want to update an item, you must tell which version you want to update. If that version doesn't match the current version of the item in the database, your update will be rejected.
>
> Imagine the following scenario. An item is created in version 0. Process A looks up that item (version 0). Process B also looks up that item (version 0). Now process A wants to make a change by invoking the updateItem operation on DynamoDB. Therefore process A specifies that the expected version is 0. DynamoDB will allow that modification because the version matches; but DynamoDB will also change the item's version to 1 because an update was performed. Now process B wants to make a modification and sends a request to DynamoDB with the expected item version 0. DynamoDB will reject that modification because the expected version doesn't match the version DynamoDB knows of, which is 1.
>
> To solve the problem for process B, you can use the same trick introduced earlier: retry. Process B will again look up the item, now in version 1, and can (you hope) make the change.
>
> There's one problem with optimistic locking: if many modifications happen in parallel, a lot of overhead is created because of many retries. But this is only a problem if you expect a lot of concurrent writes to a single item, which can be solved by changing the data model. That's not the case in the Imagery application. Only a few writes are expected to happen for a single item: optimistic locking is a perfect fit to make sure you don't have two writes where one overrides changes made by another.
>
> The opposite of *optimistic locking* is *pessimistic locking*. A pessimistic lock strategy can be implemented by using a semaphore. Before you change data, you need to lock the semaphore. If the semaphore is already locked, you wait until the semaphore becomes free again.

The next route you need to implement is to look up the current state of a process.

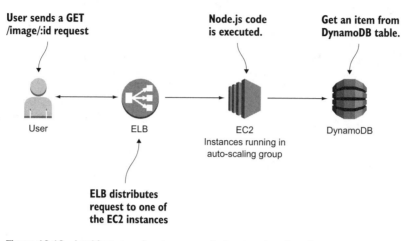

User sends a GET /image/:id request

Node.js code is executed.

Get an item from DynamoDB table.

User

ELB

EC2
Instances running in
auto-scaling group

DynamoDB

ELB distributes request to one of the EC2 instances

Figure 13.12   Looking up an image process in Imagery to return its state

LOOKING UP AN IMAGERY PROCESS

You'll now add a route to the Express application to handle GET /image/:id requests. Figure 13.12 shows the request flow.

Express will take care of the path parameter :id by providing it within request .params.id. The implementation needs to get an item from DynamoDB based on the path parameter ID.

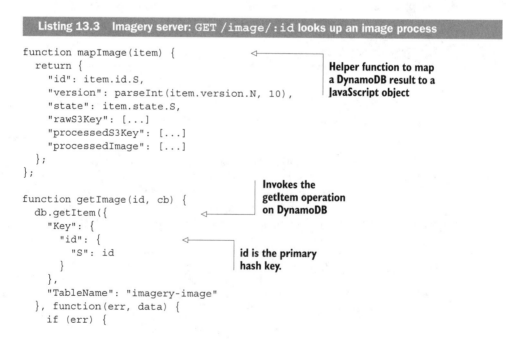

Listing 13.3   Imagery server: GET /image/:id looks up an image process

```
function mapImage(item) {
  return {
    "id": item.id.S,
    "version": parseInt(item.version.N, 10),
    "state": item.state.S,
    "rawS3Key": [...]
    "processedS3Key": [...]
    "processedImage": [...]
  };
};

function getImage(id, cb) {
  db.getItem({
    "Key": {
      "id": {
        "S": id
      }
    },
    "TableName": "imagery-image"
  }, function(err, data) {
    if (err) {
```

Helper function to map a DynamoDB result to a JavaScript object

Invokes the getItem operation on DynamoDB

id is the primary hash key.

```
      cb(err);
    } else {
      if (data.Item) {
        cb(null, mapImage(data.Item));
      } else {
        cb(new Error("image not found"));
      }
    }
  });                                                    ◁──┐  Registers the
}                                                            │  route with
app.get('/image/:id', function(request, response) {    ◁────┘  Express
  getImage(request.params.id, function(err, image) {
    if (err) {
      throw err;
    } else {
      response.json(image);             ◁──┐  Responds with the
    }                                       │  image process
  });
});
```

The only thing missing is the upload part, which comes next.

UPLOADING AN IMAGE

Uploading an image via POST request requires several steps:

1. Upload the raw image to S3.
2. Modify the item in DynamoDB.
3. Send an SQS message to trigger processing.

Figure 13.13 shows this flow.

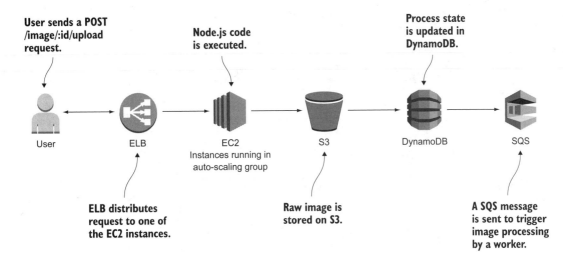

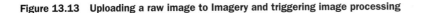

Figure 13.13 Uploading a raw image to Imagery and triggering image processing

The following listing shows the implementation of these steps.

Listing 13.4   Imagery server: `POST /image/:id/upload` uploads an image

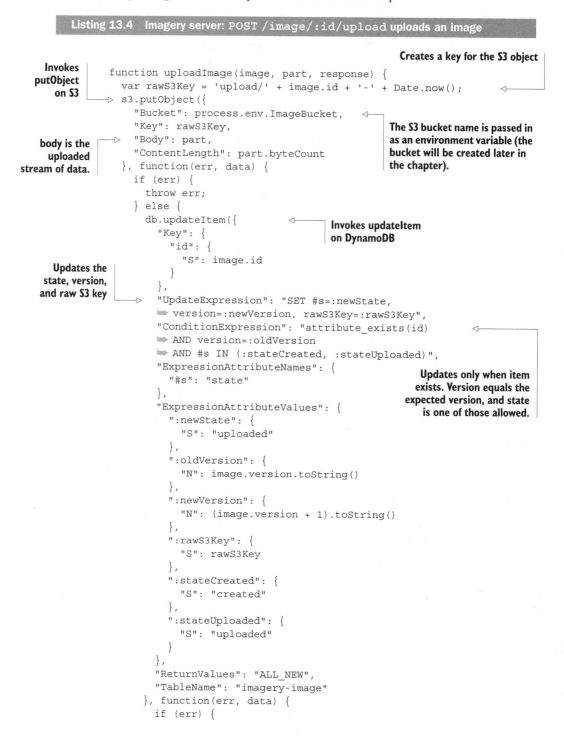

Creates a key for the S3 object

```
function uploadImage(image, part, response) {
  var rawS3Key = 'upload/' + image.id + '-' + Date.now();
  s3.putObject({
    "Bucket": process.env.ImageBucket,
    "Key": rawS3Key,
    "Body": part,
    "ContentLength": part.byteCount
  }, function(err, data) {
    if (err) {
      throw err;
    } else {
      db.updateItem({
        "Key": {
          "id": {
            "S": image.id
          }
        },
        "UpdateExpression": "SET #s=:newState,
          version=:newVersion, rawS3Key=:rawS3Key",
        "ConditionExpression": "attribute_exists(id)
          AND version=:oldVersion
          AND #s IN (:stateCreated, :stateUploaded)",
        "ExpressionAttributeNames": {
          "#s": "state"
        },
        "ExpressionAttributeValues": {
          ":newState": {
            "S": "uploaded"
          },
          ":oldVersion": {
            "N": image.version.toString()
          },
          ":newVersion": {
            "N": (image.version + 1).toString()
          },
          ":rawS3Key": {
            "S": rawS3Key
          },
          ":stateCreated": {
            "S": "created"
          },
          ":stateUploaded": {
            "S": "uploaded"
          }
        },
        "ReturnValues": "ALL_NEW",
        "TableName": "imagery-image"
      }, function(err, data) {
        if (err) {
```

Invokes putObject on S3

body is the uploaded stream of data.

The S3 bucket name is passed in as an environment variable (the bucket will be created later in the chapter).

Invokes updateItem on DynamoDB

Updates the state, version, and raw S3 key

Updates only when item exists. Version equals the expected version, and state is one of those allowed.

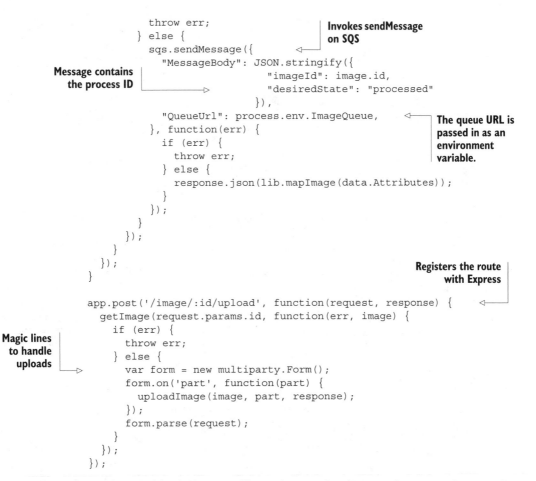

```
                        throw err;
                    } else {
                        sqs.sendMessage({
                            "MessageBody": JSON.stringify({
                                "imageId": image.id,
                                "desiredState": "processed"
                            }),
                            "QueueUrl": process.env.ImageQueue,
                        }, function(err) {
                            if (err) {
                                throw err;
                            } else {
                                response.json(lib.mapImage(data.Attributes));
                            }
                        });
                    }
                });
            }
        });
    }

app.post('/image/:id/upload', function(request, response) {
    getImage(request.params.id, function(err, image) {
        if (err) {
            throw err;
        } else {
            var form = new multiparty.Form();
            form.on('part', function(part) {
                uploadImage(image, part, response);
            });
            form.parse(request);
        }
    });
});
```

The server side is finished. Next you'll continue to implement the processing part in the Imagery worker. After that, you can deploy the application.

13.3.3 Implementing a fault-tolerant worker to consume SQS messages

The Imagery worker does the asynchronous stuff in the background: processing images into sepia images while applying a filter. The worker handles consuming SQS messages and processing images. Fortunately, consuming SQS messages is a common task that's solved by Elastic Beanstalk, which you'll use later to deploy the application. Elastic Beanstalk can be configured to listen to SQS messages and execute an HTTP POST request for every message. In the end, the worker implements a REST API that's invoked by Elastic Beanstalk. To implement the worker, you'll again use Node.js and the Express framework.

SETTING UP THE SERVER PROJECT

As always, you need some boilerplate code to load dependencies, initial AWS endpoints, and so on, as shown in the following listing.

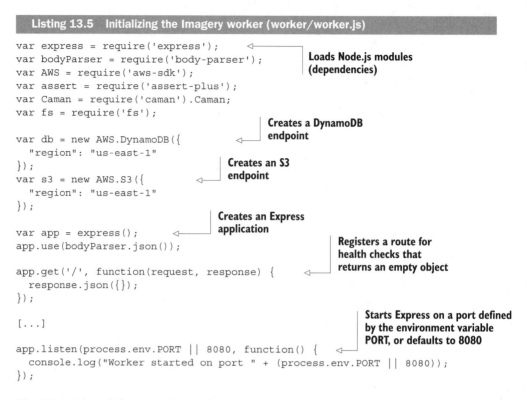

Listing 13.5   Initializing the Imagery worker (worker/worker.js)

```
var express = require('express');            Loads Node.js modules
var bodyParser = require('body-parser');     (dependencies)
var AWS = require('aws-sdk');
var assert = require('assert-plus');
var Caman = require('caman').Caman;
var fs = require('fs');
                                             Creates a DynamoDB
var db = new AWS.DynamoDB({                   endpoint
  "region": "us-east-1"
});                                          Creates an S3
var s3 = new AWS.S3({                         endpoint
  "region": "us-east-1"
});
                                             Creates an Express
var app = express();                         application
app.use(bodyParser.json());
                                                  Registers a route for
                                                  health checks that
app.get('/', function(request, response) {        returns an empty object
  response.json({});
});
                                                  Starts Express on a port defined
[...]                                             by the environment variable
                                                  PORT, or defaults to 8080
app.listen(process.env.PORT || 8080, function() {
  console.log("Worker started on port " + (process.env.PORT || 8080));
});
```

The Node.js module caman is used to create sepia images. You'll wire that up next.

HANDLING SQS MESSAGES AND PROCESSING THE IMAGE

The SQS message to trigger the raw image processing is handled in the worker. Once a message is received, the worker starts to download the raw image from S3, applies the sepia filter, and uploads the processed image back to S3. After that, the process state in DynamoDB is modified. Figure 13.14 shows the steps.

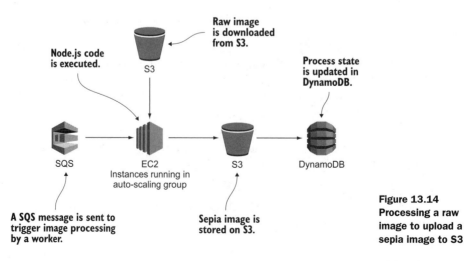

Figure 13.14
Processing a raw
image to upload a
sepia image to S3

Instead of receiving messages directly from SQS, you'll take a shortcut. Elastic Beanstalk, the deployment tool you'll use, provides a feature that consumes messages from a queue and invokes a HTTP POST request for every message. You configure the POST request to be made to the resource /sqs. The following listing shows the implementation.

> **Listing 13.6   Imagery worker: POST /sqs handles SQS messages**

```
function processImage(image, cb) {        ◁──┐  The implementation of processImage
  var processedS3Key = 'processed/' + image.id + '-' + Date.now() + '.png';
  // download raw image from S3              isn't shown here; you can find it in
  // process image                          the book's source folder.
  // upload sepia image to S3
  cb(null, processedS3Key);
}

function processed(image, request, response) {
  processImage(image, function(err, processedS3Key) {
    if (err) {
      throw err;
    } else {                          Invokes the updateItem
      db.updateItem({          ◁──┘  operation on DynamoDB
        "Key": {
          "id": {
            "S": image.id
          }
        },                                          Updates the state, version,
        "UpdateExpression": "SET #s=:newState,  ◁── and processed S3 key
        ➥ version=:newVersion, processedS3Key=:processedS3Key",
        "ConditionExpression": "attribute_exists(id)  ◁──┐ Updates only when an
        ➥ AND version=:oldVersion                        item exists, version
        ➥ AND #s IN (:stateUploaded, :stateProcessed)",  equals the expected
        "ExpressionAttributeNames": {                     version, and state is
          "#s": "state"                                   one of those allowed
        },
        "ExpressionAttributeValues": {
          ":newState": {
            "S": "processed"
          },
          ":oldVersion": {
            "N": image.version.toString()
          },
          ":newVersion": {
            "N": (image.version + 1).toString()
          },
          ":processedS3Key": {
            "S": processedS3Key
          },
          ":stateUploaded": {
            "S": "uploaded"
          },
```

```
            ":stateProcessed": {
               "S": "processed"
            }
         },
         "ReturnValues": "ALL_NEW",
         "TableName": "imagery-image"
      }, function(err, data) {
         if (err) {
            throw err;
         } else {
            response.json(lib.mapImage(data.Attributes));    ◁──┐ Responds with the
         }                                                        process's new state
      });
   }
  });
}

app.post('/sqs', function(request, response) {           ◁──┐ Registers the route
  assert.string(request.body.imageId, "imageId");              with Express
  assert.string(request.body.desiredState, "desiredState");
  getImage(request.body.imageId, function(err, image) {   ◁─────────────┐
    if (err) {                                     The implementation of getImage is
      throw err;                                      the same as on the server.
    } else {
      if (request.body.desiredState === 'processed') {
        processed(image, request, response);        ◁───────┐ Invokes the processed function if
      } else {                                                 the SQS message's desiredState
        throw new Error("unsupported desiredState");           equals "processed".
      }
    }
  });
});
```

If the POST /sqs route responds with a 2XX HTTP status code, Elastic Beanstalk considers the message delivery successful and deletes the message from the queue. Otherwise the message is redelivered.

Now you can process the SQS message to process the raw image and upload a sepia image to S3. The next step is to deploy all that code to AWS in a fault-tolerant way.

13.3.4 *Deploying the application*

As mentioned previously, you'll use Elastic Beanstalk to deploy the server and the worker. You'll use CloudFormation to do so. This may sounds strange because you use an automation tool to use another automation tool. But CloudFormation does a bit more than deploy two Elastic Beanstalk applications. It defines the following:

- S3 bucket for raw and processed images
- DynamoDB table imagery-image
- SQS queue and dead-letter queue
- IAM roles for the server and worker EC2 instances
- Elastic Beanstalk application for the server and worker

It takes quite a while to create that CloudFormation stack; that's why you should do so now. After you've created the stack, we'll look at the template. After that, the stack should be ready to use.

To help you deploy Imagery, we created a CloudFormation template located at https://s3.amazonaws.com/awsinaction/chapter13/template.json. Create a stack based on that template. The stack output `EndpointURL` returns the URL that can be accessed from your browser to use Imagery. Here's how to create the stack from the terminal:

```
$ aws cloudformation create-stack --stack-name imagery \
--template-url https://s3.amazonaws.com/\
awsinaction/chapter13/template.json \
--capabilities CAPABILITY_IAM
```

Now let's look at the CloudFormation template.

DEPLOYING S3, DYNAMODB, AND SQS

The following CloudFormation snippet describes the S3 bucket, DynamoDB table, and SQS queue.

Listing 13.7   Imagery CloudFormation template: S3, DynamoDB, and SQS

```
{
  "AWSTemplateFormatVersion": "2010-09-09",
  "Description": "AWS in Action: chapter 13",
  "Parameters": {
    "KeyName": {
      "Description": "Key Pair name",
      "Type": "AWS::EC2::KeyPair::KeyName",
      "Default": "mykey"
    }
  },
  "Resources": {
    "Bucket": {                                    ◁── S3 bucket for uploaded and
      "Type": "AWS::S3::Bucket",                        processed images, with web
      "Properties": {                                   hosting enabled
        "BucketName": {"Fn::Join": ["-",
        ["imagery", {"Ref": "AWS::AccountId"}]]},  ◁── The bucket name contains
        "WebsiteConfiguration": {                       the account ID to make the
          "ErrorDocument": "error.html",                name unique.
          "IndexDocument": "index.html"
        }
      }
    },
    "Table": {                                     ◁── DynamoDB table
      "Type": "AWS::DynamoDB::Table",                   containing the
      "Properties": {                                   image processes
        "AttributeDefinitions": [{
          "AttributeName": "id",
          "AttributeType": "S"
        }],
        "KeySchema": [{                            ◁── The id attribute
          "AttributeName": "id",                        is used as the
          "KeyType": "HASH"                             primary hash key.
```

```
      }],
      "ProvisionedThroughput": {
        "ReadCapacityUnits": 1,
        "WriteCapacityUnits": 1
      },
      "TableName": "imagery-image"
    }                                      SQS queue that receives
  },                                       messages that can't be
  "SQSDLQueue": {                    ◁──── processed
    "Type": "AWS::SQS::Queue",
    "Properties": {
      "QueueName": "message-dlq"
    }
  },                                       SQS queue to trigger
  "SQSQueue": {                      ◁──── image processing
    "Type": "AWS::SQS::Queue",
    "Properties": {
      "QueueName": "message",
      "RedrivePolicy": {            ◁──── If a message is received more
        "deadLetterTargetArn": {"Fn::GetAtt":   than 10 times, it's moved to
        ["SQSDLQueue", "Arn"]},              the dead-letter queue.
        "maxReceiveCount": 10
      }
    }
  },
  [...]                                    Visit the output with
},                                         your browser to use
"Outputs": {                               Imagery.
  "EndpointURL": {                  ◁────
    "Value": {"Fn::GetAtt": ["EBServerEnvironment", "EndpointURL"]},
    "Description": "Load Balancer URL"
  }
}
}
```

The concept of a dead-letter queue needs a short introduction here as well. If a single SQS message can't be processed, the message becomes visible again on the queue for other workers. This is called a *retry*. But if for some reason every retry fails (maybe you have a bug in your code), the message will reside in the queue forever and may waste a lot of resources because of many retries. To avoid this, you can configure a *dead-letter queue (DLQ)*. If a message is retried more than a specific number of times, it's removed from the original queue and forwarded to the DLQ. The difference is that no worker listens for messages on the DLQ. But you should create a CloudWatch alarm that triggers if the DLQ contains more than zero messages because you need to investigate this problem manually by looking at the message in the DLQ.

Now that the basic resources have been designed, let's move on to the more specific resources.

IAM ROLES FOR SERVER AND WORKER EC2 INSTANCES

Remember that it's important to only grant the privileges that are needed. All server instances must be able to do the following:

- `sqs:SendMessage` to the SQS queue created in the template to trigger image processing
- `s3:PutObject` to the S3 bucket created in the template to upload a file to S3 (you can further limit writes to the upload/ key prefix)
- `dynamodb:GetItem`, `dynamodb:PutItem`, and `dynamodb:UpdateItem` to the DynamoDB table created in the template
- `cloudwatch:PutMetricData`, which is an Elastic Beanstalk requirement
- `s3:Get*`, `s3:List*`, and `s3:PutObject`, which is an Elastic Beanstalk requirement

All worker instances must be able to do the following:

- `sqs:ChangeMessageVisibility`, `sqs:DeleteMessage`, and `sqs:ReceiveMessage` to the SQS queue created in the template
- `s3:PutObject` to the S3 bucket created in the template to upload a file to S3 (you can further limit writes to the processed/ key prefix)
- `dynamodb:GetItem` and `dynamodb:UpdateItem` to the DynamoDB table created in the template
- `cloudwatch:PutMetricData`, which is an Elastic Beanstalk requirement
- `s3:Get*`, `s3:List*`, and `s3:PutObject`, which is an Elastic Beanstalk requirement

If you don't feel comfortable with IAM roles, take a look at the book's code repository on GitHub at https://github.com/AWSinAction/code. The template with IAM roles can be found in /chapter13/template.json.

Now it's time to design the Elastic Beanstalk applications.

ELASTIC BEANSTALK FOR THE SERVER

Let's have a short refresher on Elastic Beanstalk, which we touched on in section 5.3. An Elastic Beanstalk consists of these elements:

- An *application* is a logical container. It contains versions, environments, and configurations. To use AWS Elastic Beanstalk in a region, you have to create an application first.
- A *version* contains a specific version of your application. To create a new version, you have to upload your executables (packed into an archive) to S3. A version is basically a pointer to this archive of executables.
- A *configuration template* contains your default configuration. You can manage the configuration of your application (such as the port your application listens on) as well as the configuration of the environment (such as the size of the virtual server) with your custom configuration template.
- An *environment* is the place where AWS Elastic Beanstalk executes your application. It consists of a version and the configuration. You can run multiple environments for one application by using the versions and configurations multiple times.

Figure 13.15 shows the parts of an Elastic Beanstalk application.

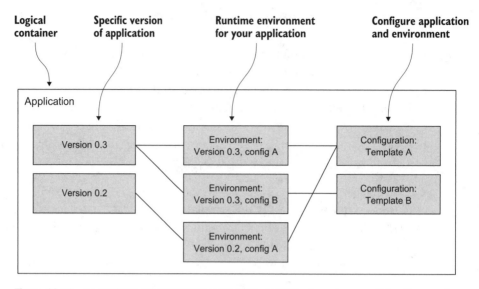

Figure 13.15   An AWS Elastic Beanstalk application consists of versions, configurations, and environments.

Now that you've refreshed your memory, let's look at the Elastic Beanstalk application that deploys the Imagery server.

Listing 13.8   Imagery CloudFormation template: Elastic Beanstalk for the server

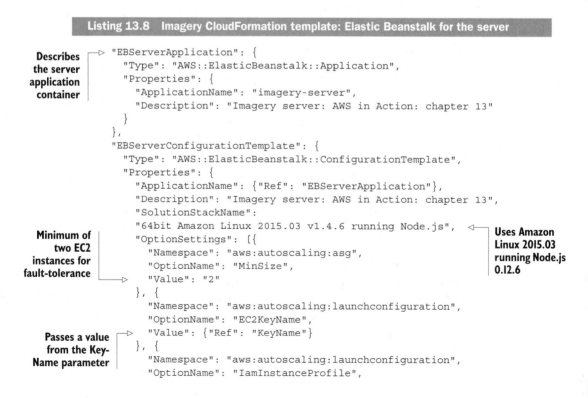

```
"EBServerApplication": {
  "Type": "AWS::ElasticBeanstalk::Application",
  "Properties": {
    "ApplicationName": "imagery-server",
    "Description": "Imagery server: AWS in Action: chapter 13"
  }
},
"EBServerConfigurationTemplate": {
  "Type": "AWS::ElasticBeanstalk::ConfigurationTemplate",
  "Properties": {
    "ApplicationName": {"Ref": "EBServerApplication"},
    "Description": "Imagery server: AWS in Action: chapter 13",
    "SolutionStackName":
    "64bit Amazon Linux 2015.03 v1.4.6 running Node.js",
    "OptionSettings": [{
      "Namespace": "aws:autoscaling:asg",
      "OptionName": "MinSize",
      "Value": "2"
    }, {
      "Namespace": "aws:autoscaling:launchconfiguration",
      "OptionName": "EC2KeyName",
      "Value": {"Ref": "KeyName"}
    }, {
      "Namespace": "aws:autoscaling:launchconfiguration",
      "OptionName": "IamInstanceProfile",
```

Describes the server application container

Minimum of two EC2 instances for fault-tolerance

Passes a value from the Key-Name parameter

Uses Amazon Linux 2015.03 running Node.js 0.12.6

```
                              "Value": {"Ref": "ServerInstanceProfile"}
Links to the IAM          }, {
instance profile            "Namespace": "aws:elasticbeanstalk:container:nodejs",
created in the              "OptionName": "NodeCommand",
previous section           "Value": "node server.js"     ⟵  Start command
                          }, {
Passes the SQS              "Namespace": "aws:elasticbeanstalk:application:environment",
queue into an              "OptionName": "ImageQueue",
environment                "Value": {"Ref": "SQSQueue"}
variable                  }, {
                            "Namespace": "aws:elasticbeanstalk:application:environment",
                            "OptionName": "ImageBucket",
Passes the S3              "Value": {"Ref": "Bucket"}
bucket into an            }, {
environment                "Namespace": "aws:elasticbeanstalk:container:nodejs:staticfiles",
variable                   "OptionName": "/public",
                            "Value": "/public"           ⟵  Serves all files
                         }]                                  from /public
                      }                                      as static files
                    },
                    "EBServerApplicationVersion": {
                      "Type": "AWS::ElasticBeanstalk::ApplicationVersion",
                      "Properties": {
                        "ApplicationName": {"Ref": "EBServerApplication"},
                        "Description": "Imagery server: AWS in Action: chapter 13",
                        "SourceBundle": {
                          "S3Bucket": "awsinaction",
                          "S3Key": "chapter13/build/server.zip"   ⟵  Loads code from the
                        }                                             book's S3 bucket
                      }
                    },
                    "EBServerEnvironment": {
                      "Type": "AWS::ElasticBeanstalk::Environment",
                      "Properties": {
                        "ApplicationName": {"Ref": "EBServerApplication"},
                        "Description": "Imagery server: AWS in Action: chapter 13",
                        "TemplateName": {"Ref": "EBServerConfigurationTemplate"},
                        "VersionLabel": {"Ref": "EBServerApplicationVersion"}
                      }
                    }
                  }
```

Under the hood, Elastic Beanstalk uses an ELB to distribute the traffic to the EC2 instances that are also managed by Elastic Beanstalk. You only need to worry about the configuration of Elastic Beanstalk and the code.

ELASTIC BEANSTALK FOR THE WORKER

The worker Elastic Beanstalk application is similar to the server. The differences are highlighted in the following listing.

Listing 13.9   Imagery CloudFormation template: Elastic Beanstalk for the worker

```
"EBWorkerApplication": {               ⟵  Describes the worker
  "Type": "AWS::ElasticBeanstalk::Application",     application container
  "Properties": {
```

```
        "ApplicationName": "imagery-worker",
        "Description": "Imagery worker: AWS in Action: chapter 13"
      }
    },
    "EBWorkerConfigurationTemplate": {
      "Type": "AWS::ElasticBeanstalk::ConfigurationTemplate",
      "Properties": {
        "ApplicationName": {"Ref": "EBWorkerApplication"},
        "Description": "Imagery worker: AWS in Action: chapter 13",
        "SolutionStackName":
        "64bit Amazon Linux 2015.03 v1.4.6 running Node.js",
        "OptionSettings": [{
          "Namespace": "aws:autoscaling:launchconfiguration",
          "OptionName": "EC2KeyName",
          "Value": {"Ref": "KeyName"}
        }, {
          "Namespace": "aws:autoscaling:launchconfiguration",
          "OptionName": "IamInstanceProfile",
          "Value": {"Ref": "WorkerInstanceProfile"}
        }, {
          "Namespace": "aws:elasticbeanstalk:sqsd",
          "OptionName": "WorkerQueueURL",
          "Value": {"Ref": "SQSQueue"}
        }, {
          "Namespace": "aws:elasticbeanstalk:sqsd",
          "OptionName": "HttpPath",
          "Value": "/sqs"                            ◁——┐
        }, {
          "Namespace": "aws:elasticbeanstalk:container:nodejs",
          "OptionName": "NodeCommand",
          "Value": "node worker.js"
        }, {
          "Namespace": "aws:elasticbeanstalk:application:environment",
          "OptionName": "ImageQueue",
          "Value": {"Ref": "SQSQueue"}
        }, {
          "Namespace": "aws:elasticbeanstalk:application:environment",
          "OptionName": "ImageBucket",
          "Value": {"Ref": "Bucket"}
        }]
      }
    },
    "EBWorkerApplicationVersion": {
      "Type": "AWS::ElasticBeanstalk::ApplicationVersion",
      "Properties": {
        "ApplicationName": {"Ref": "EBWorkerApplication"},
        "Description": "Imagery worker: AWS in Action: chapter 13",
        "SourceBundle": {
          "S3Bucket": "awsinaction",
          "S3Key": "chapter13/build/worker.zip"
        }
      }
    },
    "EBWorkerEnvironment": {
      "Type": "AWS::ElasticBeanstalk::Environment",
```

Configures the HTTP resource that's invoked when an SQS message is received

```
    "Properties": {
      "ApplicationName": {"Ref": "EBWorkerApplication"},
      "Description": "Imagery worker: AWS in Action: chapter 13",
      "TemplateName": {"Ref": "EBWorkerConfigurationTemplate"},
      "VersionLabel": {"Ref": "EBWorkerApplicationVersion"},
      "Tier": {                          ◁────────┐  Switches to the worker
        "Type": "SQS/HTTP",                          environment tier (pushes
        "Name": "Worker",                            SQS messages to your app)
        "Version": "1.0"
      }
    }
  }
}
```

After all that JSON reading, the CloudFormation stack should be created. Verify the status of your stack:

```
$ aws cloudformation describe-stacks --stack-name imagery
{
  "Stacks": [{
    [...]
    "Description": "AWS in Action: chapter 13",
    "Outputs": [{                              Copy this output into
      "Description": "Load Balancer URL",      your web browser.
      "OutputKey": "EndpointURL",
      "OutputValue": "awseb-...582.us-east-1.elb.amazonaws.com"  ◁────┘
    }],
    "StackName": "imagery",
    "StackStatus": "CREATE_COMPLETE"    ◁──────  Wait until CREATE_COMPLETE
  }]                                             is reached.
}
```

The `EndpointURL` output of the stack is the URL to access the Imagery application. When you open Imagery in your web browser, you can upload an image as shown in figure 13.16.

Go ahead and upload some images. You've created a fault-tolerant application!

Cleaning up

To find out your 12-digit account ID (878533158213), you can use the CLI:

```
$ aws iam get-user --query "User.Arn" --output text
arn:aws:iam::878533158213:user/mycli
```

Delete all the files in the S3 bucket `s3://imagery-$AccountId` (replace `$AccountId` with your account ID) by executing

```
$ aws s3 rm s3://imagery-$AccountId --recursive
```

Execute the following command to delete the CloudFormation stack:

```
$ aws cloudformation delete-stack --stack-name imagery
```

Stack deletion will take some time.

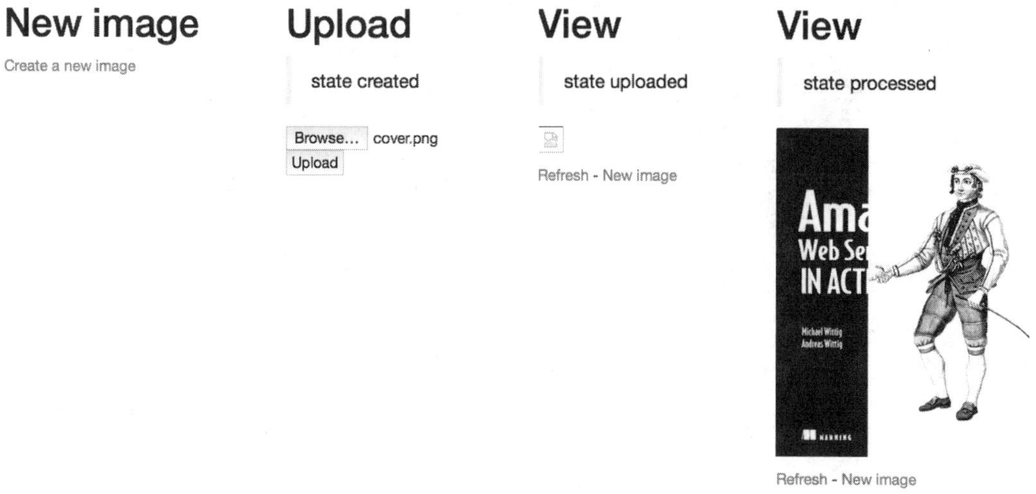

New image

Create a new image

Upload

state created

Browse...   cover.png
Upload

View

state uploaded

Refresh - New image

View

state processed

Am
Web Se
IN ACT

Michael Wittig
Andreas Wittig

MANNING

Refresh - New image

Figure 13.16   The Imagery application in action

13.4   Summary

- Fault-tolerance means to expect that failures happen. Design your systems in such a way that they can deal with failure.
- To create a fault-tolerant application, you can use idempotent actions to transfer from one state to the next.
- State shouldn't reside on the server (a stateless server) as a prerequisite for fault-tolerance.
- AWS offers fault-tolerant services and gives you all the tools you need to create fault-tolerant systems. EC2 is one of the few services that isn't fault-tolerant out of the box.
- You can use multiple EC2 instances to eliminate the single point of failure. Redundant EC2 instances in different availability zones, started with an auto-scaling group, are the way to make EC2 fault-tolerant.

Scaling up and down: auto-scaling and CloudWatch

This chapter covers

- Creating an auto-scaling group with launch configuration
- Using auto-scaling to adapt the number of virtual servers
- Scaling a synchronous decoupled app behind an ELB
- Scaling an asynchronous decoupled app using SQS
- Using CloudWatch alarms to modify an auto-scaling group

Suppose you're organizing a party to celebrate your birthday. How much food and drink do you need to buy? Calculating the right numbers for your shopping list is difficult:

- How many people will actually attend? You received several confirmations, but some guests will need to cancel at short notice or show up without letting you know in advance, so the number of guests is vague.

363

- How much will your guests eat and drink? Will it be a hot day, with everybody drinking a lot? Will your guests be hungry? You need to guess the demand for food and drink based on experiences from previous parties.

Solving the equation is a challenge because there are many unknown factors. Behaving as a good host, you'll order more food and drink than needed to have a solid buffer, and no guest will be hungry or thirsty for long.

Planning to meet future demands is nearly impossible. To prevent a supply gap, you need to add extra capacity on top of the planned demand to prevent running short of resources.

The same was true when we planned the capacity of our IT infrastructure. When procuring hardware for a data center, we always had to buy hardware based on the demands of the future. There were many uncertainties when making these decisions:

- How many users would need to be served by the infrastructure?
- How much storage would the users need?
- How much computing power would be required to handle their requests?

To avoid supply gaps, we had to order more or faster hardware than needed, causing unnecessary expenses.

On AWS, you can use services on demand. Planning capacity is less and less important. Scaling from one server to thousands of servers is possible. Storage can grow from gigabytes to petabytes. You can scale on demand, thus replacing capacity planning. The ability to scale on demand is called *elasticity* by AWS.

Public cloud providers like AWS can offer needed capacity with a short waiting time. AWS is serving a million customers, and at that scale, it isn't a problem to provide you with 100 additional virtual servers within minutes if you need them suddenly. This allows you to address another problem: typical traffic patterns, as shown in figure 14.1. Think about the load on your infrastructure during the day versus at night, on a weekday versus the weekend, or before Christmas versus the rest of year. Wouldn't it be nice if you could add capacity when traffic grows and remove capacity when traffic shrinks? In this chapter, you'll learn how to scale the number of virtual servers based on current load.

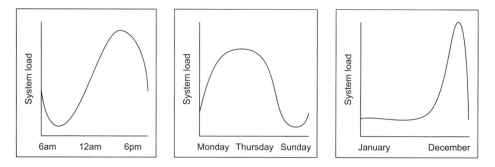

Figure 14.1 Typical traffic patterns for a web shop

Scaling the number of virtual servers is possible with *auto-scaling groups* and *scaling policies* on AWS. Auto-scaling is part of the EC2 service and helps you to scale the number of EC2 instances needed to fulfill the current load of your system. We introduced auto-scaling groups in chapter 11 to ensure that a single virtual server was running even if an outage of an entire data center occurred. In this chapter, you'll learn how to use a dynamic server pool:

- Using auto-scaling groups to launch multiple virtual servers of the same kind
- Changing the number of virtual servers based on CPU load with the help of CloudWatch
- Changing the number of virtual servers based on a schedule, to be able to adapt to recurring traffic patterns
- Using a load balancer as an entry point to the dynamic server pool
- Using a queue to decouple the jobs from the dynamic server pool

---

Examples are 100% covered by the Free Tier

The examples in this chapter are completely covered by the Free Tier. As long as you don't run the examples for longer than a few days, you won't pay anything. Keep in mind that this only applies if you created a fresh AWS account for this book and nothing else is going on in your AWS account. Try to complete the examples of the chapter within a few days; you'll clean up your account at the end of each example.

There are two prerequisites for being able to scale your application horizontally, which means increasing and decreasing the number of virtual servers based on the current workload:

- The servers you want to scale need to be *stateless*. You can achieve stateless servers by storing data with the help of a service like RDS (SQL database), DynamoDB (NoSQL database), or S3 (object store) instead of storing data on local or network-attached disks that are only available to a single server.
- An entry point to the dynamic server pool is needed to be able to distribute the workload across multiple servers. Servers can be decoupled synchronously with a load balancer or asynchronously with a queue.

We introduced the concept of the stateless servers in part 3 of this book and explained how to use decoupling in chapter 12. You'll return to the concept of the stateless server and also work through an example of synchronous and asynchronous decoupling in this chapter.

14.1 Managing a dynamic server pool

Imagine that you need to provide a scalable infrastructure to run a web application, such as a blogging platform. You need to launch uniform virtual servers when the number of requests grows and terminate virtual servers when the number of requests shrinks. To adapt to the current workload in an automated way, you need to be able to launch and terminate virtual servers automatically. The configuration and deployment of the blogging platform needs to be done during bootstrapping, without human interaction.

AWS offers a service to manage such a dynamic server pool, called *auto-scaling groups*. Auto-scaling groups help you to

- Run a desired number of virtual servers that can be adjusted dynamically
- Launch, configure, and deploy uniform virtual servers

As figure 14.2 shows, auto-scaling consists of three parts:

- A *launch configuration* that defines the size, image, and configuration of virtual servers
- An *auto-scaling group* that specifies how many virtual servers need to be running based on the launch configuration
- *Scaling policies* that adjust the desired number of servers in the auto-scaling group

Because the auto-scaling group references a launch configuration, you need to create a launch configuration before you can create an auto-scaling group. If you use a template, as you will in this chapter, this dependency will be resolved by CloudFormation automatically.

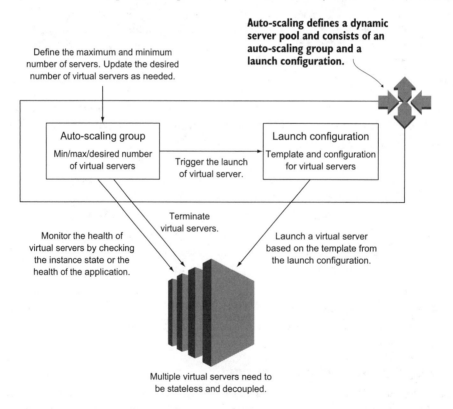

Figure 14.2   Auto-scaling consists of an auto-scaling group and a launch configuration, launching and terminating uniform virtual servers.

If you want multiple servers to handle a workload, it's important to start identical virtual servers to build a homogeneous foundation. You use a launch configuration to define and configure new virtual servers. Table 14.1 shows the most important parameters for a launch configuration.

Table 14.1   Launch configuration parameters

Name	Description	Possible values
ImageId	Image from which to start a virtual server	ID of Amazon Machine Image (AMI)
InstanceType	Size for new virtual servers	Instance type (such as t2.micro)
UserData	User data for the virtual server used to execute a script during bootstrapping	BASE64-encoded String
KeyName	Name of the SSH key pair	Name of an EC2 key pair
AssociatePublicIpAddress	Associates a public IP address with the virtual server	True or false
SecurityGroups	Attaches security groups to new virtual servers	List of security group names
IamInstanceProfile	Attaches an IAM instance profile linked to an IAM role	Name or Amazon Resource Name (ARN, an ID) of an IAM instance profile
SpotPrice	Uses a spot instance instead of an on-demand instance with the maximum price	Maximum price for the spot instance per hour (such as 0.10)
EbsOptimized	Enables EBS optimization for the EC2 instance offering a dedicated throughput to EBS root volumes with the IOPS defined in the image (AMI)	True or false

After you create a launch configuration, you can create an auto-scaling group referencing it. The auto-scaling group defines the maximum, minimum, and desired number of virtual servers. *Desired* means this number of servers should be running. If the current number of servers is below the desired number, the auto-scaling group will add servers. If the current number of servers is above the desired number, servers will be terminated.

The auto-scaling group also monitors whether EC2 instances are healthy and replaces broken instances. Table 14.2 shows the most important parameters for an auto-scaling group.

If you specify multiple subnets with the help of VPCZoneIdentifier for the auto-scaling group, EC2 instances will be evenly distributed among these subnets and thus among availability zones.

Table 14.2   Auto-scaling group parameters

Name	Description	Possible values
DesiredCapacity	Desired number of healthy virtual servers	Integer
MaxSize	Maximum number of virtual servers; scaling limit	Integer
MinSize	Minimum number of virtual servers; scaling limit	Integer
Cooldown	Minimum time span between two scaling actions	Number of seconds
HealthCheckType	How the auto-scaling group checks the health of virtual servers	EC2 (health of the instance) or ELB (health check of instance performed by a load balancer)
HealthCheckGracePeriod	Period for which the health check is paused after the launch of a new instance, to wait until the instance is fully bootstrapped	Number of seconds
LaunchConfigurationName	Name of the launch configuration used to start new virtual servers	Name of a launch configuration
LoadBalancerNames	Load balancers at which auto-scaling registers new instances automatically	List of load-balancer names
TerminationPolicies	Policies used to determine which instance is terminated first	OldestInstance, NewestInstance, OldestLaunchConfiguration, ClosestToNextInstanceHour, or Default
VPCZoneIdentifier	List of subnets in which to launch EC2 instances	List of subnet identifiers of a VPC

Avoid unnecessary scaling with a cooldown and a grace period

Be sure to define reasonable Cooldown and HealthCheckGracePeriod values. The tendency is to specify short Cooldown and HealthCheckGracePeriod periods. But if your Cooldown period is too short, you'll scale up and down too early. If your HealthCheckGracePeriod is too short, the auto-scaling group will launch a new instance because the previous instance isn't bootstrapped quickly enough. Both will launch unnecessary instances and cause unnecessary expense.

You can't edit a launch configuration. If you need to make changes to a launch configuration, follow these steps:

1. Create a new launch configuration.
2. Edit the auto-scaling group, and reference the new launch configuration.
3. Delete the old launch configuration.

Fortunately, CloudFormation does this for you when you make changes to a launch configuration in a template. The following listing shows how to set up such a dynamic server pool with the help of a CloudFormation template.

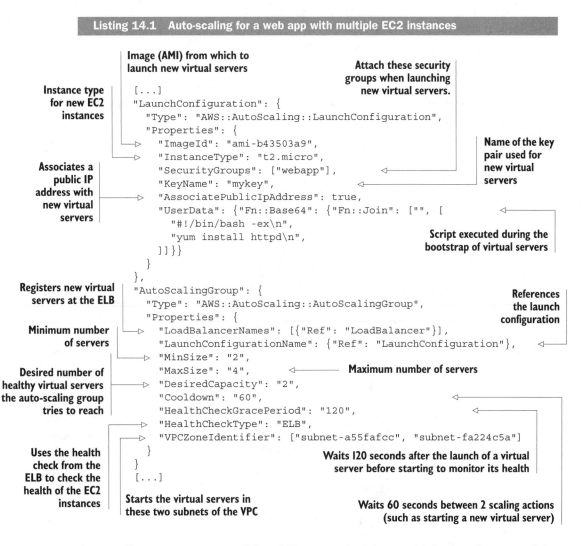

Listing 14.1 Auto-scaling for a web app with multiple EC2 instances

Image (AMI) from which to launch new virtual servers

Instance type for new EC2 instances

Attach these security groups when launching new virtual servers.

Associates a public IP address with new virtual servers

Name of the key pair used for new virtual servers

Script executed during the bootstrap of virtual servers

Registers new virtual servers at the ELB

References the launch configuration

Minimum number of servers

Desired number of healthy virtual servers the auto-scaling group tries to reach

Maximum number of servers

Uses the health check from the ELB to check the health of the EC2 instances

Waits 120 seconds after the launch of a virtual server before starting to monitor its health

Starts the virtual servers in these two subnets of the VPC

Waits 60 seconds between 2 scaling actions (such as starting a new virtual server)

```
[...]
"LaunchConfiguration": {
    "Type": "AWS::AutoScaling::LaunchConfiguration",
    "Properties": {
        "ImageId": "ami-b43503a9",
        "InstanceType": "t2.micro",
        "SecurityGroups": ["webapp"],
        "KeyName": "mykey",
        "AssociatePublicIpAddress": true,
        "UserData": {"Fn::Base64": {"Fn::Join": ["", [
            "#!/bin/bash -ex\n",
            "yum install httpd\n",
        ]]}}
    }
},
"AutoScalingGroup": {
    "Type": "AWS::AutoScaling::AutoScalingGroup",
    "Properties": {
        "LoadBalancerNames": [{"Ref": "LoadBalancer"}],
        "LaunchConfigurationName": {"Ref": "LaunchConfiguration"},
        "MinSize": "2",
        "MaxSize": "4",
        "DesiredCapacity": "2",
        "Cooldown": "60",
        "HealthCheckGracePeriod": "120",
        "HealthCheckType": "ELB",
        "VPCZoneIdentifier": ["subnet-a55fafcc", "subnet-fa224c5a"]
    }
}
[...]
```

Auto-scaling groups are a useful tool if you need to start multiple virtual servers of the same kind across multiple availability zones.

14.2 *Using metrics and schedules to trigger scaling*

So far in this chapter, you've learned how to use an auto-scaling group and a launch configuration to launch virtual servers. You can change the desired capacity of the auto-scaling group manually, and new instances will be started or old instances will be terminated to reach the new desired capacity.

To provide a scalable infrastructure for a blogging platform, you need to increase and decrease the number of virtual servers in the dynamic server pool automatically by adjusting the desired capacity of the auto-scaling group with scaling policies.

Many people surf the web during their lunch break, so you might need to add virtual servers every day between 11:00 AM and 1:00 PM. You also need to adapt to unpredictable load patterns—for example, if articles hosted on your blogging platform are shared frequently through social networks.

Figure 14.3 illustrates two different ways of changing the number of virtual servers:

- Using a CloudWatch alarm to increase or decrease the number of virtual servers based on a metric (such as CPU usage or number of requests on the load balancer)
- Defining a schedule to increase or decrease the number of virtual servers according to recurring load patterns (such as decreasing the number of virtual servers at night)

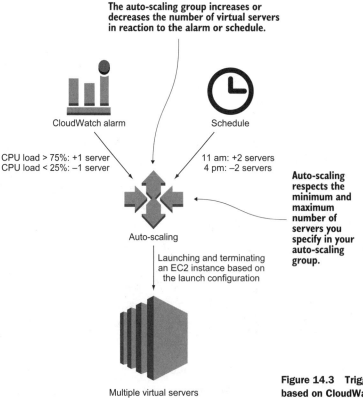

The auto-scaling group increases or decreases the number of virtual servers in reaction to the alarm or schedule.

CloudWatch alarm

Schedule

CPU load > 75%: +1 server
CPU load < 25%: –1 server

11 am: +2 servers
4 pm: –2 servers

Auto-scaling respects the minimum and maximum number of servers you specify in your auto-scaling group.

Auto-scaling

Launching and terminating an EC2 instance based on the launch configuration

Multiple virtual servers

Figure 14.3 Triggering auto-scaling based on CloudWatch alarms or schedules

Scaling based on a schedule is less complex than scaling based on a CloudWatch metric because it's difficult to find a metric to scale on reliably. On the other hand, scaling based on a schedule is less precise.

14.2.1 Scaling based on a schedule

When operating a blogging platform, you might notice recurring load patterns:

- Many people seem to read articles during their lunch break, between 11:00 AM and 1:00 PM.
- Requests to your registration page increase heavily after you run a TV advertisement in the evening.

You can react to patterns in the utilization of your system with different types of scheduled scaling actions:

- One-time-only actions, creating using the `starttime` parameter
- Recurring actions, created using the `recurrence` parameter

You can create both types of scheduled scaling actions with the help of the CLI. The command shown in the next listing created a scheduled scaling action that sets the desired capacity of the auto-scaling group called `webapp` to 4 on January 1, 2016 at 12:00 (UTC). Don't try to run this command now—you haven't created the auto-scaling group `webapp` to play with.

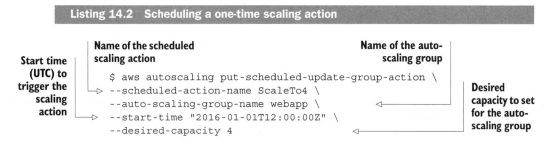

Listing 14.2 Scheduling a one-time scaling action

You can also schedule recurring scaling actions using cron syntax. The next listing sets the desired capacity of an auto-scaling group to 2 every day at 20:00 UTC. Don't try to run this command now—you haven't created the auto-scaling group `webapp` to play with.

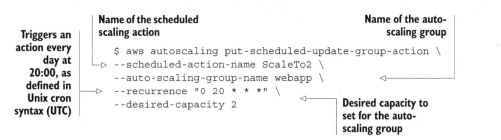

Listing 14.3 Scheduling a recurring scaling action that runs at 20:00 o'clock UTC every day

Recurrence is defined in Unix cron syntax format as shown here:

```
* * * * *
| | | | |
| | | | +- day of week (0 - 6) (0 Sunday)
| | | +--- month (1 - 12)
| | +----- day of month (1 - 31)
| +------- hour (0 - 23)
+--------- min (0 - 59)
```

You could add another scheduled recurring scaling action to add capacity in the morning that you removed during the night. Use scheduled scaling actions whenever the load on your infrastructure is predictable. For example, internal systems may be mostly needed during work hours, or marketing actions may go live at a certain time.

14.2.2 *Scaling based on CloudWatch metrics*

Predicting the future is a hard task. Traffic will increase or decrease beyond known patterns from time to time. For example, if an article published on your blogging platform is heavily shared through social media, you need to be able to react to unplanned load changes and scale the number of servers.

You can adapt the number of EC2 instances to handle the current workload with the help of CloudWatch and scaling policies. CloudWatch helps monitor virtual servers and other services on AWS. Typically, a service publishes usage metrics to CloudWatch, helping you to evaluate the available capacity. To trigger scaling based on the current workload, you use metrics, alarms, and scaling policies. Figure 14.4 illustrates.

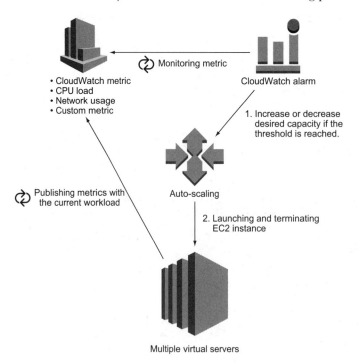

Figure 14.4   Triggering auto-scaling based on a CloudWatch metric and alarm

An EC2 instance publishes several metrics to CloudWatch by default: CPU, network, and disk utilization are the most important. Unfortunately, there is currently no metric for a virtual server's memory usage. You can use these metrics to scale the number of virtual servers if a bottleneck is reached. For example, you can add servers if the CPU is working to capacity.

The following parameters describe a CloudWatch metric:

- `Namespace`—Defines the source of the metric (such as AWS/EC2)
- `Dimensions`—Defines the scope of the metric (such as all virtual servers belonging to an auto-scaling group)
- `MetricName`—Unique name of the metric (such as `CPUUtilization`)

A CloudWatch alarm is based on a CloudWatch metric. Table 14.3 explains the alarm parameters in detail.

Table 14.3 Parameters for a CloudWatch alarm that triggers scaling based on CPU utilization of all virtual servers belonging to an auto-scaling group

Context	Name	Description	Possible values
Condition	`Statistic`	Statistical function applied to a metric	`Average`, `Sum`, `Minimum`, `Maximum`, `SampleCount`
Condition	`Period`	Defines a time-based slice of values from a metric	Seconds (multiple of 60)
Condition	`EvaluationPeriods`	Number of periods to evaluate when checking for an alarm	Integer
Condition	`Threshold`	Threshold for an alarm	Number
Condition	`ComparisonOperator`	Operator to compare the threshold against the result from a statistical function	`GreaterThanOrEqualToThreshold`, `GreaterThanThreshold`, `LessThanThreshold`, `LessThanOrEqualToThreshold`
Metric	`Namespace`	Source of the metric	AWS/EC2 for metrics from the EC2 service
Metric	`Dimensions`	Scope of the metric	Depends on the metric, references the auto-scaling group for an aggregated metric over all associated servers
Metric	`MetricName`	Name of the metric	For example, `CPUUtilization`
Action	`AlarmActions`	Actions to trigger if the threshold is reached	Reference to the scaling policy

The following listing creates an alarm that increases the number of virtual servers with the help of auto-scaling if the average CPU utilization of all virtual servers belonging to the auto-scaling group exceeds 80%.

Listing 14.4   CloudWatch alarm based on CPU load of an auto-scaling group

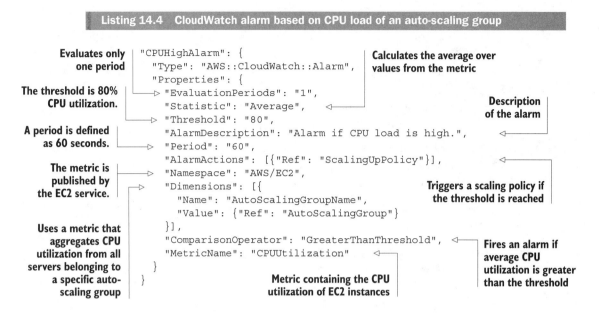

If the threshold is reached, the CloudWatch alarm triggers an action. To connect the alarm with the auto-scaling group, you need a *scaling policy*. A scaling policy defines the scaling action executed by the CloudWatch alarm.

Listing 14.5 creates a scaling policy with CloudFormation. The scaling policy is linked to an auto-scaling group. There are three different options to adjust the desired capacity of an auto-scaling group:

- ChangeInCapacity—Increases or decreases the number of servers by an absolute number
- PercentChangeInCapacity—Increases or decreases the number of servers by a percentage
- ExactCapacity—Sets the desired capacity to a specified number

Listing 14.5   Scaling policy that will add one server when triggered

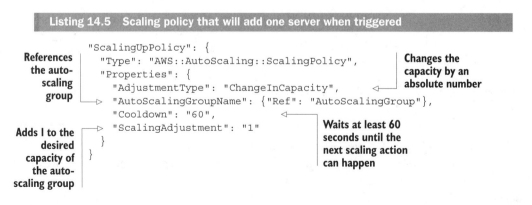

You can define alarms on many different metrics. You'll find an overview of all namespaces, dimensions, and metrics that AWS offers at http://mng.bz/8E0X. You can also publish custom metrics—for example, metrics directly from your application like thread pool usage, processing times, or user sessions.

Scaling based on CPU load with virtual servers offering burstable performance

Some virtual servers, such as instance family t2, offer burstable performance. These virtual servers offer a baseline CPU performance and can burst performance for a short time based on credits. If all credits are spent, the instance operates at the baseline. For a t2.micro instance, baseline performance is 10% of the performance of the underlying physical CPU.

Using virtual servers with burstable performance can help you react to load spikes. You save credits in times of low load and spend credits to burst performance in times of high load. But scaling the number of virtual servers with burstable performance based on CPU load is tricky because your scaling strategy must take into account whether your instances have enough credits to burst performance. Consider searching for another metric to scale (such as number of sessions) or using an instance type without burstable performance.

Many times it's a good idea to scale up faster than you scale down. Consider adding two servers instead of one every 5 minutes but only scaling down one server every 10 minutes. Also, test your scaling policies by simulating real-world traffic. For example, replay an access log as fast as your servers can handle the requests. But keep in mind that servers need some time to start; don't expect that auto-scaling can double your capacity within a few seconds.

You've learned how to use auto-scaling to adapt the number of virtual servers to the workload. Time to bring this into action.

14.3 Decoupling your dynamic server pool

If you need to scale the number of virtual servers running your blogging platform based on demand, auto-scaling groups can help you provide the needed number of uniform virtual servers, and a scaling schedule or CloudWatch alarms will increase or decrease the desired number of servers automatically. But how can users reach the servers in the dynamic server pool to browse the hosted articles? Where should the HTTP request be routed?

Chapter 12 introduced the concept of decoupling: synchronous decoupling with the help of ELB, and asynchronous decoupling with the help of SQS. Decoupling allows you to route requests or messages to one or multiple servers. Sending requests to a single server is no longer possible in a dynamic server pool. If you want to use auto-scaling to grow and shrink the number of virtual servers, you need to decouple your server because the interface that's reachable from outside the system needs to

Synchronous decoupling

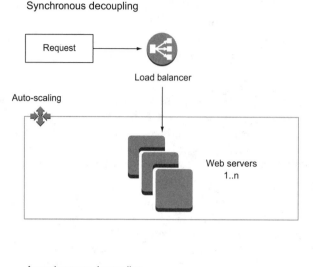

Asynchronous decoupling

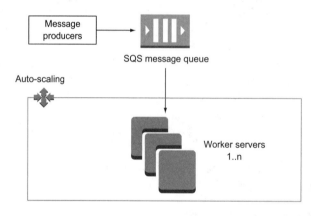

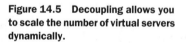

Figure 14.5   Decoupling allows you to scale the number of virtual servers dynamically.

stay the same no matter how many servers are working behind the load balancer or message queue. Figure 14.5 shows how to build a scalable system based on synchronous or asynchronous decoupling.

A decoupled and scalable application requires stateless servers. A stateless server stores any shared data remotely in a database or storage system. The following two examples implement the concept of a stateless server:

- *WordPress blog*—Decoupled with ELB, scaled with auto-scaling and CloudWatch based on CPU utilization, and data outsourced to RDS and S3
- *URL2PNG taking screenshots of URLs*—Decoupled with SQS (queue), scaled with auto-scaling and CloudWatch based on queue length, data outsourced to DynamoDB and S3

14.3.1 *Scaling a dynamic server pool synchronously decoupled by a load balancer*

Answering HTTP(S) requests is a synchronous task. If a user wants to use your web application, the web server has to answer the corresponding requests immediately. When using a dynamic server pool to run a web application, it's common to use a load balancer to decouple the servers from user requests. A load balancer forwards HTTP(S) requests to multiple servers, acting as a single entry point to the dynamic server pool.

Suppose your company is using a corporate blog to publish announcements and interact with the community. You're responsible for the hosting of the blog. The marketing department complains about page speed in the evening, when traffic reaches its daily peak. You want to use the elasticity of AWS by scaling the number of servers based on the current workload.

Your company uses the popular blogging platform WordPress for its corporate blog. Chapters 2 and 9 introduced a WordPress setup based on EC2 instances and RDS (MySQL database). In this last chapter of the book, we'll complete the example by adding the ability to scale.

Figure 14.6 shows the final, extended WordPress example. The following services are used for this highly available scaling architecture:

- EC2 instances running Apache to serve WordPress, a PHP application
- RDS offering a MySQL database that's highly available through Multi-AZ deployment
- S3 to store media files such as images and videos, integrated with a WordPress plug-in
- ELB to synchronously decouple the web servers from visitors
- Auto-scaling and CloudWatch to scale the number of web servers based on the current CPU load of all running virtual servers

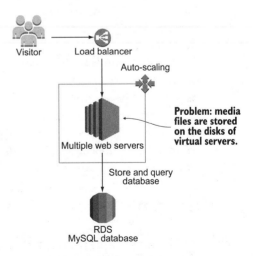

So far, the WordPress example can't scale based on current load and contains a pitfall: WordPress stores uploaded media files in the local file system as shown in figure 14.6. As a result, the server isn't stateless. If you upload an image for a blog post, it's only available on a single server.

This is a problem if you want to run multiple servers to handle the load. Other servers won't be able to service the uploaded image and will deliver a 404 (not found) error. To fix that, you'll

Figure 14.6 WordPress running on multiple virtual servers, storing data on RDS but media files on the disks of virtual servers

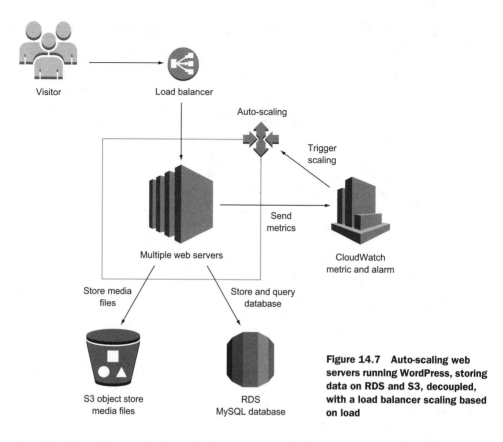

Visitor

Load balancer

Auto-scaling

Trigger
scaling

Send
metrics

Multiple web servers

CloudWatch
metric and alarm

Store media
files

Store and query
database

S3 object store
media files

RDS
MySQL database

Figure 14.7   Auto-scaling web servers running WordPress, storing data on RDS and S3, decoupled, with a load balancer scaling based on load

install a WordPress plug-in called *amazon-s3-and-cloudfront* that stores and delivers media files with the help of S3. You're outsourcing the state of the server as you did with the MySQL database running on RDS. Figure 14.7 shows the improved version of the WordPress setup.

As usual, you'll find the code in the book's code repository on GitHub: https://github.com/AWSinAction/code. The CloudFormation template for the WordPress example is located in /chapter14/wordpress.json.

Execute the following command to create a CloudFormation stack that spins up the scalable WordPress setup. Replace $BlogID with a unique ID for your blog (such as awsinaction-andreas), $AdminPassword with a random password, and $AdminEMail with your e-mail address:

```
$ aws cloudformation create-stack --stack-name wordpress \
--template-url https://s3.amazonaws.com/\
awsinaction/chapter14/wordpress.json \
--parameters ParameterKey=BlogID,ParameterValue=$BlogID \
ParameterKey=AdminPassword,ParameterValue=$AdminPassword \
ParameterKey=AdminEMail,ParameterValue=$AdminEMail \
--capabilities CAPABILITY_IAM
```

It will take up to 10 minutes for the stack to be created. This is a perfect time to grab some coffee or tea. Log in to the AWS Management Console, and navigate to the AWS CloudFormation service to monitor the process of the CloudFormation stack named wordpress. You have time to look through the most important parts of the Cloud-Formation template, shown in the following two listings.

Listing 14.6 Scalable and highly available WordPress setup (part 1 of 2)

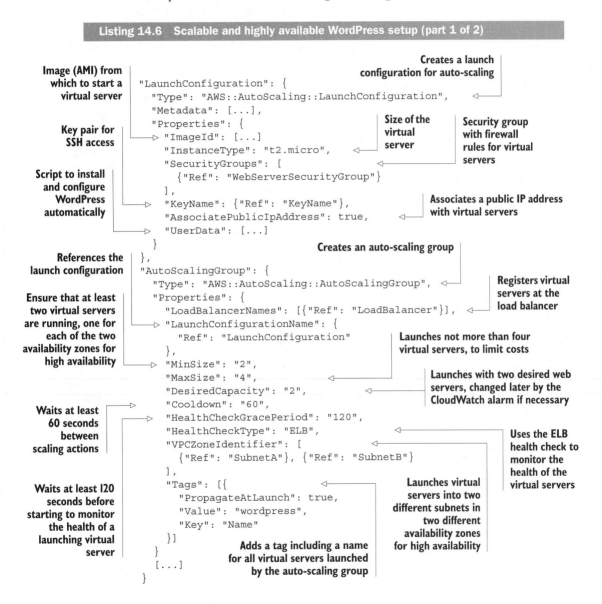

Image (AMI) from which to start a virtual server

Key pair for SSH access

Script to install and configure WordPress automatically

References the launch configuration

Ensure that at least two virtual servers are running, one for each of the two availability zones for high availability

Waits at least 60 seconds between scaling actions

Waits at least 120 seconds before starting to monitor the health of a launching virtual server

Creates a launch configuration for auto-scaling

Size of the virtual server

Security group with firewall rules for virtual servers

Associates a public IP address with virtual servers

Creates an auto-scaling group

Registers virtual servers at the load balancer

Launches not more than four virtual servers, to limit costs

Launches with two desired web servers, changed later by the CloudWatch alarm if necessary

Uses the ELB health check to monitor the health of the virtual servers

Launches virtual servers into two different subnets in two different availability zones for high availability

Adds a tag including a name for all virtual servers launched by the auto-scaling group

```
"LaunchConfiguration": {
  "Type": "AWS::AutoScaling::LaunchConfiguration",
  "Metadata": [...],
  "Properties": {
    "ImageId": [...]
    "InstanceType": "t2.micro",
    "SecurityGroups": [
      {"Ref": "WebServerSecurityGroup"}
    ],
    "KeyName": {"Ref": "KeyName"},
    "AssociatePublicIpAddress": true,
    "UserData": [...]
  }
},
"AutoScalingGroup": {
  "Type": "AWS::AutoScaling::AutoScalingGroup",
  "Properties": {
    "LoadBalancerNames": [{"Ref": "LoadBalancer"}],
    "LaunchConfigurationName": {
      "Ref": "LaunchConfiguration"
    },
    "MinSize": "2",
    "MaxSize": "4",
    "DesiredCapacity": "2",
    "Cooldown": "60",
    "HealthCheckGracePeriod": "120",
    "HealthCheckType": "ELB",
    "VPCZoneIdentifier": [
      {"Ref": "SubnetA"}, {"Ref": "SubnetB"}
    ],
    "Tags": [{
      "PropagateAtLaunch": true,
      "Value": "wordpress",
      "Key": "Name"
    }]
  }
  [...]
}
```

The scaling policies and CloudWatch alarms follow in the next listing.

Listing 14.7   Scalable and highly available WordPress setup (part 2 of 2)

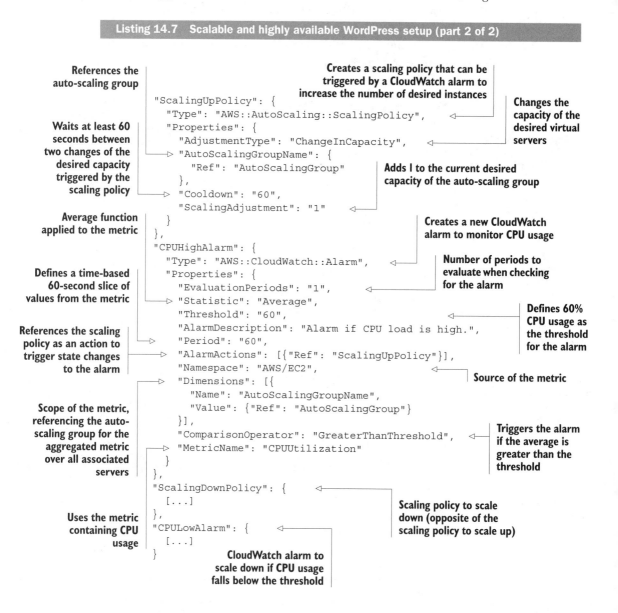

Follow these steps after the CloudFormation stack reaches the state CREATE_COMPLETE to create a new blog post containing an image:

1   Select the CloudFormation stack wordpress and switch to the Outputs tab.
2   Open the link shown for key URL with a modern web browser.

3 Search for the Log In link in the navigation bar and click it.

4 Log in with username `admin` and the password you specified when creating the stack with the CLI.

5 Click Posts in the menu at left.

6 Click Add New.

7 Type in a title and text, and upload an image to your post.

8 Click Publish.

9 Move back to the blog by entering the URL from step 1 again.

Now you're ready to scale. We've prepared a load test that will send 10,000 requests to the WordPress setup in a short amount of time. New virtual servers will be launched to handle the load. After a few minutes, when the load test is finished, the additional virtual servers will disappear. Watching this is fun; you shouldn't miss it.

NOTE If you plan to do a big load test, consider the AWS Acceptable Use Policy at https://aws.amazon.com/aup and ask for permission before you begin (see also https://aws.amazon.com/security/penetration-testing).

Simple HTTP load test

We're using a tool called *Apache Bench* to perform a load test of the WordPress setup. The tool is part of the `httpd-tools` package available from the Amazon Linux package repositories.

Apache Bench is a basic benchmarking tool. You can send a specified number of HTTP requests by using a specified number of threads. We're using the following command for the load test, to send 10,000 requests to the load balancer using two threads. `$UrlLoadBalancer` is replaced by the URL of the load balancer:

```
$ ab -n 10000 -c 2 $UrlLoadBalancer
```

Update the CloudFormation stack with the following command to start the load test:

```
$ aws cloudformation update-stack --stack-name wordpress \
--template-url https://s3.amazonaws.com/\
awsinaction/chapter14/wordpress-loadtest.json \
--parameters ParameterKey=BlogID,UsePreviousValue=true \
ParameterKey=AdminPassword,UsePreviousValue=true \
ParameterKey=AdminEMail,UsePreviousValue=true \
--capabilities CAPABILITY_IAM
```

Watch for the following things to happen, with the help of the AWS Management Console:

1 Open the CloudWatch service, and click Alarms at left.

2 When the load test starts, the alarm called `wordpress-CPUHighAlarm-*` will reach the `ALARM` state after a few minutes.

3   Open the EC2 service and list all EC2 instances. Watch for two additional instances to launch. At the end, you'll see five instances total (four web servers and the server running the load test).

4   Go back to the CloudWatch service and wait until the alarm named `wordpress-CPULowlarm-*` reaches the `ALARM` state.

5   Open the EC2 service and list all EC2 instances. Watch for the two additional instances to disappear. At the end, you'll see three instances total (two web servers and the server running the load test).

The entire process will take about 20 minutes.

You've watched auto-scaling in action: your WordPress setup can now adapt to the current workload. The problem with pages loading slowly in the evening is solved.

> **Cleaning up**
>
> Execute the following commands to delete all resources corresponding to the Word-Press setup, remembering to replace `$BlogID`:
>
> ```
> $ aws s3 rb s3://$BlogID --force
> $ aws cloudformation delete-stack --stack-name wordpress
> ```

14.3.2 *Scaling a dynamic server pool asynchronously decoupled by a queue*

Decoupling a dynamic server pool in an asynchronous way offers an advantage if you want to scale based on your workload: because requests don't need to be answered immediately, you can put requests into a queue and scale the number of servers based on the length of the queue. This gives you a very accurate metric to scale, and no requests will be lost during a load peak because they're stored in a queue.

Imagine that you're developing a social bookmark service where users can save and share their bookmarks. Offering a preview that shows the website behind a link is an important feature. But the conversion from URL to PNG is slow during the evening when most users add new bookmarks to your service. Customers are dissatisfied that previews don't show up immediately.

To handle the peak load in the evening, you want to use auto-scaling. To do so, you need to decouple the creation of a new bookmark and the process of generating a preview of the website. Chapter 12 introduced an application called URL2PNG that transforms a URL into a PNG image. Figure 14.8 shows the architecture, which consists of an SQS queue for asynchronously decoupling and S3 to store generated images. Creating a bookmark will trigger the following process:

1   A message is sent to an SQS queue containing the URL and the unique ID of the new bookmark.

2   EC2 instances running a Node.js application poll the SQS queue.

3   The Node.js application loads the URL and creates a screenshot.

4 The screenshot is uploaded to an S3 bucket, and the object key is set to the unique ID.

5 Users can download the screenshot of the website directly from S3 with the help of the unique ID.

A CloudWatch alarm is used to monitor the length of the SQS queue. If the length of the queue reaches the limit of five, a new virtual server is started to handle the workload. If the queue length is less than five, another CloudWatch alarm decreases the desired capacity of the auto-scaling group.

The code is in the book's code repository on GitHub at https://github.com/AWSinAction/code. The CloudFormation template for the URL2PNG example is located in /chapter14/url2png.json.

Execute the following command to create a CloudFormation stack that spins up the URL2PNG application. Replace $ApplicationID with a unique ID for your application (such as url2png-andreas):

```
$ aws cloudformation create-stack --stack-name url2png \
--template-url https://s3.amazonaws.com/\
awsinaction/chapter14/url2png.json \
--parameters ParameterKey=ApplicationID,ParameterValue=$ApplicationID \
--capabilities CAPABILITY_IAM
```

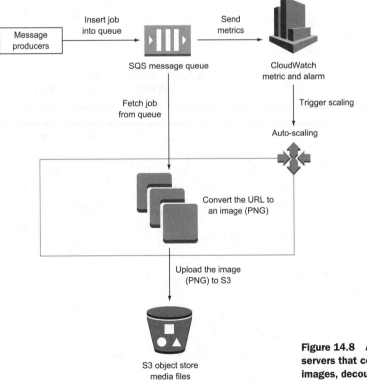

Figure 14.8 Auto-scaling virtual servers that convert URLs into images, decoupled by an SQS queue

It will take up to five minutes for the stack to be created. Log in to the AWS Management Console, and navigate to the AWS CloudFormation service to monitor the process of the CloudFormation stack named url2png.

The CloudFormation template is similar to the template you used to create the synchronously decoupled WordPress setup. The following listing shows the main difference: the CloudWatch alarm monitors the length of the SQS queue instead of CPU usage.

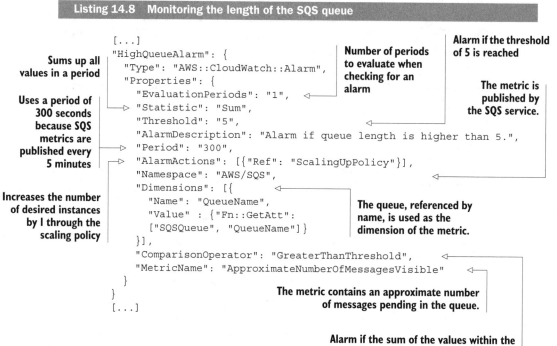

Listing 14.8   Monitoring the length of the SQS queue

```
[...]
"HighQueueAlarm": {
  "Type": "AWS::CloudWatch::Alarm",
  "Properties": {
    "EvaluationPeriods": "1",
    "Statistic": "Sum",
    "Threshold": "5",
    "AlarmDescription": "Alarm if queue length is higher than 5.",
    "Period": "300",
    "AlarmActions": [{"Ref": "ScalingUpPolicy"}],
    "Namespace": "AWS/SQS",
    "Dimensions": [{
      "Name": "QueueName",
      "Value" : {"Fn::GetAtt":
      ["SQSQueue", "QueueName"]}
    }],
    "ComparisonOperator": "GreaterThanThreshold",
    "MetricName": "ApproximateNumberOfMessagesVisible"
  }
}
[...]
```

Sums up all values in a period

Uses a period of 300 seconds because SQS metrics are published every 5 minutes

Increases the number of desired instances by 1 through the scaling policy

Number of periods to evaluate when checking for an alarm

Alarm if the threshold of 5 is reached

The metric is published by the SQS service.

The queue, referenced by name, is used as the dimension of the metric.

The metric contains an approximate number of messages pending in the queue.

Alarm if the sum of the values within the period is greater than the threshold of 5

You're ready to scale. We've prepared a load test that will quickly generate 250 messages for the URL2PNG application. New virtual servers will be launched to handle the load. After a few minutes, when the load test is finished, the additional virtual servers will disappear.

Update the CloudFormation stack with the following command to start the load test:

```
$ aws cloudformation update-stack --stack-name url2png \
--template-url https://s3.amazonaws.com/\
awsinaction/chapter14/url2png-loadtest.json \
--parameters ParameterKey=ApplicationID,UsePreviousValue=true \
--capabilities CAPABILITY_IAM
```

Watch for the following things to happen, with the help of the AWS Management Console:

1 Open the CloudWatch service and click Alarms at left.

2 When the load test starts, the alarm called `url2png-HighQueueAlarm-*` will reach the `ALARM` state after a few minutes.

3 Open the EC2 service and list all EC2 instances. Watch for an additional instance to launch. At the end, you'll see three instances total (two workers and the server running the load test).

4 Go back to the CloudWatch service and wait until the alarm named `url2png-LowQueueAlarm-*` reaches the `ALARM` state.

5 Open the EC2 service and list all EC2 instances. Watch for the additional instance to disappear. At the end, you'll see two instances total (one worker and the server running the load test).

The entire process will take about 15 minutes.

You've watched auto-scaling in action. The URL2PNG application can now adapt to the current workload, and the problem with slowly generated screenshots for new bookmarks is solved.

Cleaning up

Execute the following commands to delete all resources corresponding to the URL2PNG setup, remembering to replace `$ApplicationID`:

```
$ aws s3 rb s3://$ApplicationID --force
$ aws cloudformation delete-stack --stack-name url2png
```

14.4 Summary

- You can use auto-scaling to launch multiple virtual servers the same way by using a launch configuration and an auto-scaling group.

- EC2, SQS, and other services publish metrics to CloudWatch (CPU utilization, queue length, and so on).

- A CloudWatch alarm can change the desired capacity of an auto-scaling group. This allows you to increase the number of virtual servers based on CPU utilization or other metrics.

- Servers need to be stateless if you want to scale them according to your current workload.

- Synchronous decoupling with the help of a load balancer or asynchronous decoupling with a message queue is necessary in order to distribute load among multiple virtual servers.

index

RELATED MANNING TITLES

Java 8 in Action
Lambdas, streams, and functional-style programming
by Raoul-Gabriel Urma, Mario Fusco,
  and Alan Mycroft

  ISBN: 9781617291999
  424 pages, $49.99
  August 2014

Functional Programming in Scala
by Paul Chiusano and Rúnar Bjarnason

  ISBN: 9781617290657
  320 pages, $44.99
  September 2014

Storm Applied
Strategies for real-time event processing
by Sean T. Allen, Matthew Jankowski, and
  Peter Pathirana

  ISBN: 9781617291890
  280 pages, $49.99
  March 2015

Big Data
*Principles and best practices of scalable realtime
data systems*
by Nathan Marz with James Warren

  ISBN: 9781617290343
  328 pages, $49.99
  April 2015

For ordering information go to www.manning.com